the
practice
of
Industrial
Relations
text and cases

the practice of Industrial Relations

DAVID A. PEACH,

School of Business Administration
The University of Western Ontario

DAVID KUECHLE

School of Business Administration
The University of Western Ontario

McGRAW-HILL RYERSON LIMITED

Toronto Montreal New York London Sydney
Johannesburg Mexico Panama Düsseldorf Singapore
São Paulo Kuala Lumpur New Delhi

The Practice of Industrial Relations

ISBN 0-07-082198-4

Library of Congress Catalog Card Number 74-11913

Printed and bound in the United States of America.

4 5 6 7 8 9 10 RRD 4 3 2 1 0 9 8

Table of Contents

PREFACE

THE PRACTICE OF INDUSTRIAL RELATIONS

This book describes industrial relations practice in Canada and the United States. It is written for managers and students of management. There are ten parts, each consisting of descriptive narrative and most augmented by actual cases to highlight the important industrial relations issues facing contemporary North American managers.

For students of management the book provides a learning vehicle for understanding industrial relations practices and for carrying on decision-making responsibilities in the field. For practicing managers it provides an informative documentary and practical reference manual.

The book is practical, not theoretical, in its approach. While its primary focus is on the Canadian scene there are frequent references and comparisons to practices in the United States, reflecting the similarity of labor management experiences in the two countries.

Supplementary teaching notes have been prepared for those who would use the book for educational purposes. To the degree that this book leads to greater understanding in this complex and specialized field our purposes are met.

* * *

A number of people have helped us along the way to the completion of this book. We are grateful to our teachers of labor relations at the Harvard Business School — James J. Healy, Thomas Kennedy and E. Robert Livernash. They will no doubt find a great deal of themselves in this book. The School of Business Administration, The University of Western Ontario, has provided not only financial support for this endeavor, but also a climate which encouraged the development and use of the material. We wish to acknowledge our appreciation to the Dean of the school, John J. Wettlaufer; to the Associate Dean and former Director of Research, Joseph N. Fry; and to the current Director of Research, David C. Shaw. The school's research efforts, including this one, have been generously financed by The Associates' Plan for Excellence. We are grateful to the individuals and companies who have supported this plan. We also owe a word of thanks to the many students who have helped in giving the contents a trial run in the classroom.

More specifically, we wish to acknowledge the assistance of Ronald Stevens, David DeYoung and James Mackay in developing some of the materials in this book. Nonie Robinson and Nancy Jamieson typed the final draft of the manuscript, catching more than a few errors and omissions in the process. Professor Fraser Isbester of McMaster University read the first draft of the manuscript and made many constructive suggestions, all of which helped improve the final product. At McGraw-Hill Ryerson, Geoffrey Burn, Penelope Grows, and Audrey Coffin were extremely helpful in providing editorial and other assistance in seeing this book into print.

Finally, we owe our thanks to a number of individuals, companies and unions who provided the basis for the cases and research studies which gave rise to this book. We are deeply grateful for their help in providing examples of "the practice of industrial relations" which we hope will make the subject come alive for the reader.

London, Ontario   DAVID A PEACH
  August 1974   DAVID KUECHLE

1. AN INTRODUCTION
TO LABOR RELATIONS

When the union's inspiration through the workers' blood shall run,
There can be no power greater anywhere beneath the sun;
Yet what force on earth is weaker than the feeble strength of one?
Solidarity forever, Solidarity forever,
Solidarity forever, for the union makes us strong.

With this rousing chorus, we begin. In this ballad we have the *raison
d'être* of the union movement:

The fundamental reason for the existence of the trade union is that
by it and through it workmen are enabled to deal collectively with
their employers. Trade unionism thus recognizes that the destruction
of the workingman is the individual bargain, and the salvation of the
workingman is the joint, united or collective bargain.[1]

In 1972, there were 2,370,600 union members in Canada.[2] This
number represented only a third of the nonagricultural paid workers in
the country, and only 28 per cent of the total civilian labor force.[3]
Obviously, not all Canadian workers had accepted the idea of "solidarity
forever." (In the United States there were approximately 19 million
union members, a slightly lower, but similar, proportion of the nonagricultural and total civilian work forces there.)

However, workers in certain sectors of the economy are highly
unionized. Over 50 per cent of the paid workers in manufacturing,
forestry, construction, transportation and utilities, and public administration are union members. In other sectors, such as trade, finance, and
service industries, the degree of unionization is very low. Table I -1(p.2)
shows Canadian union membership as a percentage of the total paid
work force by major industrial classifications and subclassifications.

While union membership in both Canada and the United States is at
an all-time high, the proportion of unionized workers has been relatively
stable for the last twenty years. Union membership grew rapidly during
and immediately after World War II. In recent years, the only major area
of growth has been among employees in government at all levels.
Although they have made efforts to do so, unions have generally been
unsuccessful in organizing most other white-collar workers.[5]

There are no statutory bars against any group of employees forming
or joining a union for the purpose of bargaining collectively with their
employer. However, some groups are excluded from coverage under the
federal and provincial labor relations acts, which means that the
employer does not have to recognize them or bargain with them. It also

TABLE I-1

Union Membership in Canada as a Percentage of the Total Paid Work Force by Major Industrial Group 1971[4]

Industry	Union Members	Paid Work Force	Union Members as a Percentage of Paid Workers
Agriculture	344	102,000	.3
Forestry	32,574	65,000	50.1
Mines Quarries and Oil Wells	73,582	126,000	58.4
Manufacturing	770,000	1,757,000	43.8
Food and Beverages	91,494	199,800	45.8
Rubber	17,303	24,200	71.5
Leather	11,373	26,900	42.3
Textile	32,606	68,700	47.5
Clothing	49,223	86,100	57.2
Wood	46,190	82,200	56.2
Furniture and Fixtures	13,816	34,200	40.4
Paper and Allied Industries	82,976	116,200	71.4
Printing and Publishing	32,632	67,800	48.1
Primary Metals	67,676	114,700	59.0
Metal Fabricating	60,829	116,800	52.1
Machinery	29,340	71,200	41.2
Transportation Equip.	112,790	141,700	79.6
Electrical Products	61,840	118,400	52.3
Chemical Products	23,512	69,300	33.9
Construction	246,206	412,000	59.8
Transportation, Communication and other Utilities	377,145	664,000	56.8
Air Transport	18,606	31,300	59.4
Railway Transport	113,221	123,400	91.8
Truck Transport	37,002	52,800	70.1
Communication	99,741	150,600	66.2
Power, Gas and Water	45,556	82,000	55.6
Trade	86,970	1,119,000	7.8
Finance, Insurance and Real Estate	2,615	363,000	.7
Service Industries*	281,978	1,894,000	14.9
Public Administration **	339,216	520,000	65.2

* Includes education, hospitals, recreation, business and personal services
** Federal, provincial and local

means that the employer is generally free to discharge these workers for union membership. Those workers excluded from coverage under the various acts include managers and those employed in a confidential capacity in matters pertaining to labor relations. Agricultural workers and those employed in the medical, dental, architectural and legal professions are also generally excluded from coverage under the labor relations acts.

Although a majority of Canadian workers are not in labor unions, unionization is almost total in many industries. Even in those industries which have remained unorganized, workers are potential candidates for unionization. A manager can therefore expect at least to face the possibility of dealing with a unionized work force no matter where he works.

What are unions like? What are their goals? How do they operate? While these questions cannot be fully answered at this point, what follows will serve as a brief introduction to labor unions in North America.

UNION SIZE AND ORGANIZATION

When the union member speaks or thinks of his union, he generally is referring to his *local* union. There are over 10,000 local unions in Canada. As its name implies, a local union is based on a relatively small physical location. It might be based on a single plant location, with the workers in that plant comprising the membership of that local. It might also be based on a specific geographic location such as a city, with all the workers in a specific craft in a city belonging to one local union.

At the second level of union organization, locals are affiliated with, and in fact usually chartered by, national and international unions. National or international unions are, in effect, aggregations of local unions.

As of January 1972, there were 437 national and international unions in Canada. They ranged in size from the six-member International Association of Siderographers[6] to the United Steelworkers, with 165,000 members in Canada. The ten largest unions in Canada, with their membership, were these:[7]

1. United Steelworkers of America	165,055
2. Canadian Union of Public Employees	157,919
3. Public Service Alliance of Canada	129,652
4. International Union, United Automobile Aerospace and Agricultural Implement Workers of America	102,933

5. United Brotherhood of Carpenters and Joiners of America	74,362
6. *Corporation des Enseignants du Québec* (Quebec Teacher's Corporation)	70,000
7. International Brotherhood of Teamsters, Chauffeurs, Warehousemen and Helpers	60,560
8. *Fédération Nationale des Services, Inc.* (Service Employees Federation)	56,603
9. International Brotherhood of Electrical Workers	56,026
10. International Woodworkers of America	53,158

Ten other unions had a membership of over 30,000:[8]

11. United Paperworkers International Union	51,500
12. International Association of Machinists and Aerospace Workers	48,392
13. Laborers' International Union	45,332
14. Canadian Food and Allied Workers	42,000
15. Service Employees International Union	38,469
16. The Civil Service Association of Ontario	38,416
17. United Association of Journeymen and Apprentices of the Plumbing and Pipefitting Industry of the United States and Canada	33,465
18. Retail Clerks' International Association	33,154
19. *Fédération Canadienne des Travailleurs de la Métallurgie, des Mines, et des Produits Chimiques* (Canadian Federation of Steel, Mine and Chemical Workers.)	31,596
20. *Syndicat des Fonctionnaires Provinciaux du Québec* (Quebec Government Employees).	30,009

These twenty unions represent over half of the unionized workers in Canada.

A look at the names of the unions listed above will show that unions are of two types, those representing workers with a particular skill, such as carpenters and plumbers, and those representing workers in a particular industry, such as the Steelworkers (USW) or the Auto Workers (UAW), or the Canadian Union of Public Employees (CUPE). The former are called *craft unions* while the latter are called *industrial unions*.

These differences are no longer as distinct as they once were. Originally, the craft unions restricted themselves to representing workers in a particular trade, and several craft unions could be found even within a particular plant. The industrial unions attempted to organize all the workers in a plant (and industry) into a single union. Now many craft unions — such as the Machinists and the International Brotherhood of

Electrical Workers (IBEW) — operate at least partially on an industrial basis, representing all the workers in a given plant, not just the skilled craftsmen with a particular trade. Industrial unions, on the other hand, have organized workers in industries other than the one for which they were founded.

Sixty-two per cent of Canadian union members belong to international unions. Fifty-one per cent of the unions operating in Canada are international unions.[9] The international character of these unions is the result of membership in both the United States and Canada. The headquarters of these unions are in the United States.

In addition to the international unions, Canada has 65 national unions. Most of the large national unions are composed of workers in the public service. There are also 263 independent unions which are based in a single locality and not connected in any way with national or international unions.

THE FEDERATIONS

Most of the 437 unions in Canada are members of either of two federations of unions — the Confederation of National Trade Unions (CNTU) and the Canadian Labour Congress (CLC).

The CNTU (in French, the *Confédération des Syndicats Nationaux* — *CSN*) was originally a confederation of Catholic trade unions, with the goal of preserving the integrity of French Canada. By 1961, the CNTU had been transformed into a federation of trade unions, and remains so today.[10] In 1972, 12 unions, with 218,526 members, were affiliated with the CNTU.[11] These unions operate only in Quebec.

The other Canadian federation, the CLC, is national in character. The CLC is composed of international unions, national unions and directly chartered local unions. Most of the international unions are also members of the AFL-CIO (American Federation of Labor—Congress of Industrial Organizations) which is the United States counterpart of the CLC.

The membership breakdown of the CLC and the CNTU is shown in Table II -1(p. 7). This table also indicates that a number of unions are not affiliated with either federation. Affiliation is *voluntary*, not compulsory. Many of these nonaffiliated unions are small local organizations. One large union, the Teamsters, is unaffiliated with either the CLC or the AFL-CIO. The Autoworkers are members of the CLC but not the AFL-CIO.

Both the CLC and the CNTU are loose associations of unions. The federations have relatively little power. They are essentially instruments for inter-union cooperation and coordination. Union organizing drives are sometimes coordinated by a federation. The federations help settle jurisdictional disputes — conflicts between two or more unions as to who will represent a group of employees or as to whose members will perform a certain type of work. Through the federations, unions have concluded nonraiding agreements — agreements that they will not attempt to "steal" members from each other. The federations also make representations to various governments on behalf of organized labor and Canadian workers in general.

The structure and functions of the CLC are replicated on a provincial and on a local basis. There is a federation of labor organizations chartered by the CLC in each province, e.g. Ontario Federation of Labour. On a local basis, there are also local labor councils, such as the London and District Labour Council, and there are organizations for specific trades, e.g. London Building and Construction Trades Council. It is possible for one union to be a member of all these groups.

CHARACTERISTICS OF THE
NORTH AMERICAN LABOR MOVEMENT

Aside from size and organization the labor movement in North America has some distinctive characteristics which are worthy of note.

STRONG LOCAL UNIONS

The basic building block of the union movement is the local union. North American unionism has been called "grass-roots" unionism because of this.

The initial organization of workers occurs at the local level, although organizing efforts may be instigated by or through the international or national union office. Most of the activities of unions are concerned with the welfare of workers *at their place of employment*. These include the negotiation of collective agreements and the handling of grievances. The activities of all union bodies above the local level are of secondary importance to those at the local level. Local unions, even as part of national and international unions, are highly autonomous, and the national or international office of the union can interfere with local affairs in only limited circumstances.[13] The dues which members pay and which are the principal source of union revenue are collected at the local level.

In contrast with this pattern, unions in many European countries are organized from the top down. These unions frequently have no organization at the plant level. Sometimes they do not even deal with individual employers on behalf of their members.

TABLE II-1

UNION MEMBERSHIP BY TYPE OF UNION AND AFFILIATION, 1972[12]

Union Type	Number of Unions	Number of Locals	Membership Number	Per Cent
International unions	99	4,914	1,411,852	59.6
AFL-CIO-CLC	84	4,463	1,195,398	50.5
CLC only	4	146	115,671	4.9
AFL-CIO only	5	8	619	*
Unaffiliated unions	6	297	100,164	4.2
National unions	68	5,278	892,691	37.7
CLC	19	2,862	401,098	16.9
CNTU	12	1,135	218,526	9.2
CCW	4	27	10,511	0.5
Unaffiliated unions	33	1,254	262,556	11.1
Directly chartered local unions	129	129	12,885	0.5
CLC	128	128	12,790	0.5
CNTU	1	1	95	*
Independent local organizations	141	141	53,213	2.2
TOTAL	437	10,462	2,370,641	100.00

*Less than 0.1 per cent

DECENTRALIZED BARGAINING

Most agreements are negotiated by a single local union for a single establishment. Over 60 per cent of unionized employees are covered by an agreement reached between a single employer and one or more unions.[14] Even where more than one employer and one or more unions are engaged in bargaining, at least some issues are always negotiated on a local level.

In some European countries, most or all bargaining takes place at the national level. In Sweden, wages and hours are determined in a single negotiation between an employers' association and a confederation of unions. In Germany, negotiations are generally conducted on a national basis for each industry.

STRONG AND WEAK UNIONS

The North American labor movement is composed of a mixture of both strong and weak national and international unions. One determinant of a union's total strength and the strength of its constituent locals is the extent to which it has organized a particular industry. The Auto Workers represent almost 100 per cent of the employees of the automobile manufacturing companies in North America. It is a large union, large enough to engage, if necessary, in effective economic combat with the large automobile companies. The Teamsters union is also very powerful. It is large, as a high percentage of the trucking industry is organized, and deals with many small, financially weak employers. On the other hand, the Oil, Chemical and Atomic Workers Union is relatively weak. It has organized less than half of the workers in industries in which it operates. Also, the nature of the manufacturing process in these industries is such that a strike puts little economic pressure on the companies. The production process is semiautomatic, and managements have been frequently able to successfully operate plants during strikes.

EXCLUSIVE REPRESENTATION

No matter what the strength of the particular union, all unions in North America operate under the principle of exclusive representation. This means that only one union may represent any particular group of employees for the purpose of collective bargaining. Procedures for the certification of an exclusive bargaining agent are written into the laws of every jurisdiction in North America.

While there may be more than one union representing employees in a plant or in a company in North America, the boundaries of each union's jurisdiction are usually delineated with care. Also, whenever more than one union is present, a rationale for the arrangement exists, either in the nature of the production process, or in the existence of groups with separately identifiable interests and a desire to be represented by different unions. In contrast, in England exclusive representation does not exist, and workers even in the same production operation or department may be represented by several different unions. Even workers working side by side doing the same job may belong to different unions.

BUSINESS UNIONISM

Perhaps the most outstanding characteristic of unionism in North America is the underlying philosophy of business unionism. Samuel Gompers, the founder of the AFL, summed up the union movement's goals when he said that workers wanted "more and ever more of the product of their labor." That meant higher wages and benefits, shorter working hours and improved working conditions. The goal was to be achieved by direct action against employers, and not by changing the economic system. Successful North American unionism has accepted capitalism and free enterprise and generally rejected socialism and radicalism in any form.

In line with this philosophy labor leaders are fairly conservative in their outlook. To many, the labor movement has lost its vitality as a result of its success. The labor movement has been accused of "sleepwalking along the corridors of history."[15] Union leaders have been accused of becoming "money-hungry, taking on the grossest features of business society." Other observers say that:

> Organized labor should function as the conscience of an industrial society speaking for those who would otherwise have no voice, and holding aloft for all to see a vision of society animated by justice. Some unions still do exactly that. But a union which ignores this duty has lost its vocation. It has become just another business, better than some, perhaps, and worse than others, and entitled to exactly that amount of respect, neither less nor more.[16]

To these observers, the labor movement can only find salvation in abandoning its long-standing support of the political-economic "system." This is unlikely to happen. Working within that system has provided North American workers with the highest standard of living in the world, and workers are unlikely to join in any efforts to radically change the "system."

LIMITED POLITICAL ORIENTATION

Along with their lack of a radical ideology North American unions have generally lacked interest in direct affiliation with political parties and in real control of the political process or the government. In many European and Latin American countries, labor unions are affiliated with political parties, or vice versa.

Unions in North America have always been interested in the political process and have followed the dictum laid down by Gompers to "reward labor's friends and punish labor's enemies." In the United States, unions have generally supported candidates of the Democratic Party and have spent large sums of money in support of candidates whom they favored. For example, United States unions provided six or seven million dollars toward Hubert Humphrey's 1968 presidential campaign, although they generally refrained from helping George McGovern's 1972 presidential campaign. In 1972 they devoted their funds and organizations instead to many other Democrats who were candidates. However, unions have on occasion supported Republican candidates or remained officially neutral. More important, unions have not been consistently able to deliver the votes of their members to officially endorsed candidates. The defeats of Adlai Stevenson in 1952 adn 1956 and the defeat of Hubert Humphrey were evidence of this. The same has been true on a state and local basis.

Canadian unions have shown more interest in affiliation with political parties than have their United States counterparts. In 1921 the unions actually formed a party of their own, the Canadian Labour Party. However, many unions refused to join, and the party was short-lived and unsuccessful.

Some unions, primarily industrial unions, affiliated with the Cooperative Commonwealth Federation (CCF) and were instrumental in the foundation of the New Democratic Party (NDP) in 1961. However, only about 13 per cent of union members in Canada are presently affiliated with the NDP through their local unions.[17] Within the party, the participating unions have helped to steer a course well to the political right. In general, they are the most conservative element within the NDP.

The support given to the NDP by Canadian unions has not always been translated into votes during elections. While the NDP has formed governments in Manitoba, Saskatchewan, and British Columbia, the party was swamped in the 1971 Ontario elections, and Ontario is Canada's most highly industrialized province. In the 1963 federal election both the Liberals and Conservatives received more votes of union members than did the NDP. In 1968, the Liberals received 46 per cent of the union members' votes, the Conservatives 21 per cent and the NDP 28 per cent.[18]

Thus, in both the United States and Canada, union support for candidates of particular parties cannot be termed either monolithic or particularly successful. While efforts will probably be made to elect candidates, labor unions will still exert as much, or more, effort to making their views known to whatever government is in power.

FACTORS INFLUENCING
INDUSTRIAL RELATIONS

Union and management interactions or relationships display almost infinite variety. The relationship between unions and management has been characterized as a challenge-response process: union challenge and management response. The challenge is dual: a negotiation challenge and a grievance challenge. The challenge and the response can be militant, moderate, or weak to the point of virtual nonexistence. The nature of the challenge and the response — whether it is militant or nonmilitant — is a reflection of how the parties use the power they have and how they tend to relate to each other as human beings.

Union-management relationships can be arranged on a spectrum, ranging from conflict to collusion. Any particular union-management relationship can be placed on this spectrum in relationship to certain key or bench-mark relationships.[19]

THE SPECTRUM OF UNION-MANAGEMENT RELATIONS

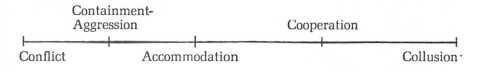

CONFLICT

In a relationship characterized as "conflict," the parties may be said to be actively attempting to "do each other in." Both the challenge and the response are likely to be extremely militant. Management does not want its employees represented by a union and will do everything in its power to see that the union is destroyed. In turn, the union is fighting for survival — on its own terms — and will do everything it can to survive, returning the company's actions tit-for-tat even if it means destroying the company.

Many of the activities which used to characterize conflict are now illegal: employer blacklists, yellow-dog contracts, the use of spies, or massive, violent picketing. Others, such as the use of strikebreakers, or moving the plant,[20] are not illegal, *per se*.

Under the law, an employer must bargain with a union which the majority of employees designate as their representative. However, the employer does not have to agree to a contract; conflict is still possible. Pure conflict, though, is rarely found today. Most employers will actively resist unionization, but if and when unionization is an accomplished fact they will attempt to develop some sort of continuing relationship with the unions.

CONTAINMENT-AGGRESSION

In a relationship characterized as containment-aggression the parties tolerate the existence of one another — but just barely. The union challenge and management response can be characterized as militant.

Management acts to restrict the degree of authority which it shares with the union. The union actively works to increase the scope of its influence. In this type of relationship the parties tend to be very legalistic, insistent on following the contract to the letter. The scope of arbitration is frequently restricted.

Jealous of their rights, the parties may engage in petty bickering. The General Electric — International Union of Electrical Workers relationship was for many years a typical containment-aggression relationship. Virgil Day, a company vice president, characterized the union as "attempting to perform a hysterectomy on the goose that lays the golden egg." When several company officers were sent to prison in the United States for violating the antitrust laws, the union President, James Carey, sent them games of Monopoly to help them pass the time.

ACCOMMODATION

Further along the spectrum is a relationship described as accommodation. Here, while still watchful of their rights, the parties are actively attempting to adjust to each other. They are learning to live with each other, even though the relationship is not always happy. They are tolerant of one another, and the union challenge is somewhat moderate. Management views the union as a channel of communication to employees rather than an obstacle to communication. A fair amount of compromise characterizes the dealings of the parties in this type of relationship. The collective bargaining agenda is conventional: wages, benefits, hours and working conditions; but management does not attempt to restrict the agenda in regard to these items as it does under containment-aggression.

COOPERATION

The collective bargaining agenda is much broader in scope under a cooperative relationship. It includes almost any matter of normal concern to management: production scheduling, prices, waste elimination, technological change, work measurement and methods analysis. The union and the workers it represents are seen as full partners in the enterprise. The two parties jointly deal with problems to the mutual benefit of both. Companies and unions that have adopted "Scanlon plans" provide examples of cooperative relationships. Few union-management relationships can be called cooperative.

COLLUSION

This final type of relationship is found where union and management are colluding to the detriment of another party. Sometimes those being harmed are the workers which the union supposedly represents. This type of unionism, known as "gangster" unionism or "predatory" unionism, is rare. The union (for a fee) signs a collective-bargaining agreement with the employer, and this effectively prevents another union from organizing employees (an existing contract is generally a bar to an organizing attempt). That agreement, called a "sweetheart contract," does not provide very significant benefits to the workers.

A legislative enquiry in Ontario in 1973 and 1974 heard testimony about union representatives receiving "payoffs" from companies in the Toronto construction industry to help ensure labor peace. These arrangements were similar to sweetheart agreements, and, in truth, were in many cases extortion rackets masquerading as trade unions.

In another variant of a collusive relationship the union and the employer conspire to help themselves at the expense of other manufacturers and the general public. A classic case of this type of relationship occurred in New York City. There the union, the International Brotherhood of Electrical Workers, represented all the workers who installed and manufactured electrical equipment. The union workers refused to install any equipment not manufactured in New York City. This provided jobs for other union members and allowed the New York manufacturers to charge New York customers very high prices for the equipment. This practice was ruled illegal by the United States Supreme Court in a famous decision, *Allen Bradley Company v. Local No. 3, IBEW*.[21]

There is probably no union-management relationship which fits neatly into one of the categories described above. Most collective bargaining relationships probably fall somewhere in between containment and accommodation. However, this brief enumeration shows that a variety of relationships are possible. The exact nature of the relationship depends on both union and management, and the parties are responsible for their relationship, whatever it is like. Generally parties get exactly the kind of relationship they deserve.

*   *   *

A number of factors influence the parties as they evolve a relationship. These factors can be differentiated into two types: those internal to the relationship and under the control of the parties, and those external to the relationship and somewhat beyond the control of the parties.

INTERNAL FACTORS AFFECTING
LABOR RELATIONS

HISTORY AND TRADITION

All union-management relationships must be viewed in a historical context. Even new relationships have a history that includes the union's organizational efforts and the response to them by the employer as well as the relationship between the employer and the employees prior to the establishment of the union.

The impact of history and tradition in a relationship can be seen in a number of ways. The parties may have a tradition of following certain wage settlements in other companies or industries in their own negotiations. Historically, certain work groups may have received a wage differential. Management may have responded only to the use of pressure tactics — wildcat strikes or slowdowns — by the union. Workers may have traditionally received a certain benefit, such as a coffee break or a Christmas bonus.

Insofar as history and tradition influence the parties' expectations about each other, rapid change cannot usually be accomplished without some upheaval. A company that has followed a set of policies designed to implement a containment-aggression relationship with the union could not logically expect to change that relationship to one of accommodation overnight. Mutual trust is earned *over time*.

Workers in the Canadian elevator industry had historically signed collective agreements based on settlements in the United States. Since the same international union and the same companies were involved in both countries, the historical pattern had considerable logic. However, in 1972/73, the Canadian branch of the union refused to go along with the pattern established by the U.S. agreements and struck the companies involved, in an attempt to achieve their own particular demands. The companies strongly resisted this move and, in fact, the dispute was resolved only by government intervention, most particularly the Ontario legislature's order for compulsory arbitration of the dispute. Thus an attempt to change a historical pattern of behavior was not easily accomplished, and it resulted in a major conflict.

NATURE OF LEADERSHIP

The personalities of leaders of both the union and management and the type of leadership they provide are major determinants of a union-management relationship.

The leadership of Edgar Kaiser, who was attempting to step out from his father's shadow, was responsible for the attempts to develop a cooperative relationship at Kaiser Steel Company. Individuals like Herbert Markley at Timken, Lemuel Boulware at General Electric and Harold Clawson at Stelco left a strong imprint on their companies' labor relations policies. During the early 1970s Cesar Chavez provided leadership that led to the organization of agricultural workers in California in the face of massive resistance. The powerful, centralized leadership of David Beck and James Hoffa was responsible for building the power of the Teamsters union. The development of the entire industrial union movement can in large part be attributed to the forceful personality and leadership of John L. Lewis.

Some union leaders, like Walter Reuther, had personalities strong enough to generate enthusiasm and trust among members so that they would follow him in whatever direction he led. His endorsement of a settlement — whatever that settlement was — was generally enough to ensure its acceptance. In many unions the leadership is diffuse or lacks the record of historical success and the charisma of a Walter Reuther. In these situations it is somewhat more difficult to reach an agreement.

UNION POLITICS

The nature of leadership is particularly important within unions, because unions are democratic institutions. Unlike management, union leadership serves at the pleasure of its constituency.

In the tradition of Orwell's pigs, all unions are democratic, but some unions are more democratic than others. Some unions, like the Printers, have an internal party system, and each party puts forth a slate of officers for each election. Other unions, like the Mine Workers, have had an entrenched leadership which seemed willing to go to almost any extreme to quiet opposition within the union. In 1974, the former President of the Mineworkers, Tony Boyle, was convicted of ordering the murder of an opponent.[22]

All unions have appointive officers. These are found particularly on the staffs of national and international unions. The number of appointive officers varies from union to union, but in almost every instance the major offices of local, national, and international unions are elective. Officers who do not perform at a level consistent with the expectations of the membership face the prospect of opposition and defeat in the next election. In addition, many unions require that new contracts be ratified by the membership before they become effective. In these unions, a membership dissatisfied with the deal their negotiator has made can reject it.

Within unions special-interest groups may exist. This is particularly true of industrial unions where the goals and outlook of the skilled members (electricians, machinists) are frequently different from those of the nonskilled or semiskilled workers in the same local. In these situations, the leadership faces the problem of responding to these often conflicting demands in a manner that will satisfy the majority.

POLICIES

Perhaps the most important determinants of the relationship between the parties are the policies adopted by the unions and management, or lack thereof.

A policy is a statement as to how an organization will act in a given situation. While leaders of most organizations believe that their actions are policy-guided, those actions frequently are not in fact so guided. Actions frequently are impromptu and often made with short-run considerations rather than long-run considerations in mind. Those companies with successful labor relations are successful because they manage by policy.[23] The same is true for unions.

Management and the union face some fundamental policy decisions in their response to each other and to collective bargaining in general. What kind of a relationship do they want? How hard are they willing to work to achieve that relationship? In general, the tone of the relationship is the result of management initiative and not union initiative.

Both parties must make policy decisions concerning the content and administration of collective agreements. These decisions must encompass a host of specific subject areas, including wage payment systems, benefit level and structure, seniority systems and discipline. The parties must determine whether and to what extent they will use or resist pressure in the pursuit of their goals. Both sides must have implementing and procedural policies for translating their goals into action.

For example, a management may decide to accept the union and to be "firm but fair" in dealing with it. In terms of discipline this basic policy may give rise to a substantive policy of administering discipline for just cause. The discipline policy may, in turn, be implemented by a policy of following a progressive disciplinary system. Detailed procedural policies would then follow to outline the specifics of the systems, such as the penalties associated with absenteeism.[24] A union could make a set of policies in the same way.

The policies adopted by the parties may be identical, may be different, or may be amenable to compromise. In any event, these policies and the extent to which they exist will influence the general relationship of the union and management and their specific actions within that relationship.

EXTERNAL INFLUENCES
ON LABOR RELATIONS

External factors influencing labor relations can be divided into six principal categories: industry characteristics, technology, socioeconomic conditions, legislation, government administration, and the judiciary.

INDUSTRY CHARACTERISTICS

The elasticity of demand for products produced in an industry and substitution availability are important industry characteristics which can influence collective bargaining. In industries where price can significantly influence demand, management will be extremely cost-conscious and tend to resist union wage demands. Where consumers can use alternate products, for instance aluminum instead of steel, or can obtain products from other markets, substituting Japanese steel for Canadian steel for example, management may be cost-conscious but also reluctant to take a strike lest customers turn permanently to the substitute product or source of supply. In some industries, such as education, medical care, or construction, there may be no available substitute for the product.

The labor cost as a percentage of the total cost of a product may well influence the parties in their relationship. In industries where labor costs are a significant cost item, such as construction, education, transportation, these costs will be monitored closely. In other industries, such as utilities, which are capital intensive and where labor costs are not as important as other costs, management may be less inclined to strongly resist wage demands.

The structure of the industry and the extent to which it is unionized, which is conditioned by the structure, are also important. Atomistic industries, such as gasoline distribution, are much harder for unions to organize totally than are oligopolistic industries like steel, or monopolies such as utilities. Unions attempt to organize as much of an industry as they can, in order to take intra-industry wages out of competition. Where they have not done this and where they are unlikely to do so, management will find competitive pressures forcing them to resist large union demands, or unions may feel compelled to make modest demands.

A final industry characteristic of note is the degree of cyclicality in sales and production. Agricultural firms, though not highly unionized, could find themselves under enormous pressure from a unionized work force at either planting or harvest time, as can other producers with seasonal production peaks. Enterprises which have seasonal or other peaks (such as supermarkets, with a weekly peak on Thursday, Friday and Saturday) are somewhat difficult for unions to organize, because they frequently employ part-time workers who are often not interested in unionization.

Cyclicality can also affect the character of the issues faced by the parties. The development of plans to provide supplemental unemployment benefits is an example. Employees in the steel and auto industries needed protection against frequent layoffs caused, in part, by the cyclicality of those industries.

TECHNOLOGY

The nature of the production technology also influences labor relations. Some process industries, such as oil refineries, are easy for management personnel to operate during a strike. Others, such as steel mills, are impossible to operate without the regular work force. A strike in the former can mean no loss of production and is not very effective. A strike in the latter is the reverse. For example, a strike at Bell Canada in 1971 and at Ontario Hydro in 1972 caused so few inconveniences that consumers hardly knew they were going on.

The nature of the technology also affects the character of the issues faced by the parties. Continuous process operations mean shift work which can present scheduling problems. Work which is dirty, such as mining, creates the issue of paid wash-up time. Some technologies, such as clothing manufacturing, are amenable to the use of incentive systems. Some highly automated industries, such as telecommunications, are not.

SOCIOECONOMIC CONDITIONS

For years the union movement was a plaything of the economic cycle, growing during good times and declining during bad. Although this is no longer true, economic conditions may well influence a union's willingness to settle and also the nature of its respective concerns in bargaining. When economic times are good, many managements are often unwilling to take a strike and are thus more receptive to union demands. When times are bad, unions may be more concerned with security than money. Recently the economic conditions of high unemployment, high inflation and low profits have made bargaining difficult.

The situation in the work environment often mirrors social conditions in the outside world. Thus in Quebec, unions and management face problems caused by the French-Canadian identity crisis, demands for French-Canadian equality, including the use of French as a working language. In both the United States and Canada, the problem of equal rights and opportunities for women is manifesting itself in the workplace. In the United States, the civil rights struggle is often carried out on the job as well as in the courts and the Congress.

LEGISLATION

Legislation is probably the greatest outside force affecting labor relations. The law has created a whole framework within which unions and management operate. Many of the parties' actions, from the recognition of the union, to the negotiation and administration of a contract, to conciliation, mediation and sometimes arbitration are carried out because the law *requires* that they be done.

The law differs in important respects between the United States and Canada. Within Canada there are 11 separate jurisdictions — 10 provincial and one federal — none of which are exactly alike in their legal requirements. In the United States most workers fall under the federal jurisdiction. A knowledge of the law under which the parties are operating is essential to understanding their behavior.

GOVERNMENT ADMINISTRATION

Governments are not only responsible for the creation of labor relations law but also for administering that law. The principal agencies for administering the law are labor relations boards, which are appointed by the government. Decisions by the boards affect every aspect of the relationship between labor and management.

Canadian boards are frequently composed of an equal number of members from labor, management and the general public. On the whole, Canadian boards have been less partisan than the National Labor Relations Board in the United States. Republican appointments to the U.S. Board have generally had a pro-business bias, while Democratic appointees have been somewhat pro-labor. It is possible for an incumbent U.S. president to formulate a board largely to his liking.

In Canada, the provincial and federal Labour ministers frequently are called to play a direct role in labor relations. These ministers are generally responsible for the appointment of conciliators, which act to help the parties resolve their differences during contract negotiations. If individual conciliators are unsuccessful, Labour ministers usually have the power to intervene a second time through the appointment of conciliation boards. The appointment of conciliators is generally compulsory in Canada as a precondition to legal strike action.

Aside from those actions which are required, governments may intervene in labor disputes in a number of other ways. In Canada Labour ministers may, if required, select arbitrators for the resolution of contract interpretation disputes. In the United States, the President has the power to seek a court order to halt strikes for 80 days if a strike or threatened strike is deemed to create a national emergency. Government may, in addition, appoint or act itself as a special mediator. Finally, the government may legislate the end of labor disputes, as the Canadian government did in the dock strike in Quebec in the summer of 1972 and the rail strike in 1973.

THE JUDICIARY

Although the role of the judiciary has been reduced from what it has been in prior years, this group still plays an important role in labor relations.

Before legislation was passed institutionalizing the present industrial relations systems, the courts time and time again handed down decisions declaring union activities illegal. Even after unions were legalized the courts frequently acted to limit the scope of their activities. Today's courts may, under limited conditions, restrict some union activities — such as picketing.

The courts may also review decisions of labor relations boards, and the definitive statements on the interpretation of the various labor relations acts are found in court decisions, particularly those of the highest courts. The courts also review, on the petition of one of the parties, decisions of arbitrators in contract interpretation disputes. Finally, violations of the labor relations acts are tried in the courts, and the courts are the only agencies which can assess penalties for violation of this legislation.

*   *   *

This introduction to the subject of labor relations is intended to be just that — an introduction. It has not attempted to tell the whole story, to explain everything. It can be used as a guide, as a list of things to look for in analyzing labor relations situations. Like most other subjects, labor relations is more complicated than it appears after a cursory examination. This note can, we hope, be the beginning to a fruitful study of the subject.

NOTES TO CHAPTER 1

1. John Mitchell, *Organized Labor*, (Philadelphia: American Book and Bible House, 1903) pp.2-4.

2. Economics and Research Branch, Canada Department of Labour, *Labour Organizations in Canada*, 1972. (Ottawa, Information Canada, 1973), p. xi.

3. Ibid., p. xix.

4. Source: Union Members, "Industrial and Geographic Distribution of Union Membership in Canada in 1971," *The Labour Gazette,* July 1973, pp. 466, 467.

Paid Work Force (main headings) "The Labour Force" Cat No 71-001 Labour Force Survey Division, Statistics Canada.

(Subheadings — Manufacturing, Transportation, Communication and Other Utilities), "Employment, Earnings, and Hours," 72-002, Monthly Employment Payroll, and Labour Income Section, Labour Division, Statistics Canada.

The figures for the subheadings under Manufacturing and Transportation, Communication, and Other Utilities are for total employees in establishments employing 20 or more employees and are annual averages for the year 1971.

5. There is some evidence that the attitudes of clerical workers are changing, however. See: Alfred Vogel, "Your Clerical Workers Are Ripe for Unionism," *Harvard Business Review*, March-April 1971, pp. 48-54.

6. A siderographer works in the printing industry, reproducing engraved steel printing plates.

7. *Labour Organizations in Canada,* op, cit., pp. xvi-xvii.

8. Ibid., p. xi.

9. Ibid., p. xxi.

10. Fraser Isbester, "Quebec Labour in Perspective 1949-1969" in *Canadian Labour in Transition, Richard U. Miller and Fraser Isbester, eds. (Scarborough, Ontario: Prentice-Hall Ltd., 1971), pp. 241-2.

11. Ibid., p. 266.

12. *Labour Organizations in Canada*, 1972, Labour Canada, Economics and Research, p. xxv, Table 3. Ottawa, Information Canada, 1973.

13. The taking over of the affairs of a local by the national or international is called a *trusteeship*.

14. Task Force on Labour Relations, *Canadian Industrial Relations*, (Ottawa: The Privy Council Office, 1968) pp. 60-2.

15. This discussion of criticisms of the labor movement is based on Derek C. Bok and John T. Dunlop, *Labor and The American Community*, (New York: Simon and Schuster, 1970).

16. Ibid., p. 32.

17. Richard Ulric Miller, "Organized Labour and Politics in Canada," in *Canadian Labour in Transition, op. cit., pp. 207-19.

18. Ibid., p. 231.

19. Benjamin Selekman et. al., *Problems in Labor Relations*, (3rd. ed.; New York: McGraw-Hill Inc., 1965), pp. 1-11.

20. In the U.S., if the only reason for relocating a plant is to avoid unionization, it is illegal.

21. 325 U.S. 797 (1945).

22. Boyle, it should be noted, was defeated by a reform slate of officers, under a special election supervised by the U.S. Dept. of Labor.

23. Sumner H. Slichter, James H. Healy, and E. Robert Livernash, *The Impact of Collective Bargaining on Management* (Washington D.C.: The Brookings Institution, 1960), p. 880.

24. Ibid., p. 882.

2. CAPSULE HISTORY OF CANADIAN LABOR RELATIONS

Ever since 1827 Canadian labor history has been dominated by the development of world capitalism, especially in the United States. While there were frequent opportunities for Canadian unions to acquire characteristics of their own, these opportunities were largely passed by, so that now there is little distinction between unions in the United States and Canada. Over 62 per cent of Canada's unionized workers are members of international unions with headquarters in the United States and with officers from both countries. Over half of all Canadian manufacturing concerns are U.S. controlled, and over 85 per cent of these are unionized.[1] Consequently there has been a commonality of personalities, a commonality of experiences and a commonality of problems between Canada and the U.S.

THE CONSPIRACY DOCTRINE

In its earliest stages Canadian and U.S. labor relations were dominated by British common law. One of the most striking features of this law was the doctrine of criminal conspiracy. Combinations of workers for purposes of collective bargaining were treated the same as conspiracies to commit murder, because, according to the early courts, their purpose was to restrain trade — a criminal act. Courts and legislatures whittled away at the conspiracy doctrine for more than a century — first reducing combinations of workers to the category of civil conspiracy — then, gradually, dropping the whole conspiracy concept. However, the doctrine held on stubbornly, and it was not until 1943 that the doctrine of civil conspiracy finally died in Ontario.

In 1871, after two generations of struggle, British unions won statutory relief from the criminal conspiracy doctrine. The following year, 1872, the doctrine received a test in Canada. This was the year that Canada's workers first demonstrated identity as a class. They were fighting for a nine-hour day, and promotion groups had been formed in many of the country's major cities to press the issue. Leading the way in Toronto was the Typographical Society. In 1872 the printers represented by that society were working six days a week, 10 hours a day, and they decided on the following demands: "A week's work to consist of 54 hours, $10 per week, 25¢ per hour for job printers."[2]

Toronto's publishers, led by George Brown, editor of the *Globe and Banner*, rejected the demand, stating that shorter hours were bad — that men would have more time to spend at home and would make a nuisance of themselves. The printers, in turn, went on strike.

Brown set out to break the strike. First he hired detectives to shadow the strikers. This resulted in several arrests on vagrancy charges and some trials on breach of contract charges wherein strikers were found guilty. Then Brown brought in strike breakers.

The next 10 days provided the first real demonstration of labor solidarity in Canada's history. The Toronto Trades Assembly, a central labor organization with 24 affiliated unions, organized a Queen's Park demonstration for April 15 in order to rally the population against the employers. Trade unionists from the Iron Moulders, Bricklayers, Masons, Cigarmakers, Bakers, Machinists, Blacksmiths and many others joined together in a march along King Street to Yonge, north up Yonge Street to College, west along College to Queen's Park. At Queen's Park 10,000 gathered and listened in apparent good spirits to a series of speeches — even while a snow storm began.[3]

The next day the employers struck back. They secured the arrest of the 24 members of the Printers Vigilance Committee, including John Armstrong, Vice President of the Toronto Printers local and later president of the union, J.S. Williams, Toronto Trades Assembly Secretary, and Edward F. Clarke, later mayor of Toronto. Employers argued that the common law forbade combinations of labor, and Magistrate McNab agreed, finding all 24 guilty. He said they were members of an illegal body, a combination.

News of the arrests and subsequent trial spread rapidly, and on April 17 around 4,000 persons gathered in Market Square. Excitement was high as speakers condemned the arrests and called for political action.

Meanwhile in Ottawa Conservative Prime Minister Sir John A. Macdonald saw this as a chance to embarrass his political opponent, George Brown, and, perhaps, gain some votes in the federal elections which would take place in several months. On Thursday, April 18, Macdonald introduced emancipating legislation patterned on the British Act of 1871. It provided that the mere combining to increase wages or to lower hours was not a conspiracy and did not violate the common law. This became the Trade Union Act of 1872 and marked an apparent end to the criminal conspiracy doctrine in Canada.

The employers were furious, but Macdonald's action, coupled with the persistence of the unions, resulted in substantial victories for the nine-hour movement. The Toronto Printers won their demands; so did those in Hamilton. Later that year the Great Western Railway signed an agreement for "54 hours a week at 58 1/2 hours pay," and the Grand Trunk Railway at Montreal instituted the nine-hour day and granted a general pay increase.

THE CANADIAN LABOUR UNION (CLU)

Following the Toronto Printers strike of 1872 Canada's first trade union center, the Canadian Labour Union (CLU), was born. The CLU was partly a product of worker solidarity demonstrated in Toronto. It was also a product of Confederation.

Confederation, in 1867, was a response to the fact that Canada's political structure had been unable to cope with the country's expanding economic forces. Railways and canals were needed, and dollars were needed to build them. In addition, there was a desire for greater independence from Britain and the United States. Confederation was followed by territorial unification brought about largely through railway building. Progress was swift, but there were serious shortcomings. Much of the immediate benefits went to large companies based in Toronto and Montreal, and inequities for employers and workers in other parts of the country were great. Thus there were moves to create a centralized labor movement to try to deal with those inequities.

Hamilton, Ontario, trade unionists pioneered the movement, and on May 3, 1872 they hosted a conference of union delegates from Toronto, Brantford and Montreal. This was probably Canada's first labor convention and resulted in formation of the CLU. A followup convention was held in Toronto on September 23 at which a constitution was adopted with a preamble as follows:

> The working men of the Dominion of Canada, in common with intelligent producers of the world, feel the necessity of co-operation and harmonious action to secure their mutual interests and just compensation for their toil, and such limitation of the hours of labor that may tend to promote their physical and intellectual well being.[4]

The convention took up problems of shorter hours, immigration, convict and child labor, and organization of the unorganized. Rules of the CLU provided for annual meetings, with delegates elected from the unions. Per capita dues were fixed at five cents quarterly per member in the case of a directly chartered local and 50 cents per member for affiliated unions.[5]

The formation of the CLU, coupled with labor's victories in the nine-hour struggles, suggested that the labor movement in Canada was on the threshold of significant advances on behalf of the country's working population. However, this was not the case. Forty-one years later, in 1913, the labor movement had succeeded in organizing less than ten per cent of the country's workers, contrasting sharply with Britain and Germany where over 22 per cent of the working population had been organized. Predominant among the reasons for labor's slow growth in Canada were the following: (a) an encumbering legal status, (b) confusion in the ideology of the movement, (c) a problem of public image, and (d) severe employer resistance.

(a) Legal Status of Unions

The Trade Union Act of 1872 permitted groups of workers to join together for higher wages and lower hours. However, the government put another law on the statute books at the same time — The Criminal Law Amendment Act. This provided penalties for violence or intimidation during organizing campaigns and strikes, and, in addition, it provided that a union-management contract was not enforceable in a court of law. Soon thereafter, in 1873, a member of the Knights of St. Crispin was arrested on a conspiracy charge under the Criminal Law Amendment Act for engaging in a strike. This was followed by more arrests and jail sentences, giving rise to demands by labor that the Act be repealed.

Unions were inhibited by the almost total absence till World War II of legislation protecting the right to organize and, once organized, requiring employers to bargain. Social legislation was almost as slow in coming. Canada's first workmen's compensation bill was enacted in 1914 in the Province of Ontario. The first Unemployment Insurance Act was passed in 1940. There were no laws providing for old-age pensions or widows' allowances until World War II.

Instances of exploitation of women and children were rampant throughout the country. Two Royal Commissions, one in 1881, another in 1887, were appointed to inquire into conditions. They subsequently published reports of children working through the night in a glass factory, a child of 8 toiling in a cotton mill earning wages of $92 a year, brutal beatings without reason, and fines. The ultimate in fines may have been reached in one tobacco plant when a boy of 14 had worked 40 hours for $1.60 but was fined $1.75 and so ended up owing the company 15 cents. The boy's father saw no future in this business and demanded the fine be returned, but to no avail.[6]

Probably the principal reason for legislative inaction regarding social conditions was the continuing conflict of powers between the federal and provincial governments. The federal government was reluctant to act on social matters, because there was general feeling that it lacked jurisdiction. As a result the responsibility fell on provincial governments, and they were slow to act. In 1880, Ontario adopted an Act regulating the hours of labor, but did not cover shops with less than 20 people, the places where abuses were most prevalent. Furthermore, no inspectors were appointed to enforce the Act until two years later, and no case of violation was brought to the courts for two more years.[7]

In Quebec, progress was even slower. In 1885 that province passed a

Factory Act prohibiting labor for women and children beyond 12 1/2 hours in a day or 72 hours per week. Employment of boys under 12 and girls under 14 was prohibited, but provision for inspection was never made, so that violations were virtually unchecked.[8]

(b) Ideology

Through the years the labor movement was consistently thwarted by confusion and disagreement about matters of ideology. Principal among the ideological issues were these two:

□ International v. national unions
□ Craft v. industrial organization

1. International unionism[9]

Until the 1860s the labor movement in Canada had been almost exclusively Canadian. Then, in 1861, there was a significant move among some of the craft organizations to affiliate with U.S. unions. Among the crafts involved were the molders and the printers. The term "international union" referred almost exclusively to unions operating both in the United States and Canada, but nowhere else. In early years the relationship was fraternal; later it became a relationship of U.S. domination that transcended individual unions and influenced the development of national-level confederations.

There were many reasons for early affiliation. The most important were the following:

□ *The underdeveloped condition of the Canadian economy*, which gave rise to the desire of many Canadians to go to the United States for jobs. The union card helped.
□ *Solidarity*. In the mid-1800s it was natural for members of crafts to seek out their own. At that time craft production was far more important than industrial production, so that members of a trade who wanted a strong union looked to members of the same trade in other locations rather than to members of other trades or unskilled workers in their own location. Most tradesmen, like carpenters, bricklayers and painters, were relatively isolated, and their Canadian members were few. It made sense to become stronger by joining a larger organization of the same trades in the United States.
□ *Money*. The more members paying dues the greater financial security in the form of strike assistance in case of a bargaining impasse.
□ *Interflow of the United States and Canadian economies*. U.S.-dominated and U.S.-owned businesses were encouraged to set up operations in Canada in order to help develop the economy and create jobs. Many did so because of the great supply of cheap natural resources and the availability of cheap labor. Labor and management both

sought consistency in their relationships, and the presence of the same union in both countries was a comfortable means toward that end.

The merits of international unionism have provided subject matter for interminable debates. Some say it was a prime factor in speeding the growth of the Canadian trade union movement which, in turn, contributed to the rapid growth of the economy in general. Others say it impeded development of a national image — that for Canada a politically oriented, socialist-inclined, industrial form of unionism would have contributed to more rapid growth and a self-sufficient, individualistic economy.

These arguments will continue without resolution. However, it can safely be said that the international union set-up was the most important single factor contributing to the nearly identical development of the U.S. and Canadian labor movements. In 1902, for example, the Trades and Labour Congress (TLC), Canada's oldest continuous labor organization, bowed to the wishes of the American Federation of Labor (AFL) and Samuel Gompers, AFL's president, in three actions at its Berlin (Kitchener), Ontario, convention. In the first instance the convention refused to seat delegates from the Montreal Federated Trades Council, lifted that council's charter, and seated instead AFL-endorsed members. Then the convention adopted an amendment to the TLC constitution by a vote of 89 to 35 not to recognize a national union in a jurisdiction where an international union existed. This effectively excluded the Knights of Labor, an industrial organization whose membership included many different crafts. The Knights, who had been founded in the United States in 1869, were geared to unskilled workers and tended to organize on a plant, rather than craft, basis. This was directly contrary to the philosophy of the AFL, a craft-oriented organization. In 1886 the Knights had combined with various Canadian craft unions to form the TLC, thus making it an all-inclusive organization.

The TLC's action of 1902 was not only a stab in the back to the Knights but also represented one of the most important events in Canadian labor history, because this, the country's largest, most influencial labor organization, had made a clear choice in favor of U.S. domination and abandoned, for the time being, one of its original reasons for being. This was punctuated by the convention's third act — the election of John Flett as president. Mr. Flett was a paid officer of an international union.[10]

In 1938 the TLC made another decision which confirmed domination by the U.S. based AFL. This involved expulsion of members affiliated with the Committee for Industrial Organization (CIO). In the prior three years Canadian union membership had increased from 280,648 in 1935 to 383,492 in 1937, the latter figure representing an all-time high for Canada. These increases were due largely to efforts of the CIO which had undertaken organization of the unorganized on an industry basis, spurred considerably by the depression of the 30s and a highly-permissive political climate under U.S. President Franklin D. Roosevelt's New Deal. The CIO's efforts in the United States had carryover effects into Canada.

The CIO was formed in 1935 when a large number of AFL affiliates, including the United Mine Workers of America, the International Typographical Union and the Amalgamated Clothing Workers, split off from the AFL as a result of a convention fight. The fight centered on the issue of whether member unions should have the right to organize on an industrial basis. John L. Lewis, President of the United Mineworkers, led the fight, and the whole thing was brought to a head when at one point in the convention Lewis walked across the floor and punched William Hutcheson, President of the United Brotherhood of Carpenters and Joiners, in the face. Lewis subsequently played a leading role in formation of the Steelworkers Organizing Committee (SWOC) in a unionization drive against the major steel companies. Several new unions were formed as a result of the CIO's efforts. These included the United Steel Workers of America (USW), the United Automobile Workers of America (UAW) and the United Electrical, Radio and Machine Workers of America (UE).

In 1036 the AFL Executive Council suspended the CIO unions on grounds that they were fostering "dual unionism." Finally in 1937 they were expelled. Throughout the 30s the two organizations competed aggressively for members without particular regard for craft or industrial distinctions. By 1937 the CIO faction actually exceeded the AFL in membership by close to 300,000. In 1938 they held a convention and formed a new federation, the Congress of Industrial Organizations. The first president of the organization was John L. Lewis.

CIO unions which were most active in Canada during the late 30s and early 40s were the USW and the UE. These and others, including national unions directly chartered by the TLC, were responsible for a dramatic increase in Canadian and TLC union membership, so that by 1948 there were 977,594 unionized workers in the country. In 1937 the CIO set up their first office in Canada, located in Toronto. At the same time the AFL was bringing pressure on the TLC executive council to follow the AFL's action of 1937 and expel all CIO affiliates. In the 1937 convention TLC rejected the AFL's stance. However, in December 1938 TLC's executive council met with the AFL executive council and were told that further delays in expulsion of CIO unions would almost certainly lead to the destruction of the TLC, because AFL unions would withdraw. TLC promptly suspended the CIO unions, thus depriving themselves of 11 international unions with around 22,000 members and succumbing once again to U.S. pressure.

Like the 1902 expulsion of the Knights of Labor the TLC's 1938 action was an important crossroads decision in Canadian union life. In 1940 the 11 expelled unions joined the All-Canadian Congress of Labour, till then a small, relatively unimportant rival of TLC. At the 1940 convention the All-Canadian Congress constitution was changed, and a new name was adopted — the Canadian Congress of Labour (CCL). CCL became the Canadian counterpart of the CIO.

The Canadian labor movement briefly asserted its sovereignty and independence in 1948 as a result of the Canadian Seamen's Union dispute, but soon after that it reverted to the old ways, featuring U.S. domination and determinism. Here were the circumstances of the Seamen's dispute:

In December 1937 the AFL created the Seafarer's International Union (SIU) in order to compete for bargaining rights on seagoing vessels with the National Maritime Union (NMU), a CIO affiliate. The AFL convention ruled that SIU had jurisdiction over seamen and fishermen in all waters of North America and Canada. TLC's president, Percy Bengough, objected, telling AFL's president, William Green, that this would create a dual representation situation, because the Canadian Seamen's Union (CSU) had been chartered by that organization in 1936 and represented the same people as the SIU would represent.

While Green and Bengough bickered, Pat Sullivan, CSU president and TLC secretary-treasurer, unexpectedly resigned both posts and organized another union — the Canadian Lake Seamen's Union. Although they had contracts with the CSU, Canadian ship owners signed a contract with Sullivan's union. This caused a strike by the CSU, whose jurisdiction was confirmed by a federal government commission. The strike started in June 1948. The companies, in turn, let loose violence on CSU members, bringing in gangsters and others to act as strike breakers. This caused the TLC to call a mass trade union conference in Ottawa to support the CSU. However, a group of Roadmen — full-time Canadian vice presidents of international unions — set up picket lines at the entrance to the conference hall and subsequently told members of the press that the meeting was composed of 98 per cent Communists and two per cent fellow travellers. The Roadmen were supporting SIU's entrance into the Canadian scene and looked upon the Sullivan-CSU clash as an opening for them to wedge their way into the picture.

On September 10, 1948, the executive council of TLC, its patience exhausted, condemned the action of the Roadmen and suspended the Brotherhood of Railway and Steamship Clerks (BRSC) whose leader, Frank Hall, was one of the principal Roadmen.

BRSC's suspension was one of the important issues presented at the September 1948 TLC convention. BRSC had sponsored the SIU in spite of the clause in TLC's constitution prohibiting affiliation of unions whose jurisdiction clashed with existing affiliates. When a vote on the issue was taken the executive council won support 545-198, indicating that in many cases the Roadmen were not supported by their own delegates.[11]

After the convention the TLC executive council met with their AFL counterparts. The AFL proposed revision of TLC's constitution so as to permit "each international union to deliver a block vote at the convention through its Roadmen." The TLC flatly refused, and on its return issued the oft-quoted statement, "*Cooperation, Yes, Domination, No!*". Thus, finally, TLC had asserted its independence.

But the new-found independence of the Canadian labor movement was short-lived, because in 1949 some strong-arm tactics by the AFL brought matters back into their former perspective. The scene was eastern Canada. Late in 1948 Canadian deep-sea shipping companies took a severe bargaining stance with the CSU. They imposed a wage cut ranging from $20 to $50 a month and abolished the union hiring hall. The CSU, 6,500 strong, voted to strike, and the companies countered by terminating bargaining relationships with the CSU and signed contracts with the SIU. The SIU had virtually no Canadian members at the time, so they were glad to get anything and accepted the proposed wage cuts.

All this represented collaborative action by the SIU and employers against an established Canadian union, member of the TLC and certified by the Canada Labour Relations Board as bargaining representative for the companies involved. On March 1, 1949, CSU picket lines in Halifax were broken by goons who boarded a Canadian National steamship and fired on the pickets from the ship. Eight striking seamen were hit.

CSU retaliated, and by May of 1949 they had tied up ports around the world — in Great Britain, Western Europe, Latin America, Africa and New Zealand. A sympathy stoppage in England by 50,000 dockers tied up 121 ships there for 74 days. Meanwhile the TLC, under severe pressure from its international union members, suspended the CSU, charging them with preventing members of affiliated unions from performing their normal work, therefore violating the sanctity of the contract. So less than one year after the *Cooperation, Yes, Dominion, No!* doctrine was proclaimed, it died.[12]

Now, in the 1970s, with rapid growth of white collar unions, professional unions, and unions of government employees, a distinct Canadian labor movement may be emerging. These newest and most rapidly growing organizations have their roots in Canada and have shown no inclination to affiliate with U.S.-based international bodies. This, coupled with the fact that many long-standing international unions are experiencing nationalist breakaways, may represent a genuine assertion of sovereignty that could reshape the entire nature of the labor scene.

2. Craft v. industrial organizations

The ideological battle between those who favored organizations according to crafts against those favoring multicraft organizations in single companies or industries has pervaded North American labor history since the early 1870s when the Knights of St. Crispin, an industrial union of shoemakers, flourished in Canada. In the 1880s the Knights of Labor emerged. They were far bigger and more important than the Knights of St. Crispin, because they represented workers in many different industries. By 1886 the Knights of Labor had at least 158 local organizations in Canada and about 1,200 members. They were strongest in Quebec and Ontario, but their membership extended as far west as Nanaimo on Vancouver Island.

The Knights of Labor survived longer in Canada than in the United States, but their demise in both countries came about for the same reasons: too-rapid growth, vacillating leadership and their acceptance of nearly everyone as members, including radicals, socialists and anarchists. The latter became involved in strikes and demonstrations of violence which not only served to give the Knights a poor image but quickly drained whatever financial strength the organization had built.

Chicago was a special Knights stronghold, and a major test for them occurred in the year 1886 as a result of the Haymarket Square riot. In that year the eight-hour movement was sweeping the United States. On May 1 upwards of 38,000 workers in Chicago staged a general strike in support of the movement. One company, McCormack Harvester, brought in Pinkerton guards and strikebreakers. On May 3 the strikers and strikebreakers clashed, bringing police to the scene. The subsequent fighting resulted in the deaths of four persons and 20 injuries. On May 4 a great protest meeting was held in Haymarket Square. More than 3,000 attended, including Chicago's mayor. Contrary to expectations the meeting was peaceful, and participants were dispersing when a detachment of 200 of Chicago's police arrived. Someone threw a bomb; the police fired. Eventually seven policemen were killed, 67 injured. Four workers were killed and more than 50 injured. The persons responsible were not immediately known, so the police combed the city for suspects. Eventually eight known anarchists were arrested and charged with murder. In an atmosphere of frenzy and fear they were immediately found guilty. Seven were sentenced to death, the eighth to 15 years imprisonment. There had been no evidence presented at the trials to connect the men with the bombing. In fact, all eight were pardoned six years later by Illinois Governor Peter Altgeld. However, when Terrence Powderly, leader of the Knights, was asked by a reporter for his reaction following the trial Powderly said "[The men] are entitled to no more consideration than wild beasts." In taking this kind of position, Powderly put a knife into the back of the Chicago strike leaders, the eight-hour movement, and his own organization. With stronger leadership and discipline the Knights might have emerged as the dominant labor force in North America. Instead they gradually faded away.

The industrial v. craft dispute came to the fore again following World War I. At that time there was industrial unrest and radicalization among workers, manifested, in part, by emergence of several new movements. One such movement came from the 1918 TLC convention. Here delegates from western provinces put forth a strong case for shifting the focus of the organization in order to promote industrial and Canadian unionism. They were summarily rebuffed; so following the convention they held a caucus of their own. This resulted in the Western Canada Labour Conference in March of 1919. Delegates to that conference agreed on a resolution which recommended severance of affiliation with international organizations and formation of an industrial organization. They called themselves the One Big Union (OBU).[13]

The terms of the conference resolution were ambiguous on two counts. First, it was not clear whether there should be secession from international unions. Second, it was not clear what attitude would be taken toward political action. Alberta's delegation had put forth a resolution calling for a united political party; however the prevailing attitude on this score was apparently negative.

As preparations went forward to conduct a referendum regarding the Western Canada Labour Conferences resolution, the Winnipeg General Strike began.[14] While the OBU did not start the strike they were active in it and reaped considerable strength from it.

The Winnipeg General Strike reflected general unrest following the war. It was not confined to Winnipeg but at one point became an interlocked general strike movement based in Winnipeg and extending west and east across Canada. The unrest was caused by the following factors: Troops were returning from the War at the rate of 3,400 per month; unemployment rates were high; employers and landlords were basking in high profits from the War. The Canadian government had not released workers interned for antiwar activity and had rescinded its ban on free speech and free assembly. There were demands for the government to cut living costs and curb profiteers, all as part of a growing dissatisfaction with the social system. A kind of native Canadian socialism was developing which paralleled, in some respects, the Russian revolution of 1917.

The strike itself was set off as a result of refusal by Winnipeg employers to deal with a newly formed metal trades council. The council was a conglomerate of various metal trades workers who had joined together to fight economic grievances. Their members at the time were earning $12 to $15 a week; but $1 in 1919 would buy only what 25 cents had bought before the war. A great number of immigrants were members of the council, many with strong socialist convictions.

The strike started on May 15 with the following demands uppermost:

1. Recognition of the council,
2. an eight-hour day and 44-hour (maximum) week,
3. double-time pay for overtime and one hour premium pay for night-shift work,
4. 85 cents per hour for skilled workers and 25 cents for apprentices.

Within 48 hours 35,000 persons in a city of 200,000 had succeeded in halting all construction and production. In addition, they froze all forms of transportation and communications. Hotels, banks and most large buildings were closed and the supply of retail goods and food was sharply reduced.

The strike was administered by a Central Strike Committee consisting of 287 delegates, three from each of 94 union locals plus five from TLC. The principal role of delegates was to decide what industrial and civic activities would be allowed to continue and to provide for essential services and supplies. They were to report back daily to their organizations.

Employers joined with governments at three levels (municipal, provincial and federal) in order to end the strike. The mayor and the majority of Winnipeg council members were hostile; so were Premier Norris of Manitoba and Prime Minister Robert Borden. Borden, reflecting his fear that anarchy might prevail, said that this was an attempt at revolution — that public servants had no right to strike.

The federal government dispatched Royal Canadian Mounted Police to Winnipeg, and they were followed on May 22 by a battalion of troops and two Lewis machine guns. On May 25 the federal government ordered postal workers back and required them to sign an agreement never to stage a sympathetic strike in the future and to disaffiliate with the Winnipeg Trades and Labour Council. The provincial government delivered an identical ultimatum to telephone workers. The municipal government ordered police and firemen back to work, subject to dismissal. Postal workers and police defied the orders and, on June 9, 190 postal workers and all members of the police force were fired. Police were replaced the same day by around 2,000 "specials," an untrained, undisciplined group, some with police records. When they made their first appearance the specials, who had been cast in the role of strike-breakers, clashed with strikers. Soon a battle erupted, with strikers and ex-servicemen on one side and specials and RCMPs on the other. Antagonists hurled bottles, brickbats and ashcan covers at each other. The specials proved to be inferior battlers, and some were hit on the head with their own clubs.

On June 17 the main strike leaders were arrested. Rev. William Ivens, one of the leaders and editor of *The Strike Bulletin,* said the RCMP had descended on his home and dragged him away in the middle of the night while his children stood by crying. The leaders were hastily taken to the Stony Mountain Penitentiary. Bail was refused. This aroused militant action across Canada in defense of the strikers. Demonstrations took place in locations from Cape Breton to Vancouver Island. On June 20, the strike leaders were released, having spent 72 hours in jail. That afternoon a large crowd gathered near the city hall, including women, children and ex-servicemen. The mayor read the Riot Act. At 2:30 PM approximately 50 mounted men, about half in red coats, half in khaki, approached the crowd swinging baseball bats. The crowd opened ranks and let them through. They stopped short, reversed direction and returned. On their return they were met by hisses, boos and a barrage of stones. With that, RCMPs and specials attacked, charging into the crowd firing revolvers. Two were killed, 30 injured. Winnipeg was placed under military control, and over 100 persons were arrested.

On June 26 the metal trades people went back to work. Others followed, but thousands were locked out, blacklisted, dismissed and otherwise discriminated against.

Aside from a compromise agreement on hours of work (from 55 a week to 50) the unions failed to attain any of their objectives, and losses were enormous. However, the Winnipeg General Strike had an important effect on Canadian labor history. It proved the folly of any general strike against the public in a free society as a means to get higher wages and fringes or improved working conditions. General strikes are most likely to be successful if their purpose is confined to dramatizing poor conditions; but as soon as members of the public are inconvenienced by virtue of deprivation or discomfort the issue switches.

In a general strike the target is almost never frozen. The Winnipeg strike brought home that lesson, loud and clear. It pointed up the need for a strong union movement equipped to exercise economic power in selected situations on a case-by-case basis, and it provided strong impetus to the growth of the One Big Union. By the end of 1919 the OBU had 41,000 members, with 100 locals, eight central labor councils and two district boards, mostly in Western Canada. However, OBU had acquired a legacy during the Winnipeg General Strike which was eventually responsible for its undoing. This legacy involved an image of radicalism and revolution and subjected the organization to almost-unreasoned resistance by employers, the government and international unions. By 1921 its membership was less than 5,300, and it ceased to be a major force. In 1956, it was largely confined to a few local unions in Winnipeg, and what was left of it became part of the Canadian Labour Congress, CLC. Possibly the OBU had been a victim of the calendar, born one year too soon.

Between 1902 and 1967 eight trade union centers connected with international unions functioned in Canada alongside the TLC and, after 1940, the CCL. These included the One Big Union, the National Trades and Labour Congress of Canada, the Canadian Federation of Labour, the All-Canadian Congress of Labour, the Workers Unity League, the Canadian Congress of Labour and the Federation of Catholic Workers of Canada (FCWC). All arose in connection with the revolt against international union domination and employer-union collaboration, and all were concerned with the issue of craft v. industrial organization.

Throughout the late 1930s and World War II the crafts v. industrial issue became blurred. It was clear to both the AFL in the U.S. and the TLC in Canada that efforts of the CIO and CCL were reaping huge rewards through industrial organization, so they decided to compete. Union membership statistics in Canada show the results: 383,492 in 1937, 711,117 in 1945, 832,697 in 1946, 912,124 in 1947 and 977,594 in 1948. The AFL and TLC were organizing both crafts and industries; CIO and CCL were doing the same. Rival unions staged bitter fights for members as unions engaged in considerable raiding and crossing of each others' picket lines. This was especially prevalent in the building trades. Finally, in the early 50s, the going got tougher. The rate of growth in union membership had begun to decline in the United States during the war and in Canada in the late 1940s. During 1954 total union membership in Canada and the U.S. remained virtually unchanged from 1953. It seemed clear that hitherto rival organizations would have to cease fighting each other and pool their resources if they hoped to extend their organization efforts.

In June 1954, the AFL and CIO, under new presidents, George Meany and Walter Reuther, signed a two-year no-raiding pact. They had come to realize that the widely prevailing union piracy and consequent jursidictional disputes had been a fruitless and costly exercise. By 1955 some 80 of the 110 AFL unions and 31 of the CIO's 33 had ratified the no-raiding agreement. Meanwhile the two federations operated a joint unity committee with Meany and Reuther playing dominant roles. There were also moves among some of the rival CIO and AFL international unions to consolidate. Then, with apparent suddenness, on February 8, 1955, the joint committee announced that full agreement had been reached for the AFL and CIO to merge.

George Meany was elected president of the new orgnization, which then had a membership of over 15 million organized workers. Except for a statement by the president of the National Association of Manufacturers that the merger "should be outlawed" and an occasional expression of conservative fears that it would mean a labor monopoly, even the organs of the business community endorsed the move and expressed the belief that it would lead to greater industrial peace. The *Wall Street Journal* expressed the belief that the merger would not enhance the monopoly status of labor, and *Nation's Business*, while suggesting that it might mean "a political powerhouse," pointed out its potential advantage for industry in reducing the incidence of jurisdictional disputes.[15]

In April of 1956 the two principal rival federations of Canada also merged, forming the Canadian Labour Congress (CLC). The CLC brought together 111 international unions and 322 federal locals with total membership of more than one million. Approximately 300,000 workers remained outside the CLC: 200,000 in independent, nonaffiliated, locals and 100,000 in the *Confédération des Travailleurs Catholiques du Canada* (CTCC). Then in September delegates to the CTCC convention voted to affiliate with C.L.C.[16]

Thus began an era in North American labor relations characterized by a shift of focus. The organizational activities and political maneuvering continued, but raiding essentially stopped, and principal attention switched to improvement of wages and working conditions for existing members.

The union movement had become a force of conservatism on the continent. It was not until the late 1960s and early 70s when a new unionism emerged to organize white collar workers, government employees and professionals that the movement started to stir from its doldrums and develop some new ideas and techniques. Until recently the issues discussed in bargaining and giving rise to strikes had hardly shifted since the 1930s.

(c) Problems of Public Image

Labor's struggles were fraught with instances of violence which almost always were blamed on labor. No matter that self-serving interest groups tended to latch onto the labor movement as a convenient forum for airing their views and that members of these groups often provoked violence.[17] No matter that labor encountered repeated instances of hostility from employers, governments and the press. The fact remained that the labor movement was often equated in the public's mind with the words radicalism, strikes, violence, intimidation. While only .18 per cent of estimated working time has been lost in strikes in the last five years, the public hears considerably more about strikes and threatened strikes than about peaceful settlements. While all but a few strikes each year are conducted peacefully and without any hint of violence, those which result in violence promptly attract newspaper reporters, politicians and special interest groups looking for an opportunity to further their self interests.

Canadian labor history is dotted with instances of violence. There were struggles in the early 1900s in the railways, mines and textile mills. After the 1930s there was a sharp decline in violence, attributed particularly to emancipating legislation. However, a few isolated instances have dotted history since then. In 1967, for example, violence erupted in London, Ontario, in association with the strike by United Steelworkers at Emco Manufacturing Company. In 1971 the same happened at Texpack Company of Brantford where the Canadian Textile and Chemical Workers staged a strike.

One of the best documented instances of violence occurred in the United States at the Carnegie Steel Company at Homestead, Pennsylvania, in 1892. The company was owned by Andrew Carnegie, an industry baron whose expressed attitudes toward the working man were probably ahead of his time. For example, Carnegie was quoted as saying, "The rights of labor to combine are no less sacred than the rights of manufacturers to produce."

Carnegie's Homestead works were directed by General Manager Henry Clay Frick. Frick was tough, stubborn and antiunion. At the time of the 1892 confrontation Carnegie was in Europe.

Carnegie's 4,000-plus workers were represented by the Amalgamated Association of Iron, Steel and Tin Workers, predecessors of the United Steelworkers. In 1892 a new contract was due. Management sought to invoke a general wage cut (not unusual in the 1800s). The union leaders balked and called a strike. Frick, in turn, locked them out and refused to negotiate. He ordered erection of barbed-wire fences around the plant and secured the services of specially sworn deputies to protect the property. The locked-out workers promptly ran the deputies out of town, believing that they were forerunners of strike breakers (scabs).

Frick then set out to crush the union. He made moves to bring in replacement workers, and the striking workers, in turn, armed themselves and stayed on 24-hour watch ready to stop any influx of scabs.

On July 6, 1892, two barges appeared on the Monongahela River, being towed slowly by a tugboat toward the Carnegie plant. They contained 300 Pinkerton detectives armed with Winchester rifles, hired by Frick to secure the property so that strike breakers could be safely brought in.

As the barges drew alongside the Carnegie mills and the tugboat dropped its load the striking workers opened fire from behind walls of steel billets. The battle raged all day from 4 AM until 5 PM — and the Pinkertons were driven back. The strikers had a small brass cannon which was set up behind some railway ties, and they proceeded to lob cannon balls directly onto the barges. However they were unable to sink the barges, so strikers poured oil into the river and set it afire.

Three Pinkertons died; several were wounded; the rest were trapped. Many ripped off their shirts and waved them in the air in surrender. The strikers then made an agreement with them: safe passage out of town in return for all their arms and ammunition.

As the Pinkertons moved through town to the railroad station they were pelted with stones and clubs wielded by women and children from the town, many of them from families of the strikers. Once they left, an uneasy calm prevailed.

Mr. Frick did not give up. On July 12 over 8,000 state militiamen arrived and established martial law in Homestead. Frick then hired 2,000 scabs. The mill started operating again, and in November the union called off the strike — totally defeated. Eventually Frick reinstated 800 of the 4,000 strikers. The Amalgamated Association was crushed. It took more than 40 years to recover.

A sequel to the early July violence occurred on July 23. On that day Alexander Berkman, an anarchist, forced his way into Frick's office and shot and stabbed the general manager. The attack was not fatal, but Berkman spent 21 years in jail as a result and was finally deported to Russia, along with Emma Goldman, a fellow anarchist, who had helped plan the attack.

Things might have been different if Andrew Carnegie had been on the scene. While he approved of the company's stance in negotiations he disapproved the employment of strikebreakers. In a letter to Prime Minister William Gladstone of England he commented on the strike, saying: "The pain I suffer increases daily. The works are not worth one drop of human blood."

To the extent that newspapers reflected the public mood one is hard-put to find any support for labor at the time of the Homestead strike. Here are some examples of newspaper comments:

> *The Independent*: "Men talk like anarchists or lunatics when they insist that the workmen at Homestead have done right."
> *The Cleveland Leader*: "... the right of every man to work for whom he pleases must and will be maintained."
> *The North American Republic*: "The first duty of the legislative

power is to emancipate the individual workman from the tyranny of his class. The individual workman should not be permitted to commit moral suicide by surrendering his liberty to the control of his fellow-workmen."[18]

In 1898 London, Ontario, was the scene of a labor dispute that involved the whole community, most members of which sided with labor and continued their support through a struggle that lasted more than a year. The dispute involved London streetcar workers.[19] The employer was a U.S.-owned company, and the union, seeking to represent the workers, was the Amalgamated Street Railwaymen of North America, an international union.

On October 27, 1898, motormen and conductors staged a strike as a result of the employer's refusal to meet with the union bargaining committee. The committee had requested wages of 16 2/3 cents an hour (from 12 cents) and a reduction in hours of work to nine a day (from 10). In addition, they sought abolition of "documents" which employees had been required to sign as a condition of employment. In these "documents" employees agreed, as a condition of employment, that they would not join a union.

On October 28, the company sought to test the strike's effectiveness by running one of the streetcars. This attracted large crowds, and the car did not move. That evening the strikers gathered at the Labour Hall. They paraded from there to the Princess Rink and were met by upwards of 5,000 citizens for a support rally.

On October 29, a Saturday, the company brought in strike breakers, at least one of whom brandished a revolver. This action enraged London's citizens, who stormed the car barns on Dundas Street. Reporters said that masses of people were crowded on the street for over a mile. On Monday, the 31st, crowds were once again assembled in the street and the Riot Act was read. The London Trades and Labour Council had printed thousands of cards and distributed them among members of the crowd. The cards carried slogans, "We walk" and "No surrender to monopoly."

London street railway service was stopped until November 11 when the parties reached apparent settlement. Wages were announced at 15 2/3 cents per hour; a nine-hour day was instituted, and the "documents" were discontinued.

But the company did not live up to its word. They continued to bar employees from joining the union and refused to hire new employees who were members. So on May 22, 1899, a second strike began, which lasted into the new year. During the next year citizens of London refused to ride streetcars. The company sought to end the strike by bribing the union leader, J.D. Marks, in order to get him to go back to work. Marks refused, and when the strikers gave no evidence of giving in the company finally relented in May of 1900. On May 1 of that year the union-citizen solidarity in opposition to the company was demonstrated by a mile-long parade of London workingmen.

(d) Severe Employer Reisistance

Employer resistance to the union movement was not confined to the bargaining table. Employers often attempted to head off unions before they ever gained a foothold, and their devices were many. Chief among them were misuse of immigrants, yellow-dog contracts, blacklists, detectives and labor spies.

1. Misuse of immigrants

Sometimes employers gave immigrants false information when they hired them as strikebreakers. During a strike at the T. Eaton Company in Toronto Alexander Redder, a cloakmaker, was brought in as a strikebreaker from Europe. Sometime later Redder discovered why he had been brought to Canada and requested money so he could get back to New York. Eaton's agent refused, causing Redder, in despair, to take his own life.[20]

2. Yellow-dog contracts and blacklists

Two of the most notorious union busting devices were "yellow-dog" contracts and blacklists. Yellow-dog contracts were documents used initially by the railroads during their feverish construction days in the West. Later they were used by other industries as well and spread throughout North America. These were contracts stipulating as a condition of employment that the worker was not, and would not become, a member of a union. Upon discovery any falsifications promptly met with discharge. Many of the early railroad workers were oriental (yellow-skinned) and willing to work at substandard wages, thus excluding unionized workers looking for more money. These orientals came to be known as "yellow dogs". Yellow-dog contracts were repeatedly upheld in the U.S. Supreme Court[21] till passage of the Norris-La Guardia Act in 1932, which prohibited their continuance.

Blacklists contained names of persons who were known to be members of unions. The lists were exchanged between employers, and if a person's name appeared on them his chances of obtaining employment were severely limited. The most prevalent use of blacklists was by the National Metal Trades Association (NMTA), an organization of employers that featured a service to members by which individuals were traced from job to job through any number of name changes. One person was known to have gone through 12 job changes and seven aliases, but he failed to escape the list. Members of NMTA were required to report any employees discharged for union activities: names of these employees were promptly published and issued to all other members of the association. The NMTA augmented the employer-reporting function with a tremendous detective staff that shadowed persons from place to place.

3. Labor spies

Labor spies were frequently used. In 1900 the J.B. King Company of Toronto hired spies to work alongside regular workers and identify any union sympathizers. Once identified the sympathizers were fired. The Canadian Pacific Railway (CPR) went even farther. They hired spies who worked their way into the union, took part in deliberations, even initiated new members. The CPR had many ways of locating "reliable" spies. In one case CPR officials succeeded in locating a lesser official of the United Brotherhood of Railway Engineers (UBRE) who was in poor health, with financial difficulties and uneasy about some past indiscretions. When CPR detectives found out about him they met him and threatened to expose him. His alternative was to sign on as a labor spy. This he did by signing the following statement:

> I, _____, organizer of the UBRE, do hereby offer my services to the Special Service Department of The Canadian Pacific Railway Company.[22]

Private police were also used by some companies. The Dominion Iron and Steel Company employed them in 1912; the Ford Motor Company employed them in the 1920s and part way through the 1930s.

These various devices — yellow-dog contracts, blacklists, spies and the like — were not confined to earlier years. While they seem to be largely under control in the United States there is evidence that blacklists and modern-day versions of yellow-dog contracts are still used in Canada. Each year there are numerous instances of persons being discharged from employment as a result of union activity. Many have been documented as unfair labor practices, but many more have taken place without documentation.

A view held by some regarding the virtue of various forms of union-busting techniques was expressed in 1902 by George F. Baer, President of the Philadelphia and Reading Railroad:

> The rights and interests of the laboring man will be protected and cared for not by the labor agitators, but by the Christian men to whom God in His infinite wisdom has given the control of the property interests of this country....[23]

Now, in the 1970s, the union movement is part of the "establish-ment." It is basically conservative and parochial in its outlook, essentially nonpolitical and relatively stable in size. In Canada its membership has risen in the past few years at about the same rate as population has grown. Increases in white collar, professional and government employee unions have been offset by decreases in blue collar ranks. As of January, 1973, there were 2.3 million union members in Canada, representing 27.2 per cent of the civilian work force. In the United States there were 19.7 million members (24.2 per cent).[24] Exceptions to the "establishment" image of the labor movement can be found in the history of labor relations in the Province of Quebec. This is discussed briefly in the next section.

THE PROVINCE OF QUEBEC[25]

The history of Canadian labor relations must necessarily consider the Province of Quebec separately. As of 1970 the population of Quebec was more than 80 per cent French-speaking and more than 85 per cent Roman Catholic in faith. For the past 150 years French-Canadian leaders have been preoccupied with maintaining the identity of their people as a distinct ethnic group in the midst of an alien Anglo-Saxon society. This position was secure, both legally and politically, by virtue of the British North America Act which gave French Canada its own separate legal and educational system in Quebec and a constitutional status equal to that of English-speaking Canada.

Over the years a distinct culture developed in Quebec based on the French language, the Roman Catholic religion and a predominately agrarian economy. With the advent of industrialization and urbanization, an outside force materialized in the province and threatened to under-mine the cultural identity of French Canadians. The principal orga-nizational structures of the new industrialism were introduced largely by English-speaking elements. These included trade unions. The ownership and control of all major commercial, financial and industrial operations were largely in the hands of English-speaking Protestants. On the other hand French Canadians were predominant in the ranks of farmers, blue collar workers, small shopkeepers, industrial proprietors, lower-paid white collar workers, civil servants and the traditional professions of law, medicine and the priesthood.

Roman Catholic Church leaders and lay nationalists in Quebec feared they would lose their cultural identity as French Canadians if they acquired the expertise of the new industrialism and associated with the

English-speaking factions. The main hierarchy of the Roman Catholic Church in Quebec therefore favored a policy of cultural separatism, and this was carried on through the church, the family and the schools, where the clergy played a leading role as teachers.

Following World War II a separate body of French Canadians, both lay and clerical, voiced a different approach. They believed that separate identity for French Canada required accommodation to the industrial system. They advocated active competition and cooperation with the English-speaking industry barons in order to compete effectively in the modern society. According to this line of thought, the clergy was expected to abandon much of its direct control over secular activities.

The French-Canadian labor movement reflected the dual nature of French Canada. It began in 1900 as a conscious effort by the Roman Catholic clergy to maintain and build a cultural identity in order to be sure that workers retained the French language and Catholic religion. Unions at the time employed a chaplain named by religious authority to take part in their counsels and assist at meetings.

In the early 1900s members of the clergy took the lead in organizing a number of new unions based on the same principles. They were successful among pulp and paper workers, asbestos workers, miners, building tradesmen, shipyard workers and longshoremen — often in the face of strong opposition from TLC and CFL organizers. They were less militant than their English-speaking counterparts, and this fact led employers to favor their presence, thus easing the job of organizing. The Catholic unions stressed harmony and cooperation between workers and employers and, in principle, prohibited the use of strikes.

In 1918, the various Catholic unions moved toward federation with the formation of the National Central Trades Council in Quebec City. Similar central councils were formed in other districts, and subsequent conferences were called to form a province-wide federation of Catholic unions. Finally in 1922 a permanent organization was established called *Confédération des Travailleurs Catholiques du Canada* (CTCC), known in English as the Canadian and Catholic Confederation of Labour.

Throughout its history the CTCC was a relatively small part of the Canadian labor movement. Its total membership never exceeded ten per cent of all union members in the country. Even among French-speaking Catholic unionists, one-half to two-thirds generally belonged to non-Catholic unions. The rivalry between non-Catholic organizations, especially TLC and CCL, contributed materially to the survival and modest growth of CTCC.

During and immediately after World War II CTCC experienced some important changes. Rapid industrial expansion drew large numbers of French Canadians into the cities where they came in contact with workers of other ethnic and religious backgrounds. Some CTCC unions ceased to be exclusively French-Canadian and Catholic, and new, aggressive lay leaders took top positions in the Federation, forcing out many of the Catholic clergy. There were glaring wage inequities between French-speaking and English-speaking workers, and the new leaders set forth to correct these. This, plus vigorous competition from CCL and TLC organizers, led to some of the most violent and spectacular labor disputes in Canada's history. The French-Catholic unions had converted from a mood of relative cooperation to aggressive militancy.[26]

As the composition of CTCC's membership changed and new leaders ascended, the organization took on many of the characteristics of TLC and CCL. Following the War the three organizations cooperated in many ventures, and soon after the merger of CCL and TLC in 1956 the CTCC voted to join the newly formed CLC. The move was spurred, in part, by the fact that the new president of CLC, Claude Jodoin, and two of the CLC's three Quebec vice presidents were French Canadians.

Following the 1956 action a number of French-Canadian unions remained outside the CLC. These groups retained a parochial outlook and hung onto vestiges of cultural separatism. Gradually their numbers increased, and they found sufficient community of interest to form a separate organization known as the Confederation of National Trade Unions (CNTU). As of 1972 CNTU was a 235,000-member coalition of 12 national and four directly chartered unions and had become one of the most powerful labor forces in Quebec.

The CNTU built itself largely as a group of industrial unions and played an important role in most of the labor disputes in Quebec during the 1960s and early 70s, starting with the Seafarers dispute of 1962. In 1968 the Confederation moved outside its collective bargaining role and began participating aggressively in political and social actions, much in the mold of European unions. In October of 1971 the CNTU published a "working paper," prepared for consideration of the rank and file, proclaiming that there was "no future of Quebec in the current economic system" and urging workers to engage in a struggle to replace the system with one "without class," controlled by the workers.

The paper was prepared with the help of a university professor, and it promptly gave rise to an open split in the leadership. Three top CNTU officials — Paul-Emile Dalpé, Jacques Dion and Amédée Daigle, challenged the leadership of the Confederation's president, Marcel Pépin, and announced that they would form a new grass-roots labor federation. They claimed that Pépin was being steered by ideologists and intellectuals who were not in step with the beliefs of the largely blue collar CNTU rank and file.

Pépin himself was a college graduate with a major in industrial relations. He held staff jobs with the CNTU for most of his career. He openly supported Rene Levesque, leader of the *Parti Quebecois*, the Quebec separatist party, and gave Levesque $900 of his own money to publish a separatist-oriented manifesto in 1967. His challengers claimed Pepin had channeled CNTU funds into radical political causes and that Pepin, himself, had used union expense money excessively. At the time of the challenges Pepin was serving a one-year jail sentence for urging workers to defy back-to-work injunctions during an 11-day public service strike in April of 1972. He quickly got out an appeal and made moves to suspend the three challengers. All three were replaced on Sunday, June 11, 1972, by men sympathetic to Mr. Pepin.

At the time of this writing the union situation in Quebec was confused. There were elements of business unionism with collective bargaining as their prime concern; these were largely represented by CLC (formerly CTCC) unions. There were vestiges of French-Canadian, Catholic-oriented separatists — mostly in places away from urban centers. And there were the CNTU unions, themselves split into factions: some advocating militant social reform and political action, other concentrating on improving wages and working conditions of its members. In the summer of 1972 a group of CNTU unions broke away from the parent to form a new organization — the *Central des Syndicats Démocratiques* (CSD), dedicated to the latter cause.

NOTES TO CHAPTER 2

1. *New York Times*, June 19, 1972, p. 51.
2. Toronto Typographical Society, *Minutes*, February 17 and 24, 1872.
3. *Ontario Workman,* April 18, 1892.
4. Canadian Labour Union, *Proceedings*, September 1873.
5. Ibid.
6. Canada, Royal Commission on the Relations of Capital and Labour (Ottawa 1889), *Evidence of Quebec*, pp 21-148.
7. Ibid., Evidence of Ontario.
8. Ibid., Evidence of Quebec.
9. For an extensive study of the growth and role of international unionism in Canada see John Crispo, *International Unionism*, McGraw-Hill, 1967.
10. Trades and Labour Congress of Canada, Seventeenth Annual Convention, 1902, *Proceedings*, pp. 46 and 73.
11. *Trades and Labour Congress Journal*, March 1949.
12. Charles Lipton, *The Trade Union Movement of Canada*, 1827-1959 (Canadian Social Publications Ltd., 1963) pp. 280-2.
13. Western Canada Labour Conference, *Proceedings*, p. 27.

14. For a detailed account of the Winnipeg General Strike see D.C. Masters, *The Winnipeg General Strike,* Toronto, 1950.

15. Foster Rhea Dulles, *Labor in America* (Crowell, 1960), pp. 390-1.

16. *Montreal Star,* September 28, 1956, p. 1.

17. Some of the more notable special interest groups which latched onto the labor movement for their own self-interest were various anarchists, Marxian socialists, Black internationalists, Lassalleans (who espoused direct overthrow of capitalism), women's rights advocates and the international Communist movement.

18. Foster Rhea Dulles, op. cit., pp 166-71.

19. For a complete history of The London Streetcar Strike see *The Industrial Banner,* 1897-1899.

20. Trades and Labour Congress of Canada, Fourteenth Annual Convention, 1899, *Proceedings,* p. 7.

21. See, for example, Hitchman Coal and Coke Company v. Mitchell, 245 U.S. 299, 38 S. Ct.65 (1918).

22. Canada, Royal Commission on Industrial Disputes in the Province of British Columbia, 1903, *Report,* p.75.

23. Foster Rhea Dulles, op. cit. p. 191.

24. The civilian work force includes agricultural workers.

25. Material in this section was taken largely from Stuart Jamieson, *Industrial Relations in Canada,* Macmillan of Canada, 1957, pages 54-9.

26. Pierre E. Trudeau, ed., *La Grève de l'amiante* (Montreal: Cité Libre, 1956).

3. LABOR LEGISLATION — AN OVERVIEW

A body of law has built up through the years which now provides a highly effective legislative, judicial and administrative framework within which industrial relations practices take place. This chapter explores the principal components of that framework. It takes a look at the historical development of Canadian and U.S. labor laws and offers some comments on their future direction.

Labor laws of Canada are similar to those in the United States. They reflect a commonality of heritage (the British common law) and a commonality of organizations and problems. Principal differences between Canadian and U.S. law are the following:

1. DECENTRALIZATION

Since 1925 the majority of Canadian workers have been covered by provincial labor laws. The Industrial Relations Disputes and Investigation Act of Canada, a national law, covers fewer than 530,000 Canadian workers, about nine per cent. In the United States over 90 per cent of the workers are covered by the National Labor Relations Act. Thus Canadian labor legislation is largely decentralized. In the United States it is largely centralized.

2. INJUNCTIVE RELIEF

Canadian labor relations are frequently influenced by the use of preventive injunctions. In the United States injunctions have been used sparingly since 1932 and are strictly controlled by legislation.

3. GOVERNMENT INTERVENTION

The laws of Canada require more frequent intervention by government bodies in negotiations and by outside persons in dispute settling. Government conciliation, for example, is required before a strike can take place. In the United States these matters are largely voluntary. However, when the U.S. National Labor Relations Board becomes involved in an industrial dispute the procedures are somewhat more formal than in Canada.

4. CONTENT OF AGREEMENTS

In Canada there are more explicit requirements regarding the content of labor agreements. For example, most jurisdictions require that a collective agreement contain a clause prohibiting strikes or lockouts during the term of agreement. There are no such requirements in the United States except by voluntary agreement by parties to a contract.

COMPONENTS OF A LEGAL FRAMEWORK FOR LABOR RELATIONS

Three basic beliefs underlie the legal framework for labor relations in Canada and the United States, and they are the central components of our industrial relations system:

1. Employees should be free to organize.
2. Representatives of employees should be able to engage employers in bargaining.
3. Employees and employers should be free to invoke meaningful sanctions in support of their positions: employees to withdraw services, employers to close their doors.

One hundred and fifty years ago all three of these components were illegal. As we trace the development of laws we will demonstrate how each of them gradually became free.

The legal framework for labor relations in any country can be measured in two ways:

1. The degree of government intervention to define limits of the three components,
2. the kinds of legal substitution the government provides for use of sanctions.

Canada and the United States have not differed materially in these measurements, although the laws in their wording might lead to the conclusion that they would differ. However, there have been variations in government intrusion based on personalities and economic and political climates. For example, the late 1960s in Canada were characterized by early intervention and forceful mediation by government representatives in labor relations matters. This was a function of the personality of an intensely active Minister of Labour, Bryce Mackasey, working under a permissive Prime Minister, Pierre Trudeau. During the same period there was a declared hands-off policy in labor relations matters in the United States. Secretary of Labor, George Shultz, backed by President Richard Nixon, believed that contract negotiations were a private matter between parties and that the government should stay out. This contrasted vividly with the subsequent Nixon economic policy, announced in August 1971 and implemented in the form of wage and price guidelines and controls until spring of 1974.

Notwithstanding differences in the wording of laws and notwithstanding short-term variations in administration brought about by differences in personalities and climates, similarities in the legal framework of the two countries far outweigh differences.

EIGHT STAGES OF GOVERNMENT INTRUSION

It is possible to trace the evolution of labor laws of any country through eight stages of government intrusion:

1. Adoption of a policy that employee organizations and collective bargaining are desirable;
2. removal of the three central components from legal disability;
3. creation of government offices of intervention to be available to parties on request (most frequently these offices take the form of mediation or conciliation);
4. imposition of government intervention as a condition-precedent to the exercise of sanctions (example: conciliation under Canada's Industrial Disputes and Investigation Act is a precondition to a legal strike or lockout);
5. imposition of public inquiry and publication of results (example: the Ontario Mediation and Conciliation Services provide for conciliation boards in some instances — these boards publish their findings and recommendations);
6. compulsory arbitration;
7. partial operation by the government;
8. seizure.

Through history Canadian and U.S. labor relations have moved closer to the eighth degree of government intrusion. Instances of total seizure and operation of a company or industry by the government have been rare. So far there have been no moves toward encompassing legislation to provide for seizure or partial seizure. However, there have been more and more laws in recent years calling for compulsory arbitration in certain instances — the most recent being Canada's Public Service Staff Relations Act, passed in 1967.

In the remainder of the chapter we will look at some of the landmark cases and legislation in the field of labor relations. In doing so we will consider both Canada and the United States, because the development of the legal frameworks in both countries was parallel: first one, then the other, moving ahead in protecting the rights of workers — then, later, in attempting to put controls on some of those rights.

MASTERS AND SERVANTS ACT

An important 19th-century encumbrance to the status of worker organizations was the Masters and Servants Act. Under this Act the decision of a worker to quit one job and move to another could result in charges of breach of contract under conspiracy sections of the Criminal Code. There were repeated instances of workers being tried and convicted under the Act for deserting employment. Sometimes they were sentenced to jail.

The Act was the subject of considerable agitation by early unions. They called it discriminatory since it made breach of contract a criminal offense for workers, whereas a contract breach was a civil offense for other persons.

In 1876 two changes in the Act were made in response to labor's urging. The first was an amendment establishing a penalty of $100 as an alternative to imprisonment; the second provided that breach of contract by an employee was not criminal, but a civil offense only.

ONTARIO MECHANICS LIEN LAW OF 1873

In the summer of 1872 a church was being built in Ottawa. On its completion the contractor obtained payment, then left town without a trace, leaving his stonecutters and masons without pay. This and other similar instances led to one of the earliest pieces of social legislation, the Ontario Mechanics Lien Law. This law provided that when work was done and wages not paid a "lien" or seizure could be placed on the employer's capital. The law was a step forward, but inadequate nevertheless, because it was operative only where unpaid wages exceeded $50, and it was obviously unenforceable against employers who vanished.

Many other abuses were prevalent in the labor scene throughout North America during the 19th and early 20th centuries, and effective legislation to deal with them was slow in coming. Chief among these abuses were child labor, prison labor and, later, the application of antitrust statutes to unions.

In 1890 the Sherman Antitrust Act was passed in the United States. It was intended as a control over business combinations that restrained trade. The Act did not specifically deal with unions. Nevertheless courts applied the Act against unions until the 1930s. This probably did more than anything to impede early growth of North American unionism.

DISPUTE-SETTLING LEGISLATION

By the early 1900s Canada was far ahead of the United States in dispute-settling legislation. In 1900 the Dominion Parliament passed the Conciliation Act, modeled after earlier provincial legislation. The Act authorized the Minister of Labour to appoint conciliation officers or conciliation boards to help settle disputes when requested to do so by representatives of the employers of workers involved.

A more comprehensive act was passed in 1903 following a long strike of trackmen on the Canadian Pacific Railroad. The 1903 Act, known as the Railway Labour Disputes Act, was limited in coverage to railroad workers. It provided for a three-man conciliation board to serve in dispute situations: one nominee to be chosen by each party, the two nominees then to choose a chairman. The board had power to investigate the causes of a dispute, to compel testimony under oath and to require production of relevant documents.

If the conciliation board failed to bring about agreement there was provision for arbitration. However, the power of arbitration boards was limited to making nonbinding recommendations. The Act contained no restraints on strikes or lockouts, and for this reason it was generally ineffective.

Provisions of the 1900 Conciliation Act and the Railway Labour Disputes Act of 1903 were combined and extended in the Conciliation and Labour Act of 1906. This, too, was inadequate and was succeeded in 1907 by the Industrial Disputes Investigation Act. The 1907 Act formed the backbone of Canadian labor legislation from that date till the present and is still on the books, mostly in its original form. It was copied in great part by the provinces, and by the United States 19 years later in that country's Railway Labor Act.

The Industrial Disputes Investigation Act (IDI) grew largely out of a rash of strikes. Perhaps the most influencial of these was the eight-month strike of Lethbridge coal field workers in Alberta which resulted in a winter fuel famine. Families suffered to the extent that they were forced to burn wood fence posts to keep warm. But that wasn't all: there were strikes of Manitoba and Ontario street railway workers and among employees of Quebec sawmills — giving rise to loud public outcries throughout the country for controlling legislation. At the time most of Canada's workers were employed by public utility and transportation companies. In the ten years 1897-1906 one-seventh of all industrial disputes accounting for over one-third of all striking workers were in these industries. Consequently the public enthusiastically backed the 1907 Act.

The new Act applied to disputes involving employees of ten or more persons engaging in mining, transport, communication, and public utility companies. The machinery it provided could be applied to any other industry if both parties consented. The philosophy underlying the Act was this: In any civilized country community private rights cease when they become public wrongs.

The Act provided for a tripartite Board of Conciliation and Investigation which had legal power to investigate disputes and compel submission of testimony and evidence. These features were derived from the 1903 Railway Labour Disputes Act. However, the new Act had a new and vitally important feature requiring postponement of any strike or lockout while investigations proceeded. Wages and working conditions were frozen during that time.

The main function of the tripartite board was to conciliate: that is, to act as a catalyst to try to get parties to come to a voluntary agreement. However, the board had power beyond conciliation by virtue of a provision calling for it to make recommendations in the event conciliation failed. The Board's findings were to include "the cause of the dispute according to the merits and substantial justice of the case." In addition, the Act required that "the Board's recommendations ... shall state in plain terms ... what in the Board's opinion ought or ought not to be done by the respective parties concerned."

The 1907 Act had many weaknesses, but these were largely overcome because this was an Act substantially agreed upon in advance by labor and management. Consequently, representatives of both were committed to make it work. Its first test came shortly after passage in 1907 when workers at the Montreal Point-St-Charles shops of The Grand Trunk Railway (now Canadian National) made plans to stage a strike in sympathy with fellow shopmen who had a dispute in Ontario. But that would have violated the IDI Act. So they didn't do it.

This and subsequent experiences caused labor to register increased coolness toward the Act. By 1916 the majority of members at the Trades and Labour Congress (TLC) convention voted for its repeal. Its biggest weakness was its failure to give protection to workers and unions against employers who took action to thwart unionization. There was no provision in the Act either protecting workers in their attempts to organize or, once organized, requiring employers to bargain.

TORONTO ELECTRIC COMMISSIONERS V. SNIDER[1]

The 1925 case of Toronto Electric Commissioners v. Snider was a court challenge to the 1907 Industrial Disputes Investigation Act based on grounds that the Dominion Government was acting beyond its proper constitutional jurisdiction. The Judicial Committee of the Privy Council of

England, bypassing the Supreme Court of Canada, upheld the challenge, declaring the Act unconstitutional. The Committee reasoned that since the Act was concerned with civil rights of employers and employees in the respective provinces there was a violation of Section 92 of the British North America Act which expressly assigned this function to the provinces.

The Canadian Parliament promptly amended the 1907 Act to restrict its application to disputes that were under the jurisdiction of the federal government. The amendment provided as well that the Act could extend to the provinces if they passed enabling legislation. Between 1925 and 1932 all provinces except Prince Edward Island did so. Two of them, Alberta and British Columbia, subsequently repealed their enabling acts and passed similar provincial laws of their own.

As a result of the Snider case the Canadian provinces became the most significant makers and enforcers of the laws in Canada. As of 1973 the Industrial Disputes Investigation Act (as amended) applied only to enumerated industries which crossed provincial lines. Crown corporations, railways, airlines, longshoring and seafaring were among those which fell into this category.

LEGISLATIVE DEVELOPMENTS IN THE UNITED STATES 1925-1940

From 1925 until 1940 the most significant legislative developments in North American labor law took place in the United States, starting with the Railway Labor Act of 1926. Many of these had profound effects on subsequent Canadian legislation and serve to this day as bases for the existing legal framework for labor relations in both Canada and the United States.

1. The Railway Labor Act — 1926

The Railway Labor Act of 1926 represented the first and only piece of negotiated labor legislation in the history of U.S. labor relations. It was initially applied to the railroads, later to the airlines. It had many features that characterized Canada's Industrial Disputes Investigation Act. In addition there were some significant differences. These included exclusive rights for unions representing a majority of members in a bargaining unit and compulsory features requiring employers to recognize and bargain with appropriate unions. Like the Industrial Disputes Investigation Act, the Railway Labor Act had many flaws, but it worked well for about ten years because labor and management were committed to it.

The Act set up machinery to deal both with disputes during a contract term and those arising after contract expiration and involving terms of a new agreement. Regarding the latter, the Act provided for a five-member National Mediation Board — the members to be appointed by the President. Disputes could be voluntarily submitted to the Board, or the Board could proffer its services if it found an emergency existed. In the event of an emergency, the Act provided a six-step procedure:

1. The National Mediation Board would meet with the parties and attempt to mediate — to secure a voluntary settlement;
2. if unsuccessful in mediation, the Board would attempt to induce the parties to submit items in dispute to binding arbitration;
3. if the parties refused arbitration a 30-day moratorium would be declared regarding any changes in pay, work rules, working conditions, or established work practices; attempts at settlement would continue;
4. if there was still no settlement and if the National Mediation Board believed the dispute would threaten substantially to interrupt interstate commerce the Board was required to report to the President;
5. if the President shared the Board's viewpoint he could create an investigatory board;
6. if an investigatory board was created it had an additional 30 days to deliver a report, and the parties were barred from changing any of the conditions which gave rise to the dispute for 30 days after receiving the report.

After expiration of all these steps, or after Step 3 if Steps 4, 5 or 6 were not undertaken, there could be a strike or lockout.

2. Norris-La Guardia Act — 1932

Since the early 1800s workers were repeatedly thwarted in their efforts to form unions and take collective action. Among their greatest enemies was the injunction, a remedy at law by which courts prohibited certain actions from being initiated or continuing on the grounds that there had been or could be a violation of the law. Violation of an injunction was dealt with through contempt-of-court proceedings.

The Norris-La Guardia Act consisted of two important parts. The first part freed unions from the threat of antitrust action. The second prohibited the use of the injunctive remedy in specified instances involving labor relations. Injunctions were barred as devices to prevent any of the following:

☐ Strikes
☐ Payments of strike benefits
☐ Aid to individuals defending or prosecuting court action in labor disputes

☐ Nonviolent picketing

☐ Peaceful assembly

Thus the injunction, long a scourge of worker organizations, was largely removed as a weapon. It could still be used in the event that unlawful acts were threatened or if there was likelihood of bodily injury or property damage and no adequate legal remedy was available. But framers of the Act believed these instances would be rare.

The Norris-La Guardia Act represented a significant step ahead of Canadian labor relations legislation in giving workers' organizations significantly more freedom. It was not until 1968 that a stab at formulating similar anti-injunction legislation was taken in Canada. Until then injunctions were used quite freely. At this writing the continued absence of specific anti-injunction legislation permitted the specter of uncertainty to persist.[2]

Mr. Justice Ivan Rand attempted to deal with injunctions in his report of 1968 which proposed changes in the Ontario Labour Relations Act. His suggestions were not adopted in legislative language. However, practices in the province had given them practical effect. Among the most important of Mr. Justice Rand's recommendations regarding injunctions were these:

1. *Ex parte* injunctions should not be sanctioned — the alleged offender must be served notice and given an opportunity to defend himself;[3]

2. in injunctive action, facts must be established by voice evidence, subject to cross examination, *unless* the alleged emergency is so great that there is not sufficent time to bring witnesses;

3. any misrepresentation or withholding of facts in injunctive action is punishable by contempt proceedings;

4. prior to issuance of an injunction it must be shown that there have been reasonable efforts to obtain police assistance, to protect property, to permit lawful entry and to prevent breach of peace. In addition, it must be shown that these efforts have failed.[4]

3. The National Labor Relations Act (Wagner Act) — 1936

The advent of the New Deal in the United States under President Franklin D. Roosevelt represented an almost revolutionary change in government attitude and policy toward organized labor.

The Wagner Act of 1936 reaffirmed three important principles established in the Railway Labor Act:

1. Workers shall have freedom to organize unions of their own choosing.

2. Workers shall be free from employer interference or domination.

3. Employers shall be required to organize and bargain with appropriate unions.

In addition, the Wagner Act created a National Labor Relations Board to investigate complaints of unfair labor practices, to prosecute offenders, and to conduct supervised elections to decide certification of unions representing the majority of workers in appropriate bargaining units.

The Wagner Act lists five unfair labor practices by managements:

1. Interference with workers' rights to organize

2. Domination of a labor organization

3. Discrimination for union activity

4. Discharge or discipline of an employee for filing charges under the Act

5. Refusal to bargain

Through the years the most frequent actions have been under the third and fifth items.

The Wagner Act established a Federal Mediation and Conciliation Service (FMCS) under which voluntary mediation services could be obtained. As of June 30, 1971, the FMCS employed 253 mediators throughout the country. Each was monitoring an average of 19 active cases.[5]

It should be noted that the Wagner Act did not provide for unfair labor practice actions against unions. This was intentional in order to give unions a relatively free path to massive organization. Economic recovery, according to Roosevelt's policy, depended on placing as much purchasing power as possible into the hands of the working population. It was not till 1947 that the pendulum shifted, and the Wagner Act was amended to provide for unfair labor practice actions against unions.

*   *   *

Passage of the Wagner Act in the United States led to strong agitation in Canada for similar legislation. At its convention of 1937 the TLC adopted a draft statute for the various provinces that was virtually identical to the Wagner Act. Within two years all provinces except two had adopted variations of the draft. The two were Prince Edward Island and Ontario.

SOCIAL LEGISLATION

Along with the move for enabling legislation for union organizing drives and dispute settling procedures, governments of Canada and the United States made rapid strides in the 30s and 40s toward enactment of much-needed social legislation. In the United States the Fair Labor Standards Act of 1938 provided for minimum wages and maximum hours beyond which premium pay would be required. Standards applied similarly to union and nonunion workers. Soon thereafter Canada adopted standards as well — somewhat more liberal than those in the United States. In 1940 the federal government of Canada enacted the Unemployment Insurance Act, marking a major breakthrough in social legislation. This was soon followed during the War by an Old Age Pension Act and a bill providing for widows' allowances.

WARTIME LEGISLATION

In 1940, as part of its war labor policy, the government of Canada issued a statement of principles which were put into operation by a series of subsequent orders-in-council. These orders prevailed until February 1944 when Wartime Labour Relations Regulations were proclaimed. These regulations represented Canada's first comprehensive labor policy since 1925 and had a direct impact on postwar legislation. Five provinces — British Columbia, Manitoba, New Brunswick, Nova Scotia and Ontario — suspended their provincial legislation and made the regulations operative as law. Ingredients of the regulations were these:

1. Workers would be free to organize;
2. employers would be compelled to engage in collective bargaining with representatives of a majority of their employees;
3. no strikes or lockouts could take place until a bargaining agent was certified and conciliation procedures were exhausted;[6]
4. employers should be free from union interference in the discharge, transfer or layoff of employees for just cause;
5. unions should be free from interference or domination by employers;
6. employees should be free from discharge for union activity;
7. disputes regarding interpretation or alleged violation of a labor agreement must be settled through orderly arrangement of the parties;
8. internal affairs of unions should be exposed to members and to the public.

The final ingredient was to be implemented through requirements that unions file copies with the Department of Labour of their constitution, bylaws and lists of officers and must, in addition, provide members with up-to-date financial statements.

In 1943 the Province of Ontario adopted the Ontario Labour Relations Act, giving expression to the 1937 draft statute proposed by TLC and to the ingredients of the wartime labor regulations. One of the most important features of the 1943 Act was a new Court of Labour. The judge of the Labour Court would decide questions of union representation (functions subsequently handled by the Ontario Labour Relations Board). Other features of the Act were these:

1. Repeal of the civil conspiracy doctrine
2. Declaration that restraint of trade would not, in itself, cause a union to be an unlawful entity
3. Declaration that a union was not a legal entity
4. All disputes arising out of interpretation of the collective agreement would be settled ultimately by arbitration
5. Courts would give legal sanctity to collective agreements

Wages during the war were regulated by Federal Government Order-in-Council 7440 issued in December of 1940. This provided that the 1926-1939 level would be the wartime norm for Canadian Workers' wages. When wages went below this level they could be raised, but the increase was limited to five per cent for any one year. The order-in-council also provided for payment of a cost-of-living bonus. Additional restrictions were imposed by succeeding orders-in-council. In 1941 P.C. 8253 was passed. This provided for a National War Labour Board with powers of investigation and recommendation on wages and working conditions. Increases in basic wages were prohibited except by permission of the Board. Two years later P.C. 8384 was enacted. This stipulated that a wage adjustment could be granted only where necessary to correct a gross inequity.

Similar wartime restrictions were in effect in the United States. The labor movements in both countries had adopted a no-strike policy, and disputes over wages, hours or conditions were submitted to the respective country's War Labor Board for final and binding determination. Men who served on these boards obtained valuable experience which stood them in good stead as arbitrators and mediators after the War.

Following the War there was considerable labor unrest caused by years of sacrifice. In 1945 the average hourly earnings for Canadian workers had been 69.4 cents per hour; the average hours worked per week was 44.3.[7] Strikes did occur during the war, but they were rare. So it was not surprising that labor sought to make up for the past six years in short order. They were stimulated in this mission by a situation of unprecedented prosperity. In late 1945, starting with the strike by the United Automobile Workers against Ford Motor Company, unions began their drive. Chrysler Local 195 at Windsor, Ontario, joined the strike. Demands included higher wages, a union shop,[8] seniority for returning service men, layoff pay and two weeks' vacation with pay.

There was considerable militancy. Mass picketing in Windsor led Labour Minister Humphrey Mitchell to believe a revolution was at hand. This view gained credence when the union withdrew members from operation of the powerhouse, causing the Association of Insurance Underwriters of Ontario to express alarm to the Ontario Attorney-General that the property was in danger. Ontario Premier Drew asked Prime Minister Mackenzie King for help, and the next day a group of Royal Canadian Mounted Police (RCMP) were sent to Windsor. The RCMPs, joined by provincial and city police, attempted to open the picket lines so that company security police could enter the power house. This caused strikers to set up a blockade of automobiles around the plant. In some areas the blockade exceeded 20 blocks in depth. Consequently the police never entered, and the company and government retreated. Mr. Justice Ivan Rand was appointed arbitrator in the dispute, and he helped bring the negotiators together to hammer out an agreement. One product of the final settlement was a form of union security which required all employees represented by the union to pay dues, although union membership remained voluntary. This was called the "Rand formula" in Canada — the "agency shop" in the United States. It represented an advancement to workers in union security, but still fell short of the union shop.[9]

The Ford strike set the stage for 1946, when 139,474 workers went on strike in locations throughout Canada. Over 4.5 million man days of work were lost. These figures represented an all-time high for the country. The strike conditions were accompanied by an increase in union membership in 1946 exceeding 120,000.

In the United States labor unrest was equally severe. Two nationwide coal strikes, a national railroad strike, and countless others set off a wave of public opinion which applied pressure on the Congress to enact controlling legislation. The 1936 Wagner Act had given unions almost unencumbered freedom to organize and provided virtually no weapons for employers to resist effectively. Furthermore, there was considerable agitation for some form of emergency powers in the hands of the federal government — similar to that which was provided in the Railway Labor Act — to intervene in disputes that threatened national health and welfare. Out of this scene the Taft-Hartley Act emerged. This was an amendment to the Wagner Act and was passed in 1947 over President Harry Truman's veto. It set the pattern for U.S. and Canadian labor legislation for the next 25 years. The Taft-Hartley Act is still on the books, with no immediate prospects of major change. It is more formally known as the National Labor Relations Act.

Among provisions of the Taft-Hartley Act was a listing of unfair labor practices which could be brought against unions. These follow:

1. Restraint of employees in their rights to organize

2. Causing or attempting to cause an employer to discriminate against an employee, or to deny employment except for failure to pay dues

3. Refusal to bargain

4. Engaging in any of several forms of secondary boycott

5. Requiring excessive or discriminatory dues

6. Causing or attempting to cause an employer to pay for services not performed

7. Engaging in any of several forms of illegal picketing

In addition to giving more power to management by virtue of these unfair labor practices the Taft-Hartley Act gave additional rights to individuals irrespective of union representation. Under Section 9a of the Act an individual could bring his own grievance to his employer and have the grievance adjusted without union intervention, provided the adjustment was consistent with the collective agreement and provided the union representative was given an opportunity to be present.

Perhaps the best-known sections of the Act were those dealing with emergency disputes, Sections 206-210. These gave the President of the United States power to delay a work stoppage for up to 80 days if he believed it imperiled the national health and safety.

As a first step in the emergency procedure the President was required to appoint a board of inquiry to discover the issues involved and to report back to him within a prescribed time limit.

The second step of the emergency procedure permitted the President, on receipt of the board's report, to direct his Attorney General to seek an injunction in the appropriate federal court to bar a stoppage for 80 days. The court had power to deny an injunction if it did not believe there was danger to national health and safety or if the industry involved did not engage in interstate commerce. So far, there has never been a denial.

From 1947 to 1972 twenty-six Taft-Hartley injunctions had been issued. On one occasion, in 1948, United Mineworkers members, led by President John L. Lewis, failed to observe an injunction, and the court found Lewis and his union guilty of both criminal and civil contempt of court. Fines of $20,000 against Lewis and $1,400,000 against the union were levied on the basis of the criminal charges. This represented the first and only attempt by union leaders to defy an injunction under this Act.

During the 80-day period the Act required that the board of inquiry be reconvened. At the end of 60 days if the dispute continued the board was required to report to the President on the then-current position of the parties and the efforts that had been made for settlement. Each party was required to state its position, and this required a statement by the employer of his last settlement offer.

Within the succeeding 15 days the Act required a secret ballot to be taken under auspices of the National Labor Relations Board among employees on strike as to whether they wished to accept the employer's final offer. This part of the procedure proved to be largely unworkable and unnecessary. Union leaders generally instructed their members to vote "no", because it cost them nothing to do so and might, through a demonstration of solidarity, result in some additional benefits. In the early 1960s longshoremen boycotted the voting, tearing up the ballots.

According to the Act, the National Labor Relations Board was required to certify results of the voting to the Attorney General within five days after expiration of the 15. If the strikers voted to accept the employer's last offer this vote was not binding on the union leaders. At the end of the 80 days if there was still no settlement the Attorney General was called on to dissolve the injunction.

The Taft-Hartley Act provided no mechanism for preventing a strike beyond 80 days. Since 1947 eighteen disputes have been settled during the 80 days; seven strikes started or resumed after the injunction expired. While far from perfect in its attempt to cope with emergency situations, the Taft-Hartley emergency sections have proved to be largely effective, and because of this there have been moves to bring U.S. railroads and airlines, still governed by the Railway Labor Act, under the same provisions. The sections have been copied by several states and were adopted virtually without change by the Province of Quebec in Section 99 of its Labour Code.

Section 301 of the Taft-Hartley Act spelled out the legal status of labor organizations, something which was not done in Canada until the 1970s. There were three principal parts to the section. Part (a) stated that suits for violations of collective agreements could be brought in the courts. Part (b) provided that unions and companies covered by the Act were bound by the acts of their agents. The second sentence of part (b) dealt with the legal entity question, stating that any labor organization may sue or be sued as an entity and in behalf of the employees whom it represented.

In all, the Taft-Hartley Act contained 47 sections, many of them defining administrative procedures for processing unfair labor practice charges and specifying ingredients of a national labor relations policy. The policy itself was concerned primarily with protection of the three central components of our industrial relations system, stated earlier.

POSTWAR PROVINCIAL LABOR ACTS — CANADA

The various Canadian provinces adopted legislation following the war that essentially incorporated most of the features of Canadian wartime legislation plus many of the features of the U.S. Taft-Hartley Act. The Ontario Labour Relations Act was adopted in 1948 and has remained essentially unchanged since then. It was typical of the acts passed by all provinces.

The principal differences between the Ontario Labour Relations Act and the U.S. Taft-Hartley Act were these:

1. Ontario contained no emergency disputes procedure. Among the provinces only Quebec and British Columbia adopted emergency measures.

2. Ontario provided for compulsory sections in collective agreements prohibiting stoppages during contract terms and requiring final and binding arbitration of disputes arising during the life of a contract. Most other provinces did the same.

3. The Ontario Labour Relations Act provided for conciliation as a compulsory precondition to a legal strike or lockout. All other provinces, but one, did the same. The Taft-Hartley Act provided only for voluntary conciliation through the services of the Federal Mediation and Conciliation Services. Either party to a dispute could apply for conciliation, or the Federal Services could assign a conciliator at the discretion of its director, but a strike or lockout could take place whether or not there was conciliation.

4. There was an important difference between the Ontario Labour Relations Act and the Taft-Hartley Act regarding enforcement. In the United States an individual could bring suit under the Taft-Hartley Act against his own union for unfair or inadequate representation. In Ontario this became possible in 1970 provided an employee could secure consent to prosecute from the Ontario Labour Relations Board.[10] Such consent was required to prosecute for any violation of the Ontario Act. In the United States no such consent was required; action to enforce the Taft-Hartley Act could be taken directly to the courts.

5. Penalties for violations of the Ontario Labour Relations Act were limited by statute. As of 1972 an individual could be fined up to $1,000, a union or company up to $10,000, for violating the Act, with each day of violation constituting a separate offense.[11] No limits were placed on penalties that could be imposed for violations of the Taft-Hartley Act.

6. Both the Taft-Hartley Act and the Ontario Labour Relations Act were based on majority rule. For example, both acts imposed a legal duty on employers to bargain with the labor organization that represented a

majority of its employees. However, the U.S. law was far more explicit in its protection of minority rights. It did this in four ways:

(a) It prohibited closed shop security arrangements.[12]

(b) It prohibited dismissal of an employee to whom membership in the union was denied or whose membership was terminated for reasons other than failure to pay regular fees, dues and assessments.

(c) It declared the right of an employer to confer with individual employees during working hours and the right of the individual employee to take grievances directly to the employer.

(d) It required union representatives to give fair representation to all members of the unit for which the union held bargaining rights, whether or not they were union members.[13] It was not until 1970 that Ontario did this by virtue of an amendment to the Ontario Labour Relations Act.[14]

Laws of the various Canadian provinces only dabbled in these matters. Closed shops could be negotiated; only a few jurisdictions prohibited dismissal of a person who had been refused union membership; the right to bring individual grievances was present only in Ontario and only after proving collusion between a union and company to deny the individual a fair hearing in the grievance procedure; the right of access was present by inference only; and the notion of "fair representation" had not been articulated except in Quebec.[15]

Postwar labor legislation in Canada did nothing to clear up the confusion surrounding injunctive remedies. In the United States the Norris-La Guardia Act had been specific in this regard, but Canada's laws were not. By 1972 it was possible to say with some degree of certainty that injunctions would be issued in labor disputes where there was a probability of property damage or personal injury, where unlawful acts were either taking place or threatened, or where no adequate remedy existed under the law. Confusion reigned over the role of injunctions in the event of picketing or union organizing activity.

GOVERNMENT EMPLOYEE UNIONISM

Since the early 1960s the greatest growth of unions occurred in the government services. In 1962 President John F. Kennedy signed an executive order extending collective bargaining rights to United States civil servants. At the same time these employees were denied the right to strike. Any disputes could be submitted on impasse to mediation and arbitration.

In 1967 the Public Service Staff Relations Act was passed in Canada. This Act similarly gave government employees the right to bargain for wages, hours and certain working conditions. It also gave them the right to strike. As bargaining units were certified to represent designated groups of employees their leaders could elect one of two options at the start of each contract regarding the action to be taken in the event of an impasse at the end of the contract term. On one hand they could elect to submit their dispute to conciliation which, if not successful, could give rise to a legal strike after a specified time period. On the other hand they could forgo the right to strike, substituting compulsory binding arbitration of all issues in dispute. As of October 1973 over 200,000 Canadian employees were covered by the Public Service Staff Relations Act. There were 109 bargaining units, 20 of which had elected the conciliation-strike option.

THE FUTURE

At present Canada and the United States have legal systems which are basically sound for the governing of labor relations. However, there are concerns about the ability of the systems to cope with changes in the social-economic systems. These changes are occurring at an ever-increasing rate, raising the question of whether any system of laws could keep pace.

Among the recent trends in labor relations that give cause for concern about the capability of the legal system to cope is the increasing tendency of unions and employers in many of North America's key industries to abandon collective bargaining. No meaningful interchange, no give and take has been observed in the United States or Canadian railroad or airline industries for many years. The longshoring and seafaring industries have typically reached an impasse before either side gave an inch — each waiting for government mediators and statutory emergency procedures to start operating before making a significant move. Public utilities have long been characterized by nonbargaining, and this is understandable, because no politically conscious public utility commissioner is willing to risk his standing with those who keep him in power by raising utility rates in order to pay for increased wage and fringe demands. Similarly no politically conscious union leader who depends for his power on the support of his constituency would place that power on the line by reducing his demands when his actions were so clearly observable. It is far better from the viewpoints of both parties for a government-appointed mediator or arbitrator to step in and recommend settlement terms. This way both sides can save face. The utility executive can claim that it was the government man, not himself, that required a consumer rate increase; the union leader can similarly put blame on the government man for his failure to get as much as he feel the members deserve.

It follows that while bargaining can take place between representatives of the government and union leaders in the government service, there are serious difficulties. Realistic exchange can hardly take place on money matters when one of the parties — the government — is on one hand an advocate charged with keeping the lid on expenditures and on the other hand a judge whose employees may ultimately be called on in mediation and arbitration procecures to recommend terms of settlement. How can the voting public rest comfortably knowing that their government representatives, charged with bargaining on their behalf, are on one hand able to transfer money by way of tax allocations to pay for any settlement they sign and, on the other hand, are maintained in office by the voting public which consists mostly of the low-to-middle income working class who reach favorably to healthy economic increases?

There are other social-economic factors that raise questions about the ability of the legal system to cope. Witness, for example, the regular practice of some companies and unions regarding conciliation requirements under Canadian law. General Motors Corporation and the United Automobile Workers, for example, abhor government involvement in the collective bargaining process. Thus, as a matter of formality, they schedule meetings with the Director of Conciliation Services at the start of each bargaining session. Typically they meet for less than ten minutes and request the conciliator to write a report indicating that he was ineffective in securing a settlement. Then, the statutory time period begins to operate so that a strike deadline comes into being, leaving the parties free to strike or lock out when the contract term expires. Consequently any expert aid which might have been secured from an outside party is consciously avoided and the parties are left to their own devices.

Perhaps the most obvious factor that raises a question about the ability of the legal system to cope is the increased willingness of people to flout the law when they believe they can gain an advantage from doing so. There are laws in many jurisdictions barring the right to strike. Some of them carry severe penalties for violations. Significant among them are U.S. laws barring the right of civil servants to strike and the laws of most states and provinces prohibiting strikes in essential services manned by policemen, firemen, teachers, doctors, hospital workers. Almost daily the news media carry stories of strikes among such employees, all of them reflecting a conscious awareness by union members and their leaders that they are violating the law, but also reflecting a belief that the violation will result in rewards that surpass the potential penalties.

As the North American social-economic system becomes more complex an increasing number of labor-management situations will fall into the category of public interest disputes. Such disputes carry the possibility of injuring third-party bystanders at least as much as the principals. Considerable attention has been devoted to devising a system of laws and practices to deal with these disputes. The Taft-Hartley Act emergency measures are probably the best devised so far, but these are not necessarily transferable to other jurisdictions. They have, themselves, demonstrated significant weaknesses and are currently undergoing examination toward possible change.

In dealing with changes in the laws we should direct our attention to the following questions:

☐ What is the public interest?
☐ Does a potential dispute affect the public so that legal interference is warranted when a union requests a wage or benefit increase that will result in price increases for essential goods and services?
☐ Is legal interference warranted only when there is a threat to the health and safety of a significant number of people?
☐ Should political officials be allowed to determine instances of public interest, or threats to health or safety?
☐ Can there be collective bargaining in instances where innocent third parties would be hurt more severely and earlier in the event of a shutdown than either of the principals to a collective agreement?

Assuming that it is possible to reach an acceptable definition of the public interest we need to ask what techniques are best for taking it into account. So far we have been unable to devise a system which calls for collective bargaining but denies parties the right to strike or lock out. All the frequently-talked-about strike substitutes have been found wanting. Compulsory, binding arbitration has limitations, because one or both sides generally believe they will gain more from an arbitrator than by bargaining; so there's no significant bargaining. Furthermore, compulsory arbitration does not necessarily prevent strikes: Witness the country of Australia where strikes have been barred since 1955, and all disputes must be submitted to arbitration if there's an impasse. In spite of this prohibition Australia experienced an average of 378 days lost in strikes per 1000 persons employed between the years 1955-64.[16]

Mediation and conciliation may be effective in averting or reducing the severity of strikes, but in cases where parties consciously ignore or avoid outside interference there is no way these devices can be helpful. Injunctions have been used, but they have been found wanting. They are repugnant to many people and difficult to enforce. During the Montreal transit dispute of 1967, for example, moves were instituted to serve 6000 separate injunctions on each of the striking workers — an impossible task.

As politicians and labor relations experts contemplate the future and propose new laws to deal with emerging problems, the informed observer can make useful inputs. In this respect it is important to remember that most laws are the product of compromise. In labor relations there is special danger that political compromise will render a law meaningless. It is important, as well, to remember that there is a tendency among political beings to try to deal with all possible contingencies through laws. Labor relations situations are too complex and changeable for that; they require a significant amount of ad hoc adjustment as new, previously unforeseen contingencies arise.

Most important of all it is necessary to understand that most politicians do not understand labor relations. This, coupled with the tendency of laymen to sit back and complain as new laws are passed, could lead to passage of laws that no party wants or can live with. It is well to remember that of the many labor relations laws dotting the history of Canada and the United States two are labeled by experts as most "successful" — the 1907 Industrial Relations Disputes and Investigation Act of Canada and the 1926 Railway Labor Act in the United States. Neither was a legal draftsman's work of art. Both became shopworn after limited periods of time. But they had one ingredient that spelled unique success: both were products of hard-nosed negotiations by representatives of labor and management. As such they had the commitment of interested parties to make them work. This element, more than any other, has been missing in recent considerations of changes in the law.

In highlighting weaknesses of the legal framework for labor relations it is important to note that the system has, by all measures of success, been extremely effective. In the period 1950-1959, for example, there were 2022 strikes and lockouts in Canada involving 976,671 workers. The total time lost during that period was 17,865,248 man days. This amounted to less than .113 per cent of total man days worked. When strikes occurred they almost always (over 99 per cent of the time) ended in some form of settlement, with employers and employee representatives resuming their relationships with only minor variations from before. This record is unparalleled in countries outside the North American continent. It is even more impressive when compared with other fields of potential conflict such as international relations.

NOTES TO CHAPTER 3

1. 55 OLR 455 (1924), I DLR 101 (1924), 2 DLR 761 (1925), AC 396 (1925), 2 DLR 5 (PC).

2. See A.W.R. Carrothers and E.E. Palmer, *Report of a Study on the Labour Injunction in Ontario*. Ontario Department of Labour, 1965.

3. *Ex parte* injunctions were used freely in Canada until the mid-1960s. These provided for issuance of prohibitive court orders based solely on the allegation of

a violation of law or probable violation of law, or actual or probable damage or injury on sworn data by an alleged offended party. Such injunctions did not require the presence of the alleged offender.

4. Ivan C. Rand, C.C., *Report of the Royal Commission Inquiry into Labour Disputes*, Queen's Printer, Province of Ontario, 1968.

5. Federal Mediation and Conciliation Service, *Twenty-Fourth Annual Report*, Fiscal Year 1971, pp. 29 and 62.

6. Statement of the first three ingredients constituted the first formal acknowledgement of the components that were long recognized as essential parts of the Canadian-U.S. labor relations scene.

7. Charles Lipton, *The Trade Union Movement of Canada*, *1827-1959*, Social Publications Ltd., 1966, p. 175.

8. Union shops required that all employees join the union within a specified time period after hiring.

9. Charles Lipton, op. cit, pp.270-1.

10. Ontario Labour Relations Act, Revised Statutes 1970, Section 90.

11. Ibid., Sections 60 and 85.

12. Closed shops required union membership as a precondition of employment.

13. Under some union security arrangements, such as open shops, agency shops (Rand Formula), and maintenance of membership, all bargaining unit members are not necessarily union members.

14. The Labour Relations Act, Revised Statutes of Ontario, 1970, Section 60.

15. A.W.R. Carrothers, *Collective Bargaining Law in Canada*, Butterworths, 1965, pp. 194-5.

16. Derek C. Bok and John T. Dunlop, *Labor and the American Community*, Simon and Schuster, 1970.

4. UNION ORGANIZATION

Nearly all managers face a union organizing drive at some time in their careers. More often than not the drive is over when the manager hears about it, and his first knowledge of its existence comes when he receives a notice of application for certification from the Labor Relations Board.

This chapter summarizes the laws governing union organizing drives and describes some of the techniques of organizing. The chapter concentrates on the laws of the Province of Ontario, with only casual reference to other Canadian jurisdictions. While laws of all Canadian jurisdictions are similar regarding union organization, readers should consult the applicable labor statutes for variations. Laws and practices in the United States are also cited, because procedures involving union organization were largely derived from that country and are likely to be influenced in the future by the same source.

* * *

Every person is free to join a union. If more than 50 per cent of the employees in a distinguishable group wish to be represented by a union they can obtain legal certification, and the employer is then required by law to bargain with them in good faith regarding wages, hours and conditions of employment. The parties are not required to come to an agreement as a result of bargaining, and if they reach an impasse the employees can stage a legal strike. Similarly the employer can effect a legal lock out. In Canadian jurisdictions the law requires entry of government conciliation services as a precondition to legal strike or lockout action; not so in the United States.

APPROPRIATENESS OF A BARGAINING UNIT

"Bargaining unit" is a term used to describe a distinguishable group of employees capable of representation by a single union. More than one union may exist in a plant, each representing separate groups of employees and governed by a separate contract. Seagoing cargo vessels, as an example, are typically manned by representatives of six separate unions, some with only one or two members aboard but each with the power to deactivate the ship if his elected bargainers fail to come to an acceptable agreement. Crews on cross-country freight trains typically are comprised of representatives of four separate unions. Airlines flight crews generally consist of representatives of three unions. Some manufacturing plants have as many as five separate bargaining units; more typically, those which are organized have two units of production employees, one or two units of distinguishable crafts and an office workers group.

It is normal for the Labour Board to issue separate representation certificates to cover distinguishable employee units — even when applied for by the same union. However in such instances the union and company often agree in negotiations to bargain for all groups to be covered by the same contract.

The bargaining unit is normally determined by agreement between the employer and union. If they cannot agree the Labour Board makes that determination. By law, the Labour Board cannot define a unit to include employees who exercise managerial functions, those who are employed in a confidential capacity in matters relating to labor relations, and certain enumerated professionals such as lawyers, medical doctors and dentists.

One of the first steps in the certification process is to determine whether the bargaining unit applied for by the union is appropriate. Employers can have a significant influence in determining appropriateness of a bargaining unit. However, their challenges are often looked upon with suspicion, because employers sometimes contest a unit merely as a means of gaining time to mount a campaign to defeat the union. If his motives are sincere, and if his arguments are well presented, an employer can be reasonably certain that the following guidelines will be used by the Labour Relations Board in determining appropriateness of a proposed bargaining unit:

1. Is the proposed unit easily distinguishable geographically or by skill or craft?

2. Has the unit been agreed upon previously during an organizing drive?

3. Is there a clear community of interests among members of the bargaining unit?

4. Are typical lines of advancement or demotion in the organization substantially confined to the proposed unit?

5. Is the proposed unit typical?

If there is disagreement on these matters the Labour Board will assign an investigating officer, called an examiner, to meet with the parties and gather evidence on the issue. Parties may produce evidence at these meetings by way of witnesses or documents. Evidence is not taken under oath, and the examiner may not seek evidence on his own to fill in gaps in the parties' presentation. Following the meeting the examiner issues a written report to the Board, copies of which are sent to the parties prior to any final determination by the Board. The report is confined to findings of fact; it contains no recommendations. Parties are then given reasonable time to object to the accuracy of the report and to request a hearing before the Board in order to argue the conclusions which they believe the Board ought to draw.

On rare occasions following receipt of an examiner's report the Board may, by request or on its own volition, visit the work site. In such a visit the Board may not gather new evidence; rather they are restricted to one purpose; to come to *understand* the evidence already gathered.

Following receipt of the examiner's report and, possibly, a follow-up hearing or an on-site visit, the Board then defines the appropriate bargaining unit. Usually this process is simple, straightforward and rapid. However, there have been occasions when it has taken a long time — sometimes up to 18 months.

In the United States the examiner has somewhat more authority than in Ontario. Aside from gathering facts from parties he may, on his own volition, visit the facilities, observe operations and, if necessary, interview some of the people in order to report back to the Board with his own recommendations on appropriateness.

LEGAL REQUIREMENTS FOR CERTIFICATION

The union requesting certification must prove to the employer or the Labor Board that more than 50 per cent of the employees in the unit want representation. Sometimes this is done by way of an election. However, in most Canadian jurisdictions it is possible to avoid an election and still obtain certification under certain circumstances. Most frequent among these are the following:

(a) Substantial preelection commitment

In the Province of Ontario the law provides that if 65 per cent or more of the employees in an agreed-upon bargaining unit sign authorization cards indicating a desire to become a member of the union and designating that union as their bargaining agent the Labour Board will grant automatic certification.[2]

It is common in Ontario for unions to seek automatic certification by virtue of the 55-per-cent rule. In 1971, over 60 per cent of all applications fell into this category.

(b) Voluntary recognition

In Ontario an employer may recognize a union as exclusive representative of his employees without involvement of the Labour Board. Any collective agreement signed by the employer under such an arrangement is valid. However, if a question of representation is raised before the

Board by another union or a group of employees the Board may declare that the original union is not legally constituted.[3]

In the United States voluntary recognition procedures are also sanctioned provided the union furnishes evidence that a majority of the employees in the desired bargaining unit wish to be represented. In addition the United States law provides for a consent election procedure. In this case the parties are in agreement on the bargaining unit, and the union has furnished proof that at least 30 per cent of the employees wish representation. Then the parties apply to the National Labor Relations Board for an immediate election. The procedures are undertaken promptly, with no further sign-ups and no hearing.

Union organizing drives are not necessarily confined to bargaining units where no union exists. Sometimes members of existing units are dissatisfied with their union and seek to replace it or drop it without replacement. Replacement drives are often referred to as raids. In early days of union activity raids were common; as of 1973 they were rare, especially among affiliates of the Canadian Labour Congress (CLC), the American Federation of Labor — Congress of Industrial Organizations (AFL-CIO) and the Ontario Federation of Labour (OFL) where internal no-raiding pacts served to limit such action. Dropping a union without replacement is known as termination of bargaining rights or sometimes, but inaccurately, as decertification.

TIMING OF APPLICATION

Organizing drives of all kinds, whether a nonunion company is involved or whether a raid is being attempted, must comply with specified laws regarding timing. If no trade union has been certified as bargaining agent for the unit claimed by the union, the union may apply at any time for certification even if it or another union failed in a representation attempt the day before. It is conceivable, however, that Labour Board would require a reasonable wait period between attempts if a union tried and failed repeatedly. In a recent case before the Ontario Labour Relations Board the same union made application for certification at the same company three successive times, each time within a week of the rejection of a former application. On the third try the Board imposed a six-month waiting period.

In cases where a union has been certified but no contract has been signed, a new application can be made by another union 12 months after the date a conciliator or mediator was appointed by the Minister of Labour to assist the parties in negotiations or, if later, 30 days after the report of a conciliation board or mediator has been issued. In some instances the Minister of Labour decides not to appoint a conciliation board. If this happens the 30-day period starts upon his making of that decision.[4]

In cases of voluntary recognition where no contract has been signed a subsequent union may not apply for certification until 12 months after signing of the voluntary agreement.

Legal raiding of existing bargaining units with valid collective agreements may take place in an open period, defined as the last two months of the contract term, in a one-, two- or three-year contract. Parties cannot escape raiding even if they sign a successor contract two months or more in advance of the open period. Under the Ontario law the maximum time period under which parties can escape raiding is 34 months, having signed a three-year agreement.

If a collective agreement is for a term of more than three years an application for certification may take place only after the start of the 35th month and before the start of the 37th month of its term, then during the last two months of each year that the contract continues in force.

CONDITION FOR SECURING MEMBERS

A union which applies for certification must furnish proof that a substantial number of employees in the designated bargaining unit want that union to represent them. Most jurisdictions require such proof to be in the form of signed membership cards. There is no prescribed form for such cards. One, used by the United Automobile Workers Union in Ontario, contains the following statement:

> I, the undersigned employee of [Company] wish to join the United Automobile, Aerospace and Agricultural Implement Workers of America, to abide by this organization's constitution and bylaws and to designate the organization as my exclusive bargaining agent.

> _____
> signed

The Province of Ontario requires that the card be accompanied by a payment of one dollar from the employee. This money is not refundable whether the union is successful or not. Furthermore it must be paid by the employee himself.[5] A card would be rendered invalid if it were shown that the money was paid by someone else. Similarly a card would be invalid if the signature was not truly that of the employee or if the employee signed under duress. Organizers from responsible unions exercise extreme care to avoid cards which are improperly signed or obtained under false pretences, because one improper card would cause the Board to disregard all other membership cards. Membership irregularities are most likely to occur when inexperienced employees are enlisted by union organizers to sign up fellow employees.

In Ontario a union must secure signed authorization cards from at least 45 per cent of the employees in the desired unit. If it has less than 45 per cent and applies for certification the union will be thrown out. If they wish to try again a new application must be filed. The cards themselves are considered valid for up to one year. However, if they are dated between six months and one year before the date of application the Board will disregard the 55-per-cent rule and order an election regardless of the number of sign-ups unless there is a fresh money payment. If cards are dated more than a year before the date of application they are considered invalid. If between 45 and 55 per cent of the desired bargaining unit have signed, an election may be ordered in which all members of the unit have an opportunity to vote. In the event of an election the majority of those voting will determine the outcome.[6]

An employee does not bind himself to vote for a union by virtue of signing a membership card and paying one dollar. In fact, the same employee may sign more than one authorization card — each for a competing union — and all would be legitimate. The card is nothing more than a demonstration of desire at the time of signing. Conditions can, and often do, change after that time. Experienced union organizers expect that up to ten per cent of the employees signing cards will vote against the union in an election. For this reason organizers are anxious to secure a 55-per-cent or higher sign-up and to do it rapidly. Statistics have consistently shown that the greater the time period between card signing and voting the greater the likelihood of a vote against the union. Similarly there has been an observed relationship between the size of the bargaining unit and the propensity of a worker to change his allegiance: the smaller the unit the more likely that the worker will switch to favoring the company.

APPLICATION FOR CERTIFICATION

When a union organizer obtains a sufficient number of cards he may apply to the Labour Board for certification. In applying, the organizer must indicate the name of the employer, the name of the union, the number of employees he seeks to have in the unit, and he must name any other parties known to be interested. In addition he must describe in detail the proposed bargaining unit. One such description follows:

All employees of W.A. McCabe Co. Ltd., Brantford, Ontario, save and except foremen, persons above the rank of foreman and members of the office staff.

Administrative procedures under the Industrial Disputes and Investigation Act, Canada's federal act, require that bargaining units spell out, in detail, the categories of all workers to be included. An exclusionary description such as the one above would be unacceptable.

In Ontario the applicant for certification also indicates whether he desires a prehearing vote.

PREHEARING VOTE

Many union organizers take advantage of a provision in the Ontario Labour Relations Act that permits an election by members of the proposed bargaining unit before a formal hearing on the merits of the application. If all documents are in order such a vote may be ordered. After the vote the ballot box is sealed, pending a hearing. If there is no challenge to the bargaining unit at the hearing or if the Board decides the appropriate unit is the same as that which voted, the results of the vote are certified.

The principal advantage to requesting a prehearing vote from an organizer's point of view is that it allows minimal time for the employer to mount an effective drive to cause those who signed membership cards to change their minds about wanting a union. There are two principal disadvantages:

1. If the employer successfully challenges the described bargaining unit the results of the prehearing vote are invalid.
2. The organizer himself may need time after application for certification to enlist more support. Any bandwagon effect that his campaign might have would be cut short.[7]

NOTIFICATION TO EMPLOYER

The Labour Board, on receipt of an application, sends a copy to the employer and invites him to submit a reply. The employer is requested to provide the Board with a list of all employees in the proposed bargaining unit as of the date of application, plus specimen signatures of each employee. On receipt of signatures a clerk from the Board compares all of them with signatures on the authorization cards.

Along with a copy of the application the Board sends a Notice of Application to the employer to be posted conspicuously at the work place. This notice indicates the proposed bargaining unit, states the date and place scheduled for a Labour Board hearing, invites interested employees to be present at the hearing, and advises employees of steps to be taken if they wish to oppose the application. Hearing dates are usually set for two or three weeks later. Another date, called the terminal date, is established for approximately a week before the hearing. This is the date by which documents, including specimen signatures, must be returned by the employer. It is also the date by which membership evidence must be filed by the union.

In practice the terminal date is strictly observed regarding membership evidence. If an employer fails to return specimen signatures by the terminal date the Board sends him a registered letter restating its request and giving five additional days. If he still fails to respond the Board proceeds according to evidence submitted and assumes that all membership cards are properly signed.

If the employer fails to return other requested documents, such as lists of employees in various categories, the Board will receive them at the hearing. If these cause the union to require a delay in order to consider them, the Board will entertain a motion to this effect.

Sometimes the Board has reason to believe that other parties are interested in the application, either from knowledge specified by the union or the employer or from its own knowledge. In such cases those parties will be informed of the application and invited to make representations. Among parties who would obviously receive notices would be other unions known to be attempting organization of the same company or an incumbent union being raided.

REPRESENTATION HEARING

The hearing normally takes place in a hearing room at the offices of the Ontario Labour Relations Board. One hearing officer and two members of the Board preside over the action.[8] The hearing is designed to accomplish four principal objectives:

1. To determine the appropriate bargaining unit.
2. To determine the number and percentage of employees in the proposed unit who have indicated a desire for membership in the union.
3. To allow the employer, individual employees, groups of employees or intervening parties such as competing unions to raise objections.
4. To indicate subsequent action.

Three forms of subsequent action may be taken: automatic certification, denial of the union's application or ordering of a representation vote. Delays in the procedure may be encountered if there are disagreements regarding the appropriate unit requiring appointment of an examiner, or if there are allegations of fraud or other improper activity in receiving signatures. Otherwise the Board's determination of action will be based solely on the number of cards submitted.

REPRESENTATION VOTE

While automatic certification is the most frequent action taken by the Board, representation votes are directed in about 40 per cent of the cases. Votes are held on the company premises at a time and place during working hours that is most convenient to the company and union involved.

The election itself is supervised by a returning officer from the Labour Relations Board accompanied by scrutineers appointed by each of the parties to the vote. Voters' names are checked off on separate lists by the returning officer and the scrutineers. In Ontario it is illegal for either the company or union to do any form of campaigning for a 72-hour period preceding the election.

In instances where a nonunion company is facing organization the ballots, furnished by the Labour Board, require the voting employee to mark an X in the space next to his preference regarding "union" or "no union." If an incumbent union is being raided by an outside union the ballots contain the names of the two unions, nothing else. In some cases two unions are competing for a nonunion bargaining unit; here the employee may vote for either of the two unions or no union — three choices. If there is no clear majority favoring any one of the three a runoff ballot is then taken between the two alternatives getting the most votes.

Usually votes are counted by the returning officer promptly on closing of the polls, and results are posted on the premises right away. In order for this to happen the parties must sign a Consent-and-Waiver form and a Certificate of Conduct of Election. These waive any right to challenge results later, even if evidence of voting irregularities is discovered.

If there is cause to believe that irregularities existed so as to invalidate the vote, one or both parties may ask for the returning officer to seal the ballot box, not to be opened until the alleged irregularities are investigated and a determination on the validity of the vote is made by the Board.

Under normal conditions the Board certifies final results in writing several days after the vote.

TERMINATION OF BARGAINING RIGHTS.[9]

Approximately one out of every five applications to the Ontario Labour Relations Board are for a declaration that a trade union no longer represents the employees in the bargaining unit — termination of bargaining rights (sometimes called decertification). Procedures for determining whether a union's bargaining rights should be terminated are identical to those for certifying a new bargaining unit, except that a vote is required even if 100 per cent of the employees indicate a desire to terminate.

The procedure for indicating a desire to terminate is somewhat different than for certification. Rather than submitting authorization cards the employees must voluntarily sign a statement that they no longer desire representation. In plants with ten or fewer employees this is often in the form of a petition; in larger plants it is more likely to consist of individually executed statements. The petition or collection of statements is then filed with the Labour Board, along with an Application to Terminate. The Board, in turn, assigns a returning officer to determine if the action was influenced by the employer. If his report is negative and if the application is timely the Board will officially terminate the relationship.[10]

UNFAIR LABOR PRACTICES

Unfair labor practices are actions by an employer or union which would tend to inhibit an employee in his efforts to exercise freedom of choice regarding unionization or, on the other hand, would tend to inhibit an employer in operating his business in a normal fashion, subject to laws permitting unionization and free collective bargaining.

A whole body of law has built up through the years around unfair labor practices. Over 80 per cent of all unfair labor practice charges concern union organization campaigns and certification procedures. If charges are levied during an organization campaign the investigation and hearing, if any, proceeds independently. The results of the unfair labor practice hearing could cause an election to be set aside. If serious enough they could bar the union from further organizing for up to six months, or, if a company is found guilty, they could result in automatic certification of the union, provided the Board is satisfied that more than 50 per cent of the employees are members of the union and the true wishes of employees are not likely to be disclosed by a representation vote.[11] The most frequent unfair labor practice charges fall into one of the following categories:

1. Intimidation, coercion, threats or promises to compel a person to join or not to join a union.
2. Persuasion of an employee during working hours to become or continue to be or refrain from becoming a member of a union.
3. Illegal strike or lockout or threat thereof.
4. Altering of rates of pay or working conditions where the probable effect would be to cause an employee to refrain from joining or to quit membership in a union, unless such alteration is in the normal course of business.

It is for the Labour Board, or the National Labor Relations Board in the United States, to determine whether an unfair labor practice existed and what, if any, remedy should be applied. In Ontario decisions of the Board may be appealed to the courts only with consent of the Board [12] and only on three counts:

1. To determine if the Board denied natural justice,
2. to determine whether the Board exceeded its jurisdiction, or
3. to determine whether the Board incorrectly denied jurisdiction.

There may be no appeal of Ontario Board decisions on the merits. This is contrary to practice in the U.S. where parties may appeal Board decisions to the courts without consent, and the courts may review the merits.

Prior to a Board hearing field officers are assigned to investigate unfair labor practice charges and try to effect a settlement. Only after the field officer makes a written report of his findings and recommendations does the Board become involved, and only then on formal appeal from the field officer's findings. The same is true in the United States.

In deciding a case on its merits the Board will be influenced by many factors. Among these are the nearness of the incident to the time of election: the nearer, the more influence it is likely to have on an employee's vote; consequently the more likely that the charge will be upheld. Another factor taken into consideration is the history of the employer's actions regarding union organizing attempts. If the employer has been known to make good on threats to discharge for union activity there is more likelihood that such threats would have intimidating influence than if he had regularly retreated from threats in the past. Consequently such an employer would be more vulnerable to an unfair practice charge.

Unfair labor practice charges are fairly common features of organizing campaigns. A substantial number of them (usually those filed by the winning party) are dropped after the Board's determination regarding certification.

Consent to prosecute is virtually automatic for applications made as a result of unfair labor practice cases, and remedies can range from fines up to $1,000 a day against offending individuals and $10,000 a day against organizations, [13] to reinstatement of discharged employees, to certification of a union seeking representation. Most often the victor in an unfair labor practice action will file for consent to prosecute and hold this fact over the head of the other party in hopes of obtaining the desired remedy without further action.

In the United States the overwhelming number of unfair labor practices which are pushed to final action result in an order by the field officer or Board for the offending party to stop doing whatever it was doing and to refrain from doing it in the future: a cease and desist order.

The relative mildness of cease and desist orders and the frequency with which they are issued often causes both unions and employers to skirt the border of unfair labor practices or even to commit blatantly illegal acts in an effort to enlist supporters or to thwart organization. Employers, of course, have more opportunity than unions to make a threat or promise stick; consequently most charges are levied against employers. For the same reason most union organizers try to keep their organizing drive secret from the employer for as long as possible, to provide minimal opportunity for the employer to retaliate.

ORGANIZING TECHNIQUES

All major unions employ field organizers. These are men who spend most of their time going from company to company attempting to organize workers. Their skills are finely honed. Their knowledge of the relevant laws is complete. They vary their techniques as the composition of the work force and problems of the employment relationship dictate.

This section is written from the viewpoint of a union organizer, not because the authors necessarily sympathize with the union point of view but because we believe that intricacies of an organizing drive can be understood best by looking at them through the eyes of one who is most frequently involved.

Some organizers are specialists within their profession. The United Steelworkers, for example, employ a man in Canada who specializes in organizing workers of Italian origin. He is Italian himself, speaks the language and appreciates the special problems of this ethnic minority. Others specialize in organizing blacks, women, or white collar professionals. Some are especially adept in organizing miners, others in organizing lumbermen.

Organizers are not elected to their positions. They are full-time employees whose tenure often transcends that of elected officers. Some of them have, themselves, formed unions to bargain for wages, hours and working conditions with their employer—the union. Now at a time in history when vistas for new organizing activity have narrowed, the skills of organizing are more finely tuned than ever before.

THE CONTACT

Most union organizing drives start with a few disgruntled workers who have done some comparing of their wages and working conditions with others in the community. Typically one or two of them call or visit the local office of a union—possibly learning about it from a friend or a newspaper article. While unions carry identifying names that tend to associate them with a certain group of workers, the competitive nature of most will lead them to express interest in any group of workers indicating a genuine desire to organize. Many unlikely associations have developed through the years as a result of this competitiveness. The Playboy Club bunnies in New York City, for example, are represented by the Teamsters Union—known generally as an organization for truck drivers; the United Mineworkers represent the dormitory maids at Yale University and the United Steelworkers represent bartenders in Timmins, Ontario.

On initial contact the union official will assess the situation and if it looks reasonably promising to him he will take the names, addresses and phone numbers of the interested employees and assign an organizer to contact them. From this time on the organizer works as strategist, educator, counselor, and companion to members of the work force in an effort to enlist enought support to secure certification, provided, of course, that he too believes there is a reasonable probability that the workers can be organized.

Sometimes union organizers themselves will take the initiative in attempting to enlist a group of workers, even if there has been no contact from members of the work force. This sort of action is most common in communities where one or two well-known nonunion companies operate amid a preponderance of unionized firms. Such companies are often a source of embarrassement and unrest for a local organizer, for one or both of two reasons. Either the managements are so enlightened that workers believe their nonunion situation is better than being unionized, thus causing some amount of envy among unionized workers, or the management has been successful in thwarting union organizing drives in the past through well-executed battle techniques and represents a seductive challenge to the union man to try again. The Dominion Foundry and Steel Company (DOFASCO) of Hamilton, Ontario has long represented a challenge to the United Steelworkers of America, who represent a large number of workers in this highly organized industrial community. DOFASCO has remained unorganized through the years by maintaining a record of progressive labor relations practices and by keeping their wage and fringe benefit packages at least equal to and sometimes ahead of the union pattern. Time and again union organizers have mounted campaigns at DOFASCO, and time and again they have been thwarted, sometimes as a result of poor organizing techniques, more often as a result of the short attention span of employees.

One of the organizer's first tasks is to form a nucleus of committed employees who will be willing to work long hours for no compensation and sometimes at considerable risk to themselves. Quite naturally this nucleus is usually made up of people suggested by those who made the initial contact. However, experienced organizers insist on meeting all members of the nucleus group for the first time in person. This way a more accurate assessment can be made as to whether the person can do the job; those who seem reluctant are promptly dropped.

While the law prohibits discrimination against employees for union activity, an employer may discharge a worker and then sit back and wait for the long, cumbersome process of unfair labor practice actions to take its course. Proving discrimination is not easy, but even if the employee prevails and is awarded his job plus full back pay the union campaign might be a matter of history. For this reason organizers are careful to spell out the risks involved and to point out the desirability of keeping the campaign quiet, at least in the early stages.

Most organizers prefer to work with a group of no more than four or five highly committed workers who can be trusted to maintain confidentiality. With information gathered from those workers about the company, its history, its personalities, its products, customers and practices giving rise to the desire to organize, the union organizer can plot his campaign.

Axiomatic with all campaigns is the need for an up-to-date, accurate list of all employees in the bargaining unit. To obtain such a list without knowledge of the employer is difficult, so organizers resort to many devices. One of the crudest, but sometimes necessary as a last resort, is to write down license plate numbers from all the cars in the company parking lot, then make a request to the Ministry of Transportation and Communications to furnish names of the owners. This provides a starting point. (Under United States law an employer is required to furnish such a list on request;[14] this is not the case in Canada.)

Having obtained a list the organizer then attempts to learn as much as he can about each person — his age, seniority, work classification, ethnic background and attitude toward a union. His attitude toward unionization may be unknown at the outset of the campaign, but as time progresses he will likely make his position known. Also the organizer tries to learn about any disagreeable working conditions, about bullheaded supervisors, and about how the company stacks up against other companies in the community in terms of wages and benefits. Most of this information can be secured from the workers who made the original approach, but an organizer is well-advised to check out all information carefully, because disgruntled workers do not always see things accurately.

Competent organizers have a good knowledge of the community, its politics, the attitude of the police force, the record of courts regarding issuance of injunctions, other unions in the area, and the nature of the news media. All of these may become important as the campaign progresses.

SIGN-UPS

Perhaps the most difficult job of an organizer is to get employees signed to membership cards as soon as possible but quietly. Probably the best way to secure committed signatures is to visit each employee at his home, but such visits are extremely time consuming. They should never seem hurried, and for maximum effectiveness the organizer should call at a convenient time, avoiding meal hours, and he should include the whole family in the conversation. He should be willing to talk about all sorts of subjects including Bobby Orr's scoring record and the Prime Minister's new baby. All this means at least an hour with each employee and, possibly, a followup visit. Most organizers consider four or five visits a day to be about the limit.

By developing a nucleus of committed employees who are willing and able to make house visits the organizer can gain considerable effectiveness and speed. Effectiveness comes from familiarity; workers will generally respond most favorably to someone they know or with whom they share a workplace. However there are risks in having fellow employees make house calls. One is that they may be unable to give satisfactory answers to questions about the union. Another risk is that they may "blow" the sales pitch through lack of sophistication, trying to hog the conversation, engaging in heated arguments or putting on pressure. For these reasons the organizer must do a hard-nosed educating job and screen out those who lack necessary skills. And for these reasons, as well, house-to-house sign-ups are not usually undertaken, except for special cases where a particular employee's signature is considered "key" for the campaign's success. Rather, the organizer and a small nucleus of employees seek to sign up people on company premises during lunch, coffee and break periods or while they are coming to or going from work. Signatures are obtained most rapidly this way, but managements also find out about the organizing drive most rapidly this way.

The first card-signing approach is normally made to those employees who are believed to be most in favor of the union. This helps build enthusiasm. It also gives greater probability of maintaining secrecy for a bit longer, because these employees are least likely to disclose the fact that organizing is taking place.

The organizer in Ontario aims for 70 to 80 per cent sign-ups and automatic certification. All organizers try to give the impression that the union is there to stay—that there is no intention of pulling out, even if the going gets tough. And they make it clear that organizing is risky—that the employer might retaliate. They set up a procedure by which authorization cards can be turned in to the organizer or to the union office as they are collected. This way the cards can be carefully checked to be sure they are properly filled out.

Union organizers are constantly on the alert for forged cards. In Canadian jurisdictions one forged card, regardless of the number of valid cards, could cause the union to lose its organizing rights at the company involved. In the United States, the knowing submission of a forged card to the National Labor Relations Board is a federal offense, and the forger may be punished by up to five years in jail and a $10,000 fine.

One way to minimize incidence of forgeries is for the organizer to insist that employees who collect signatures write their own name on each card as a witness. Presumably an employee will be reluctant to forge a card bearing his name.

Generally organizers do not divulge the number of sign-ups to anyone until they have a substantial majority. There are two reasons for this: first, the employer might use the information in planning a campaign to defeat the union; and second, it might cause discouragement, if the number is low, or laxity, if it is high, among members of the organizing committee.

RESISTANCE

Most organizing drives encounter resistance after an early surge of sign-ups. Usually this comes when the organizing committee moves from securing signatures of those favorable to the union to those who are less certain. Here, more than at the earlier stages, the organizer must use his knowledge about the company, its problems, and the union and its ability to cope with those problems. The organizer takes on the role of a salesman; he who knows his customer best and who is well acquainted with the commodity he is selling—the union—usually succeeds best. It is at this stage in the campaign that the organizer often chooses to reveal himself. He does this for two reasons: first, the employer is likely to find out anyhow, because employees with doubts often go to him with questions; and second, a wide-open, above-the-board campaign can sometimes yield a fair number of sign-up cards caused by a bandwagon effect, especially if there is a large, enthusiastic base of employees who have already signed.

Sign-ups usually continue throughout the campaign. A rule of organizing is that no more than one organizer should ever approach an employee at one time—lest there be an impression of intimidation. Most often the sign-up campaign is augmented by distributing leaflets at plant gates, by announcements of the drive through the media and sometimes by scheduling an open meeting.

One veteran organizer said that he often used the "rainy day" technique to sign up recalcitrant, but "key," employees. This involved making house contacts on cold, rainy, miserable days. If done with humility and sincerity the workers sometimes signs a card out of sympathy, expressing the belief that if someone believes in the union so much that he is willing to go out on such a miserable night it must be worth signing.

GENERAL MEETINGS

Open general meetings are less frequently held in modern organizing drives than they were in the 1930s and '40s. This is because in today's sprawling cities they are usually poorly attended, and a sparsely populated meeting often dampens enthusiasm. Even with a good turnout there is danger that some formerly enthusiastic employees will lose their enthusiasm—especially if they are forced to listen to a number of long-winded speeches. Veteran organizers have a series of rules that help guide them in holding general meetings. These include the following:

1. Don't hold a meeting unless you are sure of good turnout.
2. If there are speeches, be sure the speaker talks sincerely, with a simple vocabulary, and briefly.
3. Be sure speakers refrain from telling off-color jokes or jokes with racial or nationality overtones.
4. Maintain a "togetherness" atmosphere, never using the phrase "you people" or the word "you".
5. Don't make wild promises.

The final item regarding wild promises reflects a material departure from earlier organizing drives. It was possible to promise a great deal in the early days, because conditions were often bad and could be improved substantially in a short time. In addition, workers were less sophisticated then, perhaps more gullible. Nowadays workers are far more knowledge-able and skeptical. They trust understatement before they trust flamboyance.

Perhaps the most important reason for avoiding wild promises is to avert subsequent disappointment. If a group of workers becomes certified and then starts bargaining with hopes of fulfilling all their promises at once the employer is likely to resist, even to the point of refusing to sign a contract. If this happens in a first negotiation the newly formed union could be destroyed.

EMPLOYER TACTICS

From an employer's viewpoint the best tactic for avoiding a union is to create and maintain working conditions such that employees believe they are best off without a union. Nearly every work force has members who espouse unionization, no matter how good the working conditions, but these people are easily overcome by the majority if it can be shown that wages and working conditions are as good or better than those at any union shop. These facts should be matters of constant awareness among members of the work force, not items that are brought up only when the union organizing drive becomes evident.

There are many devices that employers can use to thwart an organizing drive, but the effect of these devices is likely to be temporary unless the employer sincerely builds toward a relationship where unions are deemed unnecessary. There are consultants who specialize in helping employers keep unions out both by designing short-term tactics and helping to build a long-term, progressive relationship. Some of these consultants are highly effective, often knowingly violating the law where it will gain them a momentary advantage, aware that risks are involved but believing the risks are low as compared to the benefits of keeping the union out. Union organizers are well aware of the tactics used by these consultants, and they have devised tactics of their own in defense. Among the employer-consultant tactics described most often by union organizers are the following:

1. Discharging or disciplining known union agitators;
2. the use of doctored statistics, such as selective wage surveys, to make employees believe conditions are better than they are;
3. making threats or promises contingent upon victory or defeat of the union;
4. secretly promoting the formation of an employees' association and encouraging the association itself to apply for certification.[15]

A shrewd union organizer will anticipate these tactics in advance and warn members of the work force to be on the lookout for them. Then, if they are used, he can say "I told you so." If they are not used he can always hold out the possibility that they might be.

Some employers make sudden changes when threatened by organization. These may indicate genuine new-found awareness that problems exist and a sincere desire to do something about them, or, on the other hand, they may represent a flurry to take the immediate sting out of the union drive. Among such changes are across-the-board wage increases, introduction of new, improved pension or insurance programs, opening up the doors of executive offices to listen to employee complaints, and organization of employee committees to create lines of communication. All these devices involve risks, even if attempted in good faith, because union leaders can claim that their mere presence caused the improvements to happen, asking workers to imagine how much more could be accomplished if the union were there all the time. In addition, the devices may be costly, well beyond the price of the improvement itself, because if the union drive is successful the existing wages, fringes and working conditions become the base on which negotiation demands are built.

The most frequent tactics used by employers to thwart unionization are those which delay certification procedures, giving the company more time to mount a campaign of its own designed to cause employees to vote "no union" in the election. One of the most frequently used delay tactics is a challenge to the proposed bargaining unit, contending for any number of reasons that it is not appropriate for bargaining, that it should be enlarged or reduced. Employers are ill-advised to use this kind of tactic unless they are prepared to live with the unit they propose, because union organizers may accede to their wishes knowing they have enough signed cards to win outright certification or an election even if the unit is changed. If the union agrees to a revised unit the issue is solved without Board interference. If they do not, the Board might prescribe the unit as the employer proposed it, and if the union is certified this then becomes a unit from which it is almost impossible to retreat. Records are heavy with cases where employers sought to change the composition of a bargaining unit so as to include assistant foremen, leadmen, salesmen, or inspectors and won their point—only to wind up with these groups organized, against the desire of both the employer and members of the included groups. Similarly, employers have succeeded in reducing the size of a proposed unit only to find the employees who are left out forming another unit of their own, covered by a separate contract.

LIBEL AND SLANDER

In the heat of a union organizing drive employers and union organizers alike need to be aware of possible actions at law for libel and slander. Libel is a malicious, false, derogatory statement in writing about an individual or group of individuals. Slander is the same, delivered orally. United States courts and some Canadian courts have ruled that unions, union representatives, employers and employer representatives can be sued when they make false statements that injure someone's reputation. In Ontario unions cannot be sued for libel or slander because they lack status as legal entities for purposes of civil action. However, union leaders can be sued in Ontario civil courts. The U.S. Supreme Court has held that the injured party can collect damages for injury to his reputation and that in addition juries can award "punitive" damages to punish the offender for his "misconduct."[16] Statements which could fall into the category of libel or slander include the following, provided they are untrue:

1. That some one is corrupt or dishonest;
2. that a union leader spends from the union's treasury for purposes inconsistent with the members' interest;
3. that a union leader or company official has a criminal record, is engaging in criminal conduct, or associates with undesirable organizations.

In some jurisdictions libel and slander actions have been upheld for a statement which was true, but where it could be shown that the person making the statement had no reasonable basis for believing it to be true at the time he made it.

EMPLOYERS' RIGHTS

Laws governing union organizing are aimed toward an ideal where there can be a genuine expression of employee preference without either party resorting to illegal or questionable tactics. A realistic employer who wishes for stability in employee relations will hope for an overwhelming victory or defeat in the organizing attempt; this will help insure that he is bargaining with people who clearly represent his employees, or, on the other hand, that there are not many unhappy employees as a result of the union's defeat. To win or lose by a close margin means that regardless of the outcome there is a substantial number of disgruntled employees.

If an employer learns that a substantial majority of his employees wish to join a union he should seriously consider granting voluntary recognition, so that the parties can get on quickly with the job of collective bargaining. However, he should recognize that voluntary recognition may be tenuous. If the true wishes of employees have not been represented there is danger that the agreement to recognize may be challenged. If a challenge is raised at any time during the first year by an employee or another union, the Ontario law places the onus on the parties to the agreement to establish that the recognized union is entitled to represent the employees. Failure to uphold the onus could result in throwing out any collective agreement which has been reached.[17] In addition the challenging union could win certification.

Employers in Ontario have demonstrated repeatedly their lack of knowledge about rights and obligations under the labor laws. Many times they make serious errors, committing blatant violations of the law and causing employees to swarm to the arms of a union. Then, finally, when they seek expert advice, it is too late—the game is lost.

On the other hand many employers, when faced with an organizing drive, act as if the jig is up, not knowing their rights, and they surrender without a whimper. Following is a list of some of the things an employer may do under the law. All of these are predicated on an employee's right under the law *not* to join, as well as to join, a union.

1. Employers have a right to express their opinions, views and sentiments regarding unions in general and the organizing union in particular.[18] This is one of the most potent weapons employers can use; yet, strangely, it is seldom utilized.

2. Employers may state their position on whether employees should or should not vote for the union, or on any other matters involved in the organizing campaign.

3. Employers may prohibit solicitation for the union on their own property on company time. Generally they must allow solicitation on free time, subject to reasonable regulations respecting safety and proper conduct.

4. Employers may prohibit distribution of union literature on premises, provided that they customarily prohibit distribution of all forms of literature.

5. Employers may increase wages, make promotions and take other personnel actions if they do so in the normal course of business and in accordance with established policy.

6. Employers may assemble employees during working hours and state opinions respecting the election, as long as they avoid threats and promises. However, if an employer does this in Ontario during the 72-hour period preceding an election or in the United States in the 24-hour period before an election, the election itself may be set aside. Employers have no obligation to give the union the same opportunity.

The following actions by an employer are illegal and could cause automatic certification if the union has a majority of employees as members, or setting aside of an election if the employer wins:

1. Promise of improvements in wages or working conditions contingent on defeat of the union,

2. granting of wage increases or making other personnel changes that are *not* in the normal course of business,

3. taking any action which the Board believes deceived the employees on vital issues to the degree that they were unable to vote freely.

While some employers give up the ghost when the union appears, others overreact. Suddenly the door to the front office opens, golf dates are cancelled and afternoon cocktails are postponed. The foremen become more friendly, more interested in the employees and their problems; a series of personal letters from the president is prepared and sent to the homes of employees stating that after an honest, thorough study the president believes, in the best interests of all concerned, that there is no advantage to having a union. Or an employee committee is organized to convince the workers that they already have an organization.

All these are legal, but if they happen all of a sudden they are likely to seem insincere. Alert union organizers are ready for such moves and often make fairly standard, but effective, countermoves. For example, if an employee committee has been formed the union will most likely attempt to force that committee to solve a knotty problem, like reorganization of a seniority system for handling promotions and layoffs, or the design of a liberal pension plan. When this happens the committee often collapses.

COLLECTIVE BARGAINING

During the later stages of an organizing campaign the union organizer usually gathers a committee of employees together to start working on bargaining demands. This helps maintain enthusiasm after most of the card signing is done and while formal certification processes are taking place. In addition to keeping the workers interested it makes for preparedness when the time for bargaining arrives. According to Ontario law the union is required to make the first move toward bargaining following certification, by giving the employer written notice. Then the law requires the parties to meet within 15 days of the giving of notice or within such further period as parties agree upon. It requires, in addition, that they shall bargain in good faith and make every reasonable effort to make a collective agreement.[19]

Once certification is secured the union organizer normally leaves the scene and puts his newly formed bargaining committee into the hands of an area representative or business agent whose job it is to negotiate contracts or to serve as adviser to local negotiating teams. In a smooth-running union the transition is easy. The organizer has refrained from wild promises and has kept the expectations of the new union members within reason. In addition, with luck, he has established a businesslike relationship with the employer so that the company and union can operate with respect for each other and genuine concern for each other's problems. However, all unions are not smooth-running, and union organizers do not always approach the job on a businesslike basis. All too often the organization phase of labor-management relations results in frayed nerves and, sometimes, violence as parties look upon the organizing drive as a battle to be won or lost. Whatever its outcome, if the organizing drive is based on less-than-honorable intentions or if antagonisms develop during the campaign there is likely to be a deleterious effect on the relationship for many succeeding years.

NOTES TO CHAPTER 4

1. The Labour Relations Act, Revised Statutes of Ontario, 1970, Chapter 232, as amended 1975. Sections 6(1) and 6(2).

2. Ibid., Section 7 (3).

3. Ibid., Sections 52 (1), (2), (3) and (4).

4. The Labour Relations Act, Revised Statutes of Ontario, 1970, Chapter 232, Section 53.

5. In some areas of Ontario a payment in kind may be substituted for cash. In lumber camps, for example, where employees rarely have cash, a pouch of tobacco has been deemed acceptable.

6. Prior to February 1971 the Ontario Law provided for determination of union representation in an election by a majority of eligible voters. This gave rise to abuses by employers, because employees who did not vote were, in effect, voting for the company. Some employers observed the polling place to discover who among their employees voted and, assuming their vote was for the union, they engaged in discriminatory practices toward those employees.

7. In the Ontario construction industry, prehearing votes are almost unheard of. The Board has devised an accelerated procedure in this industry so that certifications are often issued within eight days of application, if all paper work is in order. Generally there are no hearings in the construction industry.

8. As of September 1972 there were 10 members of the Ontario Labour Relations Board (two of whom were full-time members), five from employer backgrounds, five from union backgrounds. In addition, there were eight hearing officers including the Board chairman, the alternate chairman and six vice chairmen.

9. The Labour Relations Act, op. cit., Sections 48 and 49.

10. Timeliness is determined by the same rules applying to a new application for certification.

11. The Labour Relations Act, op. cit., Section 7 (4).

12. Ibid., Section 90.

13. Ibid., Section 85.

14. Excelsior Underwear Inc., Saluda Knitting Inc. and Amalgamated Clothing Workers of America, AFL-CIO, 61LRRM1217, 156NLRB11 (February 4, 1966).

15. While the Ontario Labour Relations Act bars certification of an employer-dominated union (Section 12) and bars acceptance of a contract with such an organization as a legal document (Section 40), this type of action is still common.

16. Linn v. United Plant Guard Workers of America, Local 114, 61LRRM2345 (February 21, 1966).

17. The Labour Relations Act, op. cit., Section 52.

18. Ibid., Section 56.

19. Ibid., Sections 13 and 14.

5. NEGOTIATION:
THEORY AND PRACTICE

Contract negotiation is probably the most visible activity in industrial relations. It is the process by which the employer and the union, as representative of the employees, meet to define or redefine the basic terms and conditions of their interdependence. The presence of the parties at the bargaining table implies interdependence through a common interest. It also implies the existence of conflict between the parties. "Without common interest there is nothing to negotiate for; without conflict, nothing to negotiate about."[1]

THE LAW

In North America, negotiations between unions and management occur not only because of common interest and conflict but also because they are required by law. Once the union is certified as the exclusive bargaining agent for a specific group of employees, the parties must negotiate with a view to the conclusion of a collective agreement.

However, other than the compulsion to bargain, the law does not impose many constraints on the negotiation process. In the United States and in some Canadian jurisdictions, the requirements of "good faith" bargaining is imposed, but the term is ambiguous and not particularly constructive. The general legislative requirement that negotiations include the subject of wages, hours of work and other conditions of employment is sufficiently broad to allow for the inclusion of almost any subject that the parties desire to discuss. However, the parties are not legally compelled to *agree* on any issue. The parties are generally free to determine the duration of their agreement. Under the law, the structure and procedure of collective bargaining are also left for the parties to determine.

The latitude given to the parties by the law in North America means that the structure, process and substantive content of the negotiations show an extremely high degree of diversity. Such diversity makes generalized comment about the negotiation of collective agreements somewhat difficult. Nevertheless, under the five broad headings of bargaining subjects, bargaining structure, bargaining pattern, bargaining power and bargaining process, this chapter will attempt to provide an introduction to the subject of labor negotiations, hopefully allowing the reader to gain some insights and appreciation for this particular aspect of collective bargaining.

SUBJECTS FOR NEGOTIATION

We have said that North American statutes provide for the negotiation of collective agreements covering wages, hours, and other conditions of employment, and that this injunction is sufficiently broad to cover almost any subject the parties might agree to discuss. The nature of the subjects discussed at the bargaining table is influenced by a number of factors. The most important of these factors are: nature of the industry or workplace, court or labor board rulings, the parties' expectations about the future, management and union policy, and the likelihood of a strike.

INDUSTRY AND WORKPLACE CHARACTERISTICS

The factor which most influences the nature of the subjects discussed during negotiations is the characteristic of the industry and workplace in which the agreement is negotiated. For example, some agreements covering employees on ships at sea specify the number of bars of soap, towels and sheets which are to be furnished by management to the crew. These items are of vital concern to ships' crews, but not to most workers in manufacturing.

The negotiation of agreements in industries with production operations which operate round-the-clock will devote much more time to scheduling problems than industries or firms with five-day, nine-to-five hours of operation. The garment industry has many small financially insecure manufacturers. In order to provide job security and earning opportunities for their membership, unions in this industry have negotiated contract provisions allowing union industrial engineers to study and make improvements in company manufacturing operations. Executives in the automobile industry would self-destruct rather than consider such a contract proposal.

When employees shift from employer to employer on a continual basis, as in construction and stevedoring, provisions designed to provide some kind of control over the hiring process are a central feature in collective bargaining. In industries which feature regular employment, management generally is not forced to negotiate over the imposition of controls on their discretion in the hiring process.[2]

COURT AND BOARD RULINGS

Aside from industry characteristics, the nature of the issues on the bargaining table may be influenced by court or administrative rulings or by changes in the law. The court decision in the Port Arthur Shipbuilding case[3] which restricted the arbitrator's ability to modify a disciplinary penalty in the absence of a provision giving him that power may have caused the parties to negotiate such an express provision. Similarly the revisions to the law which attempt to nullify the Port Arthur doctrine by stating that in the absence of any provisions to the contrary the arbitrator has the right to modify disciplinary penalties may now cause the parties to add such express provisions to the agreement.

Recent changes to the Canada Labour Code were designed to encourage the parties to negotiate protection for workers displaced by technological change. The Public Service Staff Relations Act, which governs collective bargaining on the Canadian Federal Civil Service, explicitly prohibits negotiation on certain subjects, such as pensions and job classification.

In the United States, rulings of the National Labor Relations Board have required companies to negotiate over certain subjects. Some companies have refused to bargain over some subjects, such as pensions, saying that the law did not require them to do so. The board has ruled otherwise. This has generally not been an issue in Canadian jurisdictions.

EXPECTATIONS ABOUT THE FUTURE

One subject which is always considered at the bargaining table is the duration of the agreement. The length of the agreement will depend on the parties' expectations about the future. If the trend of future events is unclear, an agreement will be of relatively short duration; the minimum time permitted by legislation is one year. Longer agreements are more common. Most agreements in North America are for two or three years, with the average term probably around thirty months. Thus, one important characteristic of collective bargaining in North America is that negotiation is not continuous but occurs only at regular intervals of two to three years.

MANAGEMENT AND UNION POLICY

Most managements have a policy of excluding certain subjects from the bargaining agenda. These are subjects over which management wishes to retain unilateral discretion. Many of these relate to company marketing policies like pricing, or financial policies like capital investment. Other areas often excluded from bargaining include purchasing and control systems. Unions have had certain policy goals in bargaining, such as a reduction in the length of the work week. Some unions by policy also refuse to discuss certain issues. Some, for example, have refused to accept incentive systems for wage payments. Other unions have refused to accept the lengthening of the work day which is usually involved in a move toward a four-day work week.

At times, however, the particular circumstances the parties find themselves in may lead to negotiations over subjects which would normally be considered outside the scope of collective bargaining. For example, a company which historically had placed a great deal of emphasis on "management rights" was faced with the prospect of closing a plant because of high operating costs. Rather than accept the closing, the union agreed to wage cuts and changes in work rules. In return, it insisted on a guarantee that the plant would remain open. The guarantee was negotiated when the company agreed to maintain a certain level of capital investment in the plant. Capital investment, in the eyes of most managers, is a subject that would or should *never* appear on the bargaining table. Yet, in this instance it did.

TRENDS IN BARGAINING

Despite the reluctance of managements to discuss certain issues at the bargaining table, one of the distinctly noticeable trends since the inception of collective bargaining has been the narrowing scope of managerial discretion. The limitations placed on managerial discretion have clearly increased over time, through the outright prohibition of certain activities (such as excessive overtime), through the requirement that management be "fair" or "reasonable" (as in discipline), or through the establishment of certain rules which must be followed (such as those governing layoffs). Management has also limited its authority by negotiating provisions that allow for certain actions only after consulting with the union, or with the union's consent.[4]

This trend is seen by some businessmen as extremely unfortunate, and some managements have been more successful than others in resisting inroads on their own discretion. Nevertheless, the trend is clear and the reality is that managerial discretion has been and probably will continue to be limited by negotiation. Thus, the question of what subjects properly belong on the bargaining table is somewhat academic, at least in the private sector of the economy.

In the public sector, particularly that segment operating under the Public Service Staff Relations Act, the question of what subjects belong on the bargaining table assumes a new dimension. We said earlier that the PSSRA excluded a number of subjects, such as pensions, from bargaining. Under these circumstances, some have argued that the exclusion of these subjects impedes bargaining. In the 1969 Canadian Postal negotiations, job security was a major issue. The Treasury Board and Post Office were precluded from making any meaningful guarantees on job security by other legislation which had precedence over the PSSRA. The 1972 Air Traffic Controllers dispute might have been resolved by agreement to a restudy and reclassification of the controllers' jobs. This course of action was impossible under the PSSRA, because the Act prohibited bargaining over job classifications.

STRIKE PREPARATIONS

In the course of some negotiations, the parties turn their attention to the subject of strike preparations and conduct. While this bargaining is often tacit, at times it is quite explicit. A great deal of care is required in shutting down some production operations, such as a steel mill. If a strike is to begin, the parties will discuss the procedure for the orderly closing down of operations. The question of management access to the plant may also be discussed. Another question which frequently occurs is the payment of premiums on employee health and insurance plans. In some instances the union will take over the payment of these premiums from the company. On more than one occasion, when the union has been short of cash, the company has continued to pay these premiums, in effect making a loan to the union.

Of course the above arrangements may not be made at all. The union-management relationships which are characterized by the arrangements such as those mentioned above are relationships in which the parties are committed to a reasonably satisfactory long-term relationship. While disagreement exists in the short run, and economic pressure in the form of a strike (and the corresponding willingness to take a strike) is being applied, the intent of that pressure is to impel an agreement so that the mutually profitable relationship can continue. The parties negotiate strike arrangements which will help preserve that long-term relationship.

One critical decision which every management must consider in terms of strike preparation is whether to attempt to continue operations during a strike. In some situations, such as electric utilities and refineries, supervisory personnel can be used to continue production. In other operations, replacements must be found for the striking employees. The employer can keep his doors open and urge the strikers to return to work, or he can hire replacements — strikebreakers, or "scabs" as they are called by unions.

The most critical factor influencing this decision is the probable union response. History shows that attempts to continue operations in the face of a strike often lead to violence. The Texpac, Dare Foods, and Artistic Woodwork strikes in Ontario are good examples. Unions have generally been successful in developing the ethic that picket lines are not to be crossed. When peaceful picket lines are crossed, striking employees may well attempt to *forcefully* prohibit entry to the struck premises.

This union response is understandable, since in many instances an attempt by an employer to continue operations is an attempt to do away with the union. At a minimum, an employer who can continue to operate during a strike is not being affected by that strike, and the union cannot hope to achieve its strike goals unless the employer is shut down.

BARGAINING STRUCTURE

The wide variety of subjects found on the bargaining table is matched by the diversity of structures within which the bargaining occurs. While most unionized workers in North America work under a contract negotiated between a single union and a single employer or a single plant,[5] negotiations occur within a number of other institutional arrangements. A single employer can bargain simultaneously with a number of unions as is the case in Canadian Postal negotiations. The reverse can also occur with a number of employers — usually combined into an employers' association — bargaining with a single union. This occurs in the construction industry, in West Coast pulp and paper and in the longshore industry. Employers' associations can also negotiate with a group of unions. Examples of this are seen in the construction industry and in the newspaper industry.

Even though unions are certified as bargaining agents for particular groups of workers, actual negotiations may take place in a structure different from these certified units. A negotiation involving a multiplant employer might involve only one union, but several different "bargaining units," since the union might well be certified as the bargaining agent for employees on a plant-by-plant basis. Thus labor board certification for bargaining purposes does not necessarily define the scope of the actual negotiations. The "election district" may be different from the "negotiating unit."[6]

The greater the scope of bargaining, the greater is the problem of satisfying all the different interest groups within the structure. For example, in the summer of 1972 a group of British Columbia woodworkers, the fallers, continued to strike after settlement had been reached and over 20,000 workers had returned to work, because they were displeased with the settlement. If the structure is to continue to exist, the constituent members must be reasonably satisfied with its performance — particularly in terms of their own peculiar interest. One way in which to handle a diversity of issues within particular negotiating arrangements is to provide for the negotiation of some issues at a lower level: company, plant or even department. Deciding which issue is to be negotiated at what level and coordinating the bargains at all levels can subsequently be problems for the parties. These arrangements must be made even in negotiations between a single employer and a single union. In the negotiations between the United Auto Workers and the "big three" auto manufacturers there are literally thousands of "local issues" on the bargaining table, and these issues must be resolved before negotiations can be completed. At times, the failure of the parties in the auto negotiations to solve local issues, particularly at key plants, has resulted in general shutdowns, even though the "main table" issues had been satisfactorily resolved.

BARGAINING PATTERN

Closely allied with the structure of bargaining is the pattern of bargaining. Some bargaining structures are based on pattern-setting and pattern-following arrangements. The primary example of this is in the auto negotiations in both the United States and Canada. The auto workers select one company as a "target" company and negotiate an agreement with that company. That agreement, whether reached with or without a strike, then becomes the pattern that the other companies are expected to follow.

In a number of instances, Canadian branches of international unions have refused to follow the pattern set in the United States by their union and United States companies. In the mid-1960s a number of locals of the Pulp, Paper, and Sulfide Workers in British Columbia refused to go along with the pattern, and actually broke away from the international to form a separate, autonomous union. In 1973 the refusal of the elevator installers union to accept the pattern set in the United States led to a long and somewhat bitter strike that was settled only by government intervention.

The concept of bargaining pattern can extend beyond the confines of a particular industry. A highly visible settlement can serve as a guideline for other negotiations that are in process. For example, the 1969 settlement between the United Steelworkers and the Steel Company of Canada set the pattern not only for the steel industry but for the nickel industry as well. The 1967 Seaway Settlement was viewed by many as a pattern-setter for Canadian industry in general — a pattern of high wage settlements which many argue (but not necessarily prove) were inflationary.

Of course, the bargaining pattern need not be national in scope. For the parties' purposes, settlements in a given province, or a region or a particular locality may be important guidelines in reaching a settlement. In this sense, the parties' expectations about what constitutes a reasonable settlement is determined by what others around them are doing.

There is some research to indicate that other settlements are more important to the bargainers, particularly the union, when the general economic environment is favorable and permissive. When economic conditions are unfavorable, unions tend to look more closely at conditions within the industry or firm as the basis for deciding what is an appropriate settlement, rather than settlements external to the industry or firm.[7]

In Quebec, under the Collective Agreement Decrees Act, the Minister of Labour has the power (through an order in council) to extend some of the terms of a collective agreement to a whole industry in a region or throughout the whole province. This feature of Quebec law is unique in Canada. Through it, the Minister on application of an interested party may extend the terms of a collective agreement as to wages, hours, vacations, job classification, apprenticeship programs and social security benefits to other firms in the industry. Thus, in Quebec, through the government's intervention, a particular settlement could have strong pattern-setting implications for even nonunion firms.

BARGAINING POWER

In 1972, a number of workers and unions including hospital workers and teachers banded together to confront the Province of Quebec with their demands for a contract settlement. In one sense, this common front was an attempt to change the bargaining structure. Yet in a very real sense it was an attempt by these unions to increase their bargaining power vis-a-vis the provincial government. This particular situation turned into a real confrontation, with additional workers drawn into the dispute and eventual jail terms for several Quebec labor leaders.

In 1969, in the United States, twelve unions coordinated their efforts in bargaining with the General Electric Company. The unions believed that they could increase their bargaining power by making simultaneous demands, and, as it turned out, striking simultaneously.

As formulated by Neil Chamberlain, the relative bargaining power in a two-party relationship can be expressed as follows:

$$\text{Bargaining Power of A} = \frac{\text{Cost to B of disagreeing with A's terms}}{\text{Cost to B of agreeing with A's terms}}$$

$$\text{Bargaining Power of B} \; = \; \frac{\text{Cost to A of disagreeing with B's terms}}{\text{Cost to A of agreeing with B's terms}}$$

If A is the employer, the greater the costs associated with disagreeing with the union's (B's) terms; that is, taking a strike, as opposed to agreeing with the union's terms, the greater the union's bargaining power. If the cost to one side of *disagreeing* with the other's terms is equal to or greater than *agreeing* to those terms, then the settlement is likely to be on the basis of the terms offered by the opposing side.[8]

The theory of bargaining power does not lend itself to detailed calculation of the exact terms of settlement, in part because bargaining power is based on the *perceived* cost of agreeing or disagreeing. These perceptions are difficult to measure and also keep changing as bargaining progresses. However, the notion of bargaining power is useful in understanding the collective bargaining process.

Collective bargaining always involves the use or the implied use of power. A showdown of power is latent in every negotiation.[9] While we normally think of labor negotiations in terms of *economic* power (the use of the strike or lockout), *moral, legal* or *political* power can also be brought to bear in labor negotiations. Power need not be directed toward conflict; it can be a force behind cooperation as well. In any event, to consider labor negotiations without considering the potential use of power by other parties and its influence on the process is to have a naive and erroneous notion of the process.

Bargaining power in large part determines how and why negotiations turn out as they do. Why, for example, have wage settlements (in recent years) in the construction industry been as high as they have? In large part, because construction firms are small and undercapitalized and cannot survive a strike. The cost of disagreeing with the union's demands is high. At the same time, of course, construction firms have been able to pass on cost increases to consumers, and the cost to construction firms of agreeing to the union's terms has not been high.

Situations in which management bargaining power is high can be seen in refineries and similar processing operations and in many public utilities. In these operations management can frequently continue to run the operations in the event of a strike. For example, a 1973 strike by employees of Ontario Hydro lasted for several months. Service to equipment was impaired but not eliminated, power supplies were not interrupted and the union settled for the amount that was offered prior to the strike. In these circumstances the cost to the company of disagreeing with the union offer (or demand) was low.

The concept of bargaining power also helps explain some of the activities of the parties prior to and during negotiations. Each party will try to maximize its bargaining power and to influence the opponent's perceptions of that bargaining power. Activities of each party will be designed to minimize the actual and the perceived costs to his opposite of agreeing with him, and maximize the costs of disagreeing.

In practice, these attempts to influence the outcome take a variety of forms. In firms or industries with seasonal variations in production, efforts to influence bargaining power may revolve around manipulating the contract expiration date. Unions often try to have the contract expire just prior to the seasonal upswing in production. Companies in turn attempt to have the contract expire near the bottom of the seasonal cycle.

Companies may attempt to have large inventories or to have large stocks in the hands of customers prior to the strike deadline. Unions may resist such efforts by refusing to work overtime or setting up a picket line which effectively stops shipments after a strike begins. In 1970 the contracts in the auto industry expired just as cars for the new model year were beginning to be produced. General Motors was the strike target of the autoworkers, and at Ste. Therese, Quebec, the company was attempting to produce as many cars as it could, so its dealers would at least have enough cars for display purposes. In order to reduce the number of cars going to dealers, the workers at Ste. Therese walked out before the contract expired.

Unions attempt to build up a strike fund to provide some income for members during a strike. The strike fund is a major element in the union's bargaining power. Unions will also attempt to ensure that other unions will respect their picket lines during a strike. The extent to which picket lines are respected is also a major factor influencing union bargaining power. These examples are illustrative of the attempts of the parties to enhance their bargaining power. Many others could be cited. The point has been made, though, that the parties will employ strategies built around increasing their own and reducing their opponent's bargaining power as part of the negotiation process in an attempt to secure a settlement close to what they believe is appropriate.

BARGAINING PROCESS

Aside from the theory of bargaining power, a number of attempts have been made to provide a theoretical rationale for the behavior of the parties at the bargaining table. These theories will be reviewed before a discussion of the actual activities at the bargaining table is attempted.

BARGAINING THEORY

J. Pen[10] begins with preference or satisfaction functions for each side. Every potential settlement thus has a certain value. These settlements have a certain *cost*, however, if the opponent refuses to agree to that settlement. In the negotiation process, each party constantly assesses the value of a settlement relative to the cost of the settlement in terms of the probability that the opponent will refuse to settle at that point. This theory suggests that the parties will use strategies designed to reduce the perceived value of a settlement to the opponent, increase the perceived costs associated with nonagreement and maximize the perceived risk that nonagreement will occur if the opponent insists on a particular settlement.

Carl Stevens[11] has formulated an "avoidance-avoidance" model of the negotiation process. This model is reproduced graphically as Exhibit I-5(p.105). Unlike Pen's model and conventional economic models where the parties are maximizing utilities, in Stevens's model, the parties are avoiding alternatives. In this model, each party has a range of alternatives between two unattractive extremes. One extreme is represented by the terms of agreement most favorable to him. (For an employer, this might be the status quo; for the union, their maximum demand.) This alternative is avoided because it carries certain negative consequences (for the employer, an inability to attract workers; for the union, the possibility of putting the company out of business). The other unattractive extreme is the opponent's demands or goal. For the company, this extreme would be represented by the union's maximum demand which could lead to economic ruin for the firm; for the union, the second unattractive extreme would be the status quo, acceptance of which could be disadvantageous to employees who might well get rid of leadership which advocated such acceptance. Generally, the tendency to avoid this second extreme is greater than the desire to avoid the other extreme.

Each party must choose an alternative between these unattractive extremes and, for a bargain to result, the positions must be the same. Negotiation becomes the process of exchanging information so that these positions can be coordinated. The information exchange includes attempts to modify the opponent's avoidance curve by influencing his perceptions of his own goals and his opponent's goals, and the relative unattractiveness of the two.

Rather than seeing negotiators as being faced with two unattractive alternatives, Mabry[12] sees each negotiator trading off penalties, or pain (i.e. loss of objectives) for rewards, or pleasure (i.e. gaining concessions). Each bargainer thus sees each possible settlement point in terms of *net*

EXHIBIT I-5

Stevens's Avoidance-Avoidance Model

Goal A Goal B
Settle on union's terms Settle on own terms
(status quo)

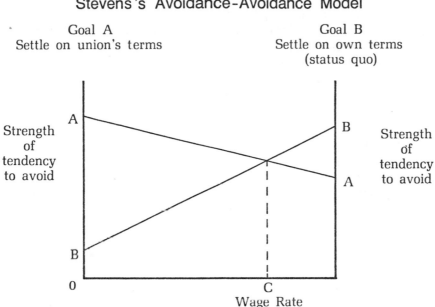

Strength
of
tendency
to avoid

Strength
of
tendency
to avoid

Wage Rate

The Line A — A represents one avoidance gradient, settling on the union's terms. The desire to avoid an outcome increases as one gets closer to it. The line B — B represents another avoidance gradient, settling on management's own terms or the status quo. At point C, the desire to avoid goal A is equal to the desire to avoid goal B, and the individual is in equilibrium.

gain, and tactics used in the negotiation process are designed to influence the opponent's view of the net gain of any settlement. In the end, both parties see a positive net gain with no greater joint advantage in any other settlement. Cross[13] has added the dimension of time, in the form of the strike deadline, to Mabry's analysis. Because of the strike deadline, anticipated net gain must be evaluated in terms of the length of time required to achieve that net gain and the costs associated with the delay.

McKersie and Walton[14] use the concept of subjectively expected utilities to explain the negotiation process. The relative attractiveness of any settlement (benefits derived vs. costs of achieving) is viewed by each side in terms of the *probability* of achieving that settlement. Each side also has a target point, which defines complete success in bargaining, and a resistance point, which defines minimum success. The bargaining process then becomes the process of manipulating the opponent's utilities *and* his assessment of the probability of achieving his goals so as to secure a settlement as close as possible to the target point.

While this brief summary hardly does justice to the various bargaining theories, some basic points should begin to emerge. Although the theories differ in detail, they present a fairly similar view of the bargaining process. Each party is constantly assessing his own bargaining goals in terms of the cost of achieving those goals. Costs are assessed, in part, by attempting to determine the opponent's goals and the extent to which he will resist particular settlements. Each negotiator attempts to make his goals attractive to his opponent, and to reduce the importance of the opponent's goal in the opponent's view. He also may influence the opponent's perception of his possible resistance to the opponent's bargaining goals. All of this is done while concealing or attempting to conceal the negotiator's own goals from his opponent. Under the pressure of a strike deadline (or a strike) this delicate ballet usually results in a contract settlement.

TYPES OF BARGAINING

McKersie and Walton note that *all* bargaining is not like that described above, that all bargaining does not involve conflicting interests or the allocation of a fixed amount of resources. Most collective bargaining negotiations do involve this type of bargaining in part, such as in wage determination. McKersie and Walton call this type of bargaining *distributive bargaining.* However, most negotiations also involve other types of bargaining. A second type of bargaining is called *integrative bargaining,* and is used to achieve mutual objectives which are *not* in conflict, or to solve problems. An example of integrative bargaining is the design of a seniority system that meets the needs of employees for job security and the needs of management for flexibility in job assignment.

At the same time that the parties are engaged in these types of bargaining, they are also engaged in two other processes: *attitudinal structuring* and *intra-organizational bargaining.* Attitudinal structuring is an attempt to influence or change the basic relationship between the parties. Intra-organizational bargaining refers to the bargaining that goes on between a chief negotiator *and his own organization,* and his efforts to convince that organization that he is obtaining the best possible bargain.[15]

Keeping in mind the fact that the parties are engaged in all four of these activities, distributive bargaining, integrative bargaining, attitudinal structuring, and intra-organizational bargaining during the negotiation process, and that the negotiation process provides the parties with opportunities for real gains and losses, will help us understand why the parties behave as they do during that negotiation process.

PREPARING FOR BARGAINING

The negotiation process does not begin at the point where the parties sit down at the table. Both unions and management devote a great deal of time and energy to preparing for negotiations. Events at the bargaining table are shaped by these efforts, and the negotiation process can properly be said to begin with these preparations.

In a sense, the preparation process is almost continuous. Once an agreement is negotiated, and the parties begin to live with or administer that agreement, problems may emerge that suggest possible revisions in the contract. As part of the process of preparing for negotiations, each side will seek suggestions for revision from their constituents.

Frequently the individuals responsible for negotiating agreements do not have the further responsibility of administering the agreement. Discussion on problems with the existing agreement with those who must live with the contract on a day-to-day basis is an important first step in preparing to negotiate another.

For the union, suggestions for revision as well as new demands will be solicited from shop stewards and from workers, sometimes in open union meetings. Some unions have special groups, such as wage-policy committees, to develop demands. Other union demands may emerge from policy resolutions passed by national or international union conventions. Management negotiators will seek the opinions of foremen and other line managers. Both sides will look at the grievance and arbitration records under the existing contract. Grievances can pinpoint trouble spots, and the losing side in an arbitration case may well wish to have the contract changed, to nullify the application of an arbitrator's award in the future.

During preparations, each side will not only develop its own demands but will also attempt to anticipate the demands which the other side is likely to make. With these in hand, cost data and counterarguments based on anticipated consequences of implementing particular proposals can be developed. Concessions implementing these demands can also be planned. For example, in 1955, the Ford Motor Company knew that it would again be faced with a demand from the auto workers for a guaranteed annual income. Prior to the negotiations the company assigned a task force the job of developing a proposal to provide an income guarantee in a way acceptable to the company. The result was the Supplemental Unemployment Benefit (SUB) Plan which was incorporated into the agreement and remains in effect today.

Another task which faces the parties prior to actual negotiations is the assembly of a bargaining team. While each side is represented by a principal negotiator, he will be joined by other individuals representing each organization. These representatives serve several functions. For one, they can provide expertise on particular subjects or problem areas. The presence of these individuals allows the bargaining agenda to be divided into segments and discussed in subcommittees. Members of the bargaining team can also serve as representatives of special-interest groups in each organization. For example, a union bargaining team might include a representative of a skilled-trades group and a management team might include a representative of production-line management. Individuals having particular influence in the two organizations might be chosen as members of the bargaining team, as might individuals who are well trusted by the other side.

The group that sits down with the chief negotiator at the bargaining table represents the varied, and sometimes conflicting, interests within each organization. This group must emerge satisfied with the negotiator's bargaining ability and also with the final settlement. They can help assure acceptance of the settlement in the wider constituency. Ultimate acceptance by that wider constituency is one reason for the large number of demands which are actually placed on the bargaining table. Acceptance of the final agreement is more likely if the members of each side believe that their problems and proposals have at least been presented and argued, even if they are not incorporated in the final agreement. The large number of issues on the table is also useful in the actual bargaining process, as we shall see shortly.

The chief negotiator for each side usually is quite experienced in negotiations. For management he is frequently an industrial relations staff specialist. Some small companies hire lawyers or other professional negotiators to negotiate for them. While members of the local union are generally involved in negotiations, frequently the chief negotiator for the union is a specialist on the staff of the national or international union. Where the chief negotiator is an "outsider" the bargaining team can help to keep the chief negotiator in tune with the realities of the work place.

AT THE BARGAINING TABLE

As they approach the bargaining table, each side has a list of demands, an estimate of the opponent's demands, and goals that define complete success and minimum success in the process that is to follow. Each side has an estimate of his strengths and weaknesses as well as those of the other side. Each side has probably made an assessment of the other's bargaining team, their strengths and weaknesses and the strategies and tactics which they are likely to follow.

The first item of business is usually a quick runthrough of each side's proposals. Sometimes elaborate presentations are made at this point. The purpose here is merely to present demands and allow for enough discussion so that they are fully understood. During the initial presentation, proposals may be represented as being equally important — vital to a reasonable settlement.

Each negotiator is, at this point, not only presenting the demands of the various interest groups which he represents but also concealing his perceptions of the minimum acceptable settlement. Unions do not always make specific monetary demands at first. Rather they ask for a "substantial" wage increase or for a "significant" increase in pension benefits. Such nonspecific demands not only conceal the union's minimum position from management but also reduce the likelihood of establishing unrealistic, unachievable goals in the minds of the membership.

Some of the demands are made to facilitate future bargaining. The initial appearance of a demand from one side of the bargaining table can usually be expected to receive a cool reception from the other side. With an eye to a continuing relationship and to future bargaining, a demand may be introduced with the thought that it will not be granted during the present negotiation, but that it will seem less novel (and perhaps less outrageous) during the negotiation of the next contract.[16]

The guaranteed annual income demand made by Walter Reuther in the early 1950s is an example of a demand which was originally made to facilitate future bargaining. The auto workers also made a demand for a company-paid dental care plan for several negotiations prior to the 1973 sessions in which a company-paid dental plan was added to the agreement.

The next stage of the negotiation process sees the parties beginning to explore each other's proposals, attempting to find out how important each proposal is to the other side while still attempting to hide the relative importance of their own proposals. A negotiator may attempt to show his opposite that one of the latter's proposals is not important or is too costly. Where facts are in dispute, an effort will be made at this point to establish mutually acceptable data.

Some clues as to the parameters of the settlement will begin to emerge at this stage, particularly to the experienced negotiator. The tone of voice, the selection of words, the arch of an eyebrow can all serve to provide clues to one's intentions. Phrases like, "I think we can work something out on that," when compared to phrases like, "We will never agree to that!" can provide real indications as to the importance of particular positions. Minor concessions may also be made at this point, as evidence of good faith and to indicate progress.

The real positions of the parties are still far from clear, however. Both sides may still be bluffing on some issues. The degree of commitment of each side to particular issues may not yet be established. In fact, attempts by one side to commit itself to achieving a particular goal may be ignored by the other side in order to keep the negotiations flexible.

At this stage of negotiations, the size of the bargaining teams may be reduced. Subcommittees may be formed to consider some proposals or problems and to work out solutions or compromises for the consideration of the whole group. As the strike deadline approaches, the first "package" offers appear. Demands are dropped, sometimes not very loudly. The party may simply fail to mention it as part of a proposed package.

Initially, package offers may be tentative: "What would you think if...." "If we give this, would you be willing to drop this demand?" "Does this proposal seem fair to you?" Agreement may be reached on some issues, pending the settlement of other more important issues, such as the size of the monetary package.

Frequently, these package offers may not be made initially at the bargaining table, particularly as the parties move closer to a settlement. "Off the record" discussions between the principal negotiators, over drinks or dinner, in the hall or even in the washroom, may produce the first and final firm offers of settlement.[17] Sometimes when settlement is reached, one party may produce one final demand, as a "sweetener." While this is sometimes successful, it rarely works more than once.

When agreement is reached, it must be reduced to writing and signed by the parties. Very often agreement is reached "in principle" with the details left for the drafting session, although at times the parties will agree to a draft of a clause at the bargaining table. In these situations, as agreements are reached they are put into writing, initialed, and then set aside until final agreement is reached on the whole agreement. Sometimes the drafting of the actual agreement is left to the lawyers of each side after negotiations have been completed.

Throughout the negotiating process each negotiator must constantly assess his own goals, the probable cost of achieving them, the goals of the other side, and the degree to which he will resist those goals. The negotiator must decide on the tactics which he will use to communicate to and to elicit information from the other side. He must decide at what point to make concessions, at what point to appear firm, how to appear to his own side to be holding out for a particular proposal while signalling to the opposing negotiator that he will drop the demand eventually. He must decide whether to and how to commit himself (and to what extent) to a particular position.

If a negotiator desires a particular settlement which he knows the other side will accept, but only with extreme reluctance, he can attempt to commit himself irrevocably to achieving that objective. He can do this, for example, by promises to his own team or by statements to the press. If he can commit himself, he may force the other side to grant that demand.[18] A union negotiator may attempt to do this by making a clear statement to the membership. He may say, for example, "I will refuse to accept a wage increase of less than $1.00 an hour." Of course, if he misjudges the willingness of the opposition to grant the demand, he may find himself out on a limb. When a negotiator has done this, his opposite number must find a way to help the opposition back down gracefully. The behavior of a negotiator must also be designed to help his opposition sell the settlement to his negotiating team.

Every negotiator faces a continual three-fold choice in negotiations: he may accept the available terms, he may attempt to improve the available terms through further bargaining, or he may break off negotiations with no intention of resuming them.[19] In labor negotiations, the strike deadline strongly influences the negotiator in his choice of a particular alternative.

THE STRIKE DEADLINE

As the strike deadline approaches, the chances that an improved offer will be forthcoming become increasingly less likely. The strike deadline forces each side to reassess its position and move toward a final offer. As the strike deadline nears, the tactic of bluffing becomes less tenable. At the zero hour there must be either a settlement or a strike. Thus, the popular picture of the parties emerging from an all-night final bargaining session has a basis in reality: a lot of action occurs in the short time before a strike deadline.

In terms of the three-fold choice, if the parties do not accept the agreement they must continue bargaining under the duress of the economic sanctions imposed by the work stoppage. At the time of the strike, one of the parties may state that his position on an issue was indeed final. He has no intention of ever making a concession on the point; he will engage in no further bargaining no matter what penalties are invoked. The decision on the three-fold choice is never easy to make, but the strike deadline forces that decision to be made.

Sometimes, if agreement is near, the parties will extend the deadline. Frequently, however, there comes a time when the strike cannot be postponed any longer.

Each side must make certain technical and organizational proceedings if there is to be a work stoppage; management must arrange for an orderly cessation of work.... Plans must be made for essential orders. Goods in process and shipments must be rescheduled. Arrangements must be made for maintenance and repair. Supervision must be alerted and scheduled to perform some of these emergency functions. Unions in turn have to organize picket lines, banners and information about the strike must be prepared with the union and the community.[20]

Beyond a certain point, these procedures cannot be delayed any longer. The preparations must be implemented and the work stoppage begun.

Another decision which each side must make is how visible it wishes its strike preparations to become. Unions frequently take strike votes, which authorize a work stoppage if there is no settlement. These are such a matter of form that they are not necessarily seen as a real threat, although they are frequently used as threats during negotiations and not merely a device for determining the views of the union membership. Other more credible union strike threats might include the renting of a strike headquarters or the open solicitation of support from other unions. Management can ship goods, make arrangements to service customers from other plants, increase security arrangements. Visible preparations for a strike may well bring charges of "bad faith" bargaining. They may also cause the other side to believe that a work stoppage is inevitable, no matter what occurs at the bargaining table, thus bringing an end to effective bargaining. Of course, if the preparations are a bluff, a threat that the party has no intention of carrying through, his credibility may be lost for future negotiations.

CONCILIATION

A special problem for Canadian negotiators is the question of how to deal with the conciliation process. With the exception of Saskatchewan, all jurisdictions in Canada require conciliation before a work stoppage takes place. Some parties make conciliation a mere formality by meeting with the conciliation officer early in negotiations, simply to fulfill the statutory requirement. Others wait until the strike deadline is near and then use the help of a conciliation officer to help reach an agreement. Others reserve their final offers until after the conciliation process. A variety of approaches to conciliation are possible, but the use of the process in negotiation must be considered by every negotiator.

At one time, in most Canadian jurisdictions, the conciliation process involved two steps: intervention by the conciliation officer and then by the conciliation board if the officer was unable to secure an agreement. The officer acted as a mediator to help the parties reach an agreement. The board also mediated but, if it could not effect an agreement, made recommendations for a settlement. While most jurisdictions still provide for conciliation boards, they are used only in exceptional disputes. Negotiators generally do not have to develop strategic plans for the use of the second stage of the conciliation process. (However, if they are engaged in an important negotiation — one with province-wide or national implications — the negotiator should anticipate second-level government intervention, and sometimes even an extra-legal third level of intervention in the form of special mediators.) Exhibit II-5 shows the duration of negotiations and settlement stage for major Canadian negotiations in 1973. The parties' expectations about the degree of intervention will clearly affect their behavior during negotiations. Also if there is any expectation on the part of management that the union membership will reject the settlement, then this may affect their bargaining behavior so that they hold back from making a final offer until after the rejection.

Collective bargaining in the Canadian Railroads is a good example of the effects of intervention. In 1973 the parties were required to proceed through the regular conciliation process and then were subject to the intervention of a special mediator and the Minister of Labour. These efforts did not head off a strike and Parliament was recalled to legislate a settlement that included the arbitration of outstanding disputes. In this situation, the parties had every reason to believe that a strike and cessation of service on the railroads (including ferry service linking Prince Edward Island and Newfoundland to the mainland) would be politically and economically intolerable. The government could be *expected* to intervene. Consequently concessions were not made as the strike deadline approached, but only as the intervention reached its final stages. In this case the final step was arbitration, and one may assume that the parties left a gap in their final positions which the arbitration board could fill with its decision.

Some union negotiating teams have the power to reach a binding settlement, while others must submit the proposals to the membership for ratification. In the late 1960s there was an increase in the number of contracts rejected by the membership, causing some to express concern as to whether collective bargaining could continue to exist if the bargains made at the negotiating table were not implemented. The "rejection phenomenon" has since declined, and there is some evidence that the problem was not as severe as it seemed, but was in part caused by divided union leadership offering conflicting advice to the membership.[22]

SOME VARIANTS IN THE BARGAINING PROCESS

This discussion of the bargaining process has been extremely general. No two negotiations even between the same parties are alike. Some negotiations are concluded quickly and easily; others are difficult and extremely time-consuming. One interesting variant to the general pattern outlined above has been practiced, among others, by General Electric. As

EXHIBIT II-5

NUMBER OF SETTLEMENTS DURING THE PERIOD JANUARY TO DECEMBER 1973[21] BY STAGE AND DURATION OF NEGOTIATIONS

Bargaining situations involving 500 or more employees, excluding the construction industry

Stage at which settled	Duration of negotiations in months										Total	
	1-3 months		4-6 months		7-9 months		10-12 months		13 months & over			
	A.*	Empls.	A.	Empls.	A.	Empls.	A.	Empls.	A.	Empls.	A.	Empls.
Direct bargaining	39	50,145	62	157,000	26	32,525	9	37,820	1	500	137	277,990
Conciliation officer	7	4,520	29	28,070	18	25,755	5	7,495	5	5,645	64	71,485
Conciliation board	-	-	1	700	5	4,180	4	17,035	2	2,610	12	24,525
Post-conciliation bargaining	-	-	11	34,730	15	12,160	3	4,140	4	39,415	33	90,445
Mediation	-	-	10	17,445	5	7,120	2	1,890	-	-	17	26,455
Mediation after work stoppage	-	-	-	-	-	-	-	-	4	9,150	4	9,150
Arbitration	1	1,600	2	1,300	3	5,150	-	-	6	18,845	18	46,995
Work stoppage	4	12,300	21	25,025	27	45,855	6	6,130	1	1,295	59	90,605
Bargaining after work stoppage	-	-	-	-	-	-	1	3,300	4	10,825	5	14,125
Other	-	-	-	-	-	-	1	900	-	-	1	900
Total	51	68,565	136	264,270	99	132,745	37	98,810	27	83,285	350	652,675

practiced by that company, it has been called *Boulwarism*, after the man, Lemuel Boulware, who developed it.

One essential feature of G.E.'s policy was effective two-way communication. The company constantly presented its views directly to its employees, and constantly sought feedback from them. During bargaining, the company listened to the union's proposals and the complete arguments behind these proposals. The company then made an offer — essentially a final offer — the terms of which were released to the employees as well as to their union representatives. The offer was generally quite attractive, although probably not close to the union's goals for maximum success. While the company would rearrange some of the components of their offer, the size of the package would not be increased. The union could accept these terms or strike; the company would not change its position. Even after a 100-day strike in 1969/70, General Electric moved only a very small distance, if even that, from its offer.

Boulwarism represented an almost perfect example of commitment tactics. The unions which bargained with G.E. bitterly resented what they called the company's take-it-or-leave-it style of bargaining. The U.S. National Labor Relations Board ruled that in practicing Boulwarism the company did not bargain in "good faith," but the board and the unions were unsuccessful in attempting to force the company to change its tactics.

The practice of Boulwarism appears deceptively easy. In truth, it requires a great deal of skill and effort. Assessing employee desires, attractively packaging the offer, and communicating not only the offer but also a host of day-to-day matters to employees is a time-consuming and difficult job.[23]

OTHER BARGAINING PATTERNS

A number of companies and unions have attempted to develop a pattern of bargaining different from the normal pattern discussed above. These attempts have been generally based on the notion that the normal "crisis bargaining" pattern is not a useful way to solve some of the pressing issues, such as automation, facing the parties. These efforts have been, in the past, a search for a better way to resolve union-management differences.

Kaiser Steel, American Motors, and Armour in the United States, and Alcan, Steinberg's, General Steelwares, and Domtar in Canada are among the companies that have made such attempts. In the United States, the steel industry, the West Coast longshore industry and the glass-container industry have also made attempts at what has been called "creative collective bargaining." Some efforts, like that at International Harvester, have been directed at improving day-to-day relationships. Others, like Domtar, have involved the formal study of critical issues away from the heat and pressure of the bargaining table. Still others, such as the human relations committee in the U.S. steel industry, were attempts to study continuously and resolve issues through continuous, noncrisis bargaining. Many of these efforts have involved the use of neutral parties as mediators in the resolution process.[24]

Some of these attempts have been successful; while others, after initial success, have been discontinued. The real point of interest here is not that there are ideal ways of negotiating but that, under the North American system of collective bargaining, the parties are free to select those strategies and tactics which they believe are most appropriate.

In fact, the number of successful attempts to apply Boulwarism on one hand and noncrisis bargaining on the other are relatively few. The negotiation of collective agreements has a relatively fixed pattern, even though alternatives are available. The obvious conclusion is that, with all its defects, the system works to the satisfaction of both union and management.

Both sides strongly resist any changes in the legal status quo that would change the system. To a great extent, the system also works for society as a whole, at least when compared with the available alternatives.

> The alternatives essentially are three. First is unilateral decision making. It reposes all power in the industrial relations field in one entity, either the employer or the state. The second is bilateral decision making. It at least precludes any one party from holding a dominating position. It, however, still eliminates an interested party: labor, management, or the public as represented by the government. The third is a multilateral approach. It overcomes the deficiency of bilateral decision making and recognizes the interplay of market and institutional forces which is inevitable in a mixed enterprise economy operating within a liberal democratic political system. The Canadian industrial relations system is multilateral. Aside from the forces of supply and demand in the labour market, it features a high degree of employer determination, trade union participation, collective bargaining, and government involvement in a variety of capacities . . . . Within industry, unions serve as countervailing power to management, and within the wider socioeconomic-political sphere, they function as potential agents for transformation in an increasingly pluralistic society.
>
> Collective bargaining is the mechanism through which labor and management seek to accommodate their differences, frequently without strife, sometimes through it, and occasionally without success. As

imperfect an instrument as it may be, there is no viable substitute in a free society....[25]

* * *

The following case series, titled "McDonald Containers, A-I," describes actual negotiations involving a large producer of folding cartons and other packaging products and its union, Local 201 of the International Paper Products and Allied Enterprises Union of America. It views the negotiations through the eyes of Mr. Clive Armstrong, the company's Manager of Industrial Relations, from initial planning stages, through various meetings, through conciliation and ultimately to settlement.

The negotiations described here did not involve a strike or a threatened strike. As such, they were typical of most negotiations. Beyond that, they offer guidelines on how to prepare for bargaining and how to conduct oneself in negotiation sessions so as to reach a just and equitable settlement.

McDONALD CONTAINERS LTD. (A)

A. CHIEF NEGOTIATOR

Last August Clive Armstrong, Manager of Industrial Relations of McDonald Containers Ltd., was on the verge of negotiating a new contract with Local 201 of the International Paper Products and Allied Enterprises Union of America (IPPU), the representative of the largest group of unionized employees of the St. Catharines, Ontario, plant. The present contract was to expire on September 14. This would be the third time Armstrong had negotiated with this local.

Clive Armstrong had served as chief negotiator in all of McDonald's contract negotiations for the past six years. Still he felt fresh pangs of excitement as each negotiation approached. Dates for the first meetings had already been set. The initial one would take place August 12.

By way of preparation Armstrong was formulating his own objectives for the upcoming rounds of bargaining. In so doing he speculated on the union's moves.

B. BACKGROUND

1. McDonald Containers

McDonald Containers was one of the largest producers of folding cartons and other packaging materials in Ontario. Sales had stabilized in the past few years at about $34 million, while profits had declined from a high of $1.5 million three years ago to $1.2 million last year. The decline in profits resulted from rising costs and increased competition.

The company had eight plants. The major products, folding cartons, were produced in six plants. There was some product overlap, because each plant was designed to serve a specific geographic area. Distance between plants made it economically unsound for one plant to absorb customer requirements for another, except in emergencies. Many of the company's packaging products were manufactured for the food industry. Of these, a large portion were for fluids, such as dairy products and soft drinks.

2. St. Catharines Division

The St. Catharines plant was McDonald's largest. It supplied over 10 per cent of the Niagara Peninsula market for containers in the food, cosmetic and hardware businesses. Since it served the fluid industry in particular, sales rose in May and continued at a high level until the heat of summer subsided.

Workers at the St. Catharines plant were represented by three unions: the IPPU, the Niagara Carton Makers Union (NCM) and the Typesetters Union. The contract with the NCM would run until next April 30 and that with the Typesetters until next August 31. These were craft unions. The former represented 30 printers while the latter represented nine lithographers. The NCM contracts usually followed the pattern set by the IPPU.

The IPPU local bargaining unit included production, maintenance, quality control, material handling and technical workers. The unit numbered 150, 38 of whom were female. The work force swelled to about 175 during the summer sales and vacation peak. Students provided most of the temporary help. Since there was a union shop these students were required to pay dues.

Skills ranged from general labor to pressmen. Pressmen were highly skilled workers akin to printers in the NCM. Básic wages for the pressmen were $4.52 per hour. The lowest rate for general labor was $3.33 for males and $2.91 for females. About 90 per cent of the work force members, including all pressmen, were eligible for incentives. The incentive system was based on time standards established by use of stop watches. After observing and timing each operation, methods engineers prescribed a certain number of "standard hours," the time in which a so-called normal performer working at average skill and efficiency could perform the necessary job assigned to him. Workers who performed their jobs faster than the standard were paid a bonus. The bonus was a percentage of the negotiated base rate.

Up till four years ago wages in the plant had been in line with other firms in the folding carton industry. Since then, wages had exceeded the industry average by about 10 per cent. However, they were below the average area rates by approximately 5 per cent. Last summer average wages at McDonald for all nonincentive hourly employees were a little over $3.50 per hour. Those on incentives averaged slightly over $3.90 per hour.

3. Union History

During World War II a plant council of workers was formed in compliance with government wartime measures. After the war the council continued as the representative of the workers and became affiliated with the International Pulp, Sulfite and Paperworkers Union. In the early 50s the workers broke from the international and formed a local of the Box Employees' Union. The local was weak, nonmilitant, and poorly led. During this period, the foremen had complete control of their departments. There were no recorded grievances. In fact, the union held meetings occasionally to quash discontent. However, rank and file militancy rose until four years ago when the Box Employees' Union was decertified and the IPPU was certified in its place. IPPU appealed to the membership on a platform of rectifying the wrongs of the weak union. It promised economic benefits. Perhaps the most important reason for the Box Employees' Union demise was that they were working under a three-year agreement calling for small annual increases. During the term of that agreement Canadian wages in general took off in spectacular fashion.

C. RECENT CONTRACTS

1. First Negotiation — Four Years Ago

Soon after the IPPU certification Clive Armstrong met with George Sheehan, the union's international representative, to negotiate the first contract. The old Box Employees contract was used as a starting point in the negotiations. Nevertheless, both men expected the negotiations to take a long time. Sheehan took a tough bargaining approach. Tension was frequent, and some conflicts arose. Armstrong was particularly upset when Sheehan informed the local newspaper of an upcoming strike vote.

This caused customers of McDonald to make arrangements for alternative supply sources and gave rise to a strong rebuke by Armstrong.

After several weeks the union applied for conciliation under provisions of the Ontario Labour Relations Act.[26] After the first conciliation meeting the company negotiators expressed concern about the apparent incompetency of the conciliator. He had led the company representatives to believe a settlement was near, but it soon became clear that he had badly underestimated the union's position. The company then requested another conciliator, and under his auspices the parties came to an agreement. It was a two-year contract, calling for a 12 per cent wage increase.

The administration of the new contract brought significant changes. In particular the grievance rate rose to a steady stream, and the foremen had difficulty adapting. They had never before experienced challenges to their authority, but they were reluctant to seek advice or counsel of the industrial relations staff, a difficult thing to do after years of autocracy.

2. Second Contract — Two Years Ago

Negotiations for the second contract took a long time. The company started off by presenting its own proposals for changes in the contract before hearing union demands. Union bargainers scoffed at this procedure and tried to ignore the proposals. Later, as the parties discussed money, George Sheehan rejected attempts by Armstrong to make industry wage comparisons. Sheehan went so far as to say the identity of McDonald's competitors and their wage rates were irrelevant. He stated that area rates provided the only fair basis for comparison.

About the time the contract expired in mid-August, the union discovered that the company had been stockpiling finished cartons at a Toronto warehouse. Sheehan was quite upset, but his irritation was tempered by the fact that the inventory was small — about a week's supply. While no work action occurred, the union leaders threatened that the membership would refuse overtime. This threat was rendered ineffective when it became evident that workers would not go along.

Once again a conciliation officer was called in. After an 18-hour session, the sides finally reached agreement on a two-year contract in the early morning hours. The wage settlement was again an expensive one for the company. The increase was applied on a cents-per-hour basis and totaled about 16 per cent.

D. RECENT DEVELOPMENTS

1. Environmental

Environmental developments were likely to have an important bearing on the current negotiations. First, there were significant economic trends: inflationary pressures were strong and wage settlements were high. At the same time unemployment had risen to levels not experienced for a decade.

Locally, the labor market was active. Numerous plant closings and threats of closings had occurred in the Niagara Peninsula area in the past two years. For a while in the spring there were threats of a brewery strike, but settlement occurred well before McDonald's negotiations started. Local strikes by civic employees were predicted in various Niagara Peninsula municipalities in August and September. In Brantford, Ontario, about 50 miles away, a manufacturer of hospital supplies had been struck by the Canadian Chemical and Textile Workers Union who were seeking a 56 cent increase on a $1.93 base rate. When the company sought to bring in strike breakers from other communities violence erupted, leading to a court injunction and more than 60 arrests. The company threatened to close down its Canadian operations if the strike continued.

Another significant environmental development concerned women's rights. The Women's Equal Employment Opportunity Act had been proclaimed in December of 1970. This act prohibited discrimination because of sex in employment conditions and hiring. It was interpreted as requiring equal wages for men and women doing the same work; but since then companies and unions had been skirmishing about its meaning.[27]

2. Union Developments

In the two prior negotiations, the union seemed to lack cohesion. There had been frequent bickering among the local bargaining committee members and between the local committee members and George Sheehan, the union's international representative.

Last fall the union vice president, Walter Stevens, resigned. Then, about three months later, an internal union uproar was caused when members came to believe that the union's executives had voted salary increases for themselves. The uproar eventually caused the union president, Julius Arthur, to resign. An international representative from the United States was called in to help smooth things over and set up an interim union executive.

Clive Armstrong was concerned that these conflicts would hinder settlement in the forthcoming negotiations. His fears seemed well-founded when the membership elected a bargaining committee before deciding on a new executive. Armstrong asked Walter Stevens, the chairman of the new bargaining committee, whether there would be a split between the executive and the bargainers. Stevens assured him that there would be no conflict, but it was hardly reassuring when Armstrong noted that none of the members of the bargaining committee were on the interim executive committee. There might be difficulties in getting union membership to ratify an agreement after it had been initialed by the bargainers.

3. Bargaining Committee

Armstrong described the members of the union bargaining committee:

George Sheehan

International representative for the IPPU in the Niagara Peninsula area. Considered a strong man by members of the local. Very persuasive with membership. Fairly democratic at negotiations. Does not force members to keep to issues at hand, often lets them go on tangents. Knowledgeable in labor relations, literature and law. Sometimes refers management to books and articles. In negotiations, actually chairs meetings for union and serves as chief negotiator. Poised, plays roles effectively.

Walter Stevens

Chairman of committee. Former vice president and department steward in the local. Late 30s. Over 20 years' service. Shipper. An average paying job. Appears to be personal friend of Sheehan's. Was active in having IPPU replace the previous union. Member of the two previous negotiating committees. Perhaps the best person to gauge feelings of the membership.

Alice Melvin

In her 30s. Eight years' service. Interested in female wages and benefits. Quiet at meetings. Apparently a behind-the-scenes disturber. A member of the union's founding executive. Former steward. A member of negotiating team two years ago.

Michael Newman

Diemaker lead hand. Fifteen years' service, early 30s. Not active in union before. Shy and not too talkative. An unknown quantity. First time on negotiating committee.

Harry Chelekian

Skilled, maintenance mechanic. Late 30s. Twelve years' service. Department steward. Concerned mainly about own area of work and himself. Talkative and overly emotional. Felt not to pull much weight with committee or members. First time on committee.

Jack Griffin

Early 30s, over seven years' service. Member of original IPPU executive. Former chief steward. Member of 1967 and 1969 negotiating teams. Not active at meetings; not a key man.

In preparing their demands for the negotiations, the union bargaining committee held two general membership meetings. Armed with ideas from the members, they met to formulate their demands.

E. MANAGEMENT PREPARATIONS

In early March, Clive Armstrong and members of his department began serious preparations for the negotiations. They surveyed wages and benefits in the industry and area; they named their bargaining committee; and they developed management proposals for changes to the contract.

The naming of the bargaining committee was a formality. The same team had negotiated in the two previous contracts.

Clive Armstrong

Chairman and chief negotiator.

Daniel Burgess

Assistant to Armstrong. Responsible, along with the personnel manager of the St. Catharines plant, for prenegotiation preparations.

John Curtis

General Manager, St. Catharines plant. He was accountable for the division's profits and had veto power over any agreement.

Frederick Lundberg

Personnel Manager, St. Catharines plant. Reported to Curtis.

William Cutts

Plant Superintendent, supervisor of the production foremen.

Ralph Reed

Manager Industrial Engineering.

John Yale

Manager of Production Planning and Material Handling.

As he did during the last negotiations two years ago, Armstrong made plans for management's proposals for contract changes to be presented at the start of negotiations. While the union had not greeted this tactic favorably, Armstrong believed it was important to give members of management an opportunity to make their viewpoints known before hearing union demands. After all, the first-line supervisors would be called on to administer the contract, and they should be made to feel that they influenced its formulation. Thus a series of meetings was held with foremen to secure their input. As a result, management prepared a 10-page proposal for changes in 32 separate contract provisions. These were condensed from significantly more proposals received from the foremen. If a foreman made a suggestion that was not incorporated into the final proposals, he was sought out and given the reasons for rejection of his suggestion.

Armstrong considered nine of the management proposals to be crucial. One of them would restrict the criteria for determining job assignments, in the event of a layoff, to seniority and ability. The present contract contained an added factor — willingness by an employee to accept a lower classification of work. Some employees were unwilling to bump downward in the event of a layoff and, because of this, they experienced difficulty when they filed for unemployment insurance. Armstrong believed the union would be receptive to removing the "willingness" criterion.

In the same vein, management was anxious to secure a contract rewording which would make "qualification" the sole criterion for filling temporary job classifications (ten working days or less). The existing contract called for a dual test: willingness and qualification.

Six of management's proposals concerned overtime distribution. They were also considered crucial. These would provide for sharing of overtime "as fairly and as reasonably as possible as circumstances permit." In addition they would provide for sharing among all qualified employees.

One additional proposal was considered important in order to clear up past confusion. This regarded group insurance coverage for married female workers. The McDonald plan was designed with the expectation that husbands would cover their wives at their place of work. Consequently, married women working at McDonald were not enrolled for married coverage unless thay made formal application. In such cases the company would pay the premium for married coverage but deduct the difference between married and single premium costs from the employee's paycheck. The company paid full premium costs on married coverage for married males. Family coverage was provided for widows and for divorced or legally separated female employees, provided they were not covered elsewhere.

Other items in management's list of proposals were considered by Armstrong to be window dressing. Mostly they dealt with improbable hypothetical situations. Nevertheless, they were included in order to pay tribute to those who put them forth. To some extent they might serve as trading horses — items to be dropped in turn for the union's dropping one or more of their demands.

*   *   *

The union negotiators insisted on holding meetings at a neutral location. The Rendezvous Motel conference room was reserved for the first three meetings. Negotiations had been held there before. Armstrong felt it was important to have a comfortable place away from the plant, thus emphasizing the importance of the proceedings and, possibly, enhancing the bargainers' own feelings of importance.

1. Bargaining Style and Strategy

Armstrong would be chairman. He insisted that there be no visible disunity or bickering on the management team. As negotiations moved into the monetary stages, management would show no outward reaction to union demands. If caucuses were called to discuss offers, they would be held away from the presence of union negotiators.

Armstrong had a healthy respect for Sheehan's bargaining ability. He believed Sheehan represented the whole strength of the union team. False emotionalism or empty threats would not be effective tools for management to use against him.

When it came time to talk money, Armstrong wanted to introduce wage comparisons from the packaging industry. He was concerned about getting McDonald's competitive situation across to the union bargainers, even if Sheehan himself displayed indifference. He expected that Sheehan would reject these comparisons and insist on making area comparisons. Most important, Armstrong would make no economic offer until all the union demands were on the table in such form that their economic value could be calculated and totaled.

Armstrong expected Sheehan to seek agreement on various union demands on a piecemeal basis. He would resist this tactic and would restrict the company's wage and fringe offer to one package. According to Armstrong:

> If you bargain item by item you discover you have no money left when you come to wages. You have to do it in a package in order to cost it properly so you know what you're giving.

During the negotiations, Armstrong would provide no news releases for the press. Also the company would never communicate directly with the members of the union outside the bargaining room. Armstrong expected the union to apply for conciliation early. Nevertheless he would try to keep everyone at the bargaining table as long as possible before that happened.

2. Anticipations

Armstrong did not know when the union would make their first concrete demands. He expected the first few meetings to focus solely on the language of the contract — not on money matters.

He did have an idea what the union's principal demands would be. He listed them:

1. Company to pay all premiums on medical insurance. At present the company paid 75 per cent of Ontario Hospital Services premiums and 100 per cent of all other welfare benefits.

2. A major pension plan revision. Armstrong was not sure exactly what form this would take, but he expected to bargain over benefits. He would insist on bargaining only regarding costs to the company.

3. Severance pay, based on years of service.

4. No contracting-out clause.

5. Cost-of-living escalator.

6. Training plan to upgrade skills.

7. More vacation time and more holidays.

3. Monetary Objectives

With negotiations about to start, Armstrong began to formulate his monetary objectives. This would be done in consultation with the Vice President of Packaging. During the consultation Armstrong would present his best guess regarding limits below which the union would strike and above which management should be willing to accept a strike.

Underlying all conversations about monetary limits was a deep concern over McDonald's long-term competitive situation in the industry. Thus, management was united in a desire to keep costs low. A budget had been set earlier in the year which included a 10 per cent increase in labor cost for the whole year. Much of this was to cushion the increases called for under the existing contract: an average of $.12 per hour effective last September 15 and $.15 per hour last March 15.

Armstrong believed that a seven-per-cent wage increase plus a one-per-cent fringe settlement would be desirable. However, he doubted whether operating managers would be willing to hold these figures if faced with a strike. These questions would have to wait until the first meeting was over.

ITEMS FOR DISCUSSION

1. Comment on Armstrong's preparation for negotiations.
2. What do you believe should be management's bargaining objectives?
3. What would be your estimation of the limits below which the union would strike and above which management should be willing to accept a strike?
4. Identify the important elements of Armstrong's bargaining strategy. Appraise each of them.

McDONALD CONTAINERS LTD. (B)

NEGOTIATIONS BEGIN

On Thursday, August 12, the negotiations began at the Rendezvous Motel. As was traditional, the parties met at 9:00 A.M. and would remain at the bargaining table until about 5:00 P.M.

> SHEEHAN (u): Well, who's paying for this?
> ARMSTRONG (oo): The company has in the past, and we will continue to do so. But we aren't if we go to conciliation!

Members of bargaining teams chuckled. They were in a jovial mood. The contract would not expire for over a month (September 14). The chief negotiators handed out copies of their demands and proposals. The union submitted 35 demands; 12 with monetary implications. The proposals were skimmed quickly. (See Exhibit 1 (p. 130) for summary of union proposals.)

> ARMSTRONG (co). I notice that the union has not stated a specific wage demand. I remind you that this will be necessary before the company can seriously consider any monetary items. Let's divide your demands into nonmonetary and monetary groups. We can start discussing the nonmonetary ones. Then, after you clarify your wage demand, we can go on.
> SHEEHAN (u): I agree to dividing them up. Oh, Clive, we would like to add to the wage demand. Could you write this in one of your sheets? Add "wage parity between male and female employees" to "substantial wage increase."

Most of the morning was spent clarifying the meaning of the demands. At noon, each group had lunch separately and talked about their initial reactions.

ARMSTRONG (co): Everything seems to be going all right.

BURGESS (co): There aren't too many surprises except the one about opening the grievance process.

ARMSTRONG (co): I wonder what Sheehan wants with that one. It could open up the process so that the union could grieve on everything from pollution to contracting out. I don't like it.

BURGESS (co): They seem to be concerned about the rights of probationary employees.

CURTIS (General Manager, St. Catharines Division): They really want to make probationary employees nonprobationary. The supervisors won't go for that.

ARMSTRONG (co): I didn't expect any female wage parity talk. I thought this was all squared away years ago.

LUNDBERG (Personnel Manager, St. Catharines Division): Maybe it was just an afterthought.

In the afternoon the negotiators delved into the union proposals in more detail. The company proposals were left aside for the moment. However, when a union demand dealt with the same article of the contract that a company proposal did, Daniel Burgess brought it up. As a result, three company proposals were discussed as well.

Tentatively, the company and union agreed on two minor points — the number of shop stewards and the company proposal regarding procedure for allocating overtime. Then, the proposal for a change in the grievance process was considered.

SHEEHAN (u): By defining a grievance as any difference between the company and union, we can make the whole process more flexible.

ARMSTRONG (co): What do you really want in doing this?

SHEEHAN (u): This will make our relationship less legalistic. We'll get used to solving more problems together.

ARMSTRONG (co): It's unworkable. If we don't agree on some issues, who decides — an arbitrator? Wouldn't this change allow you to grieve anything from changing the position of the flag pole to contracting out?

SHEEHAN (u): Well, yes it would allow us to discuss questions of that sort. But we have nothing specific in mind.

Time elapsed. The parties agreed to continue to go over the union submission at the following meeting.

Armstrong gave his reactions to the first session:

It started off pretty well. It seems as if the union is going to keep any bickering outside the meetings. The only disruptions concerned Harry Chelekian. He often gets off on a tangent and they try to quiet him down. This was expected. Everyone else is running true to form. George Sheehan and I are doing most of the talking.

I presume Sheehan is going to play a waiting game. He comes on strong with theoretical talk at first but not concrete wage demands. We will try to get through the union's nonmonetary questions quickly. No reason to delay. We want to discuss our own demands. We'll agree to their requests if they are reasonable. I'll keep reminding Sheehan that he has to put a wage demand on the table before we can talk money. There is no pressure yet until we finish the discussion of the language of the contract.

As for these nonmonetary language changes, Dan Burgess is preparing a comparison of our proposal with theirs in cases when we both want to change the same articles. He also will get comments from the people concerned regarding the language demands about departmental matters. This way we can refer to the demands quicker and have an idea what it is really about. Dan is also costing the monetary demands where possible mainly because we have no wage demand. This material will be necessary in a few weeks when we really get down to bargain money.

EXHIBIT 1 (McDonald, B)

Summary of Union Proposals Submitted at First Meeting Between Local 201, IPPU and McDonald Containers Ltd.

A. Contract changes

1. Probationary employees — no summer rate for students
   - grievance possible on discharge and layoff
   - rehiring according to service.
2. Grievance — means any difference between union and company
   - lengthen filing period to 30 days and shorten reply by company to three days (the existing contract called for 15 days and five days)
   - possible to go to arbitration without going through grievance steps.
3. Hiring — seniority criteria if qualified.
4. Hours of work— 48-hours notice of shift change or time-and-a-half pay
   - new hours for two shift operations (the existing contract called for shifts from 7 A.M. till 4 P.M. and 4 P.M. till 12:30 A.M.)
   - some departmental and job changes
5. Local issues — re-evaluate some job classifications
   - adjust some rates
   - coveralls for some workers
   - powerhouse: own union steward, one bulletin board, time-and-a-half on Saturday and double time on Sunday.
6. Overtime — voluntary
   - list of overtime kept for calendar year.

B. Benefits

1. Holidays and Vacations
   - add floating holiday at convenience of employee
   - increase number of weeks' vacation
   - add $25 per week vacation bonus
   - take vacation within year of anniversary date
   - leave granted for more categories of deaths among family members.
2. Severance Pay
   - one week's pay per year service
3. Welfare
   - company to pay 100 per cent of welfare package

- add benefits — disability
- life insurance — two times wages
- sick benefits 60 per cent wages for 52 weeks
- semiprivate hospital benefits
- any future savings in premium for government welfare schemes goes to employee.

4. Pension
   - improvement
5. Wages
   - substantial increase
6. Parity
   - equal female-male wages

*   *   *

ITEMS FOR DISCUSSION:

1. Comment on first meeting. Is there significance to the fact that the initial dialogue concerned the union's demands?
2. Why does management insist on costing the monetary demands?
3. What position would you take regarding the various union proposals?
4. As chief company negotiator how would you proceed the next day?

McDONALD CONTAINERS LTD. (C)

TWO MORE SESSIONS

The parties met again on Monday, August 16, and Wednesday, August 25. The company agreed to a number of minor changes in the contract and reached an understanding that health premium savings would be passed on to employees and/or the company in the event the government decided to discontinue premiums.

However, the company once again took a firm stand in refusing to pay welfare premiums for married women on the same basis as for married men. The union offered a minor compromise on this item, but Clive Armstrong stood firm. Armstrong also rejected the union's wish to have an impartial industrial engineer re-evaluate a number of job classifications which they considered out of line.

The rest of the day was spent clarifying and discussing the company proposals. The union accepted some of the company proposals, including the desire to deny seniority rights to students. Other proposals were held for consideration at the next meeting.

On Wednesday, the 25th, the third meeting was held. Armstrong continued to direct bargainers' attention to company proposals. The union discussed these proposals with no objection. However, they felt many were uncalled-for and unnecessary. It was agreed to meet again the following Wednesday and Thursday to complete discussion of the nonmonetary items.

REFLECTIONS

Clive Armstrong expressed pleasure with the progress so far. He was pleased that the union was seriously considering the company proposals.

One aspect of the meetings concerned Armstrong: "I've been on the receiving end of some difficult questions from the union about some of these proposals we made. I figured they were important, because the foremen had submitted them. However, I'm finding that there is little defense for many of them. I have had to back down on a few, and I feel a little silly."

The next week Armstrong had a meeting with his team about some of the questionable issues:

> I discovered, after all, that the supervisors weren't really concerned about some of these things I was supposed to argue in favor of. The foremen will probably just think I gave in but they are putting me in a bad position. I won't defend items which mainly arise out of hypothetical situations. I've learned something — next time we'll take a closer look at these proposals and find out just how important they really are. Now I'll have to withdraw them, but at least the foremen will know they have been discussed.

It was still too early to consider strike preparations. Armstrong anticipated reaching final agreement on as many proposals as possible. He was hoping Sheehan would make a monetary demand soon. He had been hounding him on this point and would continue to do so. He felt it was still early for the union to call for conciliation.

*   *   *

ITEMS FOR DISCUSSION

1. Why was Armstrong anxious for the union to make a specific monetary demand?
2. Evaluate Armstrong's comments regarding management's proposals which were apparently without defense.

3. Why do you believe Armstrong continued his opposition to payment of full welfare premiums for married women?

McDONALD CONTAINERS LTD. (D)

On Monday, Aguust 30, the parties continued bargaining on language and nonmonetary items.

The company presented a new proposal on the administration of vacations.

Pensions were brought up, and it was decided to have a life insurance company representative join the negotiators the following afternoon to answer questions and clarify technical points concerning various pension plans and their costs. Armstrong, while agreeing to invite an insurance representative to meet with the parties, emphasized that any costs from a new pension plan would be part of the package settlement and would be negotiated on a basis of cents-per-hour costs to the company, not on the basis of pension benefits to employees. He reiterated that no agreement could be reached on part of the economic package until the union made a full monetary proposal.

The union brought up female parity questions again. Armstrong said that costs arising from giving married females full married welfare benofito woro part of tho oconomic package. Regarding the issue of equal wages for male and female, the union claimed that some female jobs were more important than male ones. The management team tried to force the union to be more specific on this point. Sheehan said that equal pay was required by the Women's Equal Opportunity Act, and the company was in violation. Armstrong suggested the parties obtain an official statement from the Ontario Labour Department on the matter.

Afterwards, Armstrong commented that he was pleased with the meeting's progress. He had hoped the union would comment on more company proposals, but he expected there would be progress in this regard the next day.

The married-women benefits question and wage parity issues had occupied considerable attention, but Armstrong was not willing to move on either issue and certainly would not give anything away at this stage without something in return. He felt Alice Melvin, in particular, was pushing the married benefits question. Her husband, a seasonal construction worker, received no benefits of this nature.

The following day was expected to be similar to Monday's session. Armstrong hoped more progress would be made to clear up the nonmonetary items and to emphasize the need for a union wage demand.

*   *   *

ITEMS FOR DISCUSSION

1. Comment on management's continued refusal to discuss monetary items outside the context of a total economic package.
2. What position should management take regarding the question of female/male parity and married-women's rights to the same group insurance coverage as married men?

McDONALD CONTAINERS LTD. (E)

FIFTH MEETING

CONCILIATION APPLICATION

The following morning, Tuesday, August 31, Clive Armstrong and his fellow bargainers sat down once again across the table from George Sheehan and the union bargaining committee. Usually, the meetings opened with some hesitation, with either Armstrong or Sheehan reminding the group where they had left off the session before. Today was different. Sheehan cleared his throat and began.

> SHEEHAN (*u*): In accordance with the company's request, the union will clarify its economic position. Any settlement must preserve the relationship in the wage and benefit package that exists with McDonald Containers and other industries in the St. Catharines area who employ the same number of employees.
>
> ARMSTRONG (*co*): That is totally unacceptable! You aren't being explicit enough as to what settlements you are referring to.
>
> SHEEHAN (*u*): You are aware of the local settlements Clive; don't play dumb.
>
> ARMSTRONG (*co*): So, I'm dumb. Just give us a better idea of where you stand.
>
> SHEEHAN (*u*): Just check the papers. We are not prepared to clarify our demands further.
>
> ARMSTRONG (*co*): We can't negotiate money until you do.
>
> SHEEHAN (*u*): Well, I think it is also time to advise the company that the union will apply for conciliation at the conclusion of this meeting.
>
> ARMSTRONG (*co*): The company is opposed to your application at this time.

SHEEHAN (u): The union feels it is necessary to speed things up and get down to some serious bargaining.

ARMSTRONG (co): Come on George, you're just trying to arm-lock the company. It isn't good to apply for conciliation when we have so many noneconomic matters yet to decide. Moreover, you haven't even put a concrete wage demand on the table yet. The conciliator will probably just tell us to go back to the table ourselves.

SHEEHAN (u): We aren't trying to pressure the company at all — we just think it will speed our discussion up a bit. We will get a settlement without any pressure tactics. Also, there will be no negotiating this in the newspaper. I understand there was a little hard feeling about this before. We will reach a settlement on our own.

ARMSTRONG (co): Let's go over as many items as possible and try to get the language questions out of the way.

SHEEHAN (u): Okay.

In the afternoon two representatives from a local life insurance company joined the meeting and discussed the subject of pensions.

SHEEHAN (u): The union is interested in two possible pension plans. One would be a final earnings plan based on 1/10th of one per cent for the best five years of earnings, and the second would be a plan based on a monthly benefit based on years of service.

The existing pension plan called for yearly payment of two per cent of an employee's career average annual earnings times years of service, with employees contributing approximately one half the amount required to buy the plan. Only 50 per cent of the employees were members of the plan.

STONEMAN (ins. co): Based on last year's payroll the increase in cost to the company of the first plan you named would be about five per cent of payroll.

BURGESS (co): That works out to 18 cents per hour from my cost data.

ARMSTRONG (co): The company position on this is that any Canada Pension Plan benefit must be integrated with any proposed plan. Secondly, the company will only negotiate from a cents-per-hour cost to the company. I would remind the union that comparable firms in the Niagara area have nothing similar to these plans. They are just too expensive.

SHEEHAN (u): We know they are costly, Clive, but there are cheaper ways of handling them. I have told the membership that there will probably be changes in the government pension plan within the next five years. We know it's costly, but the present plan is not really adequate.

ARMSTRONG (co): It's part of the economic package.

SHEEHAN (u): Let's leave this for now and we'll get more information on it another time. We still have other business to discuss.

At this point, noneconomic items were reviewed. The union withdrew many of their proposals, including extending time for filing a grievance, voluntary overtime, longer notice for shift changes. Similarly, the company dropped about ten proposals. A few proposals were adopted. For example, students working in the summer would not obtain seniority rights.

The union held most of the remaining company proposals for further consideration. It was decided to meet again to clear up these items. The next session was set for Tuesday, September 7.

REFLECTIONS

The following day Clive Armstrong discussed the August 31 meeting with his assistant, Daniel Burgess.

ARMSTRONG (*co*): I was surprised that Sheehan mentioned conciliation, Dan. I really thought he would wait a week or so until some money was on the table.

BURGESS (*co*): Sheehan was trying to lighten it though — he kept saying positive things about reaching a settlement.

ARMSTRONG (*co*): That's right Dan. I also recall him mentioning no publicity to the paper. I blasted him about that a few years ago and he made a point of bringing it up.

BURGESS (*co*): Sheehan is softening a bit.

ARMSTRONG (*co*): I think he realizes we're a pretty good outfit and doesn't want to rock the boat as hard as he has in the past.

BURGESS (*co*): He does want a more harmonious relationship. But he has a monetary objective — and he wants to get it.

ARMSTRONG (*co*): Right — and we don't know if he was bluffing about conciliation. We'll wait and see if we get the notice from the Labour Department. In fact, maybe Sheehan even called the papers right after the meeting. We don't know what he is doing.

BURGESS (*co*): What issues are important at this stage, Clive?

ARMSTRONG (*co*): The wage and benefit parity between male and female is the main one. Sheehan keeps talking about discrimination. You know as well as I do those jobs are not really comparable. Anyway the cost of those demands is just too much.

BURGESS (*co*): The pension situation is changing.

ARMSTRONG (*co*): It looks like Sheehan is backing down on pensions. He's trying to convince their side that it isn't worth the money.

BURGESS (*co*): You've been pretty noncommittal so far, Clive.

BURGESS (*co*): I think I'll just wait on that one. I don't really know for sure, but I think Sheehan wants me to close the door on pensions.

BURGESS (*co*): Sheehan can sell them without our help. The only guy who is really sharp is the new man — Newman.

ARMSTRONG (*co*): He's got a head on his shoulders but I don't know how much influence he has.

BURGESS (*co*): Being shy and rather green as far as union affairs are concerned he may not try to do much. Stevens still is close to Sheehan. He must be Sheehan's link to the membership.

ARMSTRONG (*co*): Next meeting we'll try to clear up all the remaining nonmonetary items and get final agreement. I dropped most of our poor proposals today.

BURGESS (*co*): The only real issues are allocation of vacations and our desire to delete "willing" from the contract (*which made the worker eligible for unemployment if he was laid off and unwilling to take a lesser-paying job*). The main question we had about overtime allocation seems to be agreed-to already.

ARMSTRONG (*co*): In the afternoon we can discuss wage comparisons. Maybe we can get more concrete demands out of Sheehan. I'll have the Vice President, Noel Ramsey, in to say a few words about our competitive position. This is the message we have to get across to the committee whether Sheehan listens or not.

BURGESS (*co*): That's a step — we have to make them realize that our competitors in the Toronto area are well under our wage levels. By the way, I've finished that comparison on wages.

ARMSTRONG (*co*): Good! I may even have copies made to give the union committee.

BURGESS (*co*): What lies ahead — a strike vote after the conciliation meeting?

ARMSTRONG (*co*): Probably. Remember, no publicity should get out to our customers or the newspapers.

BURGESS (*co*): We meet with Mr. Kickhoeffer (*Executive Vice President*) and Mr. Ramsey (*Vice President, — Packaging*) on Friday about objectives for settlement and where we stand.

ARMSTRONG (*co*): Right now my objectives for a settlement are coming down to six per cent in wages. Maybe I'm too optimistic — it's still too early.

MEETING WITH VICE PRESIDENTS

It was Friday, September 3. The following Tuesday, another bargaining session would be held. A week from then the contract would expire. Clive Armstrong sat down with his immediate superior, Executive Vice President William Kickhoeffer, and Noel Ramsey, Vice President of Packaging, to discuss the negotiations.

Armstrong reported that recent wage settlements in the area had been in the seven to nine per cent range. Consequently, he believed McDonald's settlement would be in this range. However, he was concerned that his own superiors might be willing to go higher.

The executives expressed reluctance to dig in their toes and fight for a low settlement. They conceded that anything above 15 per cent was out of the question, but there were indications that they would give in to 10 or even 15 per cent settlement if faced with a strike. However, the men did not take a firm position in the matter; rather they decided to wait until the union put forth an initial demand before deciding on an economic limit.

The men decided to make a preliminary study of their situation should a strike be necessary. They did not want to stockpile. Staff personnel were assigned the task of discovering which major commodities could be produced at their other plants and in what quantities. They knew that there was little extra capacity elsewhere. There was some concern whether the unions in other plants would accept the work. It was hoped the study would be completed by September 10, the day when an executive meeting was scheduled to discuss the progress of the negotiations.

*   *   *

ITEMS FOR DISCUSSION

1. Evaluate Armstrong's assessment of the union's position regarding priority of demands. Do you share his belief that parity for women was most important and that Sheehan was backing down on pensions?
2. How should an appropriate economic package be determined?
3. Beyond what limits would you advise management to take a strike?
4. What, if any, preparations should be made for a strike?

MCDONALD CONTAINERS LTD. (F)

SIXTH SESSION

On Tuesday, September 7, the bargaining resumed. Sheehan informed Armstrong that formal application had been made to the Ontario Labour Relations Board for conciliation. Mr. Noel Ramsey, Vice President, attended the session all day.

Daniel Burgess gave the union a list of the tentative nonmonetary agreements reached so far. Sheehan stated he was still not fully in accord with the changes in method of overtime allocation. He informed the company that another IPPU local had a workable arrangement which might resolve the difficulty and promised to distribute a copy of this agreement later in the day. Otherwise, he said the union felt the language changes were acceptable.

Some additional items concerning wage adjustments were discussed. Most were detailed, but minor, changes. Some tentative agreements were reached.

A representative from another life insurance company joined the meeting to answer some additional questions concerning pensions.

SHEEHAN (*u*): What would it cost to provide the present pension benefits to employees not presently enrolled in the plan?

RUSSELL (*insurance co*): It would cost the company an additional $7,200 per year.

BURGESS (*co*): This, combined with the present cost of roughly $15,600, would make the total company contribution $22,800. This is 5.5 cents per hour.

SHEEHAN (*u*): Are the costs different between deposit administration and guaranteed annuity types?

RUSSELL (*insurance co*) Both cost the same amount.

ARMSTRONG (*co*): Remember, we won't negotiate benefits, just cost, George, and it will come off the wage settlement.

SHEEHAN (*u*): Well, we agree that the company must know what any plan will cost and that it should be fixed. We also know it will be part of the economic package and consequently would affect the wage increase. I think we should hold this matter.

Mr. Russell was excused at this point.

SHEEHAN (*u*): Clive, this guy is just selling life insurance. I recommend getting a third party, a consultant, in to advise us on the best way to spend our money.

ARMSTRONG (*co*): It is probably the best thing to do if we want to change the pension plan, but I'm not paying for a consultant.

That afternoon Armstrong reviewed the position of the St. Catharines plant in terms of industry wage rates and Niagara Peninsula area industrial wage rates.

ARMSTRONG (*co*): Our division's wage rates are substantially higher than our major competitors' in Toronto, even considering the fact that the major competitors have recently concluded union negotiations. We are below the Niagara area rates, but we can't compete effectively if we try to meet those rates. Mr. Ramsey, the Vice President of Packaging, can give a more detailed picture of our competitive position.

RAMSEY (*co*): This division is experiencing severe competition in all sales areas. General sales lost so far this year, compared to last year, amount to approximately $900,000. This represents 18,000 hours of lost machine activity. Specialty rates are experiencing severe competition. American imports threaten the future growth of three of our most important product lines.

SHEEHAN (u): The union recognizes the problems the company is experiencing. However, your employees have a problem of their own, and they have their own responsibilities to meet. We expect a fair and reasonable settlement based on other settlements in the community. If this results in lost business and layoffs of employees, it cannot be helped.

Discussion continued. Ramsey emphasized his figures with charts. The union bargaining committee sat quietly. Sheehan was more formal than usual, apparently out of respect for the presence of the Vice President.

As the meeting ended one of the union bargaining committee members was overheard by Armstrong as he said to a colleague: "Well, it was the same old record over again. More crying."

Armstrong drove Ramsey home and dropped in for awhile to discuss the day's bargaining.

ARMSTRONG: Well, I guess that's it until conciliation. No meeting is set. I'm fed up with having to remind them there's more business to get cleared up — we still have a lot of wage adjustments to talk about.

RAMSEY: Sheehan is a bright negotiator, seems to have the committee in control.

ARMSTRONG: Right, but he was formal today — trying to impress everyone.

RAMSEY: Relations still seem to be good, no threats and flares of temper.

(*Phone rings.*)

RAMSEY: For you Clive — it's Fred Lundberg (*Personnel Manager*).

ARMSTRONG: Hi, Fred. What's up?

LUNDBERG: Listen Clive, Walt Stevens grabbed me after the meeting. They want to meet again. They said next Tuesday the 14th, to clear outstanding nonmonetary things.

ARMSTRONG: I guess they need time to do their homework. Thanks.

Clive Armstrong left shortly thereafter. The next day he reviewed what had transpired over the past day or two and began to plan for the next week:

I guess we didn't really accomplish much out of the wage discussions — they think we're crying wolf. The quarterly report is coming out next month showing a profit decline — maybe it will emphasize our problems.

I still want to get Sheehan to put something on the table — a real wage demand. So far he's trying to get us to agree to some side issues which involve money and then build on top of it. We can't fall into that trap.

We will have to outwait Sheehan. If we put some offer out before conciliation, that will be where we start to negotiate from. It is best to hold off — let Sheehan make a ridiculously high demand and then reply really low.

When it comes to fringes, we will have to watch not to give them their pick. Better fringes, especially vacations and holidays, will have to be applied elsewhere in the plant and may spread to other plants if we give them here. We can't go too much out of line.

Next week we'll have to meet with our own bargaining committee about the wage adjustments to decide where we stand. I can't try to defend something that just isn't defensible, as we did with some of the foremen's ideas.

*   *   *

On Monday, September 13, the day before the contract officially expired, Clive Armstrong received a copy of a request for conciliation filed by Sheehan on the 10th. A copy had been sent to him by Sheehan, but there was not yet an official notification from the Labour Department. Armstrong wondered whether the union had, in fact, made application.

In the afternoon, Armstrong met with the company's executive committee to relate negotiation progress. He informed the committee of data from recent newspaper clippings indicating the union had demanded increases of from 7.6 to 9.6 per cent in wages. He expressed the belief that the union would settle for about nine per cent, and he encouraged intensification of the study of available capacity in the case of a strike.

In the meeting the executives arrived at a general set of goals — to settle between seven and nine per cent total package. While Armstrong would try for a lower settlement he knew he might have to accept something higher. The executives had not set an upper limit.

Armstrong reflected on what might happen, although he knew it would be close to a month before a legal strike could be held:

I'm not really pleased at the prospect of settling high. The company might be willing to take a short term loss of profits in order to secure its competitive position in the long term. Yet we can't continue settling higher than our competitors indefinitely.

It's hard to tell at what point Sheehan would go on strike. He would have to know we were serious. He'll test us in case we're bluffing. If we threaten him we will have to be willing to carry it through. If Sheehan knows we mean it, he might go to the membership and sell our best offer. But we have to be willing to risk it.

That afternoon Armstrong was walking toward his office and met Michael Newman, a member of the bargaining committee. Both men stopped and said hello and talked briefly about the negotiations.

> ARMSTRONG (co): These wage negotiations are quite confusing, with no one laying their cards on the table.
> NEWMAN (u): Right.
> ARMSTRONG (co): What would you do if you were me, Mike?
> NEWMAN (u): I don't know. You know Sheehan hasn't even told us what he thinks the wages should be.
> ARMSTRONG (co): Well, how the hell is the company supposed to negotiate with you?

*   *   *

ITEMS FOR DISCUSSION

1. What is the significance of the union's apparent application for conciliation?
2. In apparently agreeing to discuss pension costs, has management strayed from its previously hard line regarding discussion of monetary items?
3. Comment on Ramsey's presence and presentation of financial information.
4. Is there significance to Armstrong's conversation with Newman?
5. What's the significance of the union's desire to meet on September 14?

McDONALD CONTAINERS LTD. (G)

FINAL MEETING BEFORE CONCILIATION

The next day, September 14, the company received official notice that the union had applied for conciliation. The contract's expiration date was midnight, but the law required that it continue in force until exhaustion of conciliation procedures. Similarly a legal strike could not take place until conciliation procedures had been completed.

The union began the meeting by agreeing to the company proposal concerning allocation of vacations.

Then, they thrashed out the question of how to allocate overtime. George Sheehan put forth a compromise plan used by another firm: this, in spite of the fact that the union had tentatively agreed to the company proposal on overtime at the first meeting. The compromise would have required assignment and sharing among workers normally doing the work on the shift.

ARMSTRONG (*co*): I don't disagree with the arrangement you propose, George. But, it is going to take some time to get it implemented. We'll have to explain it to the foremen and make sure it is understood. It will probably be easier just to solve it as we proposed.

SHEEHAN (*u*): Well, I disagree. Once you get it in, it will solve the overtime question once and for all.

ARMSTRONG (*co*): Okay, it's agreed as long as we add the one stipulation we mentioned.

CHELEKIAN (*u*): What about how I got cut out of overtime a few years ago....

The discussion on overtime continued between Sheehan and Armstrong. Chelekian continued talking about a personal problem which had happened years ago. Ralph Reed made a sarcastic remark. Laughter broke out on both sides of the table until Chelekian flushed. He lost his temper and, for some reason, chose Dan Burgess as a target for venting his emotion.

CHELEKIAN (*u*): Okay Burgess, I'll get you. You're going to have grievances coming out your ears.

STEVENS (*u*). Shut up Harry!

CHELEKIAN (*u*): You too Stevens; I'll deal with you at lunch.

A pause of stifled snickering and pursed lips lasted momentarily. Although such asides had been frequent regarding Chelekian, they had not reached such a peak of emotion before.

SHEEHAN (*u*): It's agreed then. I'd like to move on to other areas on which we can agree.

Both sides made further comments on other items which had not been settled.

SHEEHAN (*u*): We can't agree to delete the word "willing" regarding changing jobs because of layoff.

ARMSTRONG (*co*): If it's left in, the man cannot get unemployment insurance.

SHEEHAN (*u*): That doesn't matter — he should get it whether he is willing or not willing to take a poorer job when he's laid off. It's his choice. The unemployment people should only be concerned whether the man is working.

ARMSTRONG (*co*): That's not how it works in reality.

SHEEHAN (*u*): It doesn't matter. We don't want it out of the contract. It would mean a man would have to take a lower classification job instead of taking a layoff.

ARMSTRONG (co): We have to tell the unemployment people he was unwilling to do so if it's still in the contract. It's to your advantage to take it out George.

No agreement was reached on this issue. The parties then agreed to some minor wage adjustments and language changes. Then the question of wage parity was brought up.

SHEEHAN (u): I have been mandated by my female constituents to reach wage and benefit parity between men and women. Thus the female rates have to be raised to the equivalent male rates. The Employment Standards Act says that all jobs of equivalent value have to be paid the same rate.

ARMSTRONG (co): That's not true — we have the Act right here. It states that the criteria for establishing equal pay for equal work depends upon equal skills, effort and responsibility. Not many female jobs are equal to the male jobs here.

SHEEHAN (u): It doesn't matter about the exact wording — I have a mandate. It's not a bargainable issue. We must have it.

ARMSTRONG (co): To do this would cost about $50,000, or 12 cents an hour. I hope the men will understand that the women will get all the wage increases this year.

SHEEHAN (u): That's a consideration, but you have to do it anyway. The government will make you do it. It's not really a cost of this settlement.

ARMSTRONG (co): Well, I've told you before — get the Department of Labour in here to look at the jobs. We won't have to raise them as you claim.

SHEEHAN (u): I don't want to get the government in. We don't want to get involved in legal process, Clive. We can work this out together.

ARMSTRONG (co): It costs too much. The company can't afford it.

RAMSEY (co): It will mean more lost sales, less work and layoffs.

SHEEHAN (u): The union is prepared to have the cost spread over the length of the contract. We want this. It is a policy of the International to eliminate wage differentials between male and female jobs. If this results in lost business and lost jobs it is of no concern of the union.

The bargainers then turned to the question of married women's benefits.

SHEEHAN (u): We've been over this one before. It is another mandate issue.

ALICE MELVIN (u): It's unfair that I should not get married benefits the same as a man.

ARMSTRONG (co): It costs too much.

SHEEHAN (u): How much?

BURGESS (co): This demand to increase welfare coverage from single to married for married females would be $10,000.

SHEEHAN (u): Those figures are wrong.

After some discussion the union conceded that Daniel Burgess's figures were correct.

A lunch break was held. Just as the company team left the room, Harry Chelekian accosted Walter Stevens. Their voices rose to shouts in the first outward display of temper among members of the union team.

In the afternoon, Clive Armstrong tried to get a more definite idea of the union's wage demands. For the first time, the voices of the bargainers on both sides were edged with tension and excitement.

> ARMSTRONG (co): Why can't you tell me what you want? Is it a big dark secret?
> SHEEHAN (u): Why should I tell you?
> ARMSTRONG (co): How can we cost anything?

At this point, Clive Armstrong, his eyes alive, directed most of his remarks to the union bargaining committee, particularly Michael Newman, and not to the chief negotiator, George Sheehan.

> ARMSTRONG (co): I've got the Vice President here — he has a right to know. How can we do our costing — how can we negotiate with you unless we know your demands?
> SHEEHAN (u): Okay. Would it make you happy if I said 90 cents over two years?
> ARMSTRONG (co): Yes. It's better than a buck.
> SHEEHAN (u) (*pulling out a publication from his notes and plopping it on the table*): This is a recent publication from the Economics and Research Branch of the Canadian Department of Labour. This states that for the first quarter of the year there was an 8.1 per cent change in negotiated base rates. Does that give you an idea?
> ARMSTRONG (co): Is that your demand?
> SHEEHAN (u): We aren't committed to anything — this figure represents federal increases, not area or provincial ones, which, as you know, are higher.
> ARMSTRONG (co): Like 9.6 per cent or thereabouts?

The negotiations turned back to the female parity questions for the rest of the afternoon. As the negotiating session ended George Sheehan made a closing comment:

> SHEEHAN (u): As you know we have applied for conciliation. The next meeting will be held with the officer. Our approach at conciliation will be not to tell the conciliation officer anything and to encourage him to hand down a no-board report so that we can enter serious negotiations afterwards. We will reach a satisfactory settlement on our own.

REFLECTIONS

Armstrong considered the September 14 meeting:

I am quite pleased with the nonmonetary agreements. The overtime settlement is really good. It's more than we wanted. It's good because it specifically outlines a method of allocating the overtime. The only agreement which may require some ironing out is the vacation scheme. But even that is okay.

It would have been better if we could take "willing" out of the contract, but that's really to their advantage. I can't see why Sheehan disagreed with it. Originally, *he* asked *me* to take it out.

The parity issue is becoming tough. However, I think Sheehan is bluffing about its importance. He just wants to be a champion to the International, because it is one of their policies. We can't afford it, and the men won't accept all the wages going to the women. Furthermore, Sheehan wouldn't have a leg to stand on if he did call the Labour Department in. I'm told there is a great deal of difference in almost all the jobs. I'm going to go into the plant in the next few days and do some of these jobs myself. I'll get a better idea of the differences, and maybe I'll stir something up.

I was pleased that I got a more concrete wage demand out of Sheehan. I don't think he planned to put anything on the table at all. That chance meeting with Newman must have riled the committee up. They probably put some pressure on Sheehan to show himself. I'm sure he showed his hand before he wanted to.

As far as that conciliation speech, I think he's joking. We'll settle it at conciliation.

The next day, September 15, the contract had expired. Nevertheless, its terms would be kept in force until there was either agreement on a new contract or a strike. On the 15th, Armstrong went into the plant and performed some of the female and male jobs in question. He became more certain of the company's position on this issue because of it. He was also intrigued by the reaction of the workers.

FEMALE WORKER: Why are you doing this, Mr. Armstrong — you're not going to put men on our jobs are you?

ARMSTRONG: No, I just want to see what the work is like after all the years I've been around here.

At a male work station, a worker asked a similar question: "You aren't going to put a girl on this job? You know they just couldn't handle it!"

UNION MEMBERSHIP MEETING

On Sunday, September 19, the union membership met. Attendance was good. First, George Sheehan discussed the progress of negotiations and described some of the demands. He stated that while he felt the pension plan presently covering the employees was not adequate, an improvement in the plan would be extremely costly. There was no apparent reaction to this from the rank and file.

However, when Sheehan commented on the female wage parity issue, there was an uproar. Many men protested that the demands would help only women and take money out of the men's pockets. The argument continued for some time.

A strike vote was taken. It was passed by a huge majority. Then the membership voted in a new executive.

Alice Melvin, the female member of the bargaining committee, was elected president. The other members were newcomers. None of the old guard (not even Walter Stevens) were elected.

Clive Armstrong heard about the meeting through the grapevine. Some workers had come to him to complain about the parity issue, claiming they weren't in favor of it. Armstrong discovered that Alice Melvin had made remarks to employees at the meeting that she was not in favor of pushing the wage parity issue. Armstrong felt this reflected the females' fear that they would have to do male jobs if equal wages were paid. He thought his visit to the plant had had its effect.

QUARTERLY REPORT

The company's quarterly report was normally published on October 15 and sent to all employees. However, on Monday, September 20, there was an article in the *St. Catharines Times* speculating on the company's expected performance and reporting parts of an interview with McDonald's President. The President said there had been a dip in profits to $522,000 in the first two quarters of the year and that in the same period last year profits were $572,000. However, he indicated that the third quarter of the current year would be somewhat improved over last year and that the full year would be only slightly below last year, barring unforeseen events.

Armstrong, on seeing the article, said: "This makes us look a little silly. Ramsey and I have been telling them of our terrible situation, and now the President says we're looking pretty good."

ARMSTRONG RE-EVALUATES HIS SITUATION

Armstrong was still concerned about the effect of the President's statement:

> The whole thing is timing. When we start sawing off around six per cent, it is going to matter who can wait it out longest. It will be tense, and I decided that I need a definite outside limit from the executive. As a result, we've beefed up the study we are doing. Only head office personnel are doing it. They are now figuring out if we can get competitors to supply some of our customers in case of a strike as well as using the extra capacity at our other plants. We are also finding out our fixed costs if there is a strike.
>
> We should have this information for the executive meeting the 24th of September. We've decided to consider the possibility of having to take a strike. This may not be the year to get tough, but at least we're considering all the options. I'd like to set a total package limit of 10 per cent a year.
>
> We aren't going to make any of our moves obvious. We don't want to threaten the union — we may end up with a walkout. We just want to be prepared.
>
> As chief negotiator, I feel much better about these negotiations with the union. My boss is trying to give me all the leverage he can. At the final meeting, I expect both the V.P.s (Kickhoeffer and Ramsey) will be there to show they're behind me all the way.
>
> As far as the conciliation meeting is concerned, it's a little early to tell. I doubt if I'll make an offer for a while. Hopefully, Sheehan will zero in on demands first. However, I expect us to settle it with the conciliator. It may take a couple of meetings.
>
> I'm not afraid of having a settlement overthrown by the membership unless we gave too little in wages to the men by agreeing to female parity. I doubt if this would happen. Sheehan must be concerned about the whole question. He must be feeling some pressure after that membership meeting.

*   *   *

ITEMS FOR DISCUSSION

1. Comment on Sheehan's apparent change in tactics.
   a) His desire to retain the present wording regarding a laid-off employee's "willingness" to do a job.
   b) His apparently premature statement regarding an economic package.
2. Comment on Armstrong's handling of the male/female parity issue. Sheehan claims this is not bargainable. What position would you take?

3. Do you share Armstrong's concern regarding the effect of the president's remarks?

4. What are prospects for settlement without a strike?

5. How do you account for the apparent difference in stated opinions regarding the conciliation process? Sheehan said he would be using it to set a deadline so that the parties could start bargaining. Armstrong said he expected to secure a settlement during conciliation.

6. Comment on the pros and cons of the Ontario law which requires that a contract must stay in force even after expiration unless parties have submitted to conciliation.

McDONALD CONTAINERS LTD. (H)

GOAL SETTING AND PREPARATION FOR CONCILIATION

On September 20 the Ontario Labour Relations Board notified the company and union that Mr. John Crowley had been designated as conciliator and would meet with the parties on Wednesday, September 29, in accordance with Section 13 of the Labour Relations Act.

The Act required the conciliator to endeavor to effect a collective agreement and, within 14 days of his appointment, report the results to the Minister of Labour (section 15). The 14-day period could be extended by agreement of the parties or by the Minister on advice of the conciliation officer that an agreement might be made within a reasonable time. If the conciliation officer was unable to effect a settlement he was required to report this fact to the Minister who then could take either of two steps: initiate procedures for formulation of a three-man conciliation board or notify the parties that he did not deem it advisable to appoint a board (section 16).

In recent years instances where conciliation boards were appointed under section 16 of the Act were rare. Neither the company nor the union expected a board to be created in the McDonald case, so that failure to settle under auspices of the conciliator would most likely result in the establishment of a strike deadline. According to the Act a legal strike or lockout could commence 14 days after the Minister released a notice to the parties that he did not deem it advisable to appoint a conciliation board [section 54(2) (b)].

[Section 54(2)(b) provided a 7-day period before which a legal strike or lockout could commence following the report of a conciliation board.]

Clive Armstrong had experienced conciliation with Mr. John Crowley in connection with earlier negotiations at another plant. The experience was not good. Consequently Armstrong expected no settlement as a result of the conciliation meeting and prepared himself and his bargaining committee for continuing negotiations after conciliation under the scepter of a strike deadline.

COMPANY EXECUTIVE MEETING

On Wednesday, September 22, the top executives of McDonald Containers met to consider a then-secret study which had been prepared by staff personnel at the head office. The study substantiated an already existing feeling that the company could not withstand a strike of more than one month. Other McDonald plants were operating at near capacity, and they were considered a poor source of alternate service to the St. Catharines plant customers. Competitors would willingly take up the slack, but the risk of losing customers to those competitors in such a case was considered high. Thus the division made tentative arrangements (unknown to operating personnel in St. Catharines) that in the event of a strike some key customers would be served by competitors who were located outside the St. Catharines market area. The added cost in freight charges would hopefully make the alternate suppliers unattractive for any long-term relationship but acceptable for a month or so. Even with these elaborate arrangements management feared that a strike of more than a month would result in a significant loss of business.

In the event of a strike it would be necessary to lay off workers who were not members of IPPU. The company decided that welfare and insurance premiums would be continued for those employees. All these plans were made with utmost secrecy. Furthermore, no one in the company wanted or expected a strike. However, there were limits beyond which they were not willing to go. These were set tentatively at 10 per cent per year in wages and fringes. If it became obvious that the union would hold firm for a settlement exceeding 10 per cent the company would "pull the plug" and activate strike plans.

CLIVE ARMSTRONG'S THOUGHTS

The rumor mill indicated to Armstrong that union membership was not willing to go on strike. However, originators of these rumors were considered apple polishers; so Armstrong greeted the information with skepticism. He did feel that membership interest in the negotiations was meager — that Alice Melvin's election as union president was a sign of apathy. Melvin had been the only serious candidate. Old-guard leaders had dropped from the scene, and younger people had not come to the fore to replace them. This apathy had been demonstrated a few days earlier when Walter Stevens, a member of the old guard and former union Vice President, contacted Daniel Burgess regarding a matter of contract administration. Stevens had no authority to do this, but the matter was pressing, and no one else took the reins.

PLANS FOR CONCILIATION MEETING

Armstrong hoped to get a signed contract during the conciliation meetings. But he was apprehensive about the reaction of Sheehan to Crowley. During the negotiations of four years ago a weak conciliator had been assigned. Sheehan promptly contacted the head of the conciliation service and arranged for a replacement — William Tunney. Tunney was able to win the confidence of both sides, and a settlement was reached in a single meeting.

Armstrong did not expect Sheehan to call for another conciliator this time. Rather, he expected that Sheehan would make a momentary appearance in order to establish a strike deadline; then he would negotiate. If Sheehan followed this tactic Armstrong would make a token economic offer. Following this, Armstrong would look for a counterdemand. If there was no counterdemand Armstrong would refuse to negotiate further and let the deadline move nearer, thus putting pressure on the union.

Armstrong believed Sheehan wanted a wage settlement between 8.1 and 9.6 per cent. If the fringe demand was fairly low the prospects for a less-than-10-per-cent settlement seemed good.

Armstrong believed that the company would gain most by waiting, and he hoped for settlement terms of less than 10 per cent. He believed there was some chance that Sheehan would try to bargain privately — outside the presence of his bargaining committee. Armstrong would resist this, believing the waiting game would have the greatest impact if members of the shop committee felt responsible themselves for the consequences. Sheehan could maintain strength while waiting; shop committee members might not be able to.

AGREEMENT ON NONMONETARY ITEMS

On September 24 at 2 P.M. a meeting took place for the purpose of affixing signatures to nonmonetary agreements reached so far. Members of both bargaining committees were present. This supposedly left only the money items to be discussed.

*   *   *

ITEMS FOR DISCUSSION

1. Comment on the conciliation procedure under the Act. As a negotiator how would this procedure influence your actions?
2. Comment on Armstrong's strategy. Under what conditions is a deadline useful in securing a settlement?
3. Comment on the company's strategy in planning for a possible strike. As a company negotiator would you feel better or worse knowing that contingency strike plans had been made?
4. Comment on the strategy of setting upper limits in advance on economic settlement terms. Do these unnecessarily hamper the negotiating team?

McDONALD CONTAINERS LTD. (I)

CONCILIATION, MEMORANDUM OF AGREEMENT AND RATIFICATION

Mr. John Crowley was appointed by the Ontario Labour Relations Board to meet with the parties as conciliator and attempt to effect a settlement. Crowley reserved a meeting room at St. Catharines' Thunderbird Inn and asked the parties to assemble at 10:30 A.M. on Wednesday, September 29.

The union and company bargaining teams arrived at the appointed hour. Mr. Crowley appeared approximately 45 minutes later, having called before to tell the parties that he'd been in an automobile accident. When he arrived he indicated that he did not want the parties to meet together. So the company team departed to a room in the inn which they had reserved for themselves. Crowley then met with the union alone. This meeting lasted until shortly before noon.

At around noon Crowley met with the company. He said he wanted to find out what their attitude was: whether they were there to get a settlement or not. Clive Armstrong stated the position taken by Sheehan earlier — that the reason he was going to conciliation was to set a deadline and get both sides negotiating. Armstrong then said: "If Mr. Sheehan has come to make an agreement, then we've come to make an agreement, but it's imperative that you find out from him what he did come here for."

CROWLEY (*conciliator*): Now look. Sheehan said you hadn't come up with any offer.

ARMSTRONG (*co*): That's right!

CROWLEY (*conciliator*): Are you prepared to?

ARMSTRONG (*co*): If you can determine whether Sheehan is here to make a deal or just go through these formalities then we'll know where we stand.

Crowley said he would go back to Sheehan. The company negotiators then went to the dining room for lunch.

After lunch the conciliator came back to the company negotiators and said that the union representatives were there to make a settlement if possible.

ARMSTRONG (*co*): All right, give us some time and we'll make up a proposal.

Crowley had a list of items given to him by Sheehan which he said were still outstanding, and he gave this to Armstrong. There were 23, including all previous monetary demands and five nonmonetary demands, the most important of which were:

1. Probationary employees shall have the right to grieve.
2. The union will have the right to grieve anything.

(Sheehan had indicated earlier the kind of things he had in mind here. One such grievance might involve the company's right to discontinue an operation.)

About one hour later, at approximately 3 P.M., the company presented Crowley with a revised proposal on money items. The company offered to pay 100 per cent of Ontario Hospital Services premiums. This was estimated to cost about $5,000, or 1.2 cents per hour. However, the company wanted to confine premium obligations for Ontario Hospital and Ontario Health Insurance coverages to the existing maxima, so that in the event of premium increases there would be no automatic requirement to pay the added amount. The company offered to replace the major medical plan with an improved plan under which the employee would pay the first $25 plus 10 per cent of the remaining costs. The existing plan provided for single employees to pay the first $25 and those with families to pay the first $75. In addition, the existing plan required the employees to pay 20 per cent of added costs. This change would cost about one quarter of a cent per hour.

Wages were tied in with increased vacation benefits and increased life insurance coverage as part of a two-year package. In the first year there would be an 11-cents-per-hour wage increase. In the second year there would be nine cents coupled with four weeks vacation for those with 19 years seniority (the existing contract called for four weeks after

20 years) and an offer to increase life insurance by $1000 for all people. The vacation and life insurance improvements were estimated to cost about 5 cents.

The conciliator took the company offer away with him and returned at 5:20 P.M. with a union counteroffer. The union offered to withdraw all nonmonetary items. Regarding monetary items they wanted the following:

1. *Wages (per hour increases)*

Effective Date	Males	Females
Date of contract signing	35¢	45¢
6 months later	10¢	15¢
One year later	35¢	45¢
18 months later	10¢	15¢

2. *Individual wage adjustments* ranging from eight to 22 cents in four job classifications.

3. *Improved vacations* as follows:

Year 1		Year 2	
Weeks	Seniority (years)	Weeks	Seniority
3	6	3	5
4	17	4	15
5	22	5	21

The union had withdrawn their earlier request for a $25 vacation bonus. The existing contract called for the following vacation schedule:

Years service	Weeks vacation
1	1
2	2
8	3
20	4
25	5

4. *Holidays* — one additional holiday to be taken at employee's discretion.

5. *Premium for power house employees* — $1 per hour for Sunday work. This was a reduction from the union's earlier demand for Sunday overtime rates for power house employees.

6. *Insurance premium reduction* — the union asked for a letter of intent indicating that any future reduction in Ontario Hospital or Health premiums would be paid to the employee as part of added wages.

7. *Life insurance coverage* — one and a half times the annual wage. The existing plan called for life insurance coverage of $1000 for all females

and between $1000 and $5000 for all male employees, the latter based on a graduated scale related to earnings.

8. *Drug costs* — complete coverage for drug costs after initial deductible amounts of $10 under single coverage and $20 under family coverage.

9. *Increased weekly indemnity* — sickness and accident benefits ($50 to $90 per week on a scale in accordance with wages) increased from 26 weeks to 52 weeks.

10. *Breadwinner clause* — family coverage for hospital and health insurance to married women on the same basis as for married men.

11. *Pensions* — monthly benefits equivalent to one per cent of the average yearly earnings for the best five years of an employee's service, employees to contribute 50 per cent of the cost.

The pension demand, estimated by the union to cost $30,000, caught company negotiators by surprise. Armstrong knew the estimated cost was low, because he had done some earlier figuring in anticipation of a demand for a noncontributory plan. At the time he discovered that contributory plans were more expensive than noncontributory plans, because they allowed for payment to those who separated from the plan before receiving benefits. Armstrong subsequently met with Sheehan and pointed this out. Sheehan said: "Yes, I know. I wanted to see if you were still awake!" This remark confirmed Armstrong's earlier belief that Sheehan was trying to give him a message: that he realized pensions were expensive and that union members were not going to pay for improved benefits. Consequently he believed the issue was merely window dressing.

Company's Counteroffer

Early that evening the company prepared a counteroffer and gave it to Mr. Crowley for conveyance to the union negotiators. It contained the following concessions:

1. *Vacations* — four weeks vacation after 18 years seniority, effective in the second year of the contract.

2. *Welfare* — 100 per cent payment for coverage under the Ontario Hospital Services Plan, with provision that premiums per month be spelled out, thereby averting the obligation to pay for increased premiums. The counteroffer did not include a limit on premiums for Ontario Health Services. So, by inference, this proviso was dropped.

3. *Individual adjustments* — the company agreed to increase the wage rate of the diemaker lead hand by four cents, letting it be known that this was done to accommodate one of the members of the bargaining committee, Michael Newman, a diemaker lead hand who, according to

Armstrong, was "obviously bargaining for himself." Armstrong told the conciliator that he believed the men who really deserved an increase were the diemakers, and if the negotiators were doing their job properly they would have requested an increase for them, not for themselves. Armstrong asked the conciliator to convey this information to Sheehan.

4. *Wages* — increases to be paid at six-month intervals, effective on ratification.

	Males	Females
Year 1		
effective on ratification	9¢	14¢
six months later	6¢	6¢
Year 2		
one year after ratification	7¢	12¢
six months later	5¢	5¢

No further offer was made on other union demands. Regarding pension, Armstrong was convinced that if the company waited long enough the demand would be dropped, because any form of increase would cut so deeply into wages that it would be distasteful.

Conciliator Calls Armstrong and Sheehan Together

At about 8 P.M. John Crowley, the conciliator, asked the two principal bargainers to meet in Crowley's room. When Armstrong arrived he found Sheehan lying on one of the beds, looking sick. Sheehan said: "Clive, what'll we do? We're not getting any place!" Sheehan said he was having trouble with his own committee — that they needed to have at least 60 cents in wages over the two-year contract period. Sheehan said he believed the company was prepared to go as high as 70 cents. Armstrong said 70 cents was too much.

> SHEEHAN (u): Let's get down to brass tacks here. What do these things cost you? For example, one of the places we're really far apart on is vacations. The cost of vacations is important; what would it be?
> ARMSTRONG (co): Off the top of my head, I don't know.
> SHEEHAN (u): What about the cost of female adjustments? We've got to bring these female rates up. We're behind the community.

Sheehan conceded that pensions were too expensive but indicated the issue was still alive. Armstrong suggested consideration of a pension plan similar to the type adopted by the automobile industry — a certain benefit amount per month. The two men then considered the cost of such a plan and agreed that 12 cents per hour would buy benefits amounting to approximately six dollars per month. With that Sheehan seemed to lose interest.

Armstrong then agreed to calculate costs on the items still outstanding. He said it would take a couple of hours.

11 P.M.

At 11 P.M. Armstrong returned to the conciliator's room with estimated costs for each of the union demands. Costs were stated in cents-per-hour equivalents. Excluding the demand for pensions, the total calculated costs were estimated by the company at 39.6 cents for the first year and 39.2 cents for the second year — a total of 78.8 cents. Sheehan looked over the figures and attacked those ascribed to vacations, calculated by the company as 4.4 cents in the first year ($19,972 total) and 4.0 cents additional in the second year ($16,133). Sheehan said: "You don't replace men on vacation!" Armstrong explained that the company hired between 40 and 60 students each summer for this purpose; that he was not prepared to back off one nickel. He conceded that his figure was a maximum but indicated the parties could stay for three weeks trying to arrive at the correct figure. Sheehan then attacked the company's figure for the "breadwinner" clause, stating that all women would not take advantage of it. This had been calculated at two cents per hour ($8000).

ARMSTRONG (co): What should (the figure) be?
SHEEHAN (u): We were just going through a list of all the women we have now, and it's not nearly that high.
ARMSTRONG (co): Do you guarantee that they're going to be here for two years? All of them? The same people? The same status? None of them are going to get married?

At this point Sheehan looked sicker than before.

ARMSTRONG (co): Are you all right?
SHEEHAN (u): I'm just tired.
ARMSTRONG (co): The total figure is 78.8 cents, without pensions.
SHEEHAN (u): Is that out of the ball park?

Armstrong, then feeling strong, resorted to some propaganda, saying: "If you stick to this position, you'll find the company acting different than before."

SHEEHAN (u): What are you planning to do out there? Are you planning to close the place down?
ARMSTRONG (co): No, we're not planning to, George, but we're not prepared to take a shellacking from you people every year, either!

According to Armstrong the statement seemed to sink in — "the first time in all of these years!"

SHEEHAN (u): I want to go back and talk to my committee.

The conciliator, meanwhile, was exhibiting impatience — saying he had to get to Toronto for a meeting the next day. Sheehan, obviously irritated, said: "John, a poor excuse is better than none at all."

As Armstrong and Sheehan left the conciliator's room Sheehan confided even more irritation with the conciliator, calling him a "damned liar" and saying that he didn't believe Crowley had an appointment the next day or that he'd had an automobile accident earlier in this day.

12:05 A.M.

Sheehan and Armstrong met again in the conciliator's room. At this point the three men agreed that all bargaining was unofficial — that the official last offer would be made at the bargaining table.

SHEEHAN (u): How would you look at this, Clive?

And he put forth the following proposal:

Wages	Males	Females
Date of contract signing	20 cents	23 cents
6 months later	10 cents	13 cents
One year later	15 cents	18 cents
18 months later	15 cents	18 cents

Vacations

	Year 1			Year 2
Weeks	Seniority/yrs		Weeks	Seniority/yrs
3	7		3	6
4	18		4	17
5	23		5	22

Welfare
- [ ] An extended health care plan,
- [ ] 100 per cent paid by company, no limit on premium, with $10 (single) and $20 (family) deductible features,
- [ ] semiprivate hospital benefits.

Life insurance
Increases of $1000 per person

Sheehan indicated the union still wanted the breadwinner clause but that pension demands had been dropped.

Crowley, the conciliator, then attempted to explain to Armstrong how the company could afford the proposed package. He said, "Your average rate is $3.67 an hour. You've already established that your limit is 10 per cent a year. That's 37 cents in the first year. If you add 37 cents to $3.67 you get $4.04. So next year you can afford 40 cents. So we're talking over two years about an increase of 77 cents."

ARMSTRONG (*co*): Thanks for your advice.

CROWLEY (*conciliator*): On top of that there won't be any increases in Ontario Hospital premiums anyway. I've got a line to the Premier on that.

ARMSTRONG (*co*): Mind your own business.

CROWLEY (*conciliator*): You're getting tired, Clive.

ARMSTRONG (*co*): I'm tired of your political philosophies, John.

Sheehan then jumped on Crowley as well, with additional invectives. Then the two men looked at each other with smiles and Armstrong said, "I'll take this away and do some costing. It looks like we're moving in the right direction."

CROWLEY (*conciliator*): I'm not going to stay much longer. You'll have to work this out yourselves or have another meeting.

SHEEHAN (*to Crowley*): Listen, I've spent all day with that committee, and I've battered them into this thing. They're not going to get away now if I have to stay here all night — or all day tomorrow either. What do you think Clive?

ARMSTRONG (*co*): George, if I have stay here till Saturday, this is not going to slip through our hands at this point. (*It was early Thursday morning.*)

CROWLEY (*conciliator*): How 'bout next week?

SHEEHAN (*u*): The hell with next week! Right now!

Armstrong went back to his committee then and told them he believed settlement was near.

1:30 A.M.

At 1:30 Armstrong returned to the conciliator's room with what he considered his final, unofficial offer. He said to Sheehan: "This is as far as we can go, George. We've stretched all the pennies."

Armstrong agreed to the union proposal on wages. On vacations Armstrong said the best he could do was four weeks after 18 years in Year One of the contract and three weeks after seven years in Year Two. He agreed with the union proposals on welfare coverage and, regarding the breadwinner clause, Armstrong said:

We will pay married coverage for females as far as Ontario Health Services are concerned.

SHEEHAN (*u*): Bullshit! I want equal treatment for females. For you to throw that in at this time is bullshit!

Armstrong and Sheehan then left the room to go back to their committees. Outside, on the patio next to the swimming pool, Sheehan took his leave. Just then John Crowley came across the patio, briefcase in hand. It was obvious he was leaving.

CROWLEY (*conciliator*): Well, the only thing you're apart on now is the breadwinner clause. If you solve that you've got an agreement.
ARMSTRONG (*co*): Where are you going?
CROWLEY (*conciliator*): I'm going home.
ARMSTRONG (*co*): Well then, leave me some carbon paper and your forms.

Crowley reached into his briefcase and withdrew the official forms on which parties normally record their memorandum of agreement. He seemed to do this reluctantly. Then he left.

Armstrong noticed a shadow next to the pool. It was Sheehan's.

SHEEHAN (*to Armstrong*): You go ahead and write up the memorandum.
ARMSTRONG (*co*): What about this breadwinner's clause?
SHEEHAN (*u*): I have a principle to uphold.

Sheehan then complained bitterly about the conciliator. While Crowley had left the official memorandum forms, he had not signed them. The signature carried no official weight, but it could be important to Sheehan when the time came to try and sell the package to union members. Sheehan told Armstrong he was going to write to the Labour Minister to complain.

Armstrong then went back to his committee to have a last hard look at the costs. Then, at about 3 A.M., he went to Sheehan, and in the company of Walter Stevens of the union team, Armstrong wrote up the memorandum of agreement. The only change from the union's last proposal involved the following wording for a "breadwinner's" clause:

It is understood that female employees are not entitled to 100 per cent coverage where husband's employer is paying for comparable coverage.

So at 3:30 A.M. on Thursday, September 30, the parties had an agreement. On the following Monday, October 4, the union members ratified it by a vote of 124 to 4. Final costs were estimated by Clive Armstrong at 30 cents in the first year, equivalent to $125,000, an increase of slightly more than eight per cent. In the second year the added costs would be 24.2 cents, roughly $100,000. The average increase for each of the two years was estimated at 7.38 per cent.

ITEMS FOR DISCUSSION

1. Evaluate the role of the conciliator. Did he aid or hinder the agreement?

2. Trace the shifting balance of power between chief negotiators as the final bargaining sessions progressed.

3. Evaluate the tactics of the chief negotiators. How might they have been more effective?

4. Evaluate the terms of settlement.

NOTES TO CHAPTER 5

1. Fred Charles Ikle, *How Nations Negotiate* (New York: Harper & Row, 1964) p. 2.

2. Derek C. Bok and John T. Dunlop, *Labor and the American Community*, (New York: Simon and Schuster, 1970), p. 216.

3. Regina v. Harry W. Arthurs et al; *ex parte* Port Arthur Shipbuilding Co., 68 C.L.L.C. 14, 136 (S.C.C. 1968).

4. Sumner H. Slichter, James J. Healy and E. Robert Livernash, *The Impact of Collective Bargaining on Management* (Washington D.C.: The Brookings Institution, 1960), pp. 947-51.

5. Bok and Dunlop, op. cit., p. 208.

6. John T. Dunlop, "The Industrial Relations System in Construction" in *The Structure of Collective Bargaining*, Arnold R. Weber, ed. (New York: The Free Press of Glencoe, Inc., 1961), p. 274.

7. J. Tait Montague, *Labour Markets in Canada* (Scarborough, Ontario: Prentice-Hall of Canada, Ltd., 1970), p. 237.

8. Neil W. Chamberlain and James W. Kuhn, *Collective Bargaining* (2nd. ed. New York: McGraw-Hill Book Company, 1965), pp. 170-1.

9. Benjamin M. Selekman, Sylvia Kopald Selekman and Stephen H. Fuller, *Problems in Labor Relations* (2nd ed; New York: McGraw-Hill Book Company, Inc., 1958), p. 4.

10. J. Pen, "A General Theory of Bargaining," *American Economic Review*, March, 1952.

11. Carl M. Stevens, *Strategy and Collective Bargaining Negotiation* (New York: McGraw-Hill Book Company, Inc., 1963).

12. B.D. Mabry, "The Pure Theory of Bargaining," *Industrial and Labor Relations Review*, July, 1965.

13. J.G. Cross, "A Theory of the Bargaining Process," *American Economic Review*, March, 1965.

14. Richard E. Walton and Robert B. McKersie, *A Behavioral Theory of Labor Negotiations* (New York: McGraw-Hill, Inc., 1965).

15. Ibid., pp. 4-6.

16. John T. Dunlop and James J. Healy, *Collective Bargaining* (Homewood, Illinois: Richard D. Irwin, Inc., 1953), p. 56.

17. Ibid., pp. 62-3.

18. Thomas C. Schelling, *The Strategy of Conflict* (New York: Oxford University Press, 1963), p. 24.

19. Ikle, op. cit., pp. 59-60.

20. Dunlop and Healy, op. cit., p. 61.

21. *Collective Bargaining Review*, no. 12, December 1973 (Ottawa: Collective Bargaining Division, Economics and Research Branch, Canada Department of Labour), p. 66.

22. James L. Stern, "Collective Bargaining Trends and Patterns," *A Review of Industrial Relations Research, vol. II,* Industrial Relations Research Association Series (Madison, Wisconsin: Industrial Relations Research Association, 1971), p. 181.

23. For further details on Boulwarism see: Herbert R. Northrup, *Boulwarism* (Ann Arbor: Bureau of Industrial Relations, Graduate School of Business Administration University of Michigan, 1964) and Herbert R. Northrup "The Case for Boulwarism," *Harvard Business Review,* September-October 1963, pp. 86-97. For a criticism of Boulwarism see: Benjamin M. Selekman, "Cynicism and Managerial Morality," *Harvard Business Review,* September-October 1958, pp. 61-70.

24. For a detailed account of these efforts see: H.C. Jain, "The Recent Development end Emerging Trends in Labour-Management Relations in the U.S.A. and Canada," *Relations Industrielles,* Vol. 20, No. 3, and July 1965, pp. 252-3, James A. Henderson; Edward R. Hintz Jr.; Jerry U. Jarrett; Robert G. Barbut and William J. White, *Creative Collective Bargaining* James J. Healy, ed. (Englowood Cliffs, N.J.: Prentice-Hall, Inc., 1965), and M. Scott Myers, "Overcoming Union Opposition to Job Enrichment" *Harvard Business Review,* May-June 1971, pp. 37-49, and William Gomberg, "Special Study Committees", *Frontiers of Collective Bargaining,* John T. Dunlop & Neil W. Chamberlain, ed. (N.Y.: Harper & Row, 1967) and Thomas Kennedy, *Automation Funds and Displaced Workers* (Boston: Div. of Research. Harvard University, Graduate School of Business Administration, 1962).

25. Task Force on Labour Relations, *Canadian Industrial Relations* (Ottawa: Privy Council Office, 1968), pp. 137-8. Reproduced by permission of Information Canada.

26. See section 13 of the Labour Relations Act of Ontario, amended in 1970 by Chapter 85.

27. See the Women's Equal Employment Opportunity Act, 1970, Statutes of Ontario 1970, c. 33, proclaimed December 1, 1970.

6. MEDIATION

Mediation as known in the field of labor relations is the intervention of a third party into negotiations in order to help produce an agreement, thus helping to prevent, or end, a strike.

There is confusion regarding the meaning of the words mediation and conciliation. Conciliation is the term used in some jurisdictions to describe the early stages of mediation required as a precondition to a strike. Mediation describes the extralegal process by which parties may voluntarily secure third-party assistance, usually after a strike date has been set. Through the years the distinction between the words has become blurred. Objectives of conciliation and mediation are essentially the same. The same persons often serve as conciliators and mediators. Thus, for purposes here, the words mediation and conciliation are considered to be synonymous.

The greatest number of labor-management negotiations, by far, are settled by the parties themselves without any outside intervention in the form of mediation or conciliation. Full-time mediators are employed by the federal governments of the United States and Canada, plus all the states and provinces.[1] In addition there are men and women who serve as ad hoc mediators, sometimes at the request of parties and sometimes on appointment by government officials. These ad hoc mediators come from all walks of life: some are retired judges, others are lawyers, priests, university professors, political office holders.

Not many mediators are well known. This is because they usually work behind the scenes without publicity. If they are successful in helping parties get a settlement they rarely receive credit; more likely the mediator himself praises the parties for their hard work and dedication when settlement is reached, and then goes on to the next job, gaining his major satisfaction from the knowledge that he helped.

When negotiators are asked to name the mediators who they believe are most effective a few individuals stand out; David L. Cole, William Simkin and Theodore Kheel from the United States, and William Dickie and William Kelly from Canada are among them. Some mediators are generally acknowledged as ineffective, and negotiators have come to regard these men as impediments to settlement. Fortunately, not many fall into the latter category.

The process of mediation is initiated most often when a representative of labor or management contacts the Director of the Mediation and Conciliation Service having jurisdiction over the negotiations and asks for help. The Director then assigns a mediator to the parties. Most often assignments are made on a rotating basis in order to give the mediators a roughly equivalent work load. Sometimes they are assigned because they have expertise in the industry involved or with the issues in dispute. Less often they are assigned on the basis of the parties' request for a particular individual.

Following appointment the mediator normally contacts the parties and arranges for a meeting at a mutually convenient time and place, not too far in the future. In Canadian jurisdictions a strike countdown begins only after a first-stage mediator has delivered his report.[2] Thus first-stage mediation is not likely to be accompanied by much of sense of urgency. In later stages there is considerably more urgency, because there is greater likelihood that a strike is either imminent or in progress. Under United States law there is no provision for first-stage mediation, so that a sense of urgency is more likely to accompany mediation in the United States.

Some mediators enter their first meeting with no advance preparation. Others research the industry, the parties and issues before going in. There are legitimate arguments for either approach. Some believe that advance preparation tends to color the mediator's opinion about what the settlement terms ought to be — that he should enter negotiations with a fresh, open mind. Others believe that mediators can be most helpful in the shortest possible time if they have advance knowledge of the particular problems facing the parties.

The first meeting is likely to be short. Here an experienced mediator determines the role he is expected to play. Usually the parties want him to act as a leader in helping them come to an agreement. Sometimes, they simply wish to go through the motions of mediation in order to fulfill statutory obligations and start the countdown toward a strike deadline.

If the mediator believes there is a desire for settlement, he will try to determine what issues still need to be resolved and the parties' present position on each of those issues. Having done this he normally moves to separate meetings with each bargaining team.

The purpose of the separate meetings, from the mediator's viewpoint, is to get some idea how far the parties are willing to go — to discover their bargaining limits. If he is successful in this regard he can use the information to assess the probability of an early agreement and then to try and get the parties somewhat nearer to each other. This is sometimes a ticklish process, rendered impossible if the parties do not trust him. The mediator will not generally disclose one party's total acceptable package to the other, because each side hopes to settle for something better. Rather, he determines how far each will yield in a series of back-and-forth probes, requiring extreme patience and a strong sensitivity to the psychology of the situation. How he proceeds varies from case to case and from one meeting to another. It involves far more than acting as a messenger boy, mechanically conveying positions from one room to the other.

One mediator gave an example to illustrate the *savoir-faire* and purposefulness with which a mediator should proceed:

I had a case where the union had asked for a 15 per cent increase in a one-year contract. Their spokesman told me he would go to 10, but not now — not until the company indicated some movement. The company was holding at 5, but said to me they would go to 7, if the union would come down a little. Both of the parties convinced me that they would go no further, and a strike seemed certain.

In some cases, if I knew the parties well, I would tell them exactly what the other said. However, in this case I simply indicated to each bargaining team in separate meetings that there was some flexibility in the other's position, but I didn't know how much. Then I said to the union: "I'd like to see you get 10 per cent or even 15, but I don't believe the company will go that high. In my opinion the most you can get is 7 or 8 per cent. I may be mistaken, but if you hold to the 10 per cent figure I think you'll have a strike."

Then I went to the company and said: "If you hold to the 5 or 7 per cent figure I can almost assure you that you'll have a strike. Now the decision is yours, and it's not for me to tell you how to spend your money, but in my opinion the settlement will eventually be 10 per cent, and I think 10 per cent might do it now. You might have to go as high as 13. If you want me to explore 7 per cent I'll give it a try, because, as I've said, the union has indicated some flexibility. But I don't think 7 per cent will get a settlement."

As the experienced mediator proceeds from separate sessions he must have a keen sense of timing. A variety of devices are available to him as the occasion seems appropriate. However, if he is convinced that the parties want a settlement and if it is clear that they are ready to move, he will continue — finally bringing them together when he thinks the settlement is ready. Before then he may alternately plead, harangue, serve as an interested listener, make suggestions and, possibly, express his own opinions. On the other hand he may simply sit quietly and take notes the whole time, without saying a word — his mere presence providing impetus for the parties to talk.

Sometimes the mediator comes to know that the principal bargainers are shackled by their own bargaining teams, and he finds some value in talking to them alone, apart from their negotiating teams. Perhaps the best known but least frequent mediation sessions have their climax in a hotel room with the two principal bargainers and the mediator hammering out final details in the wee hours of the morning with reporters hanging around outside waiting for the word: *Is there a settlement or a strike?*

The language of mediation is unique. It should be understood and appreciated by experienced bargainers, because sometimes this understanding is useful for their needs. In the example cited earlier, the mediator was saying to the employer that while the union was officially holding to 15 per cent they would take 13. An experienced negotiator would immediately understand the language. He would also understand that the union would not present the proposal directly across the table because to do so would weaken their position. Suppose, for example, they came down to 13 per cent and management promptly countered with 11. Having already conceded two per cent, some of their members might have lowered their sights enough so that another two per cent would not seem sufficient to warrant a strike.

Another illustration of the language was provided by the mediator in reference to the same example. As the strike deadline became imminent he called the sides together. The union still held to 15 per cent, but the mediator knew they would go to 13. He also knew the company was not ready to go that high. There was no point in separating them, because everyone knew how everyone else felt. So he made a suggestion: "Here's an idea. I suppose both of you will disagree with me but I'll try it out on you anyhow. Why not try out a longer term contract? Say 18 months — giving 7 per cent now and 6 per cent 18 months from now, so that the figure will come out to 13 per cent?"

This was a risky move for a mediator to make, and it could have resulted in disaster if the parties did not respect and trust him. Furthermore, it could have caused the negotiating sessions to collapse if he made a slip in language. Suppose, for example, he said: "The union has told me they will settle for 13 per cent, maybe even 10 per cent, and I know the company can afford it!"

If the mediator has displayed a genuine desire to help, the parties might be receptive to a suggestion such as the one illustrated. However, an experienced negotiator should be wary of the possibility that such a suggestion could be made at the wrong time or by a mediator who did not enjoy the trust of the parties. In such an event the tactic could shatter whatever good had been accomplished so far. Thus negotiators should look out for the possibility, and if they fear that an ill-timed suggestion on settlement terms is forthcoming they should tell the mediator to hold back.

It is important to bear in mind that mediators have virtually no power. If they make a suggestion for terms of settlement or if they express their own viewpoints regarding the conduct of the parties these views carry no weight beyond the force of their own persuasive impact. Furthermore, mediators have no vested interest in the outcome of negotiations. The company and union must live together with the product of their agreement. Consequently the mediator's interest in helping to secure a settlement extends no farther than his pride in doing a job well. In some men this is considerable; in others it is negligible.

INGREDIENTS OF EFFECTIVE MEDIATION

There is no standard formula that characterizes effective mediation. Mediators' styles vary from one person to another and with a given person from one circumstance to another. In fact, a number of mediators have said that they believe they must vary their approaches merely to avoid stereotyping themselves, thus making it difficult for parties to plan bargaining strategies based on a mediator's next anticipated move. Nevertheless, there are some elements of conduct and technique that are common to any effective mediator.

One well-known mediator, a former high official in the government of Ontario, said that the job of mediation is to create conditions such that the parties desperately want to settle. He made nonsettlement, or unreasonable delays in settlement, physically disagreeable courses of action. He arranged for uncomfortable accommodations, with stiff chairs, poor ventilation and bad lighting. He made it a practice to enter the first meeting late — apologize for the poor accommodations and then state confidently that by their mere presence the parties had indicated a desire to settle, and he said that this desire obviously transcended any physical discomfort they might experience.

Since this mediator rarely became involved in a dispute unless it was of substantial importance he was able to tell the parties with credibility that he had informed the news media that the parties were ready for settlement. Then he would light up a strong cigar, invite others around the table to do the same and announce: "Gentlemen I have cleared my calendar for as long as is necessary to get a settlement. Now let's get down to work."

As the hours wore on, and bargainers became more uncomfortable, it became more and more evident that the mediator meant exactly what he said. Negotiators came to believe that he never ate or relieved himself during a bargaining session. Occasionally, when settlement was near, he would lock the door and say, "No one is leaving here until I have a signature from both sides."

This mediator, like all effective mediators, made it clear that he was in charge, that he shared the parties' desire for reaching agreement, and that he was prepared to stay with them for as long as necessary. Some parties came to believe that settlement was more important to the mediator than to themselves, and more than one was heard to say: "We signed that one for old Charlie." Although his techniques were unorthodox his procedure for getting a settlement contained elements that characterize nearly all effective exercises in mediation. The most important of these elements are listed and discussed next.

Learn about the negotiators.

Most experienced mediators are already acquainted with one or more of the members of the negotiating teams. It is useful, and sometimes vital, to know all the members who are likely to have an impact on the proceedings. One negotiator, the personnel officer for a town council in Ontario, described an incident to emphasize this point. The incident involved a bargaining session in which the employer's negotiator had been having an especially difficult time with members of his own team, most notably a gas station attendant who had never made more than $4,000 a year. This team member was astounded to learn that city employees were making in excess of $2.50 an hour and adamant in his opposition to any increase in wages. When the mediator appeared the chief negotiator told him about his problem, and the mediator responded by taking the recalcitrant team member aside in private and telling him the facts of life. From that point on the gas station attendant was quiet, and the negotiations proceeded smoothly.

Mediators have a number of ways in which they learn about members of the negotiating teams. If they are assigned to a particular company-union relationship that has experienced mediation before, they try to consult with the earlier mediator who was involved. In addition, they read the written report filed by that mediator. Perhaps the most important thing to learn is whether it is possible to level with a particular negotiator and whether he will do the same with a mediator.

Some mediators use a more direct approach. They call each of the chief spokesmen aside at an early stage and ask them to give their assessments regarding various members of their own and the opposing teams. In addition they ask for information about the position and background of each negotiator. From this information, and from his own observations, the mediator then gains a pretty good idea of what to expect from each person.

Clarify the demands.

Most often the outstanding demands are defined in a joint meeting at the start of the mediation process. By having all bargainers in attendance the mediator can discover whether everyone is on the same wave length regarding the demands.

Professional negotiators are usually prepared and will lay out the demands clearly and concisely at the start, without embellishment. Sometimes, but rarely, they present the mediator with a written brief.

However, there are some negotiators who do not rate as professionals and who come into mediation meetings with objectives that are "different from" or "in addition to" the desire to secure a settlement. Some, for example, try to use the initial mediation meeting to deliver an oration on the virtues of their own position and the intransigence of the opposition. If the mediator suspects this is going to happen he might let the orator proceed. After he has said his piece he often feels better for it, and the mediator can then say, "Now let's get down to business." Other times, when he believes an oration will be detrimental to settlement prospects, the mediator will try to avoid a joint meeting and ask for the list of demands in separate sessions.

Once he identifies the demands the mediator sets about the sometimes tedious task of learning which of them are more important. Some mediators consciously put the demands into categories, a process that involves placement of priorities, some demands being more important than others. Although negotiators usually maintain that each of their demands is as important as another, there are almost always some that they are prepared to trade away. The mediator tries to learn which demands each negotiator considers essential and which ones he looks upon as expendable. One mediator goes at it directly, saying: "All right, you've told me what you want. Now what'll it take to settle?"

Sometimes this is difficult for a mediator to determine. Two frequently used devices help in this regard. He may ask the parties to explain each demand, occasionally injecting a hint of his own reaction. One mediator, for example, often asks the following: "Could you give me an explanation for that particular demand? To a bystander it sounds a little ridiculous." Another mediator, known for his gentlemanly manner, sometimes reacts to a demand by saying, "Surely this issue is not going to hold up an agreement!" The other way a mediator can help determine which demands are most important is to listen to the spokesman, then say he would like to hear from one of the other members of the bargaining team on the same subject. Solidarity usually indicates importance; division of opinion indicates the opposite.

Bertram A. Powers, president of the printers union, issued a warning, somewhat in awe, to his union colleagues regarding the propensity of mediator Theodore Kheel to categorize demands:

> Here's where you have to watch your step. He has these lists, and he will say, "What are the issues? Let's group them." You have to watch out as he shuffles the groups around. His term for issues he thinks you will trade on or give away is "succeptible to solution," and if you let one of your major issues get into that definition you're in trouble.[3]

It is normal practice for union representatives to enter negotiations with a great many contract proposals: many to mollify political factions in the union, others to be traded away in bargaining. Management, in self defense, has learned to formulate a few frivolous proposals of their own. An effective mediator tries to sort out the frivolities.

In the process of learning about the demands, and sorting them out, the mediator is often successful in resolving some of them. One union representative described the work of a mediator in his attempt to learn the importance of a demand by the union for a Cooperative Wage Survey (CWS) job evaluation system. The mediator called the parties into separate meetings and asked the union spokesman, "Is this issue a strike issue?" The spokesman said no but it was a matter of principle with the union that they make a start toward some systematic method for establishing wage categories. The company had registered bitter opposition to CWS, so the mediator asked their spokesman why they were opposed. He learned then that the company feared that it was a device for the sanction of featherbedding. Then the mediator went back to the union, conveyed the company's fear to them and asked if they would be willing to write a guarantee that there would be no featherbedding. They said yes, thus opening the way for a discussion of how they could introduce some meaningful job evaluation program, not necessarily CWS.

Become aware of the parties' needs.

Mediocre mediators concentrate solely on the issues. Those who are truly effective concentrate on issues only in context of the personal needs of individuals at the bargaining table. One especially articulate mediator stated a rule that guides his efforts:

> In every phase of discussions the mediator must concern himself not with interests of the principal parties, the union and the company, but with the needs of their representatives. The representative (chief negotiator) must not only do a good job, but his client (the constituency) must be convinced he has done one.

In general, managements are most concerned with the cost of a settlement. Unions are mostly concerned with the form, or appearance, that the settlement projects to the members. The mediator has many tools at his disposal to help appeal to these needs. These include the extended contract and the use of percentage figures. For example, if management will not agree to a five-per-cent increase over the existing base rate in each year of a two-year contract, perhaps it will agree to a five-per-cent increase over the current base in each year of a three-year contract. That way the employer gets an extra year of labor peace plus a subtle modification in the cost. If a worker earns $100 a week, a five-per-cent raise in the first year of a three-year contract brings him to $105. In the second year, he draws $110; the new pay raise is not five per cent but slightly over 4.75 per cent. In the third year the increase — from $110 to $115 — is slightly more than 4.5 per cent. Union leaders can report back to their members that they will receive three five-per-cent increases.[4] Management, on the other hand, can report annual increases over the three years averaging only 4.75 per cent.

Take the heat off.

An important function of mediation is to help take heat off the parties. The effective mediator allows some heat to develop, because it may promote settlement. But if he feels that one side or the other is getting angry to the detriment of negotiations he will try to separate them. In this respect he should be especially aware of experienced bargainers, who may be displaying anger as a bluff. They are sometimes play-acting, with a specific objective in mind.

When the parties are apart they usually plead their own case with the mediator. He listens perfunctorily until he feels the heat has dissipated, then tries to bring the conversation back to the real essence of why they are there — to come up with a proposal that the other side will accept. Usually, in doing this, he relies on figures, ignoring emotions. Sometimes he applies heat himself — by playing the "Devil's Advocate" with each party separately — arguing against their proposals. This can sometimes help the parties sharpen their own positions and also allows them to vent their anger at the mediator instead of the opposing side.

A negotiator for a paper carton manufacturing firm described a mediation session he experienced in late 1971 that illustrates how transference of anger can lead to a settlement. The time was well before contract deadline time when the union requested mediation. The management negotiator was reasonably convinced that the request was made for no other purpose than to start the clock running to establish a strike deadline, so he went to the mediation meeting with no expectation of reaching settlement and a chip on his shoulder from his past experiences with the same union representative, all of which had been disagreeable.

The mediator was late, having called the parties to say he had been in a minor automobile accident. When he arrived, about two hours after the appointed time, he made no apology, but said he could only spend a short time because he had another appointment early the next morning. Then he asked the parties if their purpose was to settle, or to set a strike deadline. Both indicated they wanted to get a settlement. This seemed to mildly irritate the mediator, but he agreed to meet with the parties on that basis. As the day progressed the mediator was able to isolate three issues: wages, male /female parity, and pensions. All were capable of resolution, and both sides began working toward settlement. However, about 10 P.M. that night the mediator called the two spokesmen together and told them he was planning to leave. The union spokesman said, "We intend to stay till there's a settlement and we expect you to do the same." Then the spokesmen met alone, complaining bitterly about the mediator's apparent lack of interest. At 12 midnight the mediator bade farewell, handing the negotiators a form on which they could indicate their settlement terms for submission to the Minister of Labour — and left. The negotiators, seething with anger, forged an agreement; then they registered a bitter complaint with the Director of Mediation Services about the conduct of the mediator — not realizing till much later that the apparent lack of interest by the mediator, whether by design or accident, probably caused them to "show him" by coming to a settlement.

Learn the limits.

Most negotiators and mediators alike agree that the mediator should somehow learn the limits beyond which the sides will not go — preferring to strike or be struck. Sometimes the parties themselves have not consciously established those limits. By going through the exercise the parties are forced to reassess their positions and to decide tentatively on the point when a strike would be more attractive than a settlement.

The process of learning limits requires great sensitivity, because both parties are naturally fearful that the other side will learn about their position and will take them for all they've got. So the mediator must learn what the parties will settle for by asking every question except that. Usually he does this by moving back and forth between separate meetings, ostensibly proposing packages for settlement and further compromises, but in fact testing the reactions of the bargainers to learn what points they would be willing to sacrifice, ultimately, to gain an agreement. This process of whittling away almost invariably leads to the answer he is seeking.

Having learned the limits, the mediator will almost never disclose them. Rather, he then goes to work trying to move each party closer to those limits. This is not generally done in one stroke, rather point by point, a little bit at a time, probably starting with the party whose most recent proposal is the closest to what the mediator thinks the eventual settlement will be.

Apply pressure.

Effective application of pressure requires an acute sense of timing. Some people believe that the timing sense cannot be taught, that it comes from experience, and that some mediators never acquire it. One critical time in negotiations is what Mediator Theodore Kheel calls the "crunch." This is an important deadline, usually when the contract expires and a strike is imminent or, if a strike is in progress, it is the last possible moment for one side or the other to settle and still profit from a particular economic factor.⁵ When such a time is drawing near the mediator may call for round-the-clock sessions. These sessions are often a test of physical endurance for the mediator and the parties alike. The mediator sometimes gains respect by apparently outlasting the parties. Sometimes the appearance of superior endurance is a hoax. One well-known Canadian mediator described a negotiating session in which he called the two sides into round-the-clock sessions — each meeting in separate rooms in the same hotel. It was after midnight when he went to the union and said, "I think we're nearing pay dirt; let me have one more go at the employer." Then he went to the employer and said the same thing in reference to the union. Both sides thought the mediator was meeting with the other, and as they waited for hour upon hour they became more and more convinced that he was making progress. In fact, the mediator had left both sides alone and gone to his own room, taken a short nap, shaved, and changed clothes. At about 4:30A.M. he reappeared, looking fresh, and called the parties together, announcing that he had detected a mood for settlement on both sides and suggesting that they meet for as long as necessary to get an agreement. The exhausted spokesmen said "no more" and came to an agreement in less than 30 minutes.

Sometimes a mediator's sense of timing tells him that he should stall. One mediator said there were two situations that would cause him to delay proceedings. One of them would be exhaustion of all intended concessions by one of the sides. To ask for anything more would likely cause them to walk out. The other would be a premature agreement when the mediator has doubts about whether constituents will give their approval. This mediator described a situation of over ten years ago when one of the major airlines reached an agreement with its pilots several weeks in advance of strike deadline, and spokesmen for both sides proudly announced a new era in industrial relations statesmanship as they notified the press that they had settled. Almost immediately the parties were called on to answer to their constituents — the union leaders to explain to members why they had not bargained till the last moment for every ounce they could get and the management negotiators to explain to their superiors why they gave in so easily. Since then the two sides have always given the appearance of bargaining till the last possible moment, emerging from the sessions only after "going to the brink." Most often, according to the mediator, they have been sitting together for days, sorting out grievances, watching television and playing cards — the agreement well in hand.

Occasionally, but not often, a mediator resorts to persons away from the bargaining in order to apply pressure. Most frequently these are higher authorities in the company or the union and, occasionally, the media. In cases where the chief bargainer on one side or the other is recalcitrant and resists the crunch, displaying unwillingness to take responsibility for a decision, the mediator may seek out the negotiator's superior in order to explain the consequences of his man's stance. Most often he does this after having consulted with his own superior — the Director of the Mediation Service or the Labour Minister — and securing permission to arrange a top-level meeting out of the hands of the designated bargainers. Such a tactic is used rarely, and it is demeaning to the negotiators. It is almost never done without knowledge of the negotiators. However, if a negotiator is aware that it might happen the mediator can often get him off center by dropping a subtle hint regarding the consequences of his recalcitrance.

The mediator is severely limited in use of media to apply pressure for two reasons: first the media are not vitally concerned with most negotiations; second, there is a risk of divulging positions in public so that one or both parties become frozen in their stance.

In cases where negotiations are newsworthy the mediator can apply considerable pressure, and he can do this without divulging anyone's position and without implying criticism. However, his use of pressure probably depends on having built up a considerable amount of trust. The following example, describing Theodore Kheel, serves to illustrate this point.

> Kheel's repeated demonstrations of his concern for the interests of the representatives have given him a reservoir of trust, and consequently he can get away with acts or appearances that would arouse suspicion if they were made by other mediators. In 1965, for instance, the newspaper publishers were negotiating with the printers' union at City Hall, and the union had announced that it planned to go on strike at 2 AM on April 1st. Kheel confronted the printers' international president, the late Elmer Brown, and the local president, Powers, at one-fifty and announced that he had seen signs of flexibility on management's side. In fact, he told them, he had notified reporters a few moments earlier that the union's strike deadline had been put off until four. "Brown and I just looked at each other," Powers recalled, "and then we scrambled around to call each of the shops before the men walked out. It was the perfect thing for Kheel to have done, really. If he had asked for the postponement, we would have had to say no." By four o'clock, the publishers and the printers had come to an agreement in principle, and the strike was averted.[6]

This instance is cited as an example of what can happen under conditions of total confidence, not as something that ought to be attempted by a mediator as a matter of course.

In special cases, make recommendations for settlement.

Union and management negotiators generally agree that the mediator who injects his personal viewpoints into the negotiations is more effective than the one who sits back and lets the parties do most of the talking. Some negotiators believe that the mediator should inject his viewpoints and more: that he has a duty to make recommendations for settlement.

Most mediators will not recommend settlement terms unless asked to do so by the parties. Some are more cautious, saying they will not make suggestions for solution unless they are reasonably certain the parties will accept — even if they are asked.

Generally, recommendations deal with specific issues and are presented in the context of "let's try this on for size." However, there are circumstances when the mediator should consider making a package recommendation dealing with all issues in dispute. Acceptance of the recommendation by both parties would result in total settlement.

According to Mr. William Simkin, former Director of the U.S. Federal Mediation and Conciliation Service, the timing of a package recommendation is normally reserved to the last few hours before a strike and only after it has become clear that there is no change that the parties can settle themselves. Sometimes package recommendations are useful when a strike is in progress, has persisted for some time, and the prospects for early settlement are dim. Such circumstances are rare.

Given one of these two circumstances, Simkin still would refrain from recommendations unless one of the following four situations was operative:

1. *Face saving.* Neither party is prepared to make a final proposal, but both will accept the proposal if made by the mediator. Both know the content of the recommendations in advance and both have privately committed themselves to acceptance. However, some combination of pride, face, politics, and awkwardness of retreating from a far-out position make it impossible for one or the other or both sides to retreat gracefully.

2. *Division in the ranks.* As in the first situation the parties know the content of the mediator's recommendation in advance, but one or both sides are divided as to its acceptability. If there is a good chance that the mediator's views will help secure strong majority acceptance and if the alternative is a certain and immediate strike or continuance of a prolonged strike, he probably should make the recommendation.

3. *Mediator's hunch.* In some situations there is no certainty that the mediator's recommendation will be accepted by anyone, but the mediator has a strong hunch that acceptance will be obtained.

If this hunch is accompanied by other factors, such as great public significance of the dispute or high cost and long duration of a pending or ongoing strike, he probably should go ahead. According to Simkin the batting average of U.S. Federal mediators in such situations has been good.

4. *Narrow the issues.* In some cases the mediator is reasonably certain that his recommended package will not be accepted. However he is similarly certain that a process of recommendation and partial rejection will substantially narrow the issues in dispute. To make recommendations in such a situation could severely limit a mediator's continuing usefulness in the particular case, but if he can leave the case in better shape for eventual settlement it might be a good move.

If the parties are so far apart that no successful recommendation can be made, and if the mediator believes that a recommendation will only muddy the negotiations and lengthen the dispute he should not proceed.[7]

Simkin made some additional points about recommendations themselves:

1. The parties should never be surprised by a recommendation thrown at them without warning.

2. Normally, recommendations should not be public recommendations. Rather they should be made privately with the negotiators; and if publicity is desired the text should be cleared with the negotiators.

3. Mediators should not make recommendations as a matter of standard practice. Otherwise the parties would likely key their bargaining strategy to a recommendation rather than normal give-and-take.

4. Sometimes the threat of a recommendation is more effective than the threat of a strike, the parties having conditioned themselves to the inevitability of a strike.[8]

One well-known Canadian mediator echoed Simkin's last point and added his own comment: that the threat of a recommendation was often more effective in getting a settlement than the recommendation itself. Sometimes one or both parties comes to believe that the mediator's recommendation will contain fewer concessions than they could gain across the table — so the threat sends them back to negotiating.

THE MEDIATOR AS ARBITRATOR

Occasionally a mediator changes hats part way through the process and assumes the role of an arbitrator. This happens only when negotiators come to realize that they have reached an impasse on certain issues and that mediation cannot help. Sometimes, but rarely, the mediator suggests arbitration; more often the negotiators ask the mediator to arbitrate. Many mediators are also skilled arbitrators, so the switch in roles is not difficult. In arbitration, the parties would state their positions and argue them in the fashion of lawyers before a judge, even bringing forth witnesses if necessary. As arbitrator the mediator performs a judicial function, and the parties agree in advance to abide by his decision.

If the parties decide to submit their dispute to arbitration, and the mediator serves as arbitrator, considerable time can be saved because there is no need to repeat the background of the case. However, there is some advantage in dismissing the mediator at this point and hiring a new man to arbitrate. This way the parties are forced to reassess their positions, to present them in a clear, logical fashion and argue them *de novo*. Many times the mediator has formed an opinion on the issues in dispute and made that opinion known, thus negating his role as arbitrator.

Should there be a mediation board?

So far the discussion has been based on the assumption that mediation is performed by a single person. This is usually the case. However, some statutes such as the Public Service Staff Relations Act of Canada[9] and the Railway Labor Act of the United States[10] provide for boards of mediation made up of more than one person, three under the Canadian Act, five under the American. Sometimes parties themselves hire a multimember board, usually consisting of a representative selected by the employer and one selected by the union. These two representatives then select a third man who acts as chairman of the board. The functions of the board are identical to those of an individual mediator. They may gain somewhat by establishing a more formal aura than an individual mediator. They may also gain from the fact that three men working together can sometimes hammer out a proposal for settlement that carries more impact than a proposal suggested by a single person.

Most often boards of mediation are established for the purpose of making recommendations for settlement. Here multiple representation can have considerable advantage in assuring each side that his chosen representative is in consultation with the chairman while the recommendations are being formulated. This helps minimize the chance that final recommendations will be specious or unworkable.

The value of a man representing each side on a board of mediation extends beyond making input to the chairman in formulating recommendations. One of his most useful functions is to tell members of his side that they are off-base. It is this function that may be important, because the parties' nominee has more freedom than the chairman to say to members of his negotiating team, "You're nuts, you're cockeyed."

PREVENTIVE MEDIATION

Until now the discussion has been concerned with mediation as an aid in dispute settling. Many employers and unions use preventive mediation, wherein outside assistance is sought long before any dispute materializes. Often this is done in preparation for bargaining, to establish a mutual framework from which give-and-take can proceed. Often times contract negotiations get bogged down with disagreements on matters of fact, such as wage rates and costs of various fringe packages. With the help of a mediator many of these matters can be cleared up, so that discussions can be confined to matters of genuine disagreement, if any. Parties who engage in preventive mediation have been enthusiastic about its value, generally expressing the view that after questions of fact are cleared up there are not many matters of disagreement. One company and union in Southwestern Ontario agreed several years ago to regularly employ a mediator at least six months before contract deadline time to help resolve issues of fact that might arise in the coming negotiations. Up till that time they had a history of crisis bargaining capped by a strike or near-strike. Since then they have regularly settled well in advance of deadline, with never an inkling of a crisis.

*   *   *

SUMMARY

Mediation should be looked upon by employers and union leaders as a settlement tool that can be used in certain bargaining situations. In general, parties who have experienced mediation have expressed the belief that the mediator was helpful. Many parties have indicated that a mediator was instrumental in preventing a strike or in shortening the duration of a strike.

Some cases have been reported where a mediator aggravated a situation and where he either prevented or delayed settlement. For this reason parties who are considering mediation as a settlement tool should be extremely careful about the selection of a mediator and the timing of his entry. They should compile lists of prospective mediators for possible future reference. Then, if the need for outside assistance becomes apparent, they should seek appointment of the man they want, and it should be made clear to the man what role he is expected to play. In the process of aiding settlement an effective mediator must at various times play the role of disciplinarian, guidance officer, educator, face saver, supporter and sop for the frustrations of bargainers. At all times he must have a keen sense of timing so as to know what role to play and when.

While a mediator has no power to force parties to settle he can exert strong influence. The influence is enhanced if he is asked by the parties to propose settlement terms or to express his opinions regarding the positions of the parties. Sometimes mediators take power from the parties if asked to arbitrate, the parties agreeing in advance that the mediator's recommendations for settlement will be final and binding.

Some jurisdictions in Canada and the United States require mediation as a precondition to strike action. Some require appointment of a mediation board with power to make nonbinding recommendations for settlement. Parties should be aware of the laws on these matters in the place where they operate and should use care to avoid application of those laws in a way or at a time that will impede settlement.

Employers and labor leaders should expand their thinking about mediation beyond the dispute-settling framework. Many times mediators can be helpful in preventing disputes by assisting parties at noncrisis times in determining facts that may form the background for negotiations to come.

The mediator represents the public interest insofar as the public is interested in minimizing labor relations strife, and he represents himself insofar as he gets satisfaction from helping others. He receives little recognition for his work, yet he is one of the most highly skilled and versatile persons in today's society. As labor relations develop greater complexity and sophistication the role of the mediator will change. He will have to acquire greater expertise in complex issues and develop more sensitivity to the fact that the parties to a collective contract are increasingly responsible to parties outside the contract — a reflection of the increased interdependence of our society. The mediator could become one of the most important and influential members of tomorrow's economic environment.[11]

NOTES TO CHAPTER 6

1. As of June 1971, 253 mediators were employed by the Federal Mediation and Conciliation Service of the United States; 22 were on the full-time employment roles of Canada's Department of Labour; the Province of Ontario employed 17.

2. First stage mediation is termed conciliation in most Canadian jurisdictions.

3. Fred C. Shapiro, "Profiles: Mediator," *The New Yorker*. August 1, 1970.

4. One mediator described his job as including "helping union representatives take lies back to the members," a statement which may be overly blunt but which has considerable authority in fact.

5. One example of such a time would be a certain number of days after a strike starts but just before workmen's compensation or strike benefits go into effect.

6. Fred C. Shapiro, *op. cit.*

7. William E. Simkin, *Mediation and the Dynamics of Collective Bargaining*, Bureau of National Affairs, 1971, pp. 102-5.

8. Ibid, pp. 105-6

9. The Public Service Staff Relations Act of Canada, TSC 19C. p-35, as amended July 7, 1972.

10. Public Law No. 257 (69th Congress), approved May 20, 1926, Section 4.

11. Material in this chapter was largely derived from a research study conducted by Professor David Kuechle with the research assistance of David DeYoung and published in *The Labour Gazette,* January and February 1974. The study involved negotiators in Canada and the United States who had recently experienced mediation. On receipt of written responses from 299 negotiators (187 from management and 112 from labor) follow-up interviews were conducted with 50 of the respondents (25 management and 25 labor). The open-ended interviews were conducted with ten men in Canada and the United States who were frequently cited by management and labor respondents alike as being outstanding mediators.

7. CONTRACT ADMINISTRATION

The most important aspect of industrial relations involves day-to-day administration of the collective bargaining agreement. The agreement itself may be a masterpiece of legal rhetoric — a model for guidance of aspiring labor lawyers — but it is little more than an impotent sheaf of papers except for the day-to-day actions of parties who are covered by its provisions.

There are virtually no restrictions placed on bargainers regarding the subjects they can cover in a collective agreement. Some jurisdictions require provisions barring the right to strike during a contract term; others require some means by which unsettled grievances can be submitted to final and binding arbitration; and some jurisdictions have no requirements or restrictions at all. With some minimal exceptions, parties are free in all jurisdictions to negotiate whatever contract clauses they wish.

The scope, the depth and the breadth of subject matter in labor agreements vary immensely from one relationship to another. Perhaps the shortest contract is one consisting of just two sentences as follows:

> The union and management agree that both shall work toward maximization of satisfaction on and off the job for each individual employee and toward maximum profitability of the company. We subscribe to the premise that these two goals are compatible.

signed	signed
for the union	for management

This contract was the product of negotiations in 1973, the 26th contract between the parties in a relationship dating back 41 years. At one point during those years the parties negotiated a contract exceeding 100 pages in length, and relations were stormy then. Soon thereafter, the company nearly fell into receivership because of ballooning costs, and the parties began to work together for their mutual survival. This most recent contract reflected a degree of trust and understanding that is uncommon in the field of industrial relations, spurred considerably by the crisis of near destruction.

Most contracts are much longer and more detailed than this. While there is no known correlation between length and detail of a contract and the nature of a relationship some clues about the degree to which each party attempts to preserve its prerogatives while holding the other at arms length can be obtained by searching to see if the contract contains a managment rights clause, and if it does what does it say? Here, for example, is the management rights clause from the agreement between the Steel Company of Canada, Limited, Hilton Works, and the United Steelworkers of America, Local No. 1005:

> The management of the plant and the direction of the working forces, including the right to direct, plan and control plant operations, and to schedule working hours, and the right to hire, promote, demote, transfer, suspend or discharge employees for just cause, or to release employees because of lack of work or for other legitimate reasons, or the right to introduce new and improved methods or facilities and to manage the plant in the traditional manner is vested exclusively in the Company, subject to the express provisions of this agreement.

This chapter examines six of the most frequently encountered issues in contract administration. These are the issues that arise most often in grievance procedures and, consequently, are dealt with most often by arbitrators. All of them are dealt with through the use of descriptive cases and require the reader to place himself or herself in the position of an administrator who is called upon to analyze the facts, make a decision, examine the possible consequences of that decision, then take steps for implementation. The issues dealt with, while typical, cannot pretend to be all-encompassing. The purpose is to develop an appreciation for the overriding importance of skillful administration in forming and developing a mature industrial relations climate. This is a job for all administrators, not for industrial relations practitioners alone. The development of skill and understanding in the subjects dealt with here should have transfer value in dealing with all forms of industrial relations issues.

A. DISCIPLINE

Many labor agreements provide management with the exclusive right to establish rules and regulations to govern the conduct of employees, and most agreements give management the right to discipline employees for "just cause." Unions generally reserve the right to challenge discipline actions through the grievance procedure. If rules and regulations are well known, nondiscriminatory and administered in a fair, unbiased manner the discipline actions based on them will most likely be upheld by an arbitrator.

Work rules cover a wide variety of topics, ranging from hours of work to expected production output; from dress, to conduct, to attendance. They are justified most often by an alleged need to maintain order, consistency and efficiency in the organization.

Unions are generally reluctant to participate in the formation of rules and regulations; rather they prefer to police their administration — challenging their efficacy in specific cases. It is easier and potentially less embarrassing for unions to challenge a rule or regulation formulated by management alone than one in which the union played a part in framing.

Most disciplinary programs are designed for the purpose of correcting behavior, not simply for punitive reasons. For this reason, discipline is frequently progressive; that is, penalties become increasingly severe as violations of rules are repeated. The first violation might bring a verbal warning, the second a written warning, the third a three-day suspension, and the fourth discharge. Penalties also are likely to vary with the seriousness of the offense. Tardiness might result in verbal warning, while smoking in an area where hydrogen gas is present might result in discharge.

In any disciplinary program it is impossible to anticipate all possible actions that might call for discipline. That is why the all-encompassing expression "just cause" is contained in most collective bargaining agreements. Managements governed by a "just cause" provision are repeatedly called on to exercise judgment in cases of misconduct, whether or not the misconduct was covered by a specific rule or regulation, and their judgment is subject to challenge by the union.

Arbitrators' decisions provide useful guidelines for the administration of discipline. They have consistently held, for example, that managements bear the burden of establishing that there has been an infraction and that the discipline assessed was fair. They have also held the view that discharge — the most severe form of discipline — is tantamount to industrial "capital punishment." Thus, a powerful burden is placed on management to establish just cause for discharge.

Certain guidelines in the administration of discipline have emerged as a result of thousands of arbitration opinions delivered through the years. Most important among them are these:

1. *If a rule or regulation is involved it must be known.* Certain acts, such as theft and sabotage, may be punished in absence of any specific rules or regulations prohibiting them, because any person ought to understand that such conduct is unacceptable. However, where conduct falls outside the generally accepted category of the forbidden, the employer's position is strongest when a plant rule is existent and known. Ideally the rule should be published, posted on company bulletin boards and a copy given to each employee.

2. *The rule must be reasonable.* The rule must be reasonably related to the orderly, safe operation of the business.

3. *The application of rules must be consistent.* An employee cannot be

disciplined for violation of a work rule unless others who have committed violations in the past have been similarly disciplined.

4. *Violations must be proven.* Dates, times, and places must be documented. Witnesses are often helpful in establishing proof.

5. *An individual must have reasonable grounds for expecting disciplinary action to follow a given act.* For some offenses the posting of a rule may be considered to be sufficient warning. For others, the employee should be warned, preferably *in writing,* that subsequent violations of the rule will lead to a specific penalty.

6. *The degree of discipline imposed must be related to the seriousness of the offense.* Discharge for theft might be an appropriate penalty, while it would not be appropriate for an initial tardiness. A rule that imposes an automatic penalty for an act, without considering extenuating circumstances, may be considered unreasonable.

7. *The discipline imposed must take the employee's past record into consideration.* An employee with a record of rule infractions may be subject to more severe disciplinary penalties than an employee with an unblemished work record. However, infractions on a individual's record cannot be held against him for an unlimited period of time. A period of time without an infraction, usually a year or longer, will usually serve to wipe the slate clean.

8. *The discipline imposed must also take into consideration the employee's length of service.* Arbitrators have held that long-service employees may be, and in many instances must be, treated differently from employees with a shorter term of service. If two employees were caught stealing, one of them with 20 years seniority and one of them with six months, the junior employee might well be discharged while the senior employee might receive a lesser penalty. The principle at work here is that discharge is a more severe penalty for a longer-term employee, in terms of the job and pension rights he is being deprived of and in terms of the greater difficulty older, longer-term employees have in finding alternative employment.

In their search for appropriate, meaningful penalties short of discharge, many managements have applied disciplinary suspensions for serious misconduct. This kind of action causes employees to experience some loss of earnings and, according to its advocates, causes some reassessment by the employee of the conduct giving rise to the suspension. However, in recent years disciplinary suspensions have been used less and less, and appropriately worded disciplinary warnings have taken their place. There are two reasons for this. First, the company may be depriving itself of an important skill — thus sacrificing productivity and know-how in order to establish their right to impose discipline, sometimes a foolish, wasteful action. Second, there are an increasing number of employees who play the rules and regulations game to the hilt — committing violations just frequently enough or serious enough to warrant a suspension but not so serious as to cause a discharge. This way, they can get some much-desired time off while not sacrificing the job itself.

One principle in administration of discipline can be stated unequivocally. That is, if an infraction occurs which might require discipline, management should always, without exception, investigate with extreme care away from the immediate "heat" of the circumstances before prescribing final punishment. The annals of industrial relations practice are replete with instances where managements, acting in haste and without adequate information, took inappropriate action, sometimes against innocent employees, with consequences that soured their industrial relations system for years to come. The burden is on management to administer justice fairly, consistently and without prejudice.

*   *   *

The following case — titled "Alberta Oil Company" — describes the efforts of one company and union to implement a system of discipline that switched the burden to the employee. Where infractions occurred the employee who committed them was counseled and required to establish reasons why he should continue in the employ of the company. The system, known as discipline without punishment, represents a new and different approach to building a corrective disciplinary system.

This case is unusual and forward-looking in its scope. Three more traditional cases, each involving questions of discipline, are found in Chapter 8, "Arbitration."

ALBERTA OIL COMPANY LTD. (A)

"Charlie, take a look at this and tell me what you think of it."

The date was April 5, 1972, and the speaker was Mr. George Fairfax, the Works Manager at the Leduc Refinery of the Alberta Oil Company. The company was a major Canadian producer, refiner, and distributor of petroleum products. The Leduc Refinery was located just south of Sarnia, Ontario, and provided gasoline and other products for markets in Ontario and parts of Quebec.

Mr. Fairfax had given Mr. Charles Maynard, his assistant, a copy of an article from *The Harvard Business Review* titled "Discipline Without Punishment."[1] The article described how a plywood mill changed its policy on discipline. The new policy was designed to modify individuals' behavior without the usual progressive punitive steps: oral and written warnings, time off without pay and, finally, dismissal.

Mr. Maynard was impressed with the approach to discipline outlined in the article, and in discussing it with Mr. Fairfax, said that the procedure was certainly superior to the one currently in use in the plant. In actuality, no overall discipline system was used in the Leduc Refinery. The foremen were not given any guidelines, although they generally followed a program of progressive discipline, beginning with a verbal warning, followed by a written warning, which was then followed by one to three days off without pay, then one or two weeks suspension, and then dismissal. Any discharge had to be approved by the Vice President of Operations, although a lesser penalty could be handled solely at the plant level.

At times, demotion to a lower-paying job was involved as a punishment. Mr. Maynard also believed that the foremen to a certain extent used discipline to set an example as much as to punish an individual.

The union, the Oil, Chemical and Atomic Workers (OCAW), frequently filed grievances over disciplinary actions, particularly those involving demotion or time off. The union's success was usually dependent on how consistent the foreman had been, but in general their challenges were often successful.

As a first step toward implementing a new policy, Mr. Fairfax circulated a copy of the article to the three plant superintendents: Paul Meryll, Refinery; Will Carruthers, Storage and Distribution; and Allen Calverly, Maintenance. These three men were intrigued by the approach outlined in the article and thought that a similar plan could be successful at the Leduc Refinery.

Since the foremen would be most affected by a change in discipline policy, Mr. Maynard suggested that a group of foremen be asked to study the article, decide whether such a system would be appropriate at the Leduc operation and, if so, develop a policy statement for use by all foremen. Mr. Fairfax appointed five of the most senior foremen to such a study committee, along with Mr. Bruce Becket, the plant Industrial Relations Manager. The foremen all had many years of service with the company; their average seniority was 25 years.

The group met several times, discussing the article, approving the concept, and developing a policy for implementing the disciplinary system at the Leduc Refinery. In general, the foremen believed that they and their fellow supervisors did not use discipline easily and often did not attempt to modify the behavior of employees soon enough. The foremen believed that the discipline without punishment system would help to change this situation, since it was not geared toward discharge as the existing system was. The foremen also believed that the problem-solving aspect of the system was in line with the overall nature of the union-management relationship and should help improve that relationship in the area of discipline.

In mid-November of 1972, Mr. Maynard and Mr. Fairfax approved the policy statement developed by the committee, and the new system became operational. The policy statement read:

Discipline without Punishment

Discipline in the work place is necessary for the maintenance of good workmanship and acceptable levels of output. Experience indicates that individuals, when given every possible and reasonable opportunity to maintain self-respect, will play a positive and satisfactory role in the company's operations. This does not mean that there will never be lapses from excellent workmanship or strict discipline. However, where self-respect is prevalent, such lapses will happen rarely and will stop promptly if brought to the individual's attention in a friendly manner. Self-respect is probably the most potent motivator of satisfactory performance and disciplined behavior in general.

Repeated violations within a relatively short interval where such friendly methods are applied indicates a lack of self-respect. When such a regrettable conclusion has been reached about an individual, we do not wish to keep him in our employ and an orderly method to terminate his services will be applied.

The following is to be adhered to in all cases of discipline:

1. No disciplinary demotion or suspension or other forms of punishment will henceforth be applied.
2. In the case of unsatisfactory work performance, infraction of company rules and operations, the following steps will be followed:

Procedures

STEP 1

The foreman will offer the worker a casual and friendly reminder on the job, being careful when doing so that he does it in such a way that he does not embarrass the worker.

STEP 2

Should another incident occur within six weeks of Step 1, the foreman will again correct it casually on the job, but will later call the individual to his office for a serious but friendly chat. He will explain the need for, and the purposes of, rules and make sure the person understands the explanation, and express his confidence that the person will, henceforth, decide to abide by them. He will also listen to any reasonable explanation the employee may bring up.

STEP 3

In the case of a further incident within six weeks of Step 2, then Step 2 is repeated with variations.
First, the foreman, along with the general foreman or another foreman, will see that the employee's union representative is present. Secondly, the employee's attention is directed to the possibility that he may dislike the work we have to offer or he may find the relatively strict industry discipline distasteful. In such a case, would it be better to look for some other job or kind of work (occupational counseling is available through the Personnel Office)? The foreman then expresses his hope that the employee will, in fact, decide that he likes the work and the company and will adapt himself to the requirements.

STEP 4

The employee who perpetrates another incident within six weeks of Step 3 will be called off the floor into the foreman's office, again in the presence of a general foreman or another foreman and a union representative. In their presence he is directed to go home for the rest of the shift and consider seriously whether he does or does not wish to abide by the company standards. He will also be told, prior to starting back to work, that he must see the Department Superintendent and that he will receive his normal pay for any lost hours, as an expression of the company's hope that he will wish to stay and abide by the rules.

STEP 5

If another incident should occur within a reasonable time during Step 4, Step 4 is repeated with two variations.
No letter is required and the employee's services are terminated.

GUIDE NOTES

There is no objection to the employee's requesting union representation at any time. However, whenever the union is involved, the Discipline Notice Form (No. 125) must be completed. For the purposes of recording Steps 1 and 2, each department will work out the administrative detail so that continuity will result.

If circumstances warrant, e.g. several incidents happen at unusually close intervals, the first three procedures may be skipped.

It is recognized that a series of minor offenses would lead to procedures in Step 5.

If no further incidents occur within six weeks of any one step, except Step 4, such step is cleared from the employee's record. Should another incident happen at another time, the last step will be repeated. Considerable time, e.g. one year, would have to elapse before Step 4 is cleared from the records.

Discovery of criminal behavior or in-plant fighting will result in immediate termination of services without preliminary steps being taken. Such behavior is taken as conclusive evidence of lack of adequate self-respect and discipline even if it happens only once.

THE FIRST DISCHARGE

On June 30, 1974, the first dismissal occurred under the new policy, with the discharge of Robert Willis, an employee with 20 years of service. At the time of his dismissal, Willis worked as a dispatcher in the Distributing Department, dispatching gasoline trucks to retail service stations. He was 42 years of age.

Until 1972 Mr. Willis was a satisfactory employee in every way. Beginning in that year, however, his absence from work became pronounced. From January to November of 1972 Willis was absent from work a total of 38 days.

On November 5, 1972, Willis was asked to report to Mr. Becket, the Personnel Manager. In a personal discussion that was noted on Willis's personnel record, Mr. Becket reviewed his attendance record and asked whether he or the company could do anything to help Willis improve his attendance record. Willis agreed that his record was far from good and acknowledged that the company could not be expected to tolerate his continued poor attendance. He said he would make an effort to improve his performance in that regard.

Willis did not miss work for the next two months. However, after the first of January, 1973, his attendance record worsened. Between January 2 and March 24 Willis was absent for a total of 36 days. The absences were a high percentage of actual working time, because Willis also took his 4 weeks of vacation during the period January 2 to March 24.

Willis returned to work on March 24 after a 30-day absence. As a result, he was required to see the company physician, Dr. Daily. After obtaining permission from Willis, the doctor sent the following memorandum to Mr. Carruthers, the Superintendent of Storage and Distribution: "This man is returned to work, on March 24, 1973, with no restrictions. He is an alcoholic with a personality disorder. He is being treated by Dr. Lowenstein (a psychiatrist) and should be kept under constant pressure to avoid drinking. His outlook for success is poor."

Mr. Carruthers was a close friend of Willis's family; he had known Willis since he was a child. He had a conversation with him on March 24, asking whether he, as a friend, could do anything to help. Willis was told that because of the routine of the dispatcher's job, the company had to be able to depend on his attendance, and if they could not do so, Willis's employment could not be continued.

On April 3 Willis reported off from work, saying he was sick. On April 8 he was again absent, this time without notification. Mr. Carruthers phoned Willis on April 8, and Willis agreed to meet with him and Carl Partlet, his union representative, late that afternoon. Willis did not appear for the meeting. Mr Carruthers made several attempts to contact Willis by phone during the next few days without success. Finally, he sent a letter advising Willis that he was to meet with Mr. Wells, the Assistant Superintendent, before reporting to work.

On April 15 Willis met with Mr. Wells and Harry Dunstable, the union President. Mr. Wells reviewed Willis's attendance record and Mr. Carruthers' prior conversation with him. Mr. Wells said that the company could not continue to employ Willis if his attendance habits did not substantially change. Mr. Willis said that he accepted that fact and expressed a belief that the company had been quite patient already.

Mr. Wells asked Willis whether he or the company could do anything to help with his drinking problem, or the marital difficulties which were a causal factor. Willis said that if he could have a few days off from work he could put his personal affairs in order.

Mr. Wells told Willis that he should take the next four days off, with full pay, to attend to these personal matters, and to decide whether he wished to continue working for Alberta Oil. He asked Willis to drop into his office with his decision before he returned to work.

On April 22 Willis returned to Mr. Wells's office. He said that he wished to continue working for the company. He said that he had been able to deal with his personal affairs to the point where they would not affect his attendance at work. Mr. Wells said that he was delighted with Willis's decision, that the company needed him and wanted him on his regular job. He pointed out, however, that any future absenteeism, except for sickness documented by a physician, would result in dismissal. Mr. Wells wished Willis good luck and offered him any help that might be required.

From April 22 to October 15, 1973, Willis missed no work. His foreman believed that his on-the-job performance had improved substantially.

On October 15 Willis called his foreman saying that he had some personal problems, was depressed and would not be reporting for work. He did not return until November 5. On his return to work he went to Mr. Wells's office and said he was prepared to resign, in the belief that he was about to be fired. Mr. Wells said that he believed Willis had made a sincere and effective effort over the past six months. His attendance from April to October showed that he had the desire and the ability to improve. Because of this effort, Mr. Wells said he was willing to see Willis return to work and attempt to improve on his recent record. Mr. Wells emphasized that as much as the company would like to keep Willis an an employee, further absenteeism would result in his dismissal.

Willis had no absences from November 1973 to January 22, 1974. However, after that date his attendance record worsened. By June 26th Willis had missed 53 days of work. On that date, Mr. Wells called Willis and union President, Harry Dunstable, to his office. He reviewed Willis's record and said that under the circumstances, he had no alternative but to recommend to Mr. Thomas Tucker, the Vice President of Operations, that Willis be discharged.

On June 30, 1974, Mr. Tucker accepted Wells's recommendation, and Willis and the union were informed of this decision at a meeting in Mr. Wells's office.

On July 6, 1974, Willis filed a grievance which said, "I contend that I have been unjustly discharged and am therefore processing this grievance on the basis of the company violation of Section 13 of the Collective Agreement."

Section 13 of the Agreement said:

Section 13
Reprimands, Suspensions and Dismissals

13.01   In the event of a decision by the Company to dismiss an employee who is a member of the Union, such decision shall immediately be subject to review by the Company and the Union, and shall, if desired by either party, be treated as a grievance in the third step of the grievance procedure in Section 15.01 of this Agreement. Failing a mutually satisfactory agreement as to justification for dismissal within two (2) days from the date such dismissal took place, the matter shall be carried through the remaining steps of the grievance procedure.

13.02   In any hearing conducted as a result of the terms of the foregoing paragraph, the employee concerned and the management representative on whose initiative disciplinary action is being taken, shall both be present.

13.03   No employee shall be reprimanded, suspended or dismissed except in the presence of a Shop Steward or a Union Executive Member. In dismissal cases the Union President or his nominee must be present. An employee may be sent home pending possible disciplinary action. In all cases and at least one hour prior to an employee being disciplined by the Superintendent, the reason or reasons for possible disciplinary action will be given to the employee in writing and the Union will also be notified in writing. This written statement shall contain no data regarding disciplinary action taken in the past.

13.04   No employee shall be suspended later than two (2) working days (excluding Saturday, Sunday and statutory holidays) after the alleged offense, or after the discovery of the alleged offense, unless this time is extended by agreement, in writing, between the Company and the Union Executive.

13.05   If it is found that an employee has been unjustly discharged or suspended, such employee shall be reinstated with pay from the date of his discharge or suspension.

13.06   Proper disciplinary action to be taken will be determined by the gravity of the offense and the time elapsed since the last offense. If an employee has not been formally disciplined for an interval of one year (two years in the case of suspension) his previous offenses will be referred to in the event that further disciplinary action is necessary. Any continuing punitive action taken at the time the employee was disciplined will cease at the expiration of the time limits set above.

13.07   A record of the disciplinary action taken will be given to the employee concerned, the Union and the Personnel Department.

After receiving the grievance, Mr. Wells called Harry Dunstable, the union President, to ask for an explanation of the union position. Mr. Dunstable said that neither Willis nor the union had received written notice of the company's intent to discharge.

Mr. Wells said that copies of a memorandum covering the content of the July 26 meeting were sent by his secretary as a matter of routine to Mr. Dunstable through the interoffice mail and to Willis at home. Mr. Dunstable said that he had never received his copy and did not believe that Willis had either.

Mr. Wells asked Mr. Dunstable if the union had any further arguments to make on the case. The answer was "no," so Mr. Wells suggested that the June 30 meeting be considered as the last step of the grievance procedure. Wells said that the company was not going to change its position, so the union's only recourse was arbitration.

On July 19 the company received a letter from the union referring the matter to arbitration, and naming its nominee to the three-man arbitration panel. The case was the first case within anyone's memory that the union had taken to arbitration.

TOPICS FOR DISCUSSION

1. If you were Mr. Wells, would you allow the case to go to arbitration?
2. In arbitration, what would be your arguments?
3. What do you think the union's arguments would be?
4. As an arbitrator, how would you rule?
5. What is your opinion of the "Discipline Without Punishment" system?

ALBERTA OIL COMPANY LTD. (B)

The Willis case went to arbitration, with the union arguing that the company had violated Section 13.03 of the collective agreement. The company argued that a memorandum of the June 26 meeting had been sent to Messrs. Dunstable and Willis as a matter of routine, although admitted that Mr. Wells did not sign the memo. The union said that the copies had never been received.

The company further argued that Willis was not dismissed as a matter of discipline, but rather because the company could no longer depend on him to perform his job on a regular basis.

The chairman of the arbitration tribunal said in his award that the company handled the matter of notification "too casually." He stated, "In situations of serious discipline or discharge for disciplinary reasons, the company should be meticulous in carrying out the requirements of the collective agreement."

However, the chairman did not view the Willis case as a matter of discipline. He said, "I'm satisfied that the second position taken by the company must be sustained, that is, that Mr. Willis was not dismissed as a matter of discipline and therefore the company was not required to comply with Section 13.03 of the agreement." In taking this position the chairman noted that the company had never disciplined or punished Willis, but in fact had done everything they could to help him out of his difficulties. He placed special emphasis on the four days off with pay that Willis was given to straighten out his personal affairs.

In conclusion, the chairman said, "It is always saddening and unpleasant to rule against a person in the circumstances of the present grievance but I see no other course open to the board. The grievance is dismissed and this board so awards."

The company continued to follow its policy of discipline without punishment, and supervision believed that it was working well. In the months following the Willis arbitration, two individuals were dismissed under this policy. The union did not challenge the company action in either instance. Also, two individuals resigned shortly after Step 4 (being sent home for the remainder of the shift, with pay). In both instances the resignations were voluntary. The individuals had concluded that a refinery was not a good place for them to be working. They said that the company had treated them fairly and that they were going to seek work elsewhere.

In late 1974, the driver of a gasoline truck was involved in a collision with a Sarnia city bus shortly after leaving the refinery. Both vehicles were extensively damaged, and several passengers on the bus were injured, although none seriously. Sarnia police found an open liquor bottle in the cab of the truck. However, charges were not laid.

An investigation by Mr. Fairfax, the Plant Manager, and Mr. Carrothers, the Distribution Superintendent, discovered that the driver of the truck, Donald Hildebrant, was known among his fellow workers as a man who "drank too much." One worker stated that he thought Hildebrandt was drunk when he came to work on the day of the accident.

Hildebrandt was an employee with fifteen years' service. His record before the accident was unblemished. The man was 53 years old, married, and had several small children.

Mr. Fairfax believed that the instance was one which demanded immediate dismissal. Mr. Tucker, the Vice President, refused to accept the recommendation, saying that he could not agree to discharge because of Hildebrant's seniority, age, and family situation.

"I'll tell you what, though," he said to Mr. Fairfax, "let's go ahead with the dismissal. If the union files a grievance, and I'm almost positive they will, I'll then change the penalty to four weeks off without pay. I think we also should take him off the driver's job until his drinking is under control."

ITEMS FOR DISCUSSION

1. What do you think of the arbitrator's opinion?

2. What do you think of Mr. Tucker's decision *re* Hildebrandt?

3. If you were Mr. Fairfax, what would you do now? Would you discipline and let grievance come?

ALBERTA OIL COMPANY LTD. (C)

Mr. Fairfax refused to agree to Mr. Tucker's plan to discharge Hildebrandt and then reduce the penalty when the union filed a grievance.

"I don't believe in playing that kind of game," Mr. Fairfax said. "We should make up our mind about what the appropriate penalty is, and then stick to our guns."

As a result, Hildebrandt was given a four-week suspension, without pay. After his return he was given another job in the refinery and not allowed to work as a truck driver.

The union did not file a grievance challenging the penalty imposed.

ITEM FOR DISCUSSION

1. Appraise the Hildebrandt incident in terms of the company's discipline policy.

B. HOURS OF WORK

The eight-hour workday and 40-hour workweek, with fixed starting and quitting times Monday through Friday, are generally thought to be the standard pattern of employment. However, many organizations operate on quite different patterns. Some production facilities, for example, operate around the clock: seven days a week, 365 days a year. Workers sometimes have starting and quitting times which vary from one week to the next. In some operations, like stevedoring, the hours are dependent on availability of work. In others, like banks and supermarkets, the hours are largely determined by the convenience of customers. In some companies the employees work four days a week, 10 to 12 hours each day, then take off the next three days. In still others there are no fixed starting and quitting times; rather the worker himself decides what hours he will work, constrained only by company expectations that he will put in a stated number of hours each week and will accommodate his schedule to others who may be dependent on his presence at certain times.[2]

Most collective agreements contain a section titled "Hours of Work." Often this spells out the starting and quitting times for all categories of employees covered by the agreement. Where more than one shift operates, the agreement will also indicate whether employees will remain on one shift or rotate from one to the other. In most union-management relations it is considered more desirable to work one shift than another; consequently premium payments are specified as inducements for those assigned to less desirable shifts. Sometimes a lesser number of hours is prescribed for these shifts either as a substitute for, or in addition to, the money inducements.

OVERTIME

Most jurisdictions in the United States and Canada prescribe limits in working time beyond which workers must receive premium pay. Similarly premium pay is required in most jurisdictions for work performed on Sundays and holidays. Some jurisdictions prohibit work on these days.

In most collective bargaining agreements there are provisions calling for premium pay for overtime work that are normally more liberal than those required by law. The subject of overtime is one of the most frequently debated subjects between companies and unions. Until recently unions expressed consistent interest in maximizing opportunities for overtime pay, and employees were generally eager to fatten their pocketbooks with time and a half or double time pay for added hours worked. As a result elaborate arrangements were worked out between many companies and unions to insure equitable distribution of overtime work. In some companies, for example, it is necessary to post lists of employees each week, with the number of overtime hours indicated next to each name. When work in a given category is available on overtime, the employee with the least number of hours who is qualified for the job must be asked first whether he wants to work. If he refuses, he is charged with the hours offered, but he is not paid; then the employee with the next fewest hours is asked. This process is repeated, with appropriate clerical adjustments being made to the lists, until a full complement of workers is secured.

The allocation of overtime work gives rise to many complaints. Sometimes, for example, a worker is skipped over in order to secure a person who is better qualified for the work. This then gives rise to claims for penalty pay. Most arrangements give some leeway to management to skip over workers in special circumstances, but many bitter battles are waged to be sure the overtime work is handled in a fair manner.

An issue of recent vintage concerns the compulsory nature of overtime. Some contracts require employees to perform overtime work at management's bidding, provided they are given adequate advance notice. In other company-union situations there is no such requirement stated in the contract, but past practice indicates that overtime work, if requested by the company, is compulsory. This means that an employee who refuses such work without good reason can be penalized for unexcused absence. Repeated refusals could lead to discipline and, possibly, discharge.

In recent years many unions have fought to eliminate compulsory overtime. This was a vital issue in the 1973 negotiations between the United Automobile Workers Union and the "Big-Three" auto producers. The union claimed that many members were no longer anxious to work extra hours for added pay, that they wanted more time to enjoy their families, to pursue leisure activities, and they did not want to be forced to work overtime at the companies' behest. Most likely the high earnings of auto workers played an important part in this apparent switch of attitude. This, plus a growing concern for improving the quality of life, for escaping the boredom and drudgery of assembly lines, played a part.

The companies opposed the demand — stating that customer demands sometimes required overtime work and pointing out that the production process could be severely crippled if some workers in a production facility agreed to work and others stayed home. After considerable haggling and after a brief strike by Chrysler workers a compromise was reached. Effective with the 1973 contract, overtime in the auto companies became voluntary after a prescribed number of hours each day or week. We can be reasonably certain that unions in other industries will be making similar inroads in the next several years and that the United Automobile Workers will raise the issue again in 1976, when the next contract will be negotiated. Voluntary overtime is apparently the ultimate goal.

*   *   *

The following case, "John Hemstead & Sons Ltd," concerns a company-union situation where the contract was not clear on whether overtime work was compulsory or voluntary. Management made certain commitments to their customers which required significant expenditures of overtime hours by the production work force in order to be met. Some of the workers balked, refused to work overtime and were threatened with discipline.

JOHN HEMSTEAD & SONS LTD.

John Hemstead & Sons Ltd. manufactured several varieties of string, rope and twine. Four years ago the company closed its baler twine plant in Springhill, Nova Scotia, and moved all operations to Halifax. As a result, about 225 new jobs were created at the Halifax plant, and baler twine came to constitute about 50 per cent of the plant's total production.

Baler twine was sold through a small number of large-volume distributors, and it was common practice in the industry to make sales commitments in the late summer of each year for delivery the following year. Last July Hemstead salesmen committed the company to delivery of 22 million pounds of twine in the next 12 months. Based on an estimated average production of 28,000 pounds per shift, the Production Manager, Mr. Jason McCleod, anticipated that delivery obligations could be met by running three shifts, each forty hours per week. This would put production operations at or near capacity for five days a week.

It was not long before the company gave signs of failure to meet expectations, producing only 1.2 million pounds of baler twine in the month of August. Thus, in September, the company, at Mr. McCleod's insistence, changed its schedule — requiring 44 hours per week on the first and second shifts and 47 hours per week on the third shift. Mr. McCleod calculated the new schedule on the assumption that most of the production employees would willingly work the overtime hours. However, the overtime work was on a voluntary basis, as it had always been in the past.

By September 29 Mr. McCleod was dismayed to discover only 1.23 million pounds of twine had been turned out in the first three weeks of the month — below the rate needed to meet sales commitments. This was because many more workers than expected had elected not to work on Saturdays. On the first Saturday in September, 15 per cent of the production workers were absent. On the second Saturday the figure was also 15 per cent and on the third it was 12 per cent. While accurate production figures were not in for the fourth week, Mr. McCleod received word on the 29th, a Friday, that more than 16 per cent of the production workers had indicated to their foremen they did not intend to work the next day, September 30. Thus, Mr. McCleod decided to institute compulsory overtime effective the following week. He posted the following notice next to time clocks in each department:

Notice

It is expected, and indeed required, that all employees work each day during the work week. Effective Saturday, October 7, scheduled overtime work will be compulsory.

Many departments are now working a 5 1/2-day scheduled work-week. Check your bulletin board or ask your foreman for the presently scheduled hours of work in your department.

To insure the security of your job, it is extremely important to maintain a good attendance record.

The following Monday, Mr. McCleod learned that 16.5 per cent of the productive work force had been absent the previous Saturday. Production for the day had been 48,000 pounds for 15 work hours. As a result, Mr. McCleod had a meeting with the production foremen on Monday morning. He said that effective the following Saturday the regular procedure for unexcused absences — used for normal workdays — would apply to overtime work. Under this procedure employees absent without good reason received an oral warning for the first offense, then for succeeding offenses a written warning and a three-day suspension. In the event of four such absences, the employee was discharged.

On November 6 Mr. Frederick Thompson, who had been absent for the fourth successive Saturday on the 4th, was discharged. His only reason for the absences was that he did not feel like working.

Mr. Thompson had received an oral warning following his absence on Saturday, October 14, a written warning for his absence on October 21, and a three-day suspension — October 30, October 31 and November 1 — for his absence of October 28. On the Monday following each of the absences he indicated that he felt 40 hours of work in a week was sufficient and that the company, under the labor agreement, had no right to insist on more.

This was the first instance where the company's unexcused absence procedure had been used in respect to refusals to work overtime. The procedure had been in existence for nearly twelve years and had never been seriously challenged by the union. In its years of existence two discharges and seven suspensions had been levied for excess unexcused absences.

The following day, November 7, Mr. Thompson filed the following grievance:

> I feel that I have worked my normal 40 hours under the terms of the contract and have been unjustly discharged. I request pay for three days of suspension and for time lost as a result of my unjust discharge.

Mr. Thompson was represented by Local 12 of the Textile Workers

Union of America (TWUA). Mr. George O'Toole, General Secretary of the local, indicated that Thompson's was a test case — that more than 200 members of the local had received warnings for Saturday absences in the last month and that all of them — if necessary — were likely to stay out on subsequent Saturdays to preserve the workers' belief that overtime never was and never should be made compulsory. According to Mr. O'Toole the union never assented to a change in hours, and the labor contract expressly forbade a unilateral change.

Prior to holding a grievance meeting to discuss the Thompson case Mr. McCleod met with Mr. O'Toole to show him the production figures and to demonstrate the need for overtime work. "I can't help it if your salesmen committed you to do more work than you can handle," said O'Toole. "We signed a contract to work 40 hours per week — no more, no less. And we've reaffirmed time and again during negotiations that overtime work — when available — is voluntary. If you want to reopen the contract, just say so, and I'll approach the membership. But I'll warn you — a reopening on this issue will reopen it on other issues as well."

Mr. O'Toole pointed out to Mr. McCleod that other alternatives were open to him. He said there were about 150 union members in the area without work and a fairly large unemployed population in Halifax which could be hired to augment the existing work force. As another alternative, Mr. O'Toole suggested that Hemstead could schedule eight hours instead of four for those who wished to work Saturdays. In this way the needed production could be attained with a reduced work force. As another, Sunday work could be scheduled. Since the contract called for double time pay on Sundays, this might attract a significant additional number of people.

Mr. McCleod rejected all three of Mr. O'Toole's suggestions — pointing out that the nature of the production operations was such that maximum efficiency was obtained only when all or nearly all workers were present. Machine operations predominated at Hemstead. With the increased production schedule, the plant operated at or near capacity during the week. To add more employees would be impossible. "More hours on Saturday or overtime on Sunday was out of the question," said Mr. McCleod, "because of the great expenses involved." Mr. McCleod had figures to show that efficiency dropped by nearly 20 per cent during overtime hours worked in September.

Mr. McCleod said employees were obligated to work the overtime if the company required it.

While honestly feeling his position was right, Mr. McCleod wondered what he should do. It seemed clear to him on the one hand that the union would not move from their position and that within a few weeks many more employees, in addition to Mr. Frederick Thompson, would face suspensions, and possibly discharge, if they continued to refuse Saturday work. This could involve some loyal, long-service employees. On the other hand, promises had been made to customers and Mr. McCleod felt he needed to assert, once and for all, the right of the company to require overtime work.

Pertinent Contract Clauses

Article I. Management

It is recognized that the employer has the responsibility of operating the business and of promoting and maintaining its welfare; it is agreed that it is to the interest of employees, as well as stockholders, that the welfare of the business be promoted and maintained.

It is further agreed that the employer must be free to exercise its best judgment along such lines, among others, as increasing or decreasing operations; removing or installing machinery or equipment, or changing its nature; the regulation of the quality and quantity of production; the relieving of employees from duty because of lack of work; the employment, laying off or re-employment and transfer of employees; maintaining discipline and efficiency of employees; the demotion, promotion or discharge of employees for cause as efficient operation of the plant shall, in the opinion of the employer, require; provided that the exercise of such functions by the employer shall be in conformity with the provisions of this contract.

Article II. A. Hours

The pay week shall begin and end at midnight Sunday night.

The regular hours of work per shift shall be eight (8) hours per day and forty (40) hours per week from Monday through Friday, inclusive, except that in those departments where the full forty (40) hours are not regularly scheduled from Monday through Friday, the regular hours of work may be less than eight (8) hours per day from Monday through Friday and as many hours on Saturday as are necessary to make forty (40) hours.

Article II. B. Schedule of Hours

A schedule of the hours of work for each shift and each group of employees, and establishing a work week, shall be prepared immediately by the employer and delivered to the local union. The union will be advised of any proposed change in schedule of hours, before adoption. Any dissatisfaction with a change in schedule of hours adopted by the employer shall be handled as outlined in Article IV, the grievance procedure of this agreement.

Article II. C. Overtime

1. All employees shall be paid one and one-half (1 1/2) their regular rates of pay for work performed in excess of eight (8) hours per day or forty (40) hours per week.
2. All employees, except firemen and engineers whose regular work week includes Sunday work, shall receive twice the regular rates of pay for work performed on Sunday.
3. Work performed on Saturday shall be paid for at the rate of one and one-half (1 1/2) times the employee's regular rate of pay, except in the following cases:
   (a) Those hours worked on Saturday as part of the regular schedule by employees in any one of the departments referred to in the exception of Section (A) above.
   (b) Those hours worked on Saturday by the third shift as part of its regularly scheduled work week of 40 hours.
   (c) Where the work is performed by engineers and firemen whose regularly scheduled work week includes Saturday work.
4. Engineers and firemen shall be paid one and one-half (1 1/2) times the regular rates of pay for work performed on the sixth day, and twice the regular rates of pay for work performed on the seventh day, in their regularly scheduled work week.

Article IV. Grievance Procedure

Step 1. Should any employee feel that he has been unjustly treated, he or his union representative, or both, may discuss the problem with his foreman in an attempt to adjust the matter promptly.

Step 2. Problems not settled in Step 1 may be appealed to the Production Manager. They shall be discussed, if appealed, within seven (7) working days of the appeal. The Production Manager shall answer in writing within seven (7) working days of the meeting.

Step 3. Problems not settled in Steps 1 or 2 may be appealed to a Board of Arbitration. In event of such an appeal each party shall choose one (1) representative who, in turn, shall select a third impartial member. Failing to agree on an impartial member, the two (2) above-mentioned representatives shall select an impartial member from a panel of seven (7) arbitrators furnished by the Department of Labour. The impartial member shall be selected by the company representative and the union representative, each alternately striking a name from the list until only one name remains.... The Board of Arbitration shall render a decision on the grievance within the scope of this Contract, and under no circumstances shall it modify or change this Contract. The decision of the Board shall be final and binding on both parties.

In considering the chances of success if he submitted the overtime issue to arbitration, Mr. McCleod went back over notes he had collected from negotiations in past years. Article II, in its present form, had been written first 22 years ago and had existed in the same form ever since. During those 22 years no employee had been forced to work overtime, although there were many instances when overtime work was performed. Until now, sufficient numbers of workers had been willing to work overtime, when needed, so it had been unnecessary to compel the employees to work more than 40 hours.

Mr. McCleod, himself, had joined the company 24 years ago, but he had not participated in negotiations until seven years later. However, there were notes in his files written by Mr. Caleb Shepard, now deceased. Mr. Shepard had been a member of the management negotiating team during the early years. The notes collected by Mr. Shepard in negotiations of 22 years ago indicated that the company's intent, in agreeing to Article II, was to give the company a right to compel overtime. On the other hand, Mr. George Franko, chief negotiator for TWUA at the time, also kept notes — shown to Mr. McCleod by Mr. O'Toole. They indicated that Mr. Franko, at the time, intended that Article II would provide for voluntary overtime work and that a company proposal for phraseology that would require overtime at the company's discretion was turned down.

Apparently the issue did not arise again until a grievance meeting that took place six years later. At that time the union had made a request to Mr. McCleod that maintenance workers should be permitted to work overtime whenever operating employees worked. The grievance was rejected by Mr. McCleod at the time — arguing that the company was not required to provide overtime work for maintenance men — that mere existence of the need for production work on overtime did not automatically call for maintenance support. The decision was not appealed.

Mr. O'Toole had taken notes on the grievance. These indicated that Mr. McCleod and other management representatives had argued that parallel rights were involved — that management did not have to provide overtime and, in turn, the employees did not have to work overtime. The union's notes contained a quote reading as follows:

> Mr. Jacks (company Personnel Manager) stated that the union could not force the management to work any employees over forty (40) hours per week, and management, similarly, could not force any employee to work over 40 hours.

Neither Mr. McCleod nor Mr. Jacks could recall Jacks' having made such a statement but neither did they rule out the possibility.

Thirteen years ago (three years after the grievance) both the company and the union addressed themselves in contract negotiations to the specific issue of whether an employee could be compelled to work overtime. Mr. McCleod's notes read as follows:

> Mr. O'Toole (chief TWUA negotiator) brought up the question of overtime — saying that foremen sometimes discriminated between one group of workers and another regarding overtime — that workers felt overtime was not compulsory. Mr. George Franko (member of the TWUA team) then commented that one group of men had been asked to work, with the idea that they *had* to work, whether or not they wanted to. Mr. Jacks (company Personnel Manager) then asked what use is an employee if we can't get him to work when we need him. Mr. Jacks added that we try to avoid overtime, because it is expensive, but he asked whether a worker whom we asked to work overtime and refuses is worth as much as one who says yes. Mr. Franko didn't answer the question but he referred to cases where a man doesn't feel like working. Mr. Jacks replied if such a man tells the foreman he doesn't feel like working for reasons of health, the foreman won't require him to work, but he wants some evidence he is ill.
>
> Mr. O'Toole pointed out the collective agreement spelled out a regular schedule of hours and said that when a man does that regular schedule he fulfills his obligations. The union objected to foremen going to individual workers to get them to work overtime and making veiled threats if they refused.

In the negotiations of 13 years ago both company and union agreed that in administering overtime a worker should be given two days' notice, if possible, in the event weekend overtime was scheduled, and that an attempt would be made to equalize overtime hours within each worker classification. Anyone who refused overtime work, the parties agreed, would be charged with the hours, as if they were worked, in calculating equal distribution. Then, several days later, the parties returned to the matter of compulsory versus voluntary overtime. Mr. McCleod's note disclosed the following:

> Mr. Franko then raised another point — that a foreman should not say to a man, "Work or suffer the consequences," if a man has a reasonable excuse. Mr. Jacks replied that if a man explains his reasons to the foreman, there should be no problem.
>
> Mr. Lanning [TWUA Steward and member of the negotiating team] asked whether under the contract the men are compelled to work. Mr. Jacks replied with a question asking if his previous reply to Mr. Franko sounded like compulsion. Mr. Lanning then said that his men wanted to know if they refused to work just because they didn't want to, would they be compelled to work. Mr. O'Toole then interrupted — asking if we could get something in writing — that the union wanted to end griping caused by foremen who ask a worker to

work along with veiled threats, "If you don't you'll have to suffer the consequences."

Mr. Dick Lanning commented that men had not been asked for a reason when they declined overtime work — that the foreman just went on to the next man. He added that practically everyone wants overtime.

Mr. Franko then said, "It's not compulsory for people to work if they are not feeling right or have other plans." Mr. Franko said the union would advise workers to cooperate, but then men want to feel they're free — without any threats.

Mr. McCleod pointed out that in the past 90 per cent of those who had been asked, worked. There could be a problem if 25 per cent refused and 15 per cent gave no reason. Mr. Franko admitted that this might present a problem but said management could not invoke a penalty under the agreement if a man refused to work.

Mr. McCleod said the company wanted men to work overtime when there is overtime work to do — that no one had been fired for refusing to work — yet. (Everyone agreed on this matter.) Mr. McCleod said these negotiations were the first time he had heard of threats being used by foremen to compel overtime — that there would be none of that in the future. Mr. Jacks added his comment — that naturally we can't compel anyone to work, and this is the first he had heard of any threat.

Mr. McCleod was not sure whether notes from past negotiations were relevant to the issue at hand, because the issue of compulsory overtime had never presented itself in day-to-day operations. He wondered whether he should approach the union representatives and ask for an agreement. To do so would be tantamount to admitting his own doubts about whether management could compel overtime under the existing contract. Also, it would risk opening other provisions of the contract to renegotiation. The existing agreement still had almost two years to run, but Mr. McCleod was aware of dissatisfaction within the union because leaders had settled for a wage increase in negotiations one year ago giving a 5.2 per cent a year increase for the next three years. Other firms in the area were signing this year for 7 per cent and more.

Mr. McCleod felt reasonably certain he could win a case if it were brought to arbitration; but the time, expense and potential damage to existing relationships all deterred him from that course of action.

C. JOB CLASSIFICATION AND JOB ASSIGNMENT

Job classification is the process by which various jobs are grouped for purposes of compensation. Those jobs which are of a similar nature or content are placed in the same classification and assigned the same wage or salary range.

In some firms the respective classifications are determined by a process known as job evaluation. There are many different plans for job evaluation. Some involve simple ranking of jobs; others involve sophisticated factor analyses.

Where a union is present, the nature of the evaluation plan is often negotiated, and the actual evaluation is frequently a joint process. The initial issues are: 1. What factors are to be measured? 2. What are people going to be paid for? Once these factors — called *compensable factors* — are determined, a secondary issue becomes: what shall the relative weights of these factors be?

Perhaps the best known job evaluation system is the Cooperative Wage Study (CWS) which was developed by the United Steel Workers of America in cooperation with 86 steel firms in the United States in the late 1940s. Now, after numerous revisions, the CWS plan is used in many industries throughout North America. Twelve factors are used to determine the proper evaluation of a job. Each of them is weighted in accordance with the chart below.[3]

Factors	Weight	Job requirement measured
1. Pre-employment training	1.0	The mentality required to absorb training and exercise judgment for the satisfactory performance of the job.
2. Employment training and experience	4.0	The time required to learn how to do the job, producing work of acceptable quality and of sufficient quantity to justify continued employment.
3. Mental skill	3.5	The mental ability, job knowledge, judgment, and ingenuity required to visualize, reason through,

		and plan the details of a job without recourse to supervision.
4. Manual skill	2.0	The physical or muscular ability and dexterity required in performing a given job, including the use of tools, machines, and equipment.
5. Responsibility for materials	10.0	The obligation imposed either by authority or by the inherent nature of the job to prevent loss through damage to materials. Both the care required and the probable monetary loss are considered.
6. Responsibility for tools and equipment	4.0	The obligation imposed on the workman for attention and care to prevent damage to tools and equipment with which he is actually working or which come under his control. Both the care and the probable cost of damage at any one time are considered.
7. Responsibility for operations	6.5	The obligation imposed on the workman for utilizing capacity of equipment or process by maintenance of pace and machine speeds. This includes planning, instructing, and directing the work of others.
8. Responsibility for safety of others	2.0	The degree of care required by the nature of the job and the surroundings in which it is performed, to avoid or prevent injuries to other persons.

9. Mental effort	2.5	The mental or visual concentration and attention required by the job for the performance of work at normal pace. Select that level which best describes the average degree of muscular exertion required throughout the turn.
10. Physical effort	2.5	The muscular exertion required by the job when the employee is performing at a normal pace.
11. Surroundings	3.0	The general conditions under which the work is performed, other than hazards, and the extent to which these conditions make the job disagreeable.
12. Hazards	2.0	The probability and severity of injuries to which the workman is exposed, assuming that the workman is exercising reasonable care in observing safety regulations.

Each of the factors is broken down into degrees, which are used to indicate the extent to which the factor is present in any particular job. Following is an example of how one of the factors, physical effort, is broken down.[4]

Factor 10, Physical Effort

Consider the muscular exertion required by the job when the employee is performing at a normal pace. Select that level which best describes the average degree of muscular exertion required throughout the turn.

Code	Job requirements	Numerical classifi- cation
A	Minimum physical exertion. Perform very light work such as sitting or standing	Base

for purposes of observations, and such
work as very light assembly and adjustment.
Plan and direct work.
Weigh and record.

B	Light physical exertion. Use light hand tools and handle fairly light materials manually. Operate crane-type controls, light valves. Operate truck or tractor. Sweep, clean up. Shovel light material.	0.3
C	Moderate physical exertion. Handle medium-weight materials. Use a variety of medium-sized hand tools for performing tradesman's work. Climb and work from ladders. Operate heavy controls and valves. Use light sledge.	0.8
D	Heavy physical exertion. Use heavy tools and handle heavy materials manually. Shovel heavy material. Use pick, heavy bars. Operate heavy pneumatic tools.	1.5
E	Extreme physical effort. Extremely heavy lifting, pushing or pulling.	2.5

In installing a new system, once the jobs are evaluated, jobs with similar (but not necessarily exact) point totals are grouped into job classifications. Finally wage rates are assigned to each classification. At the Steel Company of Canada, for example, jobs are grouped into 28 job classes, with about a nine-cent-per-hour wage difference between each classification.

ADMINISTRATIVE PROBLEMS

Once a job evaluation plan has been installed, administrative problems are likely to be encountered in two types of situations, one involving a new or changed job and one involving technological change.

With new jobs, the issue is the evolution of the job and its classification. Since the process is subjective, there is room for disagreement. Since the classification influences the rate of pay for a job with perhaps a ten or more cents per hour difference between one classification and another (and this over the life span of the job) there is an incentive for the employee and the union to attempt to place the job in the highest possible classification. There is a similar incentive for management in the opposite direction. Both parties face the constraint of keeping the classification and pay of new jobs more or less in line with that of existing jobs.

Changes in existing jobs create similar problems. When changes are made the issue becomes: have enough duties been added or subtracted to merit a change in the classification? Under most systems, minor changes should not result in a change of classification; but when are changes major and minor? Employees can naturally be expected to resist a downward classification, simply because of its impact on earnings.

Aside from mere changes in jobs, technological change can create real problems under a job evaluation system. The problems occur when changes created by the technological change are such that the factors used in the existing system cannot provide for the maintenance of earnings levels which existed prior to the change. For example, suppose a manufacturing process is automated so that now all the machine operator has to do is push a button, rather than make complicated adjustments to the machine. The skill level required for operation has obviously declined. In a plan where the factor of skill has a relatively large weight in the job evaluation system, the job could be expected to be reclassified at a lower level. The employee would be faced with a wage cut, and under circumstances like these the parties are frequently under pressure to change the *plan* so that earnings opportunities can be maintained.

JOB ASSIGNMENT

The process by which individuals are placed in various job classifications is called "job assignment." This process may also cause problems, because it immediately sets in motion the process of comparison. Two persons working side by side in a work team are sometimes expected to perform different, but complementary, tasks and are paid different wages. Sometimes they even share incentive earnings, though their base wages are different. This is the situation in the case that follows, titled "R. G. Williamson Company Ltd." The Williamson case raises many issues, but the matter of job assignments is perhaps the most important.

R. G. WILLIAMSON COMPANY LTD.

The Weapons Division of R. G. Williamson Company produced swords, épées and sabers used in the sport of fencing and by various theatrical and motion picture groups as props and garnishments for "period" costumes. About 45 production workers were employed in the division.

The final operations in the production of these weapons involved straightening, grinding, straightening again, then inspection. A team of four men worked on these operations. Each member of the team received an hourly rate based on his classification and, in addition, received a

group incentive bonus for each weapon turned out. The first straightening operation was performed on a mechanical straightening press,
operated by a man classified as "Straightener B." From the press the
weapon went to a grinder operator who removed small burrs. Also he
produced a high luster and semisharpness to the blades. Following
grinding, the weapon went to a Straightener A who, working with an
inspector, provided the final touches with an assortment of mallets,
hammers and a small hand press. The inspector placed the weapon in a
jig, made several measurements and applied the final polishing touches
with a buffer. While tolerances were not severe, it was essential that the
weapons used for fencing comply with requirements of the Amateur
Athletic Union.

While the straighteners, the grinder and the inspector worked in
close proximity, only the Straightener A and inspector were dependent
on each other. Typically the grinder and the Straightener A had a backlog
of weapons ahead of them so that they could do their jobs without
waiting for the Straightener B. The inspector almost never had a backlog.

For nearly six weeks prior to September 25, Frank Staiger, the
Straightener A, was absent because of illness. As a result, Hugh Lovell,
the Straightener B, was transferred temporarily to Staiger's work, and a
relatively new man was placed on Lovell's job — operating the press.
Since the Straightener A's job required considerable experience and an
expert touch, Staiger's job was rated higher than Lovell's, and Staiger's
higher hourly rate was assigned to Lovell for the time he was on the job.
However, Lynn Peters, the replacement on the straightening press, was
considerably slower than Lovell, and the group's incentive earnings fell
drastically. Members of the crew complained repeatedly to foreman Roy
Anderson, in an effort to have the incentive rate adjusted while Peters
developed his skill on the job. As an alternative the men asked for a
guaranteed minimum wage equivalent to their average earnings before
Staiger became ill.

On the morning of September 25, Mr. Lovell, who had been most
vociferous about the poor incentive earnings since Staiger's illness,
reported to the plant nurse — complaining of headaches. He had told his
foreman that he did not think he could continue work that day. Roy
Anderson, the foreman, promptly notified the union steward that if
Lovell left the plant the other three men on the incentive team would have
to be laid off. Heeding Lovell's complaints, the nurse sent him home at 11
A.M. Anderson then informed Messrs. David Davies, the grinder, and
Robert Douglas, the inspector, that they were being laid off at 12 noon for
the remainder of the shift which ended at 3 P.M. Peters remained at work
for the rest of the day to build a bank for the others. Article V, Paragraph

3 of the Collective Agreement, titled, "Seniority," provided for temporary layoffs as follows:

> Layoffs for a period of one (1) week or less shall be deemed temporary and shall not be subject to the provisions of this Article, provided there is reasonable justification for such temporary layoff. The seniority section of the contract contained an elaborate procedure governing layoffs of more than one week. In essence, the worker with least seniority in the plant in the classification affected got laid off, but the chain reaction caused by departmental, then divisional, layoffs often involved five or six displacements preceding the eventual layoff.

This provision had been negotiated five years earlier and had been part of company-union agreements since then. Davies and Douglas punched out at 12 noon, but the next day both men filed grievances — stating that their layoffs were not justified and demanding pay for the three hours missed. Their steward, Frank Wiesner, argued that there was not reasonable justification for the layoffs. At 11 A.M., when Lovell left the plant, there was a sufficient backlog of work so that both men could have worked their regular jobs for the remainder of the shift. Wiesner observed that there were plenty of weapons to keep Davies going and that Peters, if necessary, could have switched to Straightener A work in order to keep Douglas, the inspector, supplied.

Foreman Anderson acknowledged there was enough work in the "bank" for Davies to fill out the shift, but stated that the backlog would have been depleted by morning and then Davies would have had to stand around waiting for Peters. "Furthermore, I had no idea whether Lovell would be in the next day," said Anderson. He continued:

> As for Douglas — his work was closely tied to the second straightener, and he had no backlog that day. Peters never tried the Straightener A work before, and it would've been unreasonable to expect him to gain any competence in the few hours remaining that day.

Steward Wiesner pointed out that other grinders and inspectors in the plant had less seniority than Davies and Douglas and, if the company could justify the need for a temporary layoff, the lesser-seniority men should have gone out — that Davies and Douglas should have been transferred. Two other grinders — Powell and Kiessling — worked that afternoon on jobs that Davies had done in the past, and both had less seniority. One inspector — Peter Blake — had less seniority than Douglas, and he worked that day on a job Douglas had done in the past.

Anderson said:

> I can't prove it, but you know as well as I that this was one of a long line of incidents by these men to get some padding in the incentive rate. They've had a lush job for years and now — with Staiger gone — they've got to eat hamburgers like the rest of us. All three men — Lovell, Davies and Douglas — have been goofing off lately — taking extra long breaks, long lunch hours and reporting to the nurse for every ache or pain. I'm not going to switch the whole shop around just to suit their whims.

"I don't know about these men goofing off," said Wiesner, "but if they are, you've got a disciplinary procedure to follow. In this situation you've violated the contract. The temporary layoff provision was not intended as a substitute for discipline."

Foreman Anderson, after hearing Wiesner's arguments, went to his superior, James Heintskill, Manager of the Weapons Division, and told him what had happened. "I may get stuck," said Anderson, "but if I have to pay these guys for doing nothing everyone in the shop will play us for fools." Anderson said that if Davies had worked on the 25th and exhausted his backlog and if Lovell had failed to come in the next day the company would have been liable for four hours' reporting pay. "I sent the two blokes home in order to avoid that possibility," said Anderson.

Article XIII of the Collective Agreement provided for reporting pay as follows:

> An employee who is instructed to report for work and finds his regular work not available, shall be given four (4) hours of work, or four (4) hours' pay in lieu of work, at the employee's current straight-time hourly rate, exclusive of shift premiums.
>
> In the event the employee refuses to accept work offered him in accordance with the provisions herein set forth, such employee shall not be entitled to the compensation mentioned above. An employee who is not notified before quitting time on any work day not to report for work the succeeding day is deemed to be instructed to report for work.
>
> If failure to provide work is due to an Act of God or a condition beyond the control of the Company, then the Company shall not be required to pay reporting pay.

"Even if we have to pay the three hours for sending them home improperly," said Anderson, "we've saved ourselves four hours' call-in pay."

Mr. Heintskill, in looking over the Collective Agreement, felt that Article II, titled "Hours of Work," might be partly applicable:

> *A Work Day.* The usual work day is defined as eight (8) hours of work in a twenty-four (24)-hour period. Except for any unpaid lunch

period provided according to prevailing practice, the hours of the work day are consecutive.

The provisions of this Article shall not be construed as a guarantee by the company of hours for work to be provided per day or per week.

"This section, plus the section on Temporary Layoffs, should support us," said Heintskill.

"I certainly don't want to take a position that I'm going to switch people all around the factory just because of a temporary situation. And if we don't apply the temporary layoff provision in this case, we won't ever be able to apply it."

This was the first time the temporary layoff provision of the contract had been used. In the past, when emergency situations occurred because of unexpected absences or temporary shortages of material, the workers affected were transferred to other jobs in their same classification or in lower classifications without any reduction in base pay. Mr. Heintskill wondered whether past practices barred use of the temporary layoff on September 25.

Article V, in addition to the temporary layoff paragraph, had the following provisions:

> For the purpose of layoffs in connection with the decreasing of the working force and for the purpose of recalling to work employees so laid off the following factors shall be considered:
> a) Ability to perform the required work;
> b) physical fitness for the job;
> c) length of continuous service.
> Where factors (a) and (b) are relatively equal, length of continuous service shall govern.
> "Ability to perform the required work," as used in this Article, shall mean that the employee possesses the required skill and ability to perform the work in a reasonably satisfactory manner, without any training, and subject to physical fitness of the employee to perform the job.

D. PRODUCTION STANDARDS AND INCENTIVES

Production standards have many forms. All of them are designed to provide a fix on probable output and to provide a benchmark against which individual performances can be compared. Sometimes rates of pay are tied directly to production standards in the form of piecework incentives. More often they are tied indirectly to the standards; those workers who consistently attain or exceed standards are rewarded more often with raises in pay and promotions than those who do not.

If production standards are set consistently and updated whenever changes in methods of operation are incorporated they are useful devices for predicting costs, for scheduling production and for locating workers who are ill-suited to the jobs to which they have been assigned. In the latter respect, a good standards program can help supervisors determine where additional training and instruction should take place and, occasionally, can help determine where replacements are needed.

In instances where production standards are tied directly to earnings by way of an incentive plan, there is far more concern by workers and their representatives about the derivation of the standards. Usually standards themselves are subject to grievance, provided there is a challenge registered within a reasonable time after they have been set. And since many standards are subject, in part, to subjective assessments by a methods engineer, long and bitter battles are sometimes fought over the question of the methods engineer's judgment in assigning a few thousandths of a second as an expected time for doing a job. Naturally, in an incentive plan, the worker figures to benefit from standards which provide them plenty of time to do a job, because any improvement he can make in actual performance to shorten that time will result in direct additions to his pocketbook.

In collective agreements covering relationships where incentive systems are in operation there are usually clauses which protect workers against capricious and frequent changes in standards. A typical clause providing such protection is the following:

Present incentive rates are not to be changed unless there has been a significant change in methods, tools, material, design or production conditions.

Such clauses are designed to protect workers from arbitrary "rate cutting" where a standard has been improperly set or where an individual worker has managed to develop his own production short cuts that allow for production (and incentive earnings) at above standard levels.

Some managements, in an effort to cut costs, try to make minor changes in method or design in order to achieve a restudy of a job and thus change the standard. Where such attempts occur, and even where changes in methods, tools, materials, or design are legitimate, another question arises: Were the changes significant enought to warrant a restudy of the job and a change in the standard? This question is often the subject of a grievance.

When a restudy is done, there is often a question of whether the new rate is fair. On changed jobs, the question of fairness is usually related to the employee's earnings levels before the change was made. If the employee does not have the same earnings opportunities under the new standard that he had under the old, he will understandably feel that his pay has been unreasonably cut.

DEMORALIZED INCENTIVE PLANS

Where jobs are not restudied as a consequence of minor changes in method, material, or design there is a tendency for incentive rates to become out of line over time. Usually in such cases earnings have gradually crept up as well. Thus old jobs are likely to have higher earnings than new jobs. Often-times workers assigned to nearly identical jobs adjacent to each other find that the earning opportunities for one are far better than those for the other, thus giving rise to complaints, grievances, and demands to make the opportunities alike. Neither companies nor union leaders are readily able to cope with such complaints, and the grievance machinery sometimes gets bogged down with cases that are extremely difficult to solve. When this occurs, and when there is general agreement that incentive earnings are unrelated to effort, the system is said to be "demoralized."

Demoralized incentive systems are intolerable for both unions and companies. From the union's standpoint they represent a split in the ranks between those who have jobs with attractive opportunities to make money and those who do not. From the company's viewpoint they often indicate higher-than-normal labor costs. In some instances the costs have been so high that companies were forced to shut their doors. More often, however, a demoralized system has given rise to a contract demand for complete revision or abolishment of the system. Such a demand is always accompanied by a high price tag, because when an incentive plan is discontinued or revised the unions usually want a guarantee that past earnings levels will be maintained.

*   *   *

A short case follows — titled "The Apex Case." This describes a production operation on which incentive earnings became higher and higher through the years as a result of management's inattention to frequent small changes in the methods of operation and as a result of so-called skill and efficiency of the operators. Now, 22 years after the operation was first put into effect, a change in methods has been prescribed by management, the standards have been adjusted, and the workers have filed a grievance which gives rise to issues that have far-reaching impact.

THE APEX CASE

The Railroad Products Division of R. G. Budd Company manufactured galvanized steel grated walkways for freight cars and diesel locomotives and sold them exclusively to the Apex Railroad Products Company in the United States. Aside from adjustments needed to accommodate differences in width and length, the various walkway sections were manufactured in the same manner. Steel sheets were sheared and notched by a press to produce strips ranging in height from two to two and one-half inches, in thickness from 3/16 to 5/16 of an inch, and in length from one and one-half to four feet. One edge of each strip was flat; the other had scallops designed for firm footing. The strips — called beam bars — were fitted in criss-cross fashions with somewhat heavier, nonscalloped, crossbars. The bars were nested in preformed notches cut on both bars at three-inch intervals. A press forced the bars together, and the galvanizing operation — following straightening and grinding — served to weld them sufficiently for the purpose they would serve.

The key operations in production of walkways were called "assemble and press." These had been essentially unchanged for the past 24 years. Two men, one working on each side of an assembly table, placed the crossbars and beam bars into a jig, which was adjusted from time to time for differences in size. There were identical assembly tables on two sides of a large ram press. When the assembly of a section was completed one of the operators pushed a button to move his table underneath the press. Then he pressed another button to activate the press — forcing the bars together via the notches — and a third button to move the table from under the press so that the assembled walkway could be removed from the jig. Work was then begun on a new assembly. The controls of the assembly tables were wired so that it was impossible for the tables on opposite sides of the press to be activated at the same time.

Operators on the assembly tables were instructed by their foremen to activate each of the three buttons only after the prior operation was completed. Thus, the button to lower and raise the press was to be pushed only after the assembly table had moved in under the press and stopped. Times were assigned to the three button-pushing operations as follows: table in — .155; press — .080; table out — .130; — (Times are expressed as fractions of minutes.) Industrial engineers recorded those times based on stop-watch observations. The total time for the three operations was .365 minutes.

Soon after the assemble-and-press operation was inaugurated the operators modified the prescribed technique in order to activate the press, thus starting the downward action of the ram while the assembly table was moving into position under the ram. A highly skilled operator could time the action so that the press ram made contact with the grating just as the table came into full position. Then, just before the pressing had been completed, the button initiating the "table-out" action was activated. Thus, the table began to move from under the press at about the instant that the ram was released. As a result of their skill in exercising these short-timing techniques, some operators were able to reduce the total time for the combined three elements to as low as .250 minutes. Consequently earnings on the assemble-and-press operation were extremely favorable. First shift operators during the past year realized earnings averaging $4.60 per hour, 44 per cent over normal; second shift earnings were $4.56 per hour, 42 1/2 per cent over normal; and third shift earnings were $4.00, 25 per cent over normal. Third shift earnings under the synchronized method were considerably below those of the first two shifts, because the third shift operated only two or three months, cumulatively, in each year, and operators on assemble-and-press had little time to become accustomed to the job before facing layoffs. Time study policy at R. G. Budd was informally acknowledged to allow 30 per cent earning opportunity on all jobs. Consequently a 30 per cent factor was added into all machine-controlled operations where operators were not able to exercise skill and effort.

The synchronized method of assemble-and-press was observed and acknowledged by supervisors in the shop and by the industrial engineers. No one discouraged it or attempted to change it. This was a favorite job in the division — one with steady employment characteristics, less than average difficulty in performance and high earnings. The only time it caused trouble was when an operator failed to time the buttons correctly so that the press ram reached the bottom of its stroke before the assembly table was in position. Sometimes this resulted in considerable damage to the table, but most often it simply caused spoilage of the walkway section to be pressed. Repair bills caused by damage from improper synchronization of the press averaged $3,212 each year for the past ten years. Repairs to the press and table from such damage resulted in an average of four days' down time each year. Because of this, foremen in the division always instructed new operators to activate the three buttons as prescribed by the original time study.

THE SUGGESTION SYSTEM

Approximately one and a half years ago R. G. Budd Company initiated a suggestion plan designed to tap the ideas of all employees for improvements that would save the company money. It was an attractive plan — providing 25 per cent of the first year's estimated savings to the successful suggestor. All employees were eligible to make suggestions, except that eligibility did not extend to those whose suggestions could be considered within his direct area of responsibility. The Industrial Relations Director, for example, could not receive an award for a suggestion to change the wording of a collective agreement which he had responsibility to negotiate. Eligibility for awards under the suggestion plan was decided upon by a committee of three — headed by the Industrial Relations Director. Whenever in doubt the committee decided questions of eligibility in favor of the suggestor — thus endeavoring to preserve the attractiveness of the suggestion system.

Last June 5 the committee received a suggestion from Mr. Philip Evans, industrial engineer assigned to the Railroad Products Division. It was a scheme for rewiring the electrical circuits for the assembly tables and press so that a fool-proof synchronized operation would result. Under Mr. Evans's suggestion, the assembly operator would push only one button — not three. When the assembly table reached a predetermined spot, the press would be automatically activated so that the ram would meet the assembled grating at the precise moment the assembly table stopped. Then, as soon as the ram released from the grating, the assembly table would automatically return to its former position. With the new system, pointed out Mr. Evans, the company would save damage caused by improper synchronization of the three buttons, would raise production of inexperienced operators, and, most important, would save the company the high incentive wages which served to make assemble-and-press such an attractive job through the years.

The suggestion committee turned over Mr. Evans's suggestion to Mr. Harry Bateman, an industrial engineer, whose job it was to investigate and determine the feasibility of cost savings ideas that were submitted. Mr. Bateman consulted with Mr. Edward Artz, Superintendent of the Railroad Products Division, and the two men lost little time in recommending that the suggestion be adopted. The total cost of rewiring the tables and press was estimated at $600. The total savings in repairs caused by improper synchronization of the buttons were estimated at $3,200 per year, and the savings on wages were estimated at $400 a year. This latter figure was, at best, a rough estimate, because neither Bateman nor Artz could know exactly how much in wages would be saved as a result of the change. Clearly the attractiveness of the job would dimish, and the company, through the years, had benefitted from the skill of assemblers staying on the job year after year. Mr. Artz observed that time used by moving assembly tables under and out from the press and by activating the press itself constituted less than 1/12 of the job. Each of the two tables was activated every four minutes, on the average, with the press coming down every two minutes. Since the total time allowed for activating the table and press was slightly over 1/3 of a minute (.365), the men were occupied in manual assembly operations for approximately 11/12 of their time — time unaffected by this change.

THE GRIEVANCE

"If the division could save on repair costs alone, the suggestion is worth adopting," said Mr. Artz. Consequently he assigned an electrician to rewire the activating mechanisms of the tables and press, and on Monday, June 15, the new system went into effect. Mr. Evans timed the tables and press that day and assigned .260 minutes — a reduction of .105 minutes from the previously-assigned time. The operators immediately filed a grievance claiming an illegal rate cut. "We've been running this job through our own skill at .250 minutes," pointed out one operator. "Now you make an 'improvement' — adding .01 to the actual time and you want to cut our rate. This is outrageous."

Mr. Joseph Majda, Contact Board representative of the union, was summoned to the division and, after talking with the operators, went to see Messrs. Evans and Artz. Mr. Majda pointed to Section 12 of the Time Study Policy of the Collective Bargaining Agreement. He said that by changing the rate, the company was in violation of this section:

> *Section 12.* Established standards and rates will remain in effect for the life of the contract unless there is a change in methods, procedures, feeds, speeds, dies, machines, jigs, fixtures, products or materials which tend to increase or decrease production. In these cases, a restudy will be made and only those elements affected by the change will be adjusted. If it appears on examination that the resulting rate is clearly out of line, a conference will be called between the Contact Board representatives for the area and management to review the factors involved in the rate to determine the best procedure for adjusting the rate.
>
> The above procedure for changing standards is based on the principle that where proper standards exist, any changes will permit the same earning opportunity as existed under the original standard.

Section 12, in its present form, had been adopted by the company and union 11 years ago. It had been the subject of repeated grievances since then — the union consistently claiming that any change of rate that reduced earnings on a job was a violation. Company representatives, on the other hand, were inconsistent in their interpretation of the section. Some agreed with the union. Others contended that earning opportunities referred to a "normal" worker expending "normal" effort on a job he could do well under the prescribed method. Such a worker, they said, should earn 100 per cent of the assigned rate. In their support these company people pointed to Section 8 of the Collective Agreement's Time Study Policy.

> *Section 8.* One hundred (100) per cent shall be considered normal. The levelled time shall reflect the performance of the average worker working efficiently at a job he can do well, working at normal effort under the prescribed methods to produce the production standard (yield) under the conditions.

Other company representatives argued that Section 12 was designed to prevent wholesale rate cutting — that rates could be changed only when bona fide methods changes occurred: this, even though both company and union agreed the rate was out of line because of sloppy time-study practices, or lucrative because operators had devised effective short cuts. Until the Apex Case arose in June this latter view had prevailed. Section 12 had never been challenged in arbitration.

Upon receiving his report from Mr. Bateman, the Industrial Relations Director had to consider three questions — all three of which were related.

1. Should a suggestion award be tendered to Mr. Phillip Evans?
2. If an award to Mr. Evans is made, what should be its amount?
3. Should the incentive rate on the assemble and press operation be reduced as a result of the rewiring?

E. SENIORITY

Seniority is a concept based on the philosophy that longer-service employees should have greater protection than those with less service. There are two basic types of seniority: benefit seniority and competitive status seniority.

BENEFIT SENIORITY

Under benefit seniority, the level of wage or fringe benefit received by an employee is related to his length of service. The length of vacations are frequently tied to years of service: for example two weeks after one year's service, three weeks after five years' service, four weeks after fifteen years' service, five weeks after twenty years' service. Severance pay is generally related to the length of the employee's service, as is the amount of pension benefits: e.g. $7.00 per month per year of service. Benefit levels under group insurance plans are often related to seniority, as is eligibility for profit sharing or other bonus arrangements. Sometimes wage levels are related to accumulated employment time or, on the other hand, to length of service in a particular job category.

COMPETITIVE STATUS SENIORITY

Competitive status seniority is used where length of service determines an employee's status vis-a-vis other employees. Competitive status seniority is used in layoffs and recalls, promotions, transfers, work assignments, shift preference, the allocation of days off and vacation times. Employees with the longest continuous service are usually the last to be laid off, the first to be recalled, are given priorities in promotions and transfer, and have their choice of work assignment, work shift and vacation time.

The concept of seniority has been accepted in many walks of life as an equitable, objective decision-making criterion. In union management relationships the concept has existed since the earliest collective agreements were signed. Generally there has been little controversy regarding benefit seniority, but the area of competitive status seniority has been the source of considerable controversy, especially as it related to promotions, job assignments and layoffs. While unions and managements agree that length of service is an important factor in determining these matters, they often tangle when seniority *v.* ability arguments arise. Most managements seek to place greatest weight on ability in making such decisions while most unions place prime emphasis on seniority.

Usually these issues are dealt with in collective agreements by way of complex contingent language. In practice, there are many types of seniority-ability provisions in agreements. The four types listed below serve to illustrate the range of such provisions:

1. Promotions will be made solely on the basis of seniority.
2. The most senior applicant shall be promoted, provided he has sufficient ability to do the job or the ability to do the job after a reasonable training or break-in period.
3. Where skill, ability, and physical fitness are relatively equal, seniority shall govern.
4. Promotions shall be made on the basis of skill, ability, physical fitness, to be determined solely by the employer.

Clauses like (1) and (4) above are rare. Employers are generally unwilling to accept seniority as the sole criterion for the promotion of employees. Employees, through their unions, are generally unwilling to give the employer unilateral control over promotions. The result of these two conflicting viewpoints is usually a contract clause like (2) or (3) above.

Clause (2) provides that as long as the senior man can perform the job satisfactorily, he is entitled to it, even if other applicants have greater ability. Under clause (3) the applicant with the greatest ability would presumably get the promotion, even if he had less seniority than other applicants.

Regardless of the type of clause found in the agreement, certain administration problems are likely to arise in promotion situations: How is "ability to do the job" to be defined? When does an employee have the ability to do the job and when does he not? What does "relatively equal" mean? How much greater must ability be to cancel out seniority? Who is responsible for determining relative weights to be given to seniority or ability? Sometimes clauses are written that do not specify the relative weights to be given to seniority or ability. For example: "Promotions shall be based on ability, seniority, skill, physical fitness."

There are certain guidelines to the resolution of seniority v. ability issues. These guidelines have been developed through the experience of unions and management with these problems and through the decisions of arbitrators.

Some of the criteria for judging ability are the following: proficiency test, experience on the job, education, production data, performance ratings, age, personality traits, and absence, tardiness and discipline records. While the acceptability of these varies according to their exact nature (particularly in arbitration), it is important from a managerial point of view to develop reasonable, appropriate, and consistent standards. Indeed, where such standards have been applied without union challenge for a number of years arbitrators have been reluctant to allow them to be discarded.

Where the seniority clause is of the "sufficient ability" type (No. 2) arbitrators have generally held that when a junior employee is promoted, management has the burden of proof in showing clearly that the senior employee was not competent to perform the job.

Where "relative ability" clauses (type 3, above) are present, most arbitrators still place the burden on management to prove that the senior employee was not qualifed, although the requirements are less stringent. In either type clause, minor differences in ability will not be sufficient to allow the promotion of a junior employee over a senior man. As a result, employers tend to follow a "head and shoulders" doctrine; that is, a junior employee may be promoted ahead of a more senior employee only when he is *clearly* superior in ability. In cases of key jobs demanding high skills, where there is considerable risk for the organization if topnotch abilities are not tapped, arbitrators, and to some extent unions, have been less willing to substitute their judgment for management's and more willing to allow management to promote the individual it believes best suited for the job.

SENIORITY IN LAYOFFS AND RECALLS

In the absence of clear differences in ability it is generally accepted that the most senior employees should have greatest job security. In most situations this means they are the last to be laid off and the first to be recalled. However, now, with the advent of supplemental unemployment benefits and the guaranteed annual income, a new phenomenon has developed. Some of these plans allow for laid-off employees to enjoy nearly 100 per cent income protection for up to a year, causing senior employees to demand and receive the opportunity to decide whether they want to work or not. Seniority provides them with the first choice in deciding whether or not to be laid off. This phenomenon is sometimes called, quite inaccurately, "juniority."

Controversies often arise concerning the right to bump during reductions in force. In situations where plant-wide seniority prevails, and where senior employees can displace junior employees in other classifications of work, there may be long chains of bumps set off by a single layoff. Because of the tremendous administrative problems involved in any chain bumping situation, managements tend to favor seniority systems which provide for exercise of bumping rights on a restricted basis — within a department and within a classification, if possible. Unions, on the other hand, tend to favor plant-wide bumping rights, unrestricted by differences in classifications, even if it means expenditure of time and efficiency in training replacements.

The result of these divergent views is frequently some sort of compromise. In some situations plant-wide seniority is workable; in others department seniority is best. Frequently, several departments with similar operations are grouped together, and labor "pools" created, through which new employees enter the plant work force and into which senior employees displaced from their department can "bump," displacing the most junior employees. The possible variations are almost endless, but the job of developing an appropriate layoff and recall system is a major item on the bargaining agenda of most unions and managements.

The main administrative problem with layoffs and recalls is in keeping good records of seniority dates and then taking the appropriate action based on those records. Depending upon the system in use, an employee may have four different seniority dates: date of hire (plant seniority), date of entry into the department (department seniority), date of job acquisition (job seniority) and date from which various benefits are calculated (benefit seniority).

*   *   *

The following case, "Port Erie Hydro," deals with a series of issues involving seniority and ability. It is presented from the viewpoint of a union leader who is faced on one hand with the job of protecting a member against arbitrary, capricious actions of managment, while at the same time protecting certain concepts involving promotability and seniority.

PORT ERIE HYDRO

On April 29, 1973, Brian Rowe received notice that, effective the following June 14, his employment with the Hydroelectric Commission of Port Erie would be terminated. Following that he would receive two weeks vacation pay, and his name would be removed from the roles on June 28. He had been discharged.

The discharge notice, sent by mail to Rowe's home, had been signed by Mr. S.W. Schofield, the Commission's General Manager. In the notice Mr. Schofield stated the reasons for termination as follows:

...unsatisfactory performance of your work, your inability to learn and your poor attitude on the job.

The next day, April 30, Rowe went looking for his union representative, Ken Tripp. Mr. Tripp was President of Local 1175 of the International Brotherhood of Electrical Workers and had held that office for the past 10 years. Local 1175 represented all employees of the Commission except those working in offices or carrying titles of foreman, supervisor or above. Rowe had been a member in good standing since 60 days following his initial employment by the Commission on January 12, 1969.

Tripp looked at the discharge notice and commented that if Rowe was such a bad employee it seemed strange that the commission was giving him six more weeks to work. He asked Rowe if he had received any prior warnings. Rowe said he had not, that the letter caught him completely by surprise.

Tripp told Rowe that as a matter of policy the union always filed a formal grievance in the event of discharge action and said that he would do that within five days. Then he asked Rowe to give him all the facts, favorable or not, that he could about himself, his work history and events which he believed might have caused the discharge action. Following his talk with Rowe, Tripp made an appointment with Mr. Schofield to learn what he could from him. Then he planned to meet with the union's grievance committee to decide what action to take. Following are the facts which Mr. Tripp believed were most vital in deciding how to proceed.

THE FACTS

Brian Rowe had been employed by the Commission on Monday, January 12, 1969, as a Storeman Learner 3 at an hourly rate of $2.62. On March 30, 1969, he was promoted to the position of Storeman Learner 2 and on April 13 to Storeman Learner 1. On August 1 of the same year he was advanced to the position of Storeman Improver 3, a so-called permanent staff classification carrying with it the removal of probationary status and obligatory membership in Local 1175. On November 30, 1969, he was promoted to Storeman Improver 2.

Assignments to various classifications and progressions through the classifications were governed by Section 42 of the Collective Agreement. This section had been in existence at least since 1958, when Tripp became an officer of the union, and probably much longer.

Section 42. The Basic Pay Scale shall be operated and interpreted as follows:
a) each employee shall be given:
   i) a trade classification,
   ii) an appointment, and
   iii) a grading...
b) In each appointment there are one or more gradings, indicated 3,2, or 1.
c) In the case of Learner Appointments 3,2 and 1, progression is considered at the end of three (3) months. Also the Commission may act to shorten the normal progression period.
d) In the case of the Improver and Junior appointments, the progression is considered at the end of six (6) months.
e) In the case of Journeymen and Senior Appointments progression is to be considered at the end of one (1) year.
f) To move from one grade or appointment to the next requires that the employee have the necessary qualities, ability, knowledge, and has been recommended to the management by the foremen and superintendents of the departments concerned. The employee is to be given a copy of the recommendation.

Until Rowe's case came to his attention Mr. Tripp had never experienced problems with Section 42. Rowe was the only person in his memory who had failed to progress at or near the prescribed time periods. In talking with Mr. Schofield the twô could recall only one instance of a man being held back even one time period.

While most individuals progressed as Section 42 would indicate, the union leaders were regularly made aware that management considered such progression to be discretionary with themselves, not automatic. It was based on recommendation of the foreman or department head, and as a matter of procedure confidential rating sheets and rating charts were completed by individual foremen at the time employees were considered for progression.

According to Mr. Schofield it was Rowe's failure to progress in a normal fashion which led to his discharge. "If people can't go to the top," said Schofield, "we don't want them."

Following his tenure as a Storeman Improver 2 Rowe was transferred at his own request to the position of Lineman Improver 3 on October 11, 1970. For four months prior to the transfer he worked as a Lineman Learner at his Storeman Improver 2's rate ($3.12). When the transfer became official he received the assigned rate for a Lineman Improver 3 - $3.34. All this maneuvering prior to the change in classification was illegal according to the contract but was not at issue now, and Tripp chose not to pursue it. The matter of contention now, and the reason for discharge, was that Brian Rowe had retained his position as a Lineman Improver 3 since then — more than 2 1/2 years. During that time Section 42 would have required his consideration for advancement five times. And here lay the crux of the problem.

The Commission was small, employing only 238 people. The union had long shared the belief with Commission management that employees should advance through the various categoies — to develop flexibility in work assignments and increase their earnings. Ideally everyone would eventually attain journeyman or senior status. In fact the union had committed itself by virtue of Section 12 of the Collective Agreement to help develop the ability of employees.

> *Section 12.* The Commission Management will recognize three (3) representatives of a Shop Committee set up by the union which will pay particular attention to:
> a) Developing, assisting and instructing junior employees in the proper carrying out of their duties;
> b) advising Commission management in regard to abilities and attainments of employees when such information is desirable.

The shop committee had never played an active role as suggested by Section 12. Indeed, up till the Rowe case, there was no apparent need for union assistance in helping develop employees, because everyone had advanced without undue delay.

Both Schofield and Rowe were in agreement that Rowe's failure to advance had been caused by a weakness in performing overhead work. All representatives of union and management acknowledged that overhead work was essential to a lineman's package of skills, but there was disagreement on whether Rowe had been given adequate opportunity to develop those skills. Also there was considerable question in Ken Tripp's mind whether Rowe was very anxious to develop overhead skills. In fact, he had given indications that he was content to remain as a Lineman Learner 3 indefinitely.

There was nothing in the contract which said that failure to advance through the various appointments was grounds for discharge, but on the other hand Rowe's continued presence as an Improver 3 could block other, more ambitious, workers from the opportunity to obtain much-needed experience to move through the classifications. For this reason it could set an undesirable precedent of mediocrity among members of the work force. Tripp, long an employee of the Commission and a journeyman lineman himself, appreciated that the Commission needed people who would rise above mediocrity. There were many ambitious young people seeking employment, and opportunities should be made available for some of the more highly qualified.

Yet, on the other hand, Rowe probably had a case. No one had warned him that his deficiencies on overhead work might cost him his job, and furthermore there was evidence that management had not given him much opportunity to perform overhead. In fact, Rowe said that for at least 24 months of his approximately-30-month tenure as an Improver 3 he had been assigned to work on the ground, including considerable time driving a "Go Devil" (service truck) and performing storeman's work, work that was not directly associated with a lineman's job. No one in management challenged those estimates.

While they were not spelled out in writing the duties of a lineman were clear. A Lineman Improver was expected to do any kind of construction, maintenance and repair work on electric lines carrying up to 600 volts. This included underground work and pole work, and it consisted primarily of the ability to string wire and make joints. Climbing ability was considered essential, as was the ability to work well in cooperation with other linemen. While management and union representatives generally agreed that it was important for linemen to develop skills so that they could pass through the grades, no one was able to describe with precision the differences between grades 3,2 and 1. According to Mr. Jason Conlin, the Commission's Line Superintendent, progression depended on subjective judgment by management. Grades, according to Conlin, were largely intended as devices for compensation.

In investigating the case Mr. Tripp was able to uncover only three rating sheets for Rowe. The first, dated April 3, 1971, contained a statement by Foreman Michael Barlow as follows:

> I recommend that this man (Rowe) stay at the above classification and appointment (Lineman Improver 3) until a little more effort is put into learning the fundamentals of line work. Brian's climbing is improving but he is very timid and awkward while on a pole, since he has spent so much time driving a "Go Devil" (this has been corrected). I think a more accurate report may be made in six months.

Mr. Barlow had been Rowe's direct supervisor since February 1, slightly over two months prior to the date of the rating sheet. He had worked prior to that as a Journeyman Lineman on maintenance and repair teams to which Rowe had been assigned and had registered complaints on more than one occasion with Mr. Conlin about Rowe's lack of flexibility and general uncooperativeness.

Mr. Barlow remained as Rowe's supervisor until December of 1971, about 10 months in all. Tripp went to see Barlow following his conversation with Schofield, and Barlow said that in his opinion Rowe "didn't seem to have much ability," that he "didn't know his left hand from his right and was shy on the pole."

Mr. Barlow said he did not believe Rowe would improve as a lineman, and for that reason he assigned him most often to storework and driving the "Go Devil" — "jobs that needed doing and that he was most qualified to do." Barlow estimated that Rowe had been on overhead work, climbing poles and restringing wire, for part of every day for approximately two weeks under his supervision.

A second rating sheet regarding Rowe was dated October 2, 1971, and it too was signed by Barlow.

> Brian is progressing favorably on underground work (splicing etc.) but I cannot truthfully recommend him to Improver 2 until he adapts himself more handily to the mechanical aspects of overhead line work.

A note was appended to the bottom of the rating sheet and signed by Mr. Peter Dobbyn, the Commission's Chief Engineer:

> On the basis of the above statement by Mr. Barlow, the attached rating sheet and my own personal observations concerning the attitude of this employee I recommend that he receive no progression at this time.

The third rating sheet on Mr. Rowe was dated April 1, 1972, and signed by Foreman Gerald Lawson. Rowe had worked under Lawson since December of 1971. According to Lawson's rating sheet:

There is not much I can do to recommend Brian Rowe in the lineman's classification. Since being with me he has been a truck driver. I have had him climb occassionally doing secondary work, also he has done some secondary U.G. (underground).

Foreman Ralph Crump appended the following note:

When speaking to Brian Rowe last fall about not doing well at line work he informed me that he did not care to climb poles. This man will not make a lineman.

A third note on the bottom of the same form was signed by Jack McCafferty, Chief Engineer:

No recommendation for appointment to higher classification.

Mr. Tripp went to see Mr. Lawson and learned that Rowe had climbed poles on only two occasions while working for him. Tripp asked Lawson whether Rowe himself had ever shown initiative by asking for more opportunity to work overhead. Lawson said he had not and added, "I don't think he was too keen to climb poles."

Mr. Lawson said he believed it would take a person from one week to one month to develop competence in climbing poles and a similar period to learn the work needed at the top of the pole. He agreed with Tripp that if a man climbed only once a week the learning process would be slowed but said it was not ncessary to climb once a day.

In his investigation, Ken Tripp uncovered some additional company work records. These showed that Rowe had been assigned to the "Go Devil" for 276 hours between July 30, 1971, and November 2, 1972. According to Tripp's calculations this amounted to slightly more than 11 per cent of the total time available during this period, allowing for vacations and holidays.

Tripp thought it was curious that Rowe had never apparently raised a grievance or complaint about his failure to advance. When he asked Rowe about this Rowe said he had complained to Mr. Barlow about his frequent assignment to the "Go Devil," to underground work and even to stores work. Once when he raised a complaint, stating that truck driving and stores work was not part of his job description, Barlow commented about Rowe's "surly" attitude. After that Rowe decided not to complain further. He said he was not a complainer by nature and that he did not wish to jeopardize his employment or advancement possibilities by being disagreeable — that a new car, a mortgage and three kids made him somewhat less prone to complain that he might have been if his obligations were not so great.

During his tenure as a Lineman Improver Rowe applied twice for an opening with the Commission as a meter mechanic. He was rejected on both occasions. First he was rejected in favor of a student on summer vacation. The commission and union were then negotiating a new collective agreement, and a rate had not yet been agreed upon for the job. The student worked on the job for about five months, then quit to go back to school, at which time Rowe applied again. This time he was told that he lacked one of the ncessary qualifications: a grade 12 education. Rowe complained then, saying that he had received a certificate of equivalent education competence from the Canadian Armed Forces, where he had served for two years before being hired by the Commission. Rowe pointed out that the same certificate had been accepted by the Commission as evidence of Grade 12 when he initially applied for work. When the Personnel Director said he would check Rowe's claim, Rowe dropped his request, explaining later to Ken Tripp that he feared discrimination if he pursued it. As it turned out the meter mechanic's rate of pay was set at 25 cents an hour above the rate Rowe was then receiving as an Improver 3 and 12 1/2 cents above the rate of a Lineman Improver 2.

While Rowe never received a formal indication beyond the rating sheets that his work as an Improver 3 was unsatisfactory or that failure to advance could lead to dismissal, he acknowledged that Mr. Conlin had talked to him on three or four occasions about his failure to progress, indicating that he needed to develop greater competence on overhead work. On one of these occasions Rowe apparently said to Conlin, "To be truthful I don't care if I ever climb another pole for five years." Conlin interpreted this to mean that Rowe lacked desire; Rowe said it was an expression of his own frustration in being unable to receive opportunities for climbing. He said that in making the remark, "I meant that I wasn't getting advanced." It was at about the same time that he applied for the meter mechanic's job, "because I was reasonably convinced I had no future as a lineman."

On one occasion, during the summer of 1972, Rowe took matters into his own hands. He asked Walt Manley, a Lineman Journeyman, to work with him on a weekend instructing him on pole climbing. Manley spent six hours doing that and said that he saw considerable improvement. He said to Tripp that he could give Rowe the training he needed to become competent if Rowe wanted him to, but indicated that he believed it would take from nine months to a year to develop sufficient overhead experience to advance from an Improver 3 to an Improver 2.

Tripp's Analysis

After talking at length with various company representatives and with Brian Rowe himself, Ken Tripp was convinced that discharge action against Rowe was unwarranted. Apparently the discharge had been for

Rowe's failure to advance, and nothing in the contract or past practice between the parties had indicated this was a cause for discipline or discharge. Furthermore no one had warned Rowe that his failure to advance could lead to discharge.

Mr. Schofield had told Tripp that the discharge was for poor performance as a Lineman Improver 3, in addition to his failure to advance.

In Tripp's opinion this position was unconvincing. If Rowe was performing so poorly as an Improver 3 why had he been kept on the job for two and one-half years? When he asked Schofield this question Schofield remarked: "If anything, we allowed him to continue too long. Are you going to crucify us for that?"

In considering what action to take, Tripp felt that three contract provisions were relevant, aside from Sections 12 and 42 already cited. These were the Appeal Against Dismissal Section, the Arbitration Section and the Management Rights Section.

> *Section 11 — Appeal Against Dismissal.* Any employee desiring to appeal against dismissal must do so in writing to the Grievance Committee not later than five (5) days from the date of dismissal. The Grievance Committee shall notify the Commission Management in writing of the appeal within five (5) days. After receipt of such letter the Commission Management shall write the Recording Secretary of the union, giving reasons for dismissal. In case of reinstatement, the employee shall be paid in full for all time lost unless otherwise provided in the final settlement by the Grievance Committee or the Arbitration Board.
>
> *Section 8 — Arbitration* Responsibility to the citizens is the mutual responsibility of both the Commission and the employees and requires that any disputes be adjusted and settled in an orderly manner without interruption of the service to the citizens. Therefore, both parties agree that if any differences occur, during the effective period of this agreement, which cannot be settled by the usual grievance procedure, such differences will be settled by arbitration as provided in the Ontario Labour Relations Act.
>
> The Board of Arbitration shall not have any power to alter or change any of the provisions of this agreement or to substitute any new provision for any existing provisions, or to give any decision inconsistent with the terms and provisions of this Agreement.
>
> *Section 13 — Management Rights* The union acknowledges that it is the exclusive function of the Commission to:
>
> a) maintain order, discipline and efficiency;
> b) hire, discharge, lay off, classify, direct, transfer, promote, demote and suspend or otherwise discipline employees; and
> c) generally manage the activities or work in which the Commission is engaged and, without restricting the generality of the foregoing,

to determine the work to be performed, the methods and schedules of performance, etc.

d) The Commission agrees that these functions will be exercised in a manner consistent with the provisions of this Agreement, and a claim that the Commission has exercised any of these rights in a manner inconsistent with any of the provisions of this agreement may be the subject of a grievance.

The grievance procedure, Section 9 of the contract, provided for three steps prior to arbitration. All steps required notice in writing stating the nature of the grievance and citing the relevant sections of the contract which were allegedly violated. All required written responses from the management. It was necessary to file a first-step grievance within five days after facts giving rise to the grievance were made known, and five additional days were provided for written responses from management following the respective grievance meetings. First-step greivances were to be presented to the direct supervisor involved in the action. The second step provided for determination by the relevant superintendent, the third for determination by the General Manager. In the case of dismissals it was normal procedure to appeal directly to the General Manager, bypassing the first two steps because, as a matter of practice, the General Manager always was involved personally in the taking of discharge action.

In his conversations with Mr. Schofield, the General Manager, Ken Tripp, encountered a technical, legalistic argument by Schofield which made him feel uneasy. Schofield claimed that an arbitration board would not have authority under the collective agreement to determine just cause for discharge. He pointed to Sections 13 and 11 of the contract as his authority. According to Schofield, Section 13 gave the Commission certain exclusive rights, including the right to discipline and discharge. Section 11, according to Schofield, gave the Arbitration Board a right to review cases of dismissal but not to apply a "just cause" test. He argued that the Board's power was limited to a review of the fact of dismissal and to satisfy itself that the Commission had some cause for what it did — that the right to discipline or discharge was unqualified by "cause" or "just cause."

In discussing these technicalities with Mr. Schofield, Tripp was referred by Schofield to a 1966 case involving the Ainsworth Electric Company and Local 105 of the International Brotherhood of Electrical Workers (IBEW). Tripp looked up the case and made the following findings.

The Ainsworth, IBEW collective agreement provided that:

The Company has exclusive rights to the following privileges, except where they are specifically modified or denied by clause or terms embodied in this Agreement. Without restricting the generality of the foregoing sentence or the jurisdiction rights of Local 105, the exclusive rights of the company include the following: To hire, displace, discharge members of working forces.

The Arbitration Board, using a prior decision by then Professor Bora Laskin (4L.A.C.1524) in its support, ruled the Board had no jurisdiction to rule on just cause for a dismissal.

The Board stated that the Ainsworth management rights clause was, in its opinion, even more restricting than the clause considered by Professor Laskin. Quoting from the opinion:

> It may well be that where a management rights clause does not contain any provision for dismissal for just cause, that in common law an action may be maintained for unjust dismissal and that a court might well conclude that a dismissal would be actionable unless just cause or proper notice were present. Still this Board in view of the wording of the collective agreement does not consider it proper to import such words into the agreement to clothe the board with jurisdiction to hear the grievance.

In the contract dealt with by Professor Laskin a management rights clause was involved which contained no just cause criterion. The final sentence of the clause stated: "These rights shall not be used in violation of the specific terms of this agreement nor to discriminate against any employee." Laskin said it would require a "decided wrench of the language" to attribute the meaning "unfair" or "unjust" to the word "discriminate." Consequently he concluded the collective agreement gave him no jurisdiction to make a binding decision. Then, interestingly, Professor Laskin gave his views on the merits anyway saying, "Lacking jurisdiction, my finding can have only the force that the company may wish to give it as a matter of moral compulsion."

All this discussion on arbitrability made it clear to Tripp that the Commission would most likely fight to uphold the discharge even as far as arbitration. Since Schofield himself had written the discharge letter there was not much likelihood of winning Rowe's reinstatement in the third-step grievance meeting.

*   *   *

Ken Tripp was reasonably convinced that the Rowe case would have to be appealed to arbitration. He had explored a compromise with various company representatives which would open the way for Rowe to move to another occupation, but the ways were barred because there were no immediate prospects for openings for which Rowe might be qualified. Furthermore, it was the Commission's policy to promote from below whereever possible in each classification — starting with a Learner. A few occupations, such as meter mechanic, required immediate qualification without a prior Learner appointment, but with the unemployment situation as it was the prospects of a highly qualified person being available for any of these occupations was extremely high. Consequently Tripp would have to fight Rowe's discharge on its merits.

In the first instance he would have to exercise care so as to word the grievance properly. Then he would have to develop arguments on the issue of arbitrability, because if an arbitration board was prevented from ruling on the merits Tripp believed all would be lost. Assuming he could get around the arbitrability issue Tripp felt reasonably confident he could win the case on its merits. He believed the company would fight hardest in upholding their contention that inability to advance is cause for discharge. However they might also try to show that Brian Rowe was incompetent as a Lineman Improver 3, a possible cause for discharge in itself.

F. UNION PRESSURE TACTICS

Sometimes union members consider grievance procedures and arbitration too cumbersome and too time consuming to satisfy their immediate needs. Sometimes they want to apply pressure to gain a bargaining advantage during negotiations for a new contract. And sometimes workers, acting without direction from their union leaders, wish to express their dissatisfaction with the way matters are being handled by their own leaders. In all these instances there is likely to be a resort to pressure tactics.

The strike is the most familiar pressure tactic. However, there are many others — some legal, some not — but all calculated to demonstrate dissatisfaction and to achieve a goal that is not considered achievable through normal bargaining or grievance procedures.

Most often pressure tactics take the form of work slowdowns, wildcat strikes, picketing, or sabotage. Usually they are short-lived and difficult to cope with, even though most collective agreements call for stiff disciplinary penalties for those who engage in such tactics.

Work Slowdowns and Wildcat Strikes

Work slowdowns are most effective in operations calling for on-time performance or tight scheduling. One variation of a work slowdown is "work-to-rule." Here workers do exactly what they are told — nothing more — and observe all precautions, whether or not the precautions are warranted. Montreal transit workers engaged in work-to-rule tactics during the 1967 negotiations with that city. At that time bus drivers made sure that all fares were collected, all change given out and all passengers seated before moving the bus. Furthermore, they used special care to move across intersections only on full green lights when no pedestrians were crossing, and they carefully avoided cutting off other vehicles. The result: buses were running far behind schedule, throwing the system into considerable confusion.

Air traffic controllers have sometimes resorted to work-to-rule tactics to call attention to their special grievances. In large, busy airports this means maintaining maximum time and distance between planes, even when weather is perfect, and directing pilots in to landings one at a time while others maintain holding patterns. During the controllers' dispute of spring 1970 in New York City the resultant backups in aircraft waiting to take off and land was horrendous, causing some aircraft to divert to other cities and some to land or take off hours late but in complete safety.

Work-to-rule tactics are virtually impossible to cope with, because no one is violating rules. Furthermore it is difficult, if not impossible, to locate leaders who initiate the practices. Frequently union negotiators and union officers are not directly responsible; rather they share concern with management for ending conditions that gave rise to the practices.

Sometimes slowdown tactics are crude and more obvious than work-to-rule tactics. Most familiar are deliberate slowdowns that often accompany the installation of new incentive rates. Automobile parts producers with incentive rates have experienced this phenomenon for the last 35 years, each time a new model change is instituted. The objective, of course, is to maximize the increments in the rate so that when incentive efforts are applied the earning opportunities will be greatest. Typically the go-slow phenomenon lasts about a month during each year. During this time a great number of rate grievances are filed, and battles are waged between union leaders, methods engineers and management representatives over a few hundredths or thousandths of a second in the assigned incentive rates: the unions wanting more, the methods engineers less, and management wanting to get production rolling.

Most obvious among slowdown tactics are those which are blatantly announced and led by worker representatives in order to satisfy an immediate need. Often these are full-fledged illegal strikes, called "wildcats." The causes of wildcats vary considerably: from alleged safety hazards to management's decision to implement a new work practice, from contracting out work to securing the reinstatement of a suspended or discharged employee. Such tactics are usually barred by law or by the contract itself and can be dealt with through application of discipline. However, if large numbers of workers are doing the same thing discipline may be impractical.

Picketing

Picket lines are usually set up as an adjunct to a strike in order to advertise the unsettled issues that gave rise to the strike and to discourage other persons from passing through until the strike is settled. If picket lines are set up in support of a legal strike they are themselves legal so long as they are confined to the place of work where the dispute exists and so long as there is no likely danger to life or property.

Generally union members refuse to cross picket lines set up by their brethren even though they, themselves, have no dispute with management and regardless of whether there are large numbers or a great degree of belligerance displayed by the pickets. Thus a small union engaged in a dispute with management can sometimes exert enormous pressure by threatening or actually setting up a picket line if there is likelihood that workers belonging to some larger union, represented at the same company, will not cross.

Sabotage

Sabotage takes many forms. It is the most insidious of all pressure tactics, because it can be accomplished by a single person and is often impossible to track down. One of the more subtle forms of sabotage was experienced a few years ago by a major U.S. international air carrier in a dispute with baggage handlers. In order to demonstrate their power the handlers— perhaps just one or two — switched baggage tags at John F. Kennedy Airport in New York, causing near frenzy among passengers as they landed in Rome or Paris and discovered that their baggage had gone on to Athens or Beirut. More obvious forms of sabotage were reported in conjunction with the slowdown and strike during March of 1972 at the Lordstown, Ohio, assembly plant of the General Motors Assembly Division in a dispute over alleged speedup tactics. Here oily rags were placed in cans and set on fire, and cars were otherwise damaged in manifestations of unrest.

Other forms of pressure tactics include study sessions, wherein workers take a few hours or a day off to hold a meeting, with the obvious intention of calling attention to their demands or grievances. Policemen and firemen have sometimes exercised a form of pressure called "the blue flu." This tactic involves mass absenteeism caused by an imaginary illness, calculated to call attention to their particular demands.

Merchant seaman have a familiar tactic called the "bed bug" routine.

If they have a grievance and do not get satisfaction in its resolution they sometimes call the Coast Guard, claiming there are bed bugs in the laundry. It is obligatory for the Coast Guard to conduct a search in response to such claims, unless they know them to be spurious. Usually, on searching, they find a bed bug or two placed in the laundry by one of the seamen. Meanwhile the vessel has been delayed several hours or days during the investigation.

Such is the nature of pressure tactics — innovative sometimes in their conception but commonplace always in their purpose.

NOTES TO CHAPTER 7

1. Huberman, John, "Discipline Without Punishment," *Harvard Business Review,* vol. 42, no. 4 (July - August 1964), p. 62.

2. The flexible hours concept, long a feature of labor-management agreements in Europe, has only recently begun to catch on in North America. See Alvar O. Elbing et al., "Flexible Working Hours: It's about Time," *Harvard Business Review,* Jan.- Feb. 1974.

3. D. H. Everest, "Steel Industry Plan," *Handbook of Wage and Salary Administration,* Milton L. Rock, Editor-in-Chief (New York: McGraw Hill Book Company, 1972), pp. 2-72.

4. Ibid. p. 73.

8. ARBITRATION

Broadly defined, arbitration is the submission of a dispute to an impartial person or persons for determination. Arbitration may be voluntary or compulsory, and the parties either agree or are required to accept the decision of the arbitrator as final and binding.

King Solomon was an arbitrator, and the use of arbitration predates the development of English common law.[1] In its early history arbitration was used to settle disputes between businessmen (*commercial arbitration*) or between countries (*international arbitration*) and is still so used. *Labor arbitration,* the arbitration of union-management disputes, first occurred in North America in 1865.[2] Although there were some very successful applications of labor arbitration prior to 1935, the real growth of the process did not begin until the late 1930s, with the legislative creation of the present industrial relations system and the corresponding increase in the organization of employees and collective bargaining. World War II added a great deal of impetus to the adoption of labor arbitration. In essence, labor arbitration is an alternative to the strike (or lockout), and since strikes and the resultant loss of production were not acceptable during the war years the use of arbitration increased during this time.

Labor arbitration can be differentiated into two basic types: that dealing with "rights" disputes and that dealing with "interests" disputes. Interests arbitration is the arbitration of contract negotiation disputes and is used when the parties cannot agree to the terms of a collective agreement. Much of the early arbitration mentioned above was interests arbitration. Interests arbitration may be compulsory or voluntary. Under Ontario law, arbitration is required (following conciliation) where there is an impasse in contract negotiation involving hospital workers.[3] The same is true for policemen and firemen.[4] Other provinces have similar legislation. In the United States during the 1968 negotiations in the steel industry, the parties could not agree on the issue of incentive coverage and agreed to submit the dispute to a three-man arbitration panel in order to avert a strike. In 1974 these same parties agreed, in advance, to submit all outstanding disputes to final and binding arbitration.

Rights arbitration is grievance arbitration, or the arbitration of *contract interpretation* disputes. Grievance arbitration is today the most widely used form of labor arbitration. Grievance arbitration may also be compulsory or voluntary. In all jurisdictions in Canada, with the exception of Saskatchewan, contract administration disputes *must* be submitted to arbitration.[5] Thus, in Canada, grievance arbitration is essentially compulsory. In the United States grievance arbitration is voluntary, but well over 90 per cent of collective agreements provide for the final and binding arbitration of grievances.

Grievance arbitration, comprising as it does the bulk of arbitration practice, is of greater interest and importance to labor-relations practitioners than is interests arbitration. This chapter will be devoted mainly to the theory and practice of grievance arbitration. The arbitration of contract negotiation disputes will be briefly discussed in a final section.

GRIEVANCES AND THEIR ARBITRATION

Arbitration is the final step of the grievance procedure. Most grievances are settled prior to arbitration, if the grievance procedure is working properly. The number of steps in a grievance procedure prior to arbitration varies from contract to contract but, since the grievance procedure is an appeal process, there are generally two or three steps between the initial grievance and arbitration. Grievances involving established policy or precedent are generally settled at the lower steps of the procedure, while the higher steps including arbitration are reserved for cases involving new policy or precedent.[6]

A recent development in contract administration is the two-tier arbitration procedure. This is used in the U.S. Steel industry and at International Nickel in Canada. Under this system, the regular arbitration process is supplemented by a more informal, less legalistic hearing. These hearings often do not involve written decisions —the arbitrator may announce his decision on the spot. These decisions are not precedent setting. Thus the regular arbitration process is still reserved for cases involving new policy or precedent.

The individuals involved in the grievance procedure vary from company to company. The process starts with the aggrieved employee and his foreman; the union representative may or may not be present at this stage. As a case progresses through the grievance procedure it involves successively higher levels of both the union and management organizations. The management labor relations staff may become involved at any point, and frequently are the final place of appeal prior to arbitration.

Most contracts require that the grievance be put in writing and that subsequent answers and appeals also be in writing, although this requirement is sometimes waived at the first step. Time limits for the filing and consideration of grievances at each step are also generally set out in the agreement. Contracts frequently provide for an expedited grievance procedure, usually by omitting certain steps. The expedited procedure is most typically used in cases involving discipline and discharge. Time limits and expedited procedures are designed to provide for a speedy resolution of the problem which exists. Speedy resolution is important in the face of potential employee hardship; it also reduces the size of retroactive costs (e.g., back pay in a discharge case) for management.

The extent to which the contractually outlined grievance procedures are actually followed depends on the relationship between the parties. Time limits may be waived, issues may be considered even though not reduced to writing, settlement may be made on a "once only" basis, etc. In general, though, before a grievance reaches arbitration, it has been well considered and discussed by the parties.

ARBITRABILITY

The fact that an issue has been considered in the grievance procedure does not necessarily mean that it can be taken to arbitration or considered by an arbitrator under the terms of the contract. That is, all grievances are not necessarily arbitrable.

Collective agreements usually put some restrictions on the type of issues that may be arbitrated. Most clauses restrict arbitration to disputes over the application, interpretation, administration, or violation of the contract. While this might seem sufficiently broad to cover any possible grievance, in practice this is not necessarily so. Under such a clause, an employee complaint that a particular management action was unfair would not be arbitrable unless it could be shown that the action violated the provisions of the collective agreement.

Strictly defined, a grievance is a charge that the contract has been violated. However, complaints of a general nature may find their way into the grievance procedure. Many managements are anxious to have any employee gripe or complaint aired, and in practice the words "complaint" and "grievance" are used interchangeably. However, in order to be *arbitrable*, a complaint must be a bona fide grievance— a charge that the contract has been violated.

Some contracts do provide for a broader scope to arbitration than application, interpretation, administration or violation of the agreement. For example, issues subject to arbitration can be extended to "any matter relating to wages, hours and working conditions not specifically covered by the agreement"; or "all grievances and controversies which cannot be adjusted by mutual consent"; or "any complaint."[7]

Some contracts eliminate certain subjects from arbitral review. In the U.S. auto industry production standards are so excluded. While a company with such a restriction in the contract might entertain a grievance on the subject it would object to an arbitration of the dispute. The U.S. trucking industry and the Teamsters' Union have what is called an "open end" grievance procedure, in which the parties decide at the point of arbitration whether to submit a case to arbitration or to strike (or lock-out) over the issue. In practice, this is a powerful tool in the hands of the Teamsters' Union, because most individual trucking firms are not financially strong enough to withstand a strike. Indeed, the very existence of such a procedure is evidence of the Teamsters' strong bargaining power. The legal preclusion of mid-contract strikes in Canada is one of the reasons why the Teamsters are a more powerful union in the United States than in Canada.

Any grievance and arbitration procedure which precludes the arbitration of any or all subjects presents the parties with the possibility of a legal strike (or lockout) to achieve an illegal end. For example, assume that a contract does not provide for the arbitration of production standards. The union is free to strike in mid-contract if it does not agree to the standards. In practice unions have refused to agree to, and have struck over, production standards until other outstanding disputes have been settled to their satisfaction. They have done so even though they did not really disagree with the production standards. Contractually, the other disputes or grievances should have been submitted to arbitration. A strike over these other issues is prohibited. For this reason most contracts, even in the United States, where mid-contract strikes are legal, do not exclude any particular dispute from arbitral review.

The elimination of certain subjects from arbitral review is much more common in the United States than in Canada. With the exception of Saskatchewan, all Canadian jurisdictions generally forbid strikes or lockouts during the term of an agreement.[8] In the United States where a union is contractually prohibited from carrying an issue to arbitration, it is permitted by the contract and the law to strike over the issues. Since such strikes are prohibited by law in Canada, specific restrictions are not placed on arbitrable subjects in collective agreements. Also, in some jurisdictions (such as Ontario) where either party is unable to secure, at the bargaining table, an arbitration clause providing for the arbitration of all differences between the parties arising from the interpretation, application, administration or violation of the agreement, that party may apply to the labor relations board to have such a clause inserted into the agreement.[9]

Who decides whether a dispute is arbitrable? In both Canada and the United States this question is generally left to the arbitrator to decide. If one party refuses to permit arbitration, the other party may ask a court to order arbitration. In the United States the Supreme Court has established that courts must order arbitration, unless there is an absolutely clear exclusionary contract provision. If there is any doubt as to whether a case is arbitrable it is to be decided in favor of arbitration.[10] In most Canadian jurisdictions legislation requires that arbitrability be determined by an arbitrator, and the courts have generally enforced this legislative dictate. A later section on judicial review will further discuss the relationship between arbitration and the courts.

Thus, a company faced with a union demand for the arbitration of an issue which the company believed to be nonarbitrable could not refuse to schedule and attend an arbitration hearing on the issue. If they did they would be ordered to do so by a court of law. In the arbitration hearing the company would first have to argue that the issue was not arbitrable, and the arbitrator would first have to decide the issue of arbitrability. If he decided the issue was arbitrable, the arbitrator would then proceed to hear and decide the case. If he decided that the issue was not arbitrable, the proceeding would stop at that point.

FORMS OF ARBITRATION

Board v. Single Arbitrator

The discussion to this point has used the term "arbitrator." In Canadian industrial relations practice, arbitration is most frequently conducted by boards of arbitration. In a study of major agreements in manufacturing by the Canada Department of Labour, 69 per cent of the contracts provided for an arbitration board, while the rest provided for a single arbitrator, or the choice of board or single arbitrator.[11] In the United States a single arbitrator is used in the great majority of cases.

Arbitration boards are generally tripartite, and usually only one member, the chairman, is a true neutral. The practice is for the parties each to select a representative to the board. The union and management representatives then select a neutral chairman, although the parties themselves can also select the chairman. Arbitration boards composed of three *neutrals* are usually used for the arbitration of interests disputes. Most contracts provide that the decision of the board shall be a majority decision, except that where there is no majority the decision of the chairman shall govern. Some contracts provide only for a majority decision, however.

The advantages of using a board as opposed to a single arbitrator lie in the ability of the partisan members to provide technical or other advice to the neutral. The use of a board also permits the mediation of contract disputes rather than strict arbitration.

Disadvantages cited in the use of an arbitration board primarily relate to the time delays involved in selecting a panel and in hearing and deciding a case. The partisan nature of the parties' representatives may mean a complete and time-consuming rehash of the proceedings during the board's deliberations. Some chairmen make deliberations only a formality and then retire to write a decision which is submitted to the other members. In these situations the partisan members are obviously superfluous. Where a majority report is required the chairman's job is made even more difficult, and chairmen sometimes find that they have to compromise their own best judgement to secure a majority vote. Delays in the procedure increase the cost of arbitration, and the presence of the partisan members alone represents an additional cost for the parties. (The parties' nominees to arbitration boards may serve without pay, particularly when they are from other companies or unions. However, nominees may also be professionals, such as lawyers, and as such are remunerated for their services.)

Ad Hoc Arbitrators v. Permanent Umpires

Arbitration board chairmen or single arbitrators can be selected for each case sent to arbitration, or the parties can select a permanent arbitrator, usually called an umpire. The permanent umpire is selected for a given period of time, such as the duration of the contract, or simply to serve at the pleasure of the parties. Normally he is paid a retainer fee. Ad hoc arbitrators are used far more frequently than permanent umpires.

The advantages of having a permanent umpire include the fact that time need not be wasted in selecting an arbitrator. The permanent umpire becomes familiar with the provisions of the parties' agreement, their day-to-day relationship, their personalities and their customary practices. Where a large number of disputes are likely to arise, a permanent umpire offers the parties a cost advantage. Finally the awards of permanent umpires are more likely to serve as guides to future action by the parties— they come to know how he is likely to rule on an issue and adjust their behavior accordingly.

On the other hand, finding an individual who the parties believe is and will continue to be acceptable is no easy task. Once the parties have selected a permanent umpire there is some danger that they will resort to his services too quickly, before really attempting to reach agreement themselves. The parties may decide to make the umpire earn his retainer, which must be paid regardless of whether his services are used. Finally, there may be a tendency on the part of a permanent umpire to "split" awards— some for the union, some for the company, without regard for the merits of the cases. Of course, in such a circumstance, the umpire would not be fulfilling his function and the parties would be wise to eliminate the use of his services. In any event, the services of a permanent umpire are useful only as long as he has the complete confidence of the parties.

Companies and unions can secure many of the advantages of having a permanent umpire simply by continuing to use an ad hoc arbitrator as long as his services are satisfactory. By using ad hoc arbitrators the parties can bring special skills, such as industrial engineering, to bear on particular cases.

Even though the parties may not be dissatisfied with a particular ad hoc arbitrator, either or both of them may feel precluded from using his services again for political reasons, particularly in the face of an adverse arbitral decision. In using many different arbitrators, the parties are subjecting themselves to the greatest drawback to the use of the ad hoc arbitrators. This is the lack of knowledge on the part of the arbitrator of the circumstances of the parties. Also, a series of ad hoc arbitrators may well provide conflicting rulings on similar issues, leaving the parties with few useful clues to appropriate future action.

SELECTING THE ARBITRATOR

The arbitration provision of the contract usually sets out the procedure for selecting the arbitrator or arbitration board chairman. Where the parties or their board nominees are unable to agree on an arbitrator, provision is made for him to be selected by an outside party: the Labour Minister, the Labour Relations Board or special agencies. The American Arbitration Association (which also operates in Canada) provides lists of arbitrators to the parties, and on their failure to agree on an arbitrator will appoint one. In Ontario, a Labour Management Arbitration Commission (LMAC) was appointed in 1968 to perform the same function. Under Ontario law, if the parties cannot agree on an arbitrator, the Minister of Labour will appoint one, on the application of either party.

The AAA submits lists of arbitrators to the parties. The parties strike the names which they find unacceptable from the lists and return them. Any name(s) not struck from both lists may then thus be selected as the arbitrator. If no name is selected additional lists will be submitted, and if the parties still cannot agree the AAA will appoint an arbitrator; but this appointment will not be an individual who has been previously rejected by one of the parties.

The AAA and Labour-Management Arbitration Commission screen individuals carefully before they are placed on the lists of available arbitrators. The AAA requires general evidence of suitability in terms of experience and education, and, in addition, prospective arbitrators must provide references from both labor and management. The LMAC is a labor-management commission, and individuals on their lists are also acceptable to both sides.

The cost of arbitration is borne equally by both parties. Arbitrators receive a fee not only for the hearing, but also for the time required to decide the case and write the decision. The minimum fee charged by arbitrators is $100 per day, and while most fees are under $200 per day some go much higher. Additional costs involved in arbitration include the arbitrator's expenses, a stenographic transcript (which is optional), and attorneys' fees if lawyers are used.

Given the fact that by definition an arbitrator is an impartial judge, one would think that the parties would not attempt to seek out, as arbitrators, individuals who are predisposed toward particular points of view. This is not necessarily so. The adversary nature of the collective bargaining process carries over into the grievance and arbitration process so that each side tries to maximize its chances of winning a case. This is done by trying to select an arbitrator who is likely to be favorably inclined toward the position of one side, or who, at a minimum, is not likely to be unfavorably disposed toward a particular point of view. As an extreme example, one arbitrator has noted that management might well like to have a Jesuit priest for a discharge case because Jesuits have a strong sense of discipline.[12]

Services are available to both unions and managements which report on the proportions of particular arbitrator's decisions which favor labor or management. Like anyone else, arbitrators, even in the absence of formal reports, develop reputations. This is particularly true in terms of specific issues. For example, a man may develop a reputation as being highly unwilling to sustain a discharge. Such an individual may find his services unacceptable to some managements, at least for this type of arbitration case.

Of course this type of speculation on the part of both unions and management is generally unfair to arbitrators. An arbitrator of any worth decides each and every case on its own merits. Arbitrators can and do get justifiably upset about their "ratings" or "reputations," but the reliance on such by the parties is indeed a reality.

Since the arbitrator's decision is to be final and binding, and since issues taken to arbitration frequently are extremely important to the parties, the acceptability of the arbitrator to both parties is of maximum importance. It is not at all surprising that so much effort is expended on choosing the right arbitrator.

What kind of people serve as arbitrators? Some individuals make a career out of arbitration. Others, such as university professors (of law, labor relations, or industrial engineering) arbitrate on a part-time basis. Legal training is often thought to be useful for arbitration work, and many arbitrators are lawyers. In Ontario, until recently, almost all labor arbitration was done by members of the judiciary. Since 1968 judges have been barred by law from acting in this capacity. In other Canadian jurisdictions arbitration is still done by judges. There are no occupational bars to arbitration, and it is and can be done by anyone, as long as he is acceptable to both parties.

THE ARBITRATION HEARING

Once the arbitrator or arbitration board is selected, the stage is set for the actual arbitration hearing. The actual conduct of the hearing depends on the preferences of the parties and the arbitrator. No two hearings will necessarily be the same. However, there are some broad similarities which can be outlined.

Although judicial in nature, arbitration is essentially an informal and even friendly procedure. Even though it is of an informal nature, the arbitration proceedings must provide for a full and fair hearing of the issue. In order to insure this (and to prevent the judicial vacation of the award on procedural grounds) the following procedures must be met:

1) All interested parties[13] must receive notice of the time and place of the hearing and must have an opportunity to attend.

2) The parties must be permitted to introduce evidence, without unreasonable restrictions.

3) The parties must be permitted to fully cross-examine adverse witnesses.

4) The parties must be allowed to make concluding oral arguments.

5) If they so desire, the parties must be allowed to file post-hearing written briefs.[14]

These requirements are reflected in the normal order of procedure in an arbitration hearing. After introductions, the arbitration hearing normally proceeds as follows:

1) Opening statement by the moving party, followed by a similar statement from the other side.

2) Presentation of evidence, witnesses and arguments by the moving party.

3) Cross-examination by the other party.

4) Presentation of evidence, witnesses and arguments by the defending party.

5) Cross-examination by the moving party.

6) Summation by both parties, usually following the same order as in the opening statements.[15]

Moving Party

The moving party is the party which has initiated the arbitration action. This is almost always the union, and the general rule is that the moving party presents his case first. However, a more general rule is that the order of presentation should serve the orderly development of the case. The latter rule explains why in discharge cases the company usually presents its case first. In doing so, the company sets forth the basis for and the facts surrounding the discharge, which are then responded to by the union.

Burden of Proof

In a lawsuit, the order of appearance is generally connected to the question of burden of proof, with the party bearing that burden being required to present his case first. In arbitration the criteria of orderly presentation are more important than the burden of proof in determining order of presentation. The doctrine of burden of proof "... is that where the evidence is exactly balanced... between the proponent and opponent of a proposition, the proponent, or the one who advanced the proposition has failed to prove it."[16] In terms of a grievance arbitration, the party which has advanced the grievance would be considered the proponent and would thus have the burden of proof. This normally would be the union. However, most arbitrators have held that the employer bears the burden of proof in discipline cases. The burden of proof in arbitration cases is generally *not* the criminal standard of "beyond reasonable doubt," but the civil standard of balance.[17] Thus the principle of burden of proof in arbitration cases comes into play only when the evidence presented by both sides is *equal*. The evidence is so rarely equal, that an arbitrator is seldom required to decide a case solely on the basis of burden of proof. In order to be assured of winning a case, however, the proponent must be sure that his evidence is greater than his opponent's. If the evidence is of equal weight, then the proponent cannot be sustained by an arbitrator.

The Issue

The arbitrator's job is to make a decision in regard to the dispute between the parties. At some point in the arbitration proceeding a clear statement of the issue (or question) to be resolved by the arbitrator must emerge, e.g., "Was John Doe discharged for just cause?" Clearly, an arbitrator cannot make a decision until he knows just what he is being asked to decide. Also, as will be shown later, an arbitrator's decision which goes beyond the bounds of the question submitted to him can be overturned by a court. Thus arbitrators are careful to have a clear statement of the issue before them.

Sometimes the parties will meet prior to the arbitration and agree to a statement of the issue. This is called a *stipulation* of the issue. The stipulated issue is given to the arbitrator prior to or at the beginning of the hearing. At the same time the parties may provide the arbitrator with a statement of the remedy sought, the contract, and any facts which are not in dispute. They may also provide him with any statement of his authority, which is different from that contained in the contract (or when no such statement exists in the contract) as well as any statement as to how they prefer the procedural details of the hearing to be handled. Taken together, this package is called a *submission* to the arbitrator.

More frequently, though, the issue will emerge in the course of the hearing. The grievance statement, as processed through the grievance procedure, may serve as a statement of the issue. At other times the arbitrator may simply pinpoint the issue during the hearing and ask the parties if they agree that this is the issue he is to decide. If an arbitrator cannot get the parties to agree to a statement of the issue he may refuse to hear the case.[18] On the other hand, he may continue to hear the case and as part of his decision provide a statement of the issue at dispute.

Other Procedural Matters

Depending on the preferences of the parties and the arbitrator, witnesses may be sworn and a transcript of the hearing taken. The arbitrator has the power to exclude witnesses (except for the directly concerned parties). That is, he may require them to leave the hearing room during the testimony of other witnesses. This is done to preserve "purity of testimony," and at the request of the parties. If the arbitrator finds it necessary he may visit the plant in order to see the physical site involved in the dispute. He may not do this without both parties being present or having the opportunity of attending. The arbitrator may call or cross-examine witnesses or he may ask for specific evidence. In doing so, arbitrators generally try to tread a fine line between gaining a complete understanding of the case and appearing to present a case for one side or the other. The arbitrator does not generally have the power to subpoena witnesses or evidence if the parties refuse to provide these voluntarily. In Ontario, arbitrators do have this power, which is given to them by statute.

PRESENTING A CASE IN ARBITRATION

The American Arbitration Association has provided a brief and useful summary of points to be remembered in presenting an arbitration case:

1. The opening statement

The opening statement should be prepared with utmost care, because it lays the groundwork for the testimony of witnesses and helps the arbitrator understand the relevance of oral and written evidence. The statement, although brief, should describe the controversy clearly, show what is sought to be proved, and indicate the relief sought.

The question of the appropriate remedy, if the arbitrator should find that a violation of the agreement did in fact take place, deserves careful attention at the outset. A request for relief should be specific. This does not necessarily mean that if back pay is demanded, for instance, it is essential for the complaining party to have computed an exact dollars-and-cents amount. But it does mean that the arbitrator's authority to grant such relief under the contract should not be in doubt.[19]

Because of the importance of the opening statement, some parties prefer to present it to the arbitrator in writing with a copy given to the other side. They believe that it may be advantageous to make the initial statement a matter of permanent record. It is recommended however that the opening statement be made orally even when it is prepared in written form, for an oral presentation adds emphasis and gives persuasive force to one's position.

While opening statements are being made, parties are frequently able to stipulate facts about the contract and the circumstances which gave rise to the grievance. Giving the arbitrator all the uncontested facts early in the hearing saves time throughout, thereby reducing costs.

2. Presenting documents

Documentary evidence is often an essential part of a labor arbitration case. Most important is the collective bargaining agreement itself, or the sections that have some bearing on the grievance. Documentary evidence may also include such material as correspondence, official minutes of contract negotiation meetings, personnel records, medical reports and wage data. Every piece of documentary evidence should be properly identified, with its authenticity established. This material should be physically presented to the arbitrator (with a copy made available to the other side), but an oral explanation of the significance of each document should not be omitted. In many instances, key words, phrases and sections of written documents may be underlined or otherwise marked to focus the arbitrator's attention on the essential features of the case. Properly presented, documentary evidence can be most persuasive; it merits more than casual handling.

3 Examining witnesses

Each party should depend on the *direct examination* of his own witnesses for presentation of facts. After a witness is identified and qualified as an authority on the facts to which he will testify, he should be permitted to tell his story largely without interruption. Although leading questions may sometimes be permitted in arbitration, testimony is more effective when the witness relates facts in his own language and from his own knowledge. This does not mean, however, that questions from counsel may not be useful in emphasizing points already made or in returning a witness to the main line of his testimony.

4. Cross-examining witnesses

Every witness is subject to cross-examination. Among the purposes of such cross-examination are: disclosure of facts the witnesses may not have related in direct testimony; correction of misstatements; placing of facts in their true perspective; reconciling apparent contradictions; and attacking the reliability and credibility of witnesses. In planning cross-examination, the objective to be achieved should be kept in mind. Each witness may therefore be approached in a different manner, and there may be occasions when cross-examination will be waived.

5. Maintaining the right tone

The atmosphere of the hearing often reflects the relationship between the parties. While the chief purpose of the arbitration hearing is the determination of the particular grievance, a collateral purpose of improving that relationship may also be achieved by skillful and friendly conduct of the parties. Thus the parties should enter the hearing room with the intention of conducting themselves in an objective and dignified manner. The arbitration hearing should be informal enough for effective communication, but without loss of that basic sense of order that is essential in every forum of adjudication.

The hearing is no place for emotional outbursts, long speeches with only vague relevancy to the issue, for bitter, caustic remarks or personal invective. Apart from their long-run adverse effect on the basic relationship between the parties, such immoderate tactics are unlikely to impress or persuade an arbitrator. Similarly, overtechnical and overlegalistic approaches are not helpful.

A party has every right to object to evidence he considers irrelevant, for the arbitrator should not be burdened with a mass of material that has little or no bearing on the issue. But objections made merely for the sake of objecting often have an adverse effect, for they may give the arbitrator the impression that one simply fears to have the other side heard.

6. The summary

Before the arbitrator closes the hearing, he will give both sides equal time for a closing statement. This is the occasion to summarize the factual situation and emphasize again the issue and the decision the arbitrator is asked to make.

As arbitration is a somewhat informal proceeding, arguments may be permitted to some extent during all phases of the hearing. There may be times, however, when the arbitrator will require parties to concentrate on presenting evidence and put off all arguments until the summary. In either event, all arguments should be stated fully.

Finally, as this will be the last chance to convince the arbitrator, the summary is the time to refute all arguments of the other side.[20]

Rules of Evidence

Arbitrators are not required to adhere to the legal rules of evidence. Arbitrators generally allow great leeway in the admission of testimony and other evidence. This is because arbitrators usually want to give the parties as much opportunity as possible to present their cases as they see fit. Also, on some occasions, arbitrators' decisions have been overturned by the courts because the arbitrator refused to admit evidence of some sort.

Thus arbitrators may admit hearsay evidence or allegations without proof. (Some arbitrators, though, will sustain objections about the introduction of this kind of testimony.) However, the admission of evidence does not necessarily mean that the arbitrator must act on it. Usually the arbitrator will admit all evidence "for what it is worth." In the case of hearsay, this is frequently not much.

Arbitrators may make a decision on the basis of purely circumstantial evidence, although they will generally refuse to accept improperly or illegally obtained evidence, or confessions which were obtained under duress. Arbitrators have treated the failure of a grievant to appear and testify at a hearing as a factor leading to the conclusion that the grievance was without merit. There is also a general consensus, in the United States at least, that the criminal law privilege against self-incrimination does not hold in the arbitration of grievance cases.

Despite the fact that evidence is freely admitted in an arbitration case, both parties can and do object during the hearing to the evidence offered by the other party. Objections that the evidence is hearsay, or is immaterial, irrelevant, or incompetent may not get the evidence removed from the record, but will serve to remind the arbitrator of the weight which should be given that evidence in considering the record of the hearing.

One rule of evidence that must clearly be followed by arbitrators is that they must not hear evidence from any source except in the presence of both parties. The operation of a tripartite arbitration board is open to this sort of error. As Curtis says:

> . . . it may afford a party an excellent opportunity for reaching the ear of the arbitrator without approaching him directly. A party ordinarily expects its nominee to make its position clear and to point up its arguments so that the chairman will give them the weight they are expected to carry. Occasionally a nominee is called upon to do more than to present evidence, which, for some reason the party does not want to produce at the hearing. Clearly the chairman who accepts evidence through such a channel is acting improperly. The party that attempts to present evidence in such a way is also acting improperly, besides risking whatever merits its case may possess.[21]

*　　*　　*

Having heard the case, the arbitrator must proceed to make a decision. He can make his decision only on the evidence placed before him by the parties. The evidence presented in arbitration cases is sometimes contradictory. The arbitrator must sift the testimony to reach the best conclusion he can as to the facts. Determination as to the weight, the relevancy and the authenticity of the evidence is part of the arbitrator's task in reaching a decision.

And yet arbitrators' decisions are not made in a complete vacuum. Standards for arbitral decisions exist in both precedent (the findings of other arbitrators) and in general rules of contract interpretation. These standards are of use to arbitrators in deciding a case, and to the parties in arguing a case.

PRECEDENT

Precedent does not have the force in arbitration that it has in civil or criminal law. Precedent in arbitration can be differentiated into two types; authoritative and persuasive.[22] Authoritative precedents are ones which must or should be followed whether the arbitrator agrees with them or not. Arbitrators are not under any obligation to follow persuasive precedents, but take them into consideration, giving them as much weight as their intrinsic merit will allow.

Examples of authoritative precedents are those set by a permanent umpire or board chairman. One of the major purposes of having such an arrangement would be voided if precedent were not followed. Decisions by ad hoc arbitrators involving the interpretation of a specific contract provision between a company and a union will generally not be reversed by another arbitrator. Thus, an interpretation given to a clause in a particular agreement by an arbitrator will stand until the agreement is changed.

The extent to which persuasive precedent affects an arbitrator really depends on the arbitrator. Some arbitrators rely heavily on precedents cited by the parties, while others do not. In almost all cases, the arbitrator will consider the precedents cited, and the parties should take care to make sure that the cases they cite are germane to the one at hand, lest the arbitrator be negatively influenced by the citing of irrelevant material. Also, reading precedent is time-consuming for the arbitrator and can increase the costs of arbitration. However, precedent can be useful to arbitrators, and it is worthwhile for the parties to seek out other cases similar to their own, if only to discover what arguments arbitrators find most cogent.

Precedent in arbitration cases can be found in several sources. Canadian cases are summarized in *Labour Arbitration Cases,* published by the Canadian Law Book Company (Toronto) in cooperation with the Central Ontario Industrial Relations Institute. U.S. citations can be found in *Labor Arbitration Reports* published by the Bureau of National Affairs, Incorporated and *Labor Arbitration Awards* published by Commerce Clearing House, Incorporated. The American Arbitration Association has recently begun a new series of reports called *Labor Arbitration in Government.* All of these reports are indexed under the subject matter of the dispute; e.g., Seniority, Discharge.

PRINCIPLES OF CONTRACT INTERPRETATION

The core of the arbitrator's job is the interpretation of the collective agreement. Certain standards exist to help him do this. These have been developed through arbitration precedents and the common law of contracts. While these standards are not absolute, they can be a useful guide to preparing arbitration cases and also in deciding whether to take cases to arbitration.

First of all, arbitrators will not interpret a contract in such a way that the application of the clause would result in an unlawful act. Similarly, where necessary, arbitrators will look at the rulings of administrative tribunals such as the Labor Relations Board and the decisions of courts (particularly the highest courts) for guidance in interpretation. Arbitrators will also interpret an agreement so that the application will not result in harsh or absurd results.

Ambiguity

The very existence of a claim for arbitration is an indication that the parties disagree over the interpretation or application of the agreement. That is, certain alleged ambiguities exist in the contract. However, the arguments that the contract language is ambiguous must be *plausible*; a mere claim that it is ambiguous is not enough, and if the words are plain and clear, the clear meaning will be applied by the arbitrator.

Even though contracts have become increasingly detailed over the years, they still contain much ambiguity. Frequently contracts are ambiguous because the parties believe that they cannot spell out in detail all the language which might be necessary. Discipline is a primary example of this type of situation. Most contracts specify that management shall discipline only for "just cause." Such a phrase is clearly ambiguous, and deliberately so, to provide the parties with a reasonable amount of flexibility in the face of the impossibility of spelling out penalties for all the conceivable disciplinary situations which might arise during the term of an agreement. Sometimes the parties provide ambiguous language in the contract because they cannot *agree* to a more specific language. At other times the language is not seen as ambiguous until the parties attempt to apply it to a specific situation. In any event, all agreements have some ambiguities; if this were not so there would be little need for arbitration.

The primary rule to be observed in the interpretation of collective agreements is that the *intent* of the parties in drafting the agreement must be preserved. Thus, where ambiguities exist, the arbitrator may examine the precontract negotiations to help determine what the clause meant to the parties at the time the agreement was signed. Where ambiguity cannot be resolved by any other way, it will be resolved by construing the language *against* the party who proposed or drafted it during negotiations. Arbitrators will also look at the contract as a whole in order to ascertain the intent of the parties with regard to a specific section; a clause would not be interpreted so as to nullify or modify another part of the agreement. However, where a contract has specific language covering the issue in dispute, that language will prevail over general language which only deals with the issue by inference.[23]

Probably the most important standard used by arbitrators in interpreting ambiguous contract language is *past practice*. If the parties have behaved in a manner that gives ambiguous language a specific meaning, then the agreement will be interpreted in light of that behavior. For example, suppose a contract has a statement which reads: "The Company shall continue to make reasonable provisions for the safety and health of its employees." Assume also that the company always provided gloves for occupants of particular jobs. In all probability, the company could not now require employees to purchase gloves for this job. Most, if not all, arbitrators would rule that the past practice of supplying the gloves free of charge, in the absence of any other evidence, gives meaning to the words, "make reasonable provisions."

However, past practice only governs in the face of ambiguous language. Clear language prevails over past practice.[24] Thus, if the contract provides for one thing and the parties have in practice followed another course, the contract language will prevail if a dispute occurs.

Discipline Cases.

Because most contracts are ambiguous with regard to discipline, and because discipline is involved in a significant proportion of cases taken to arbitration, the subject of discipline deserves special mention. Over the years, arbitrators have developed standards for interpreting whether there is "just cause" for discipline. Arbitrators have generally held that:

1. Policies must be known and reasonable; an individual must have reasonable grounds for expecting a disciplinary action to follow a given act.
2. Violation of policies must be proven.
3. The application of rules and policies must be consistent— employees cannot be singled out for discipline.
4. Where workers are held to a standard, that standard must be reasonable.
5. Adequate training must be provided by employers.
6. The job rights of employees must be protected from capricious, arbitrary or discriminating action.
7. Employees with long service generally deserve greater consideration than those with short service.[25]

Sometimes arbitrators will find that just cause for discipline exists but that the particular penalty imposed by the company is too harsh. They then substitute a lesser penalty. Some contracts preclude arbitrators from doing this. Under these clauses, if the arbitrator determines that just cause for discipline existed, then the penalty imposed by management must stand.

In a decision by the Supreme Court of Canada, arbitrators were found not to have the power to modify disciplinary penalties, except where they were specifically given that power by the contract or the stipulation of the parties.[26] However, this court decision has been modified by legislation in several jurisdictions including Alberta, Ontario and the Federal jurisdiction. Thus, in arbitrations under these jurisdictions, arbitrators do have the power to modify disciplinary penalties, except where precluded from doing so by contract provisions.

PAST PRACTICE WHERE THE CONTRACT IS SILENT

Where contract language is ambiguous, arbitrators will rely on past practice of the parties to help determine what the language means. But what about situations where there is no contract language covering the issue, but a practice exists? Does the existence of a practice constitute an implied agreement, precluding its change during the term of an agreement? This question goes to the heart of the most contentious issue in arbitration. It relates to management's ability to make changes during the term of an agreement in the absence of explicit contractual restrictions.

"Reserved Rights" Theory.

Managements have generally argued that prior to collective bargaining they had unilateral control over wages, hours and all other conditions of employment. This unilateral control, or "management right" still exists except where *specifically limited by the collective agreement*. Thus, where the contract is silent about an issue, such as the "right" to subcontract out work, management has the right to take unilateral action. A past practice, unless specifically mentioned in the contract, is not binding on management and may be withdrawn at any time.

"Status Quo" Theory.

Some contracts have clauses which are designed to insure continuance of established practices. Even where such clauses do not exist, unions have argued that the "status quo" at the beginning of the agreement, modified by practices that have been accepted during the agreement, should be maintained until the parties agree otherwise.[27] Thus any practices which exist at the beginning of an agreement must remain in force during the term of the agreement, unless the parties agree to a change. Following this theory, management does *not* have the right to make unilateral changes in wages, hours or conditions of employment during the term of an agreement, even if the contract is silent on the matter.

In Canada, arbitrators have generally followed the reserved rights theory.[28] In the United States, arbitrators have attempted to find some middle ground between the reserved rights and status quo positions. For example, in the United States, where the contract is silent in regard to subcontracting, arbitrators have generally held that management does not have the unilateral right to subcontract work normally done by employees in the bargaining unit if it results in layoffs or the impairment of an established employee benefit (such as overtime), except where this is a drastic change in underlying conditions of the jobs in question.[29] In Canada, where the agreement is silent, arbitrators have permitted management to subcontract without any restrictions at all.[30]

In the United States arbitrators have used the following criteria in judging management's right to make changes during the term of an agreement: 1) the action must be exercised in good faith, 2) for compelling business reasons, and 3) with due regard to the interests of the parties. In Canada, despite the fact that arbitrators have generally followed the reserved rights doctrine, there is evidence that if the good faith criterion were not present, the management decision would be reversed. This would occur if management was planning a unilateral step to which it knew the union would object, but remained silent about the matter *during contract negotiations,* so as to obtain the protection of the statutory no-strike clause. This would be regarded as "bad faith" bargaining, with management not providing appropriate data so that they could later take the unilateral action and the union would be powerless to stop that action. Mid-contract strikes are prohibited, and if the union went to arbitration, the arbitrator might be expected to follow the reserved rights doctrine and allow the action. However, because of the good faith principle, a Canadian arbitrator might well not sustain the management action. Also, in a Canadian case in which the issue was whether management had the unilateral right to establish an incentive plan, the arbitrator said that management did not have the right. The question was whether the wage rates established in the contract were minimum rates or the sole basis for employee remuneration. The arbitrator said that an incentive plan could so distort the agreed-upon wage structure that the management right to introduce it unilaterally was prohibited.[31] In this decision, the arbitrator seemed to question the effect of the action in terms of the interests of the parties. Thus despite the general drift of Canadian arbitration decisions, management's right to introduce change in mid-contract where there is no prohibitive language is *not* clearly established.

JUDICIAL REVIEW

If one of the parties is dissatisfied with the arbitrator's ruling he may apply to the courts to have that ruling overturned or reversed. (Or should he fail to honor the award, the other party may petition the courts for enforcement.) Few cases are appealed to the courts, partially because there are very limited grounds for appealing cases. Courts will set aside arbitrators' decisions only under special circumstances. Judicial interference with arbitral decisions is somewhat more common in Canada than it is in the United States.[32]

In both the United States and Canada, courts will vacate arbitrators' awards only if:

1. The arbitrator has exceeded the scope of his authority.

2. There is venality (bribery, fraud, corruption, bias) on the part of the arbitrator.

3. There are procedural defects in the proceedings such as *ex parte* hearings, or if the parties of interest are excluded, or if time limits set in the grievance procedure have not been observed.

Where there is venality or a procedural defect, the arbitration is said to lack natural justice. An arbitrator can be found to have exceeded his jurisdiction if the issue is not arbitrable, or if he ruled on a matter not submitted to him by the parties, or exceeded the authority granted to him by collective agreement. In terms of the last point, most contracts provide that the arbitrator cannot add to, amend, or modify any provisions of the agreement. Also, as has been seen above, other contracts place specific restrictions on the arbitrator, such as allowing him only to determine whether there was just cause for discipline, and not whether the penalty was appropriate.

In Canada, another ground exists for judicial appeal of arbitrators' decisions. That ground is error of law on the face of the record. This can occur where the award is ambiguous, or when the arbitrator has made a "manifest error" in the proceedings such as wrongful admission or rejection of evidence. It can also occur when he interprets the agreement erroneously. Except in Ontario, an error of law is grounds for vacating an award only where it is a *collateral* error of law; that is, when it does not involve the very thing referred to the arbitrator. Thus, if a clause is submitted to an arbitrator for interpretation, his interpretation *of that clause* cannot be challenged. However, if he has erroneously interpreted *another* clause in reaching his decision or has improperly excluded evidence in reaching his decision, his award can be vacated. As an example of an error of law in a collateral issue, the Supreme Court overturned an arbitrator's decision to sustain a discharge because it found that he had disregarded a relevant provision of the agreement.[33] The Court did not challenge the arbitrator's interpretation of the clause he relied on but said that he should have considered another clause which provided a more suitable basis for a decision.

The question of whether an issue is a collateral issue of law is for the Court to decide. The Court decides what the issue before the arbitrator was and in making that decision then regulates all other issues to collateral status. In practice, the principle of collateral error of law has been used by Canadian courts to review and reverse arbitrators' decisions in a fairly wide-ranging manner.

Arbitration in Ontario has been viewed as being required by statute.[34] For this reason, the Court will also review and vacate an award there if it finds that the arbitrator has made an error of law *in deciding the specific dispute submitted to him.* This is largely a question of judgment; so, if the Court disagrees with an award of an arbitrator, it may vacate that award on the grounds that the arbitrator has interpreted a clause so as to give it a meaning that it "cannot reasonably bear."[35] In brief, in Ontario, if the Court disagrees strongly with the arbitrator's award, it may vacate that award.

The concept of error of law on the face of the record is not an easy one to master. Its use by Canadian courts offers the parties much greater opportunity to have arbitrators' decisions reviewed by the courts than their counterparts in the United States. Whether this is good or bad is a matter of opinion. Clearly though, if arbitration is to be a viable substitute for industrial warfare, the institution and the decisions reached thereunder must be generally accepted by both of the parties. Appeals to superior bodies must be minimized as much as possible. The delays involved in judicial review and the appearance that one party is attempting to avoid an award can only serve to reduce the attractiveness of arbitration as a means of settling industrial relations disputes.

INTERESTS ARBITRATION

In form and process, interests arbitration is the same as rights arbitration. The substance differs, however. Rights arbitration concerns the application, interpretation, or administration of an existing agreement. Interests arbitration involves the actual determination of the terms of the agreement.

In the North American labor relations system, the terms of a collective agreement are normally determined by the parties through collective bargaining. Disputes between the parties in the negotiation process are essentially conflicts of interests, which are not normally viewed as amenable to settlement by rule of law. These disputes are normally left to the parties to resolve, and sometimes this results in the use of the strike (or lockout). The function of the strike here is to force the other side to change its bargaining position, to help effect an agreement.

The alternative to the self-resolution of interests disputes is some form of arbitration, which may be voluntary or compulsory. In some countries, notably Australia, interests disputes must be submitted to final and binding arbitration. In some North American jurisdictions, interests disputes involving certain parties (e.g. firemen, policemen) must also be submitted to arbitration. In other instances, such as under the Federal Public Service Staff Relations Act,[36] the arbitration of interests disputes is voluntary.

PROS AND CONS

Where compulsory interests arbitration is provided for by legislation in North America, the presumption is that the public interest precludes any interruption of a product or service that would be caused by a strike or a lockout. Where there is no public interest involved (and both labor and management generally argue that this is true of most disputes in the private sector of the economy) both parties are generally opposed to interests arbitration, particularly when it is compulsory.

Many arguments are advanced against compulsory interests arbitration. Opponents claim that it destroys the bargaining process: "If the parties are not faced with the consequences of refusing to settle, their desire, determination, or even ability to settle dwindles."[37] Interest disputes are complex, and no clear criteria exist for third parties. For example, what should wages be? What seniority system is appropriate? Is there any objective way of determining these issues?[38] The use of and the decisions under compulsory arbitration are said to be subject to political pressure.[39] Compulsory arbitration may not prevent strikes, but may actually result in an increase in strike activity; strike activity is higher in Australia under compulsory arbitration than it is in the United States or Canada.[40]

Not all of the evidence is against compulsory interest arbitration. Under the operation of the Ontario Hospital Disputes Arbitration Act, there is evidence that the operation of compulsory arbitration has not led to the breakdown of collective bargaining in that industry.[41] There have, however, been complaints about the length of time needed under this system to get a contract settlement.

STANDARDS

Compulsory interests arbitration is part of the North American labor relations scene, and will probably continue to be so. Even though interests disputes are complex, and criteria for decisions are often ambiguous and conflicting, such criteria exist and have been used.

Of course, the standards to be used by arbitrators can be set by statute or they can be agreed to by the parties prior to the arbitration. Where these conditions do not exist, the arbitrator must determine the criteria for making the decision, and the parties' arguments would include reference to the suitability of particular criteria.

The Public Service Staff Relations Act provides that the following factors shall be considered by the arbitration tribunal:

a) The needs of the Public Service for qualified employees;

b) the conditions of employment in similar occupations outside the Public Service, including such geographic, industrial or other variations as the Arbitration Tribunal may consider relevant;

c) the need to maintain appropriate relationships in the conditions of employment as between different grade levels within an occupation and as between occupations in the Public Service;

d) the need to establish terms and conditions of employment that are fair and reasonable in relation to the qualifications required, the work performed, the responsibility assumed and the nature of services rendered, and

e) any other factor that appears to be relevant to the matter in dispute.

Other criteria which have been used in interests arbitration include:

1. The prevailing practice in an industry, a similar industry, in a geographic area or in an industry in a given geographic area.

2. The cost of living.

3. A living wage.

4. The ability of the employer to pay.

5. The competition faced by the employer in both wage and product markets.

6. General wage movements, i.e., the percentage wage increase granted in an industry or in general.

7. Productivity.

8. Past practice.

9. Expectations of the parties as evidenced by their negotiating positions.

10. The public interest.

"LAST BEST OFFER" ARBITRATION

An interesting variation in interest arbitration is "last best offer" arbitration. Under this plan, the arbitrator or arbitration board must choose between the final negotiation position of the parties. The parties must make a final offer (their last best offer) and the arbitrator must choose one or the other; no compromise is possible.

This type of interest arbitration has been used in negotiations between civil servants and the governments of Michigan and Wisconsin in the United States. It has been used as well in a number of municipalities in the United States, particularly in contract negotiations between the cities and their firemen and policemen. Last best offer arbitration has been proposed as an alternative for ending National Emergency Disputes in certain industries in the United States (rail, trucking, airline, longshore and maritime) but has not been enacted into law.[42]

In general, where last best offer arbitration is used or proposed, the process can be invoked by either side after bargaining has proceeded for a certain length of time. Depending on the law or the parties' agreement, the parties can submit either a final offer on the entire collective agreement, or on only those items which are still in dispute. Most plans call for an exchange of final proposals, and then a brief period in which further negotiation is allowed. The proposals are then submitted to the Arbitration Board, which must select one of the two final offers. The Boards are usually not permitted to compromise or to attempt to mediate a settlement. Often the Board is prohibited from considering as evidence any prior bargaining positions of the parties. The parties are generally free to attempt to reach a negotiated settlement before the Board reaches its decision but, once the Board makes a decision, the decision is final and binding, and the parties are not permitted to deviate from it. Very often the Board must make its decision within a certain period of time, such as two weeks or 30 days.

As originally proposed, last best offer arbitration was intended to be so unattractive a proposition that the parties would be compelled to reach a negotiated solution prior to the actual arbitrated decision.[43] How such a scheme would actually work if the parties were unable to reach a settlement themselves has been questioned by some observers. If the parties failed to make reasonable final offers, the arbitrator could be faced with an almost impossible dilemma. Also, many issues in collective bargaining, such as work rules, manning and technological change are not suited to "either-or" resolution. Finally, the process has "win-lose" overtones, and the party whose position was not accepted by the arbitrator might cause trouble, if only to save face.[44]

Despite these objections, many people find the idea of last best offer arbitration fascinating, and in all likelihood this type of interest arbitration will be given at least trial usage in a major dispute in the near future.

*   *   *

The following section consists of three cases. All three are taken from transcripts of actual arbitration hearings and all involve matters of discipline. The opinions and awards of arbitrators are not included; rather readers are expected to consider the evidence, define the issues and decide how they would resolve those issues if they were the arbitrator. Students of industrial relations can use these cases as mock arbitration experiences by taking sides as union and management and presenting the facts through witnesses before an actual arbitrator for his decision.

In the field of industrial relations it is important for students and practitioners alike to develop their ability to look at all cases from an arbitrator's point of view. Arbitration is considered the ultimate step in deciding grievances and occurs relatively infrequently in most union-management settings. However, the relative power of disputing parties is often determined by a considered judgment as to how an arbitrator would decide the issues giving rise to a dispute.

TIDEWATER INDUSTRIES LTD.

Tidewater Industries Ltd. maintained three production facilities and a warehouse in the Toronto area. The company employed twelve men as roving repair and maintenance men for transportation equipment. Six were assigned to the first shift, four to the second, and two to the third. The foreman, Lyle Lane, worked on the first shift and assigned work to the men by way of written work orders — some in response to emergency calls from foremen in the various facilities, others as routine maintenance jobs. The men seldom had any supervision when they performed their work. They traveled from one plant to another in a company truck loaded with tools and spare parts necessary for the jobs to be done.

The two men assigned to the third shift were Mr. Norman Stanley and Mr. Charles Onasch. Mr. Stanley was titled a truck mechanic, Mr. Onasch a lubrication mechanic. They worked as a team, and their regular hours were 11 P.M. till 7 A.M. Mr. Stanley had worked for the company for the past eight and a half years, Mr. Onasch for the past three.

Last April the company was harried by a series of thefts at the warehouse, and a decision was made to hire a man to carry on surveillance. The company secured the service of Mr. Steven Jennings, a private detective, who was assigned to do actual work in the warehouse as a part-time inventory clerk. Mr. Jennings' place of work was at a desk in a balcony overlooking most of the floor area. He was so placed that anyone on the floor would have difficulty seeing him.

Mr. Jennings planned to spend three days a week at the warehouse — one on each shift. On Wednesday, April 12, he worked the third shift and, while he did not report observing any thefts, he did report seeing two men — later identified as Norman Stanley and Charles Onasch — enter the warehouse sometime between 4 A.M. and 5 A.M. According to Mr.

Jennings the men looked around the building for a while, then worked on the lift trucks and other transportation equipment until around 6:30 in the morning — when Mr. Jennings left. Mr. Jennings reported the same behavior by the men on five subsequent Wednesdays — April 19, April 25, May 3, May 10, and May 17.

The following week Mr. Jennings started working the third shift on Tuesdays, and on Tuesday, May 23, he reported observing Mr. Stanley and another employee (not Mr. Onasch) entering the warehouse at about 3: A.M. and staying until he (Jennings) left around 6:30 A.M.

On Tuesday, May 30, according to Mr. Jennings, Messrs. Stanley and Onasch came to the warehouse at about 1 A.M. They walked around for a while, then Mr. Stanley found a folded carton, placed it on the floor, put some hampers around it, and apparently went to sleep. He did not arise until 4:30 A.M., after which he and Mr. Onasch performed their usual maintenance tasks as observed earlier. During the time Mr. Stanley slept or rested, Mr. Onasch was not visible to Mr. Jennings.

With the exception of June 6, when they worked from 1:45 A.M. until quitting time, Mr. Jennings reported that all through June — the 13th, 20th and 27th — Mr. Stanley and Mr. Onasch followed the pattern they had set on May 30. While the time of arrival at the warehouse and the time for starting work varied, Mr. Jennings said he regularly observed Mr. Stanley making rather elaborate preparations for a comfortable resting place and then sleeping for about three hours. Mr. Onasch, meanwhile, was out of Mr. Jennings' sight.

On July 5, a Wednesday, the production manager, Mr. Leonard Birts, asked Lyle Lane, supervisor of Messrs. Stanley and Onasch, to report to the third shift that night and observe along with Mr. Jennings. Lane reported the same kind of behavior. Messrs. Stanley and Onasch arrived at the warehouse at 12:45 A.M. Mr. Stanley prepared a resting place and apparently went to sleep and Mr. Onasch disappeared from sight at 1:15. Mr. Stanley arose at 4:55, replaced the carton on which he had rested along the wall, and rearranged the hampers. Mr. Onasch reappeared, and both went to work till quitting time.

Mr. Lane reported what he had seen to Mr. Marvin Fuller, the Manager of the Maintenance Department. Mr. Fuller, after conferring with his superior, Mr. Birts, decided to discharge Messrs. Stanley and Onasch. He left word for them to report to him before starting their shift the next day, July 6. Mr. Fuller would come in at 11 o'clock to meet them. It was then that Mr. Fuller told the two men they had been discharged.

Messrs. Stanley and Onasch were members of Local 2101 of the International Brotherhood of Electric Workers (IBEW), exclusive bargaining agent for Tidewater's production and maintenance employees at all four Toronto locations. The next morning, July 7, they went to the IBEW business agent, Mr. Gordon Hellman, admitted they had been sleeping during working hours in the warehouse and asked Mr. Hellman to process a grievance on their behalf for reinstatement. Mr. Hellman agreed with the two men that discharge was too severe a penalty for sleeping on the job, especially in view of their good record as Tidewater employees since they were hired. Neither had a blemish on his personnel record and both had enjoyed regular merit increases. On the day they were fired both were earning the maximum rates of pay for their respective classifications. Since IBEW had won representation rights 10 years earlier, no employee, to Mr. Hellman's knowledge, had been discharged for sleeping on the job.

Mr. Hellman presented all these points to Mr. Fuller at a first-step grievance meeting held on Monday, July 10. Mr. Fuller agreed that Messrs. Stanley and Onasch had unblemished personnel records and acknowledged that, while two or three men had been caught sleeping on the job before, all were given warnings. But Mr. Fuller pointed out that the other cases were, in his opinion, far less serious. In the first place, the others had apparently dozed off inadvertently. In this case Messrs. Stanley and Onasch had deliberately planned to sleep and made certain physical arrangements to do so. Furthermore, said Mr. Fuller, Messrs. Stanley and Onasch were in a greater position of trust than many other employees. They worked without supervision most of the time and were often the only employees in the warehouse on the third shift. While the warehouse was protected by an automatic ADA alarm system, this system was deactivated by Messrs. Stanley and Onasch when they entered the building — giving them some added responsibility for plant protection.

If activated, the ADA alarm system set off a loud siren and bell inside the warehouse and caused a set of lights to flash outside each entrance door. In addition, the system registered at a central location, and it was necessary for a company representative to come to the scene in order to stop the various warning devices. Mr. Stanley had a key for deactivating the system upon entering the building and for reactivating it on leaving. It was possible to reactivate the system once the men had entered the building, but they did not normally do so — nor were they so instructed. In light of the recent wave of thefts from the warehouse Mr. Fuller said this protective aspect of their jobs had become especially critical.

Mr. Hellman expressed great surprise and concern that Messrs. Stanley and Onasch should have been held responsible for protection of the warehouse. Neither man was trained nor even instructed to the effect that they had any responsibilities beyond those of maintenance and repair of transportation equipment. Mr. Lane, on questioning from Mr. Hellman, said he had never instructed the men that they had plant protection responsibilities but pointed out that all employees had a responsibility to be attentive to their work and said he hoped that if his men observed something amiss, they would report it. Mr. Fuller, by way of clarifying his position, said he wanted to make it clear that he did not expect Messrs. Stanley and Onasch to apprehend thieves if they were seen, but that he believed any loyal employee would report unusual actions they observed. "Someone could have set the building afire and they'd never have known it!" said Mr. Fuller.

In the grievance meeting Mr. Fuller said the two men had been discharged for two offences: 1) deliberately sleeping on the job, 2) falsification of records.

The first, in itself, said Mr. Fuller, was sufficient justification for discharge in view of its deliberate nature. However, because of the good records of both men and the company's past treatment of those caught sleeping, he would be willing to convert the penalty to a suspension without pay. However, the second offence was far more serious. Both men had turned in job reports for July 5, indicating eight hours of work. The company had published Personnel Policies — posted on all bulletin boards — stating causes for suspension or discharge without warning. These included falsification of records. Mr. Lane produced the work records turned in by Messrs. Stanley and Onasch. These can be found in Exhibit 1 (p.260-70). The reports, signed by the men, indicated they had worked eight hours each. "They even charged their half-hour lunch period to a job," observed Mr. Fuller.

Mr. Fuller then asked Mr. Lane if all the jobs reported had been completed. Mr. Lane said, "Yes, to the best of my knowledge, they were!"

Messrs. Stanley and Onasch objected to the charge that they had falsified records. Both claimed that they had been instructed to charge all hours to some job — to allocate the full eight hours among the jobs performed regardless of the time actually required to do them. They admitted the times were not accurate in that they did not measure the actual time spent on each job — that they encompassed breaks, lunch periods and even bull sessions. Mr. Fuller interjected — "and sleeping!"

Mr. Lane confirmed that he had instructed the men to allocate the jobs among their shift hours but said it was the responsibility of the men, in his opinion, to use the full eight hours on preventive maintenance inspections if work orders are not sufficient to provide a full eight hours of work. "Sometimes the repair jobs take a lot longer than I expect," said Mr. Lane. "Sometimes they're just routine. I can't know in advance how long each will take. We have a charge number for general maintenance," said Mr. Lane, "but these men, to my knowledge, have never used it!" "It's the first I've heard about it," said Mr. Stanley. "Likewise," said Mr. Onasch.

After hearing the arguments, Mr. Fuller refused to change his action, contending the discharges should stand. Mr. Hellman then appealed to the second step of the grievance procedure presided over by Mr. Leonard Birts, Production Manager. No new arguments were presented, and Birts upheld Fuller's position. According to the procedure Mr. Birts delivered a written reply as follows:

> I hereby uphold the discharges of Messrs. Norman Stanley and Charles Onasch for their actions on the third shift beginning at 11P.M. on Wednesday, July 5.
>
> The two employees were observed by their supervisor to have deliberately slept for a lengthy period during their scheduled shift and to have falsified their work records for the period in question.
>
> This is a clear violation of published company policy, subjecting the violators to immediate discharge without warning.
>
> I find the action of the manager of the maintenance department warranted by the circumstances of this case and by prior precedents within the company.

There had been three previous instances of discharge for falsification of records. Two, which took place four and a half years ago, involved one employee's deliberately punching the time card of another who had asked him to do so as a favor to cover his leaving before the shift ended. Both men had been fired. The other discharge for falsification involved an incentive worker who regularly reported producing more parts than were substantiated by actual count. That took place almost exactly three years before.

Having failed to get a satisfactory answer from Mr. Birts, Mr. Hellman took the case to the third step of the procedure. This involved the presence of Mr. Donald Oswald, Industrial Relations Director of Tidewater. Oswald upheld the earlier positions and, at the request of Mr. Hellman, gave a written opinion. Mr. Hellman prepared then to take the case to arbitration.

Mr. Oswald's written opinion reads as follows:

> The two employees, Messrs. Stanley and Onasch, were discharged without prior warning because of falsification of their work records. They admit that they did, indeed, falsify their work records by reporting that they were servicing machines and equipment during periods when, in fact, they were not. They urged that the opinion of Mr. Leonard Birts, Production Manager, who affirmed the supervisor's action, be reversed or modified and that they be given another chance because of their periods of service with Tidewater over seven years in one case, three in the other, and because they consider the action of the supervisor arbitrary and harsh.
>
> For several years it has been a widely published company rule that

any employee found guilty of certain acts is subject to immediate discharge without our usual series of warnings; among these acts is falsification of records. The adoption of this rule and the publicity given to it constitute full warning. To adopt such a rule and then to apply it only after an additional warning to a guilty employee would involve such a relaxation of necessary disciplinary procedure as, in effect, to revoke the rule.

It has been alleged that others have been lax in writing up their time records, that the time actually recorded for doing a job has been extended to include time devoted to breaks and lunch periods and even to conversation, that others have fallen asleep on the job, and that such other situations have not always led to immediate dismissal. While it is clear that such laxity should be vigorously discouraged, it is also clear that there is a difference between the kind of human weakness involved in these previous incidents and the calculated misbehavior of the present case. I know of no example of deliberate and planned falsification of records which has not led to dismissal without warning.

The discharges are upheld!

EXHIBIT 1 (TIDEWATER)
JOB REPORTS FOR
NORMAN STANLEY AND CHARLES ONASCH
JULY 5

JOB REPORT

SHIFT 3
Date: July 5*

Location	Work Order No.	Equipment	Nature of Work	Labor Hours
Warehouse	113	Clark	Weekly inspection & repair drive motor	2.0
Warehouse	113	Raymond	Weekly inspection & chain adjustment	2.0
Warehouse	113	Clark	Weekly inspection & hydraulic control adjustment	2.0
Warehouse	16	Automatic floor scrubber	Weekly inspection	1.0
Plant 1	110	Raymond	Replace two 130 amp fuses	1.0
			TOTAL HOURS	8.0

Signed: _____

Norman Stanley

JOB REPORT

SHIFT 3

Date: July 5*

Location	Work Order No.	Equipment	Nature of Work	Labor Hours
Warehouse	113	Ray Reach	Weekly inspection & height adjustment	2.0
Warehouse	205	Yale	Weekly inspection	1.0
Warehouse	205	Automatic	Weekly inspection	1.0
Warehouse	87	Conveyor	Lubrication	2.5
Plant 2	18	Floor washer	Weekly inspection	1.5
			TOTAL HOURS	8.0

Signed: _____

Charles Onasch

*Workers on third shift recorded dates as of the shift starting time.

EXHIBIT 2 (Tidewater)

Personnel Policies

Rules of Conduct

Among causes for suspension or discharge without warning are:
1. *Drinking* or being under the influence of liquor while on company premises.
2. *Pilfering* or *theft* of company property or personal property of others.
3. *Falsification* of records.
4. *Claiming sickness benefits under false pretences.*
5. *Failure to notify supervisor of absence* without a good reason.
6. *Gambling:* placing or accepting bets on the races, buying or selling number pool tickets or any other gambling activity.
7. *Other misconduct* detrimental to the best interests of the company.

EXHIBIT 3 (Tidewater)

Grievance Procedure

In the event of any complaint or grievance arising under the terms or provisions of this Agreement, including a question as to just cause discharge, the employee affected or his Union representative shall have the right to use the following procedure.

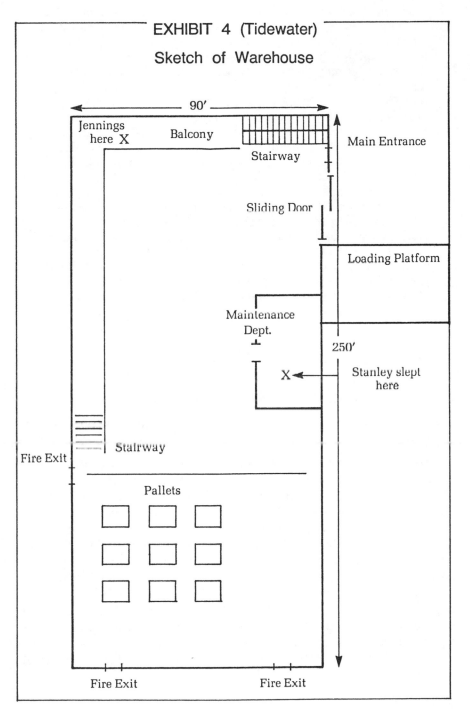

EXHIBIT 4 (Tidewater)

Sketch of Warehouse

Step 1

If an employee has a complaint he may present it to his foreman. In a discharge case he may present it to the manager of his department.

Step 2

If the employee has not been satisfied in Step 1, he or his Union representative may present his grievance to the Production Manager.

Step 3

If the employee has not been satisfied in Step 2, he or his Union representative may request a written decision from the Production Manager and may appeal to the Industrial Relations Director who shall hold a meeting within five (5) working days of the appeal in an effort to arrive at a satisfactory solution. A decision must be delivered within ten (10) working days of the meeting.

Step 4 The employee or the Union representative may request a written decision from the Industrial Relations Manager for appeal to arbitration. Such written decision must be delivered within ten (10) working days of the request. The arbitrator shall be chosen by mutual agreement of the parties. In absence of such agreement he shall be appointed by the Minister of Labour. His decision will be final and binding on both parties except the arbitrator shall have no authority to alter the terms and conditions of this agreement.

PIERRE DÉRY

On September 24, Mr. Pierre Déry filed the following grievance:

> *J'ai été renvoyé sans juste cause. Je demande la rétraction de mon renvoi et plein compensation.*

On the day of his discharge, September 23, Mr. Déry was working as a Production Operator in the Assembly Department (B-2) of Roetes Motors on a job known as option drilling. He was required to drill holes in various locations of the car body using a hand-operated power drill. The number of holes, their size and location depended on the options the finished car was to have, such as power steering, convertible top, power brakes and radio. In total there were 14 different option packages requiring between four and eight holes, each hole having a predesigned location.

Roetes Motors was located in Upton, Ontario, a town with a population of approximately 12,000 located on the St. Lawrence River east of Kingston. The plant employed 500 hourly workers, of whom approximately 350 were French-speaking Canadians.

On September 23, Mr. Déry was classified as a probationary employee but was entitled to grieve under the procedure of the Master Agreement. Under Section 13A of the agreement, after 30 days of employment, an employee, even though still classified as "Probationary", had access to the normal grievance procedure for questions of layoff and discharge for just cause. The union, United Automobile Workers, Local 2768, represented probationary employees, but they did not become members of the union until they acquired seniority rights. Section 13 of the agreement (Probationary Employees), Section 4 (Grievance Procedure) and Section 2 (Management Rights) are reproduced as Exhibits 1, 2 and 3 (pp.277-280).

The probationary period was designed to give the company an opportunity to assess the capability of newly hired employees before they were given permanent status. From the union's point of view, this eliminated unnecessary paper work in connection with union membership for individuals who might be employed for only a short period of time. In the past three years, 75 men had been hired by Roetes Motors as probationary employees. Of these, 45 gained seniority rights. No employee had been kept on probationary status for longer than 60 days.

Mr. Déry was hired on the previous July 24. He was first assigned to the job of "Sanding Wet Deck" in the Paint Shop. On July 31, he transferred to the body shop to work under Foreman Gregory Landry. The following day, August 1, he was reassigned to the assembly department to work under Foreman Leslie Curran. He worked as an option driller under Mr. Curran until his discharge.

Immediately after being discharged Mr. Déry contacted Mr. Jacques Poirier, the union steward, and filed a grievance. Mr. Déry claimed his discharge was unjust and in addition clearly violated Paragraph 20 of the Agreement:

No person shall be discriminated against for purposes of hiring, firing or promotion because of race, creed, religion or political beliefs.

Mr. Déry was an active member of the Quebec Separatist Movement and aired his views on and off the job. He claimed that neither his foreman nor management in general was sympathetic to his views, and were using his alleged poor work record as an excuse to discharge him.

The first and second steps of the formal grievance procedure were waived. This was normal at this plant in discharge cases. At the third step of the procedure, management was represented by Mr. Fred Campbell, Plant Manager, Mr. C. Sequin, Industrial Relations Manager, and Mr. Leslie Curran, Foreman, assembly department. Union representatives were Mr. S. Payne, Chairman of the Shop Committee, Mr. J. Poirier, Steward, and Mr. Pierre Déry. The following information was disclosed at the third step hearing, and Mr. Campbell was faced with the decision of whether to grant or deny Mr. Déry's grievance.

*   *   *

Mr. Déry's first job was as a "Wet Deck Sander." He reported to Foreman Claude Cayouette and was required to sand manually areas of the car body where the machine sanders could not operate, for example, along door and window edges. Mr. Déry was assigned to work with another employee for one and a half days. The company contended that no training was required on this job, because the new man learns from the employee with whom he was working. However, after a day and a half both the utility man and Mr. Cayouette instructed Mr. Déry on the proper sanding procedure and the requirements of his job, commenting that the normal learning procedure did not appear to be sufficient. Mr. Cayouette stated that after three days Mr. Déry was inept and consistently missed unsanded areas.

According to Mr. Déry, he received no indication either formally or informally that his performance was below par. He recalled Mr. Cayouette instructing him, but said he felt that the instruction was given only to improve his efficiency. He said Mr. Cayouette had shown him methods to simplify and speed up his work: things not readily apparent to a new man. When questioned about the instruction provided by the fellow wet deck sander Mr. Déry replied that the instruction consisted of:

Here's your sandpaper. Just do what I do.

On July 31, Mr. Déry was transferred to the body shop where Mr. Gregory Landry assigned him to the job of production helper. His duties were to supply materials and tools required by other production men. After observing Mr. Déry for one day Mr. Landry commented:

Déry was extremely nervous and unsure of himself. I could tell in five minutes that he would never be a good worker. These political radicals usually aren't worth a damn anyway.

Mr. Landry had become aware of Mr. Déry's political leanings during the morning coffee break. Mr. Déry had been extolling the advantages of Separatism to the other workers. Mr. Landry had overheard the conversation and, being a strong Liberal supporter and a believer in that party's "One Nation" policy, he couldn't restrain himself and joined the discussion. At one point he made the comment to Déry:

All you radicals should be shipped to a desert island and then blown to hell!

Later that day Mr. Déry was transferred to the assembly department. At the time Déry accepted the transfer without argument, but he and others in the department interpreted this as a transfer dictated by

Landry's personal animosity to Déry. Mr. Landry later admitted that Déry was transferred in an attempt to isolate him physically from other employees — because of his political views. Mr. Seguin, the Industrial Relations Manager, said that if he had known Mr. Déry's political views, he probably would not have hired him in the first place.

On August 1, Mr. Déry began working as an option driller for Mr. Leslie Curran. Three option drillers worked on each shift. Each car required a certain number of holes to accommodate options which were installed further down the production line. The number and location of the holes depended on the options specified on a metal plate fastened to the firewall of the car. The specific options to be built into a car were also listed on a production ticket which accompanied the vehicle as it moved down the production line. Each of the 14 option packages had a code number, for example, the power steering and power brake option was known as A-31 and required the drilling of six holes. Exhibit 4(p.279) is a depiction of a firewall plate with option A-31 marked as an example. The points at which holes were to be drilled were clearly marked on the firewall. In the case of option packages which required the drilling of holes in the car body, such as adjustable rear-view mirror, radio antenna, and power windows, the exact location of these holes was also clearly marked by an indented X mark on the car body. Holes drilled in the firewall were 1/2" in diameter. Holes drilled in the body were 1/4", 15/32" or 1/2" in diameter.

Mr. Déry was placed on the production line to observe and learn the procedure from a fellow worker. On the second day, he received one hour's instruction from Mr. Henry Arsenault, the utility man. After the hour Mr. Arsenault left Mr. Déry on his own with instructions to call on him if he needed assistance. After two days on the job Mr. Déry, according to Mr. Curran, "was visibly unsure of himself." Mr. Curran said he personally instructed Déry on the proper sequence for drilling the holes and on the proper way to achieve maximum benefit from the power-operated drill. Again on August 14, 20, 26 and 29 Mr. Curran instructed Déry on the proper method for doing his job, showing him how to sequence the holes to increase his speed. Curran received numerous complaints from subsequent production departments during the time Déry was on the job — all complained of misplaced and missed holes. Cars with misplaced or missed holes, or holes of the wrong size, had to be removed from the assembly line to have the mistakes corrected so that the option equipment could be installed. Curran commented:

> After two weeks, Déry hadn't acquired the skill normally achieved after three or four days. No one has ever taken more than a week to learn this job. His mind must be on his hair-brained political ideas. It's sure not on his job.

Déry claimed that all instructions that he received, with the exception of those given by Henry Assenault, were given in English. He had difficulty understanding English, especially in the noisy surroundings and he said Curran's instructions were not always clear to him.

"Usually," Déry explained, "I would wait until Mr. Curran had left and then ask a fellow employee for a translation." The fact that instructions were not given in French, according to Déry, was in itself a discriminatory practice:

They knew when they hired me that French was my language!

The language used by the foremen in the plant varied according to the preference of the individual foreman. Foreman Curran spoke a little French and understood more than he was able to speak. He rarely used French in the plant, however. The application form was in both French and English, while the employment interview was almost always conducted in English.

Déry further explained that his arrival on the job corresponded with a period when cars were being produced for dealer showrooms. Sometimes 10 or 12 cars would come down the line, each with a different option package. Déry commented:

I had to ask the man across from my work station for help. I never had a chance to learn the options and was forced to miss holes because I didn't know where the holes went. On a production line people are too busy to explain each option as it comes through. They have their own work to do. It took me quite a while to learn all the options but I know most of them now.

On at least two occasions Déry explained that he was unable to do his job because the utility man had his tools. On another occasion his drill hose broke and it was cut off and reattached to the drill instead of being replaced by a new hose. Déry complained that with the short hose he was unable to reach holes on the far side of the car. Only after a day was the hose repaired correctly. Curran said he was unaware of this instance, but George Martin, maintenance electrician, confirmed Déry's story.

In summary Déry stated:

I was nervous at first, but it was a new job and I had some difficulties. I received no written complaints about my work, although Curran did offer suggestions on several occasions. I attempted to explain the reasons for my poor performance but he was always too busy to listen.

On September 22, Curran discovered Déry using a 15/32-inch drill instead of the regular 1/2-inch drill. He reprimanded Déry and pointed out that while he might not know the difference on first sight, he could have seen the number 15 embossed on the drill stem. Curran acknowledged that the 32 was obscured. Déry said that the utility man had removed the 1/2-inch drill and not returned it. He asked whether it wasn't better to drill holes anyway even if they were 1/16 inch too small. According to Déry, Curran replied, "Of course not," and walked away.

On the following day, during a check on operations, Curran discovered 25 incorrectly drilled cars. He went directly to Déry's work station and found him again using a 15/32-inch drill. Curran grabbed the drill, removed the bit and smashed it on the floor. This was at 1:30 in the afternoon. Curran severely reprimanded Déry and ordered him to report to his office at the end of the shift. Déry received his discharge immediately upon reporting to Curran's office.

EXHIBIT 1 (PIERRE DÉRY)

Section 13 of Collective Agreement

Probationary Employees

A. An employee shall be a "Probationary Employee" until he has acquired seniority rights, at which time he shall become a Seniority Employee. The retention of Probationary Employees shall be solely at the discretion of Management and there shall be no responsibility for the re employment of Probationary Employees who are laid off or discharged. However, any claim by a Probationary Employee made after 30 days of employment that his layoff or discharge is not for just cause may be taken up as a grievance. Such claims must be stated in detail in writing at the time of the filing of the grievance.

B. An employee shall acquire seniority rights when he has worked ninety (90) days in any consecutive six (6)-month period terminating during the life of the agreement. Management, should they decide that the probationary employee is satisfactory prior to the ninety (90) days, may grant seniority rights.

EXHIBIT 2 (PIERRE DÉRY)

Section 4
GRIEVANCE PROCEDURE

All grievances arising between employees and the Company shall be dealt with as speedily and effectively as possible by cooperative effort on the part of both the Union and local Management in accordance with the following procedure.

STEP 1

Any employee having a grievance, or one designated member of a group having a grievance, should first take the grievance up with his Foreman who will attempt to adjust it.

STEP 2

If the grievance is not adjusted at Step 1 the grievance shall be reduced to writing on an Employee Grievance Form. The aggrieved and his union steward shall meet with the Department Superintendent or Department Head within two days of submitting the written grievance. The Superintendent shall give his decision in writing not later than two working days following the completion of the grievance discussion.

STEP 3

If the written decision of the Superintendent or Department Head is not satisfactory the grievance may be referred to the Shop Committee who may request a meeting with management. The Shop Committee may, within 5 days of receiving the written decision from Step 2, appeal the decision to management. Management, consisting of the Plant Manager or his designated representatives, will meet within 3 working days of receiving the grievance and render its written decision within 5 days of the grievance discussion.

In cases of discharge, the First and Second Steps of the grievance procedure may be waived at the discretion of the aggrieved and his representatives.

STEP 4

If the written decision of management at Step 3 is not satisfactory to the Union Representatives and/or the aggrieved the grievance may be submitted to final and binding arbitration. The arbitrator shall be jointly selected from a list of 5 arbitrators agreed upon as satisfactory to both union and management. The arbitrator's decision in a case shall be rendered within thirty (30) days from the date on which the case was submitted to him. The cost of arbitration shall be divided equally between the Union and the Company. An Arbitrator shall not alter, add to, subtract from, modify or amend any part of this Agreement.

EXHIBIT 4 (PIERRE DÉRY)

EXAMPLE OF FIREWALL PLATE

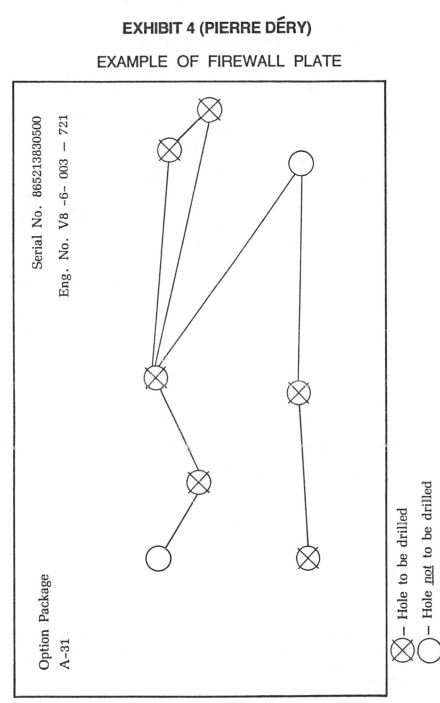

EXHIBIT 3 (PIERRE DÉRY)
Section 2

MANAGEMENT'S RIGHTS

Except as otherwise expressly and specifically provided in this Agreement, the Union recognizes and agrees that the supervision, management and control of the Company's business, operations, working force and plant are exclusively vested in the management of the Company. Without limiting the generality of the foregoing, the Union recognizes and agrees that the right to plan, direct, and control the Company's business, methods, operations, and working force; to hire, promote, transfer and lay off employees, and, lawfully and for just and proper cause, to demote, discipline, suspend or discharge employees, and the right to determine the hours, schedules, and assignments of work, the work tasks and standards of performance for employees, and the right to change, relocate, abandon, or discontinue any production services, methods, or facilities, or to introduce new or improved materials, methods, or facilities, and to purchase or otherwise acquire and utilize materials and services from such sources as is deemed desirable by the Company, is vested exclusively in the management of the Company. The foregoing shall not be taken, however, as a limitation upon the rights of the Union to represent the employees covered hereby in the procedures provided in this Agreement.

ALEXANDER BERT LTD.

A CASE OF ALLEGED DRUG USE

On September 8, 1974, Mrs. Frieda Thorenson filed this grievance:

I was given a leave of absence on Tuesday, August 31, 1974, at which time I went to the hospital because I was sick. On Friday, September 3, 1974, I received a telegram from the company stating I was dismissed.

Action requested by me is that I be reinstated in the company to my former position, without any loss of seniority and that I be paid for all straight time and all overtime hours which I might have worked but lost because of the action taken by the company.

The aforementioned discharge notice issued by the company on September 3, 1974, read:

On Tuesday, August 31, 1974, you reported for work under the influence of unprescribed drugs. This is a direct violation of item 2 of the established plant rules and regulations, clearly posted on the main bulletin board in the plant.

You are hereby informed that your employment with this company has been terminated for:
a) being under the influence of unprescribed drugs;
b) medical unfitness.
The termination is effective Friday, September 3, 1974.

The posted rule to which reference was made read:

Any employee committing any of the following acts shall be disciplined by reprimand, suspension or dismissal depending upon the seriousness of the offense and the past record of the employee...
2) Reporting for work or being present on company property under the influence of alcohol or unprescribed drugs, or bringing alcoholic beverages or unprescribed drugs on to the premises.

The discharge notice and subsequent grievance arose out of incidents at the Alexander Bert, Limited, plant in Chatham, Ontario, on August 31, 1974. At seven-thirty on the morning in question, Mr. Steven Rolfe, foreman in one of the machine shops, became concerned about one of his employees, Mrs. Frieda Thorenson. He described her as behaving "as though someone was sticking pins in her. She was twitching and jumping around, chewing something violently." He further explained that he had observed Mrs. Thorenson in a similar state before, but not with such pronounced symptoms.

Out of concern for her safety, Mr. Rolfe changed Mrs. Thorenson's work, along with two other women, to that of racking in the plating shop. (The term "racking" referred to the placement of light-weight plated metal sheets into wooden racks for storage and, later, shipment. It was simple, not dangerous, manual work.) Rolfe took this action at about 8:00 .. About fifteen minutes later he noticed a number of employees standing back from the operation, staring at Mrs. Thorenson. He said:

She was behaving very irregularly. She was still chewing violently; she was moving around all over the place, with very exaggerated body movements — jerking. She was also fumbling with some parts; she dropped one part.

Mr. Rolfe was unsure of what to do about the situation, so he sought more expert advice in the person of Mr. Frank Hall, the Personnel Manager. Rolfe was instructed by Hall to accompany Thorenson to the first-aid office. This he did, and he left her there, not to see her again until 11:00 A.M. Mr. Hall came to the first-aid office around 8:30 and found Mrs. Thorenson lying on the bed, but with both legs on the floor. She was perspiring heavily and, when asked what was happening, she spoke very rapidly making it very difficult to make out what she was saying. Hall said:

She went on and on for five or ten minutes, telling about her emotional problems at home; she said her nerves were bad. She was talking about someone who had been hurt in the back of a truck some time ago. She said she had taken some nerve pills, but she had not had any drug at that time. Speed was one of the drugs she mentioned, but not at that time.

The company nurse, Mrs. Margorie McMahan, was there at the time and suggested that Mrs. Thorenson rest for a while. Mrs. McMahan said she would look in on her occasionally and that she would promptly summon a doctor if she believed it was necessary.

Hall left Mrs. Thorenson and returned about 12:15 to find her sleeping. He woke her and accompanied her to Mrs. McMahan's office, adjoining the first-aid room, to use the telephone to call her husband. Hall said her body movements were still very exaggerated and that her eyes were "flashing around."

Miss Janice Nelson, secretary to the personnel manager, stayed with Mrs. Thorenson for the morning. She gave a similar description of Thorenson's actions. She said that Mrs. Thorenson was chewing something quite violently; she had difficulty sitting still — crossing and uncrossing her legs. According to Nelson, Mrs. Thorenson was constantly looking at her fingers, at times digging under one nail with the nail of another finger. Miss Nelson reported seeing a skin rash on Mrs. Thorenson's hands. She said that Mrs. Thorenson would not look at her, and for the most part, talked and hummed to herself. In answer to a question she did not give a complete answer; she used disjointed words. It was necessary to repeat questions three or four times before she would reply. Miss Nelson, like Hall, described the woman as perspiring profusely.

Meanwhile the personnel manager had arranged for Mrs. Thorenson to see her physician at 3:00 P.M. at the Chatham General Hospital. Dr. Arthur Hodgson, the company's doctor, was instructed to consult with the woman's doctor and to report his findings to the personnel department. He did so. Mrs. Thorenson's doctor was Richard Gilman, assistant professor in the Department of Community Medicine in a nearby university who had a small private practice. Dr. Gilman said that he had seen Mrs. Thorenson on August 13, when she complained of a skin problem. She had told him that she believed her skin problem was due to crystals of methedrine coming out of her skin and that there were insects crawling under her skin. Dr. Gilman prescribed a tranquilizer, describing the phenomenon described by Mrs. Thorenson as "hallucinations."

Dr. Gilman stated that when Mrs. Thorenson arrived at the hospital on August 31 she was very distraught, was hallucinating, and appeared to be in a psychotic condition. He described the skin condition on her hands and said the area under her fingernails appeared to have been "dug at" by her fingers or possibly a sharp instrument. Her hallucinations took the form of insects crawling under her skin and snakes crawling on her face. Dr. Gilman said that all of these symptoms strongly suggested that Mrs. Thorenson had been taking drugs — "most likely methedrine (speed)." He stated that to reach the point of hallucinations from speed required prolonged, heavy use, that a single dose would not give that result. He further remarked that it was unlikely that the excessive perspiration was caused by methedrine, but that with street purchases of the drug one could not be certain of what other drugs or substances might be included in the mixture.

After examining Mrs. Thorenson and performing some tests, Dr. Gilman determined she was under the influence of methedrine and decided to admit her to the hospital. He said that at the time "she was not medically fit for anything." She agreed to undergo treatment, but on September 4 she discharged herself. The doctor believed that she should have remained in the hospital for at least a week, and then she should have entered one of two rehabilitation centers for drug users. He could offer no opinion as to why Mrs. Thorenson discharged herself from the hospital.

Mrs. Thorenson said that she had been taking drugs off and on for about a month prior to August 31. She attributed her condition to emotional disturbances at home; her husband had been unemployed for over a year. She admitted taking methedrine early in the morning on the day prior to August 31, but said she felt no ill effects from it. She said she had obtained the drug that day from a friend, who earlier had procured it for himself by prescription from a doctor. Mrs. Thorenson claimed to have two witnesses who could be called upon to testify that she had not acted abnormally on August 31.

Paul Martin, president of Local 1212 of the United Auto Workers, the representative of Alexander Bert workers, said the company had been too severe in its discipline. No one had previously been disciplined for drug abuse, but he cited three cases wherein the company had discharged employees for suspected alcohol intoxication. Three of the four employees involved in these cases were reinstated as a result of arbitration hearings. Mr. Martin cited Mrs. Thorenson's flawless work record over the seven years she had served the company as further evidence of injustice. He stated,

> The company suggests that Mrs. Thorenson wantonly disregarded its rules and regulations. This is incomprehensible, given her desperate personal situation. She could not afford to lose her job. If, as the company contends, she was under the influence of some drug, then I submit that it was involuntary. Involuntary ingestion of a drug cannot be separated from the contraction of measles. It is only when

the afflicted person refuses treatment, that we can condemn her. Mrs. Thorenson did submit to treatment. Management has acted irresponsibly; no arbitrator will let it pass.

While this was the first disciplinary action taken at Alexander Bert Ltd. for alleged drug use, managers in the area were becoming increasingly concerned that the drug problem would eventually surpass the problem of alcoholism among factory employees.

NOTES TO CHAPTER 8

1. Frank Elkouri and Edna Elkouri, *How Arbitration Works* (rev. ed., Washington, D.C.: BNA Incorporated, 1960), p. 2.

2. Robin W. Fleming, *The Labor Arbitration Process* (Urbana: The University of Illinois Press, 1965), p. 2.

3. *Ontario Hospital Labour Disputes Act,* S.O. 1965, ch. 48.

4. *The Police Act,* R.S.O. 1960, ch. 298. *The Fire Departments Act,* R.S.O. 1960, ch. 145.

5. Some jurisdictions, e.g., Federal, B.C., provide that disputes arising out of the interpretation or application of the contract shall be settled by arbitration "or otherwise" or "such other method as may be agreed upon." Mid-contract strikes are prohibited, and the parties have in fact found no viable alternative other than arbitration.

6. Sumner Slichter, James, J. Healy and E. Robert Livernash, *The Impact of Collective Bargaining on Management* (Washington, D.C.: The Brookings Institution, 1960), p. 722.

7. Economics and Research Branch, Canada Department of Labour, *Collective Agreement Provisions in Major Manufacturing Establishments* (Ottawa: The Queen's Printer, 1964), p. 23.

8. In some jurisdictions, strikes may be permitted in mid-contract if the parties are unable to agree on the implementation of technological change.

9. A.C. Crysler, *Handbook of Employer-Employee Relations in Canada* (Don Mills, Ontario: CCH Canadian Limited, 1969), p. 128.

10. This basic rule, and the definitive statements on arbitrability and the courts' role in the arbitration process is found in a simultaneously issued set of opinions called "The Trilogy": *United Steelworkers of America v. American Manufacturing Company, (1960),* 363 U.S. 564; *United Steelworkers of America v. Enterprise Wheel and Car Corporation, (1960),* 363 U.S. 593; and *United Steelworkers of America v. Warrior and Gulf Navigation Company, (1960),* 363 U.S. 574 and also in a later decision: *John Wiley and Sons Incorporated v. Livingston, President of District 65, Retail Wholesale and Department Store Union, (1964),* 376 U.S. 543.

11. "Collective Agreements in Manufacturing (Part IV)," *The Labour Gazette,* September, 1967, p. 570.

12. Fleming, op. cit., p. 78.

13. This could include a foreman who might be affected if a discharged employee

were allowed to return to work, or an employee who might lose his promotion if a claim to the job by another employee were allowed by an arbitrator.

14. Clarence M. Updegroff, *Arbitration and Labor Relations* (Washington, D.C.: The Bureau of National Affiars, Inc., 1970), pp. 244-5.

15. American Arbitration Association, *Labor Arbitration* (New York: American Arbitration Association, 1966), pp. 16-17.

16. Updegroff, op. cit., p. 252.

17. A.W.R. Carrothers: *Labour Arbitration in Canada* (Toronto: Butterworths, 1961), p. 124.

18. C.H. Curtis, *Labour Arbitration Procedures* (Kingston, Ontario: Department of Industrial Relations, Queen's University, 1957), p. 51.

19. In Canada, the ability of the arbitrator to modify penalties in discipline cases presents special problems. This will be discussed later.

20. American Arbitration Association, op. cit., pp. 17-19.

21. Curtis, op. cit., p. 67.

22. Elkouri and Elkouri, op. cit.

23. Paul Prasow and Edward Peters, *Arbitration and Collective Bargaining* (New York: McGraw Hill Book Company, 1970), p. 59.

24. Ibid.

25. Slichter, Healy and Livernash, op. cit., pp. 657-8.

26. *Regina v. Arthurs et. al ex parte Port Arthur Ship-Building Co.*, 68 C.L.L.C. 14, 136 (S.C.C. 1968).

27. Paul C. Weiler, *Arbitration and Social Change*, Task Force on Labour Relations, Study No. 6 (Ottawa: Privy Council Office, 1969), p. 6.

28. Ibid.

29. Prasow and Peters, op. cit., p. 47.

30. Weiler, op. cit., pp. 7-8.

31. Ibid., p. 26.

32. George W. Adams, "Grievance Arbitration and Judicial Review in North America," *Osgoode Hall Law Journal*, December, 1971, p. 491.

33. *Re Columbia Packing Co. Ltd., and Amalgamated Meat Cutters and Butcher Workmen of North America*, Local 212, 62 C.L.L.C. 15, 408 (B.C.S.C. 1962).

34. The Ontario law, as opposed to that of other provinces, does not allow the parties to select any alternative methods of dispute settlement other than arbitration. Arbitration tribunals have thus been viewed by the courts as statutory tribunals, whose awards are reviewable in higher courts.

35. Adams, op. cit., p. 503.

36. R.S.C. 1970, ch. 72, sec. 68.

37. Herbert R. Northrup, *Compulsory Arbitration and Government Intervention in Labor Disputes* (Washington, D.C., Labor Policy Association, Inc., 1966), p. 183.

38. Donald J.M. Brown, *Interest Arbitration*, Task Force on Labor Relations, Study No. 18 (Ottawa: Privy Council Office, 1968), p. 26.

39. The Brotherhood of Railway Trainmen, *The Pros and Cons of Compulsory Arbitration* (Cleveland, Ohio: The Brotherhood of Railway Trainmen, 1965), p. 48.

40. Northrup, op. cit., pp. 179-211.

41. Brown, op. cit., p. 214.

42. For a discussion on the proposal to amend the National Labor Relations Act in the U.S., see Benjamin Aaron, "National Emergency Disputes: Some Current Proposals," *Proceedings of the 1971 Annual Spring Meeting, Industrial Relations Research Association Series,* (Madison, Wisconsin: Industrial Relations Research Association, 1971), p. 470. For a description of a municipality's experience with the process see Gary Long and Peter Fenille, "Final Offer Arbitration: 'Sudden Death' In Eugene," *Industrial and Labor Relations Review,* January 1974, pp. 186-203.

43. Carl M. Stevens, "Is Compulsory Arbitration Compatible with Bargaining?" *Industrial Relations,* February, 1966, pp. 38-52.

44. Byron E. Calame, "'Best Offer' Arbitration Critics," *The Wall Street Journal,* June 14, 1972, p. 16.

9. GOVERNMENT EMPLOYEE UNIONISM

Perhaps the most significant trend in North American labor relations is the emergence and rapid growth of government employee unionism. During the last ten years this has been the area of greatest membership growth, by far, stimulated primarily by the passage of enabling legislation at all levels of government — federal, provincial, state and local.

The Canadian postal case documents this trend among public service employees in Canada's federal government. These people were essentially unorganized in 1967; but three years later, in 1970, they had over 200,000 members. With such rapid growth it was necessary for unions, employers and administrative agencies of government to make rapid adjustments. There was not the luxury of aches and pains associated with slow growth, but rather the challenge of total adjustment from being suddenly dropped into a strange environment.

The tendency, at first, was for persons knowledgeable in the field of labor relations to transfer most of their assumptions, beliefs and practices from the private sector. In large part this worked; but in still larger part it presented vexing problems of adjustment. Entirely new issues were raised, including these:

- ☐ Should employees in the public service have a right to strike?
- ☐ If there is no right to strike what, if any, power can employees have at a bargaining table?
- ☐ What are appropriate criteria for determining economic packages for public service employees?
- ☐ Can representatives of the government serve as effective negotiators when they are constantly watched and second-guessed by politicians?
- ☐ How can rules and regulations formulated by a collective bargaining agreement be brought into concert with the traditions and practices of a bureaucracy?

*   *   *

Within the next few years government employee unions will become pattern setters for their private-sector brethren, not because they seek that role but rather because they represent employees of the largest employer in the country. Their wages and fringe packages will largely represent the economic policies of the government in power, and as those economic policies pervade the private sector other unions and private employers will have little choice but to follow.

For these reasons, the student of labor relations in the 1970s should be well acquainted with special issues presented by government employee unionism. The postal case which follows is presented with this in mind.

CANADIAN POSTAL NEGOTIATIONS
1972 - 1973

On February 16, 1973, nonsupervisory postal workers across Canada voted for acceptance of a new labor agreement. This marked conclusion of the fourth collective agreement between the Treasury Board of Canada, representing the employer, and the Council of Postal Unions (CPU), the bargaining agent for employees. The CPU was composed of two unions: the Canadian Union of Postal Workers (CUPW) and the Letter Carriers Union of Canada (LCUC). Together these unions represented about 28,000 employees, including 12,600 Postal Clerks, 11,900 Letter Carriers, 2,200 Mail Handlers, 700 Dispatchers and 500 Mail Service Couriers.

The most recent agreement covering these parties had extended for a 30-month period from October 1, 1969, to March 26, 1972, and provided for an average annual increase of 6.8 per cent. According to Treasury Board figures total straight-time payroll costs for nonsupervisory postal workers had increased 40.5 per cent from 1967 till 1973 — from $148,223,844 to $208,188,564. This compared with an increase of 36.2 per cent over the same period for the public service as a whole.

Terms of the new agreement — to run until December 31, 1974 — included pay increases as follows:

☐ 38 cents per hour effective the first pay period following ratification,

☐ 14 cents per hour effective 10 months after ratification,

☐ 13 cents per hour effective 15 months after ratification.

The average annual compound increase was calculated at 6.61 per cent.

The agreement did not provide for retroactivity of hourly increases; rather it provided for a lump-sum payment for full-time employees of $400 for the period March 27, 1972 (the expiration date of the old contract) till December 31, 1972, and $66 per month for the period January 1, 1973 for the first pay period following ratification. Part-time letter carriers were given half of these sums to cover the same periods.

There were also improvements in fringe benefits, the most important of which included the following:

1. *Work on a day of rest*
   Double time on second day of rest in a week, provided the first day of rest had been worked.

2. *Vacation leave*
   Four weeks after 16 years (had been 4 after 18), five weeks after 30 years (no previous provision for five weeks).

3. *Medical and hospital*
   Employer to pay 50 per cent of the hospital premiums in addition to previous obligations.

4. *Uniforms and protective clothing*
   Boot and glove allowances increased to $84 from $70, and $8 from $5 per year respectively.

Perhaps the most important provisions involved issues of technological change and job security. These were dealt with, in part, by amending the grievance procedure so that matters involving job classifications could be included, and by establishing a manpower committee to engage in consultation regarding proposed technological changes. The committee was given authority to discuss all matters of mutual interest including:

i) the effect of change on working conditions and on the work force,

ii) job descriptions and job contents arising from the introduction of change...,

iii) wages to be paid to changed jobs and new jobs,

iv) the relationship between change and hours of work.

A new wage schedule was formulated with hourly rates assigned to various levels as follows:

Level	Increments	Feb. 26 1973	Dec. 17 1973	May 17 1974
1	Minimum	$3.32	3.46	3.59
	1st Year	3.39	3.53	3.66
	2nd Year	3.46	3.60	3.73
	3rd Year	3.53	3.67	3.80
2	Minimum	3.50	3.64	3.77
	1st Year	3.57	3.71	3.84
	2nd Year	3.64	3.78	3.91
	3rd Year	3.71	3.85	3.98
3	Minimum	3.69	3.83	3.96
	1st Year	3.76	3.90	4.03
	2nd Year	3.84	3.98	4.11
	3rd Year	3.92	4.06	4.19
4	Minimum	3.82	3.96	4.09
	1st Year	3.90	4.04	4.17

	2nd Year	3.98	4.12	4.25
	3rd Year	4.07	4.21	4.34
5	Minimum	3.90	4.04	4.17
	1st Year	3.99	4.13	4.26
	2nd Year	4.07	4.21	4.34
	3rd Year	4.16	4.30	4.43

Part-time
Letter Carrier   3.73   3.87   4.00

The job titles which corresponded to various levels were as follows:

Level

1   Coder
2   Mail Handler
3   Letter Carrier
         Part-time Letter Carrier
         Mail Services Courier
         Supervisory Mail Handler
4   Postal Clerk
5   Mail Dispatcher
         Supervisory Letter Carrier

LEGISLATIVE BACKGROUND

By early 1973 more than 200,000 government employees were represented by bargaining agents certified under the Public Service Staff Relations Act. The Act designated the Treasury Board of Canada as the employer. This was done in order to promote consistent employee relations policies in the government service, something that was considered unlikely to transpire if each department negotiated its own contract. A particularly unique feature of the Staff Relations Act required the various government employee unions to choose in advance one of two alternative methods for dispute settlement to be used in event of a deadlock. This choice had to be made prior to each round of bargaining. On one hand they could submit the items in dispute to a board of conciliation with a subsequent right to strike if they did not agree with the board's recommendations (sect. 86). Or, on the other hand, they could submit their dispute to final and binding arbitration (sect. 70). As of October 1, 1973, 109 bargaining units had been formed in the public service. Eighty-nine had chosen binding arbitration as their means of settlement. Twenty, including the Council of Postal Unions, had chosen conciliation with the eventual right to strike.

The Public Service Staff Relations Act established an independent board, chaired by Professor Jacob Finkelman, to resolve disputes arising out of the Act and to exercise administrative responsibilities connected with bargaining. The board reported directly to Parliament. Among its responsibilities was the designation of appropriate bargaining units. The board determined that an appropriate unit for the postal workers included letter carriers, clerks, dispatchers and mail handlers. Thus the CUPW and LCUC, which had combined earlier for purposes of collective bargaining, were certified as one entity, the Council of Postal Unions.

Section 56 of the Public Service Staff Relations Act restricted areas of negotiations in the public service to those not already covered by other legislation. The Public Service Employment Act, for example, dealt with matters of employment including hiring, merit rating, promoting, demoting, transfer, layoff or release — thus apparently excluding these from consideration of the postal negotiators. Pensions were excluded from consideration, because they were covered by the Public Service Superannuation Act. Matters involving redress of poor working conditions, while subject to grievance procedure under the contracts, sometimes required involvement of the Public Works Department for their correction. And matters concerning the impact of technological change, a prime concern of the Council, could be considered via consultation, but no effective action could be taken because layoffs, and effects thereof, were subject to provisions of the Public Service Employment Act.

THE 1972/73 NEGOTIATIONS

Negotiations began on February 10, 1972. A total of 57 meetings were held 4 in February, 13 in March, 8 in April, 6 in May, 7 in June, 11 in July and 8 in August. On August 23 the unions announced that they would apply for a conciliation board, and on December 14, 1972, the conciliation board reported its findings and recommendations. The majority of the union's bargaining committee rejected the conciliation report; but when union membership voted on January 7 and 8, 1973, on whether to accept their majority bargaining committee's position, the membership overrode the committee. This forced resumption of negotiations. Following five meetings, a memorandum of agreement was signed on January 24, 1973. On February 15, 1973, postal workers finally ratified the new contract — 73 per cent of the 24,000 workers who voted expressed approval. There was no general strike, but a number of work stoppages occurred in various parts of the country during the period of negotiations, many of which were only incidentially related to the negotiations.

The chief spokesman for the CPU was James Mayes, First Vice President of the Letter Carriers Union (LCUC). Mayes had been chief spokesman in the 1969/70 negotiations as well. Other members of the union committee were:

Roger Decarie, President, LCUC;
Alex Power, President, Toronto Local Union, LCUC;
Alex Edey, President, Hamilton Local Union, LCUC;
Donald Harrison, Winnipeg, LCUC;
Jim McCall, President, CUPW;
Wayne Mundle, President, Campbellton, N.B., Local Union, CUPW;
Lou Murphy, President, Toronto Local Union, CUPW;
Frank Pasacreta, Research Director, Vancouver Local Union, CUPW;
Paul Lachance, President, Quebec City Local Union, CUPW.

Claude P. Parent, Director, Staff Relations Branch, Post Office Department was chairman of the Management Committee. Mr. Parent was hospitalized from mid-June of 1972 until the second week in July. During that time George Orser, member of the Staff Relations Division, Personnel Policy Branch, Treasury Board Secretariat, acted as chief negotiator and continued to play a major role in negotiations after Parent's return. Mr. Orser was the only member of management's committee who was not from the Post Office. There were seven others on the committee. These included men from Staff Relations Headquarters, officers from the field and one operational representative from headquarters.

BARGAINING MANDATE

The negotiating authority of the management team derived from a mandate prepared by the team, submitted to the Director of Staff Relations for the Treasury Board, then reviewed in general terms by a Senior Coordinating Committee and submitted by the Deputy Secretary of the Treasury Board to the Board's President. The Senior Coordinating Committee in this case consisted of the Deputy Postmaster General, John Mackay, the two Assistant Deputy Postmasters General, Lionel Barriere and Gordon Sinclair, and Claude Parent.

Aside from reviewing the bargaining mandate, this committee consulted with negotiators on all major items of policy and tactics. They also formed a connecting link between bargainers and the two relevant ministers: the Postmaster General and the President of the Treasury Board.

EARLY NEGOTIATIONS

Three pre-negotiation meetings took place prior to February 10. These covered such matters as location and schedule of meetings and the composition of bargaining teams. As in the 1969/70 negotiations the Council of Postal Unions (CPU) made a request for simultaneous translation facilities. As they had done before, management negotiators said they would endeavor to provide such facilities if the Council was prepared to share the costs.

There was no apparent problem with language among negotiating team members. Negotiations were conducted in English, and those members with a French-Canadian background were essentially bilingual. The Council did not raise the matter again, nor did management.

During one of the early meetings management negotiators said that the government was prepared to live with the existing contract and to confine bargaining to matters of wages and the term of the agreement. They recognized that there were problems with the wording of some sections of the contract, but they pointed out that the contract was only 15 months old and needed more time in operation in order for people to discover for certain whether provisions needed changing.

The Council rejected this idea, and in the meeting of February 10 they proposed changes in 43 articles of the old agreement. In addition they put forth three new articles for adoption. In total, they raised approximately 160 separate issues. It appeared to management negotiators that they were looking for almost a complete revision of the contract. None of these demands concerned monetary terms except to say they wanted a "substantial" increase.

The principal reason for the great number of demands stemmed from the nature of the Council itself. Demands had been prepared following solicitations among members across the country. A national committee of the Council, composed of approximately 20 officers, received and passed on the demands to their bargaining representatives. Council bargainers could be sure that by the time a demand reached the bargaining table a considerable number of people supported it. While the team itself was probably not serious about pushing all demands they did treat them all as politically serious. By presenting them in formal bargaining they paid heed to various groups of constituents.

It was impossible for management negotiators to know which of the 160 or so demands were most important. However, two issues seemed to pervade most of them: job security and classification. And these issues had been anticipated by management.

The job security issue had been raised during the 1969/70 negotiations and involved concern by the Council and management alike with the need for the Post Office to modernize in order to meet the rapidly increasing demands on its services. Automatic equipment had already been introduced in some locations; in others it was imminent. New techniques for sorting and coding mail were being designed and implemented, and all these raised anxieties among workers concerning possible loss of jobs, the possibility of transfer, the desire for retraining, and the possibility of doing things differently from the way people had been accustomed to doing them for the past 24 years.

THE CLASSIFICATION ISSUE

Closely related to matters of job security were issues surrounding job classification, and these came to a head about three months after negotiations started — presenting the management team with a strategy dilemma.

The existing classification system for Post Office employees had been introduced in 1966 and 1967 and had existed unchanged since then. This defined various skill levels. Rates of pay were negotiated for each of these levels. As new skills were called for because of modernization or changed methods, positions affected were not reclassified. The job level and assigned rate remained unchanged even though there was a clear difference in skills required.

Until May of 1972 the classification issue had not been specifically raised. However, everyone knew it lay in the wings, and it all came to a head during a special meeting called by management at the Post Office Department Headquarters to discuss the mechanization of Ottawa's Alta Vista Post Office, which was then under way. Management was careful to hold this meeting in a location away from the regular negotiating meetings, which took place in Place Bell Canada, and to call it a consultation meeting only. Management believed the issues involving job classification were made exclusive matters for their determination by law. However, they believed that union negotiators should be informed about what was taking place, because the consequences might bear heavily on negotiations.

Section 7 of the Public Service Staff Relations Act provided the unilateral authority regarding classification which management was ever careful to retain. The section is quoted here:

> *Section 7. Right of employer.* Nothing in this Act shall be construed to effect the right or authority of the employer to determine the organization of the Public Service and to assign duties to and classify positions therein.

As a matter of practice the union became involved in classification issues only in a consultative role, as management described, point-rated, and determined the appropriate level for a job. Similarly they became involved if an employee raised a grievance regarding appropriate classification. However, in formulating the actual job description the union never became involved, and the Treasury Board Secretariat made it clear to their negotiators that this practice must be maintained. So when the Ottawa modernization became imminent bargainers were faced with the issue of whether to bring it up at all, lest it be construed as a negotiable issue. Some members of the management team actually advocated delay of any modernization until after the contract was signed.

The Ottawa modernization involved introduction of a new job — that of "coder operator." This job was similar to that of a key-punch operator and called upon a person to read a letter code (the number, letter combination now assigned to nearly all Canadian addresses) and to punch keys that translated the code into a series of bars to be printed on the envelope. Then the envelope was placed in an automatic machine, which, through a set of electric eyes, was equipped to read the bars and sort the letters. This operation would apply to all mail and would eventually eliminate the need for manual sorting. Manual sorters, who were classified as Level 4 workers, were considered to be among the most skilled of all post office employees. In some locations they needed to possess instant recall of more than 5000 points of knowledge in order to do their job, and they were required to undergo periodic examinations to test that recall.

The new coder operator job was determined by management, through application of their classification plan, to be Level 1. No great tests of memory were involved, and key-punching skills were largely mechanical. In the expiring contract there was no rate for a full time Level 1 employee. There were some employees designated Level 1, but all of these were part-time. Consequently, management indicated that a full-time Level 1 rate would be one of their requirements in the new contract and that for the present a $2.94 hourly rate would be assigned to the job.

Union representatives claimed that the Level 4 designation should be maintained — that the coder operator was sorting mail, no matter that he was sorting mail through a mechanized process. It had always been that way, and it should stay that way.

Lying beneath the Ottawa situation were anxieties concerning other locations as well. Coding machines had been purchased and were awaiting installation in at least 14 other locations. And there were other issues: what about all the jobs that had been changed since 1966/67 without a formal change in level? Did the Post Office contemplate downgrading them now? Supervisory letter carriers presented a case in point. In recent years their jobs had been changed so that they were no longer called on to supervise. Probably these jobs should carry a Level 3 designation — that assigned to a letter carrier; at most they should be Level 4. However, as of then, they were considered Level 5, because of their former supervisory role.

Issues surrounding the coder were discussed in four separate "non-negotiation" meetings. Council representatives grew increasingly restive, and they finally walked out on the fourth meeting — held in late June.

The reason for the walkout was that the Council believed these were matters for negotiation and that the employer had changed conditions of employment after notice to bargain had been given. Thus, they contended, management had violated the Public Service Staff Relations Act. Later, in September, they brought a case before the Staff Relations Board alleging violation of Section 51 of the Act. The Board delivered its decision on the matter on October 18.

Meanwhile Post Office management went ahead and introduced the new coder in Ottawa. They hired a coder operator, assigning an hourly rate of $2.94, equal to that of part-time Level 1 employees. This did not dispose of the issue, and while the general issue of job classification hung over the negotiations from beginning to end it was not faced directly at the bargaining table until the conciliation phase. In the early stages the most important issue, from management's point of view, concerned timing.

TIMING AND THE ELECTION

1972 was a federal election year. This was certain, but no one — even at the ministerial level — apparently knew *when* it would be. As negotiations began, the best guess appeared to be late spring, probably June. Management negotiators discussed at length what strategy, if any, they ought to adopt in light of pending elections. These discussions included members of the Senior Coordinating Committee. Two views prevailed — both predicated on the assumption that a conciliation board would almost certainly be appointed. One group of management bargainers felt the government should try to move matters along in order to get to conciliation in a hurry — before the election. This would help keep bargaining issues out of the campaign. Another group favored delaying as long as possible, for two reasons: 1) no one on the team could predict the election day, and 2) if conciliation were undertaken and the appropriate time limits expired so as to put the Council in a legal position to strike, they would be able to govern all major events from then on. They could decide when and where to strike, and, in so doing, they could use their power to embarrass the government and, possibly, to extract more-than-reasonable concessions at a time when the government could not politically afford to take a tough stand.

As it turned out union negotiators made it apparent that they were in no great hurry to settle. Furthermore, the election did not take place until October 30. So the timing issue assumed less importance during June and July, but it became of paramount importance when the union applied for conciliation on August 23.

Reasons for the union's apparent reluctance to move ahead with bargaining probably centered around a series of internal events. Among these were the following:

1. *Officer elections.* The trienniel convention of the Letter Carriers Union (LCUC) was scheduled for the last week in August. There would be a complete election of officers, and they would consider the issue of merger with CUPW. At its most recent convention the Council of Postal Unions had written a provision into their constitution empowering the executive to seek a merger. The LCUC constitution did not have such a provision, and there would likely be a fight as to whether they should have one. The LCUC and CUPW had been uneasy bedfellows ever since designation of CPU for bargaining purposes, and while internal difficulties were observed mainly in CUPW there was some degree of factionalism in LCUC as well.

2. *Internal Problems of CUPW.* James McCall, CUPW's President, had been a compromise candidate at that union's most recent election, held in Calgary. His election had depended on support of the Quebec delegation led by Marcel Perreault. Perrault led a demonstration in Ottawa that summer to picket the CUPW headquarters protesting the slowness of negotiations and complaining that he had not been kept informed of what was happening at the bargaining table.

The Perreault demonstration and other instances gave cause for management bargainers to question whether union negotiators were actually speaking for the membership. Later events in January 1973 bore out management's concerns in this regard.

REGIONAL RATES

On May 3 the Management Committee presented detailed pay proposals based on regional rates of pay and a 36-month agreement. As in previous negotiations, the unions flatly rejected the idea. Small locals, which would have benefited, voted against the proposal in an all-for-one, one-for-all kind of demonstration. The issue remained alive until August, when it seemed apparent that it was to become a whipping force against management in the forthcoming LCUC convention. Then on August 10, about two weeks before the convention, management dropped the issue, much to the surprise of the union. Soon thereafter the unions somewhat surprised management with a request for appointment of a conciliation board on August 23.

CONCILIATION

Section 52 of the Public Service Staff Relations Act provided for assistance of a conciliator upon request by either party to a contract. Section 77 provided for establishment of a conciliation *board* on request of either party. While nothing in the Act specified that the appointment of a conciliation board must be preceded by action of a single conciliator it had been practice in the past for the Council of Postal Unions to request a conciliator. Then, after delivery of the conciliator's report, a full board had been requested and appointed. Thus it was a surprise to management negotiators on August 23 when the union asked immediately for a board.

Management opposed the request, arguing that the intent of legislation was that a conciliation officer should deliver his report as a condition-precedent to appointment of a board. To many observers it appeared that management's real purpose was to stall for time. The federal election had not been announced, but such announcement was felt to be imminent. The election itself would follow the announcement by no more than 60 days. If a conciliation board was established its report could be expected about 47 days afterwards, according to time limits established in the law and expected administrative delays.[1]

The unions would have a right to strike seven days after delivery of the board's report.[2]

If, on the other hand, a conciliation officer were to be appointed under section 52 there would almost certainly be a board appointed after that, and an additional 14 days or more would be spent, because the conciliation officer must, under Section 53, report to the Chairman of the Public Service Staff Relations Board within 14 days from the date of his appointment or "within such longer period as the chairman shall determine."[3] Consequently, management objected to the appointment of a board — arguing that appointment of a board should be held in abeyance until after a conciliator, appointed pursuant to management's request, had exhausted his efforts to effect a settlement.

Management argued further that the Council had not bargained in good faith and that according to Section 50 of the Act parties must make "every reasonable effort to conclude a collective agreement." Since the Council had not made a counteroffer following management's withdrawal of its proposal for regional rates, management contended that the Council had not fulfilled the intent of Section 50. Union leaders termed this a stall tactic.

All these arguments were heard by Chairman Jacob Finkelman of the Public Service Staff Relations Board on September 5 in regard to the union's application for a conciliation board. Finkelman, in delivering his opinion on September 11, upheld the Council in all respects and announced establishment of a board. He said that in his opionion the appointment of a conciliator would not "serve the purpose of assisting the parties in reaching agreement," pointing out that one of the parties had looked upon his appointment "as an obstacle that must be removed with all possible haste...." Thus, said Finkelman, "the conciliator's chances of succeeding in his efforts are reduced to the vanishing point."

Regarding management's argument concerning good-faith bargaining, Chairman Finkelman said, "I cannot bring myself to believe that it was the intention of Parliament in enacting Section 77 to declare that the establishment of a conciliation board should turn on a consideration as to whether every change of position by one side had been met by a change of position by the other."

Then the Chairman indicated concern that the parties might undertake conciliation for the purpose of establishing a legal strike date, and he delivered a short written essay, as follows:

> ...The purpose of establishing a conciliation board is to assist the parties in reaching agreement. A conciliation board is not to be regarded as a mere legal hurdle that contestants must leap over to reach the goal of a strike. To regard it as such would be to imply that industrial relations in the Public Service of Canada in this decade of the twentieth century has not moved beyond the stage of a slightly controlled primitive blood feud. This is not to say that democratic society has devised a perfect method for dealing with industrial disputes that totally eliminates the need to resort to strike in some circumstances. But it would be highly improper and dangerous for the common weal to focus attention on the possibility of a strike rather than on the possibility of a peaceful settlement of the issues in dispute.

Between the date of hearing and the date of Finkelman's decision the federal election was announced. It would be held on October 30. The conciliation report would most likely be delivered after that date, and legal strike action during the campaign would be impossible.

Pursuant to Mr. Finkelman's decision to establish a conciliation board, each of the parties designated its representative. The government nominee was Bruce H. Stewart, a Toronto lawyer. The Council chose William Walsh, a labor consultant from Hamilton. Walsh had served as the Council's nominee to the conciliation board set up during the 1969/70 negotiations. Mssrs. Stewart and Walsh subsequently agreed upon Mr. Owen Shime, a vice chairman of the Ontario Labour Relations Board, as Chairman of the Board. However, their agreement was reached on October 3, slightly after the five-day limit provided in the law for that purpose, so, while Shime became the designee, his appointment came officially as the result of nomination by Mr. Finkelman.

On September 25, 27 and 29 counsel for the parties met with Mr. Finkelman to present briefs on matters in dispute so that he could formulate terms of reference for the conciliation board, required under Section 83 of the Public Service Staff Relations Act.

It soon became obvious to Mr. Finkelman that matters in dispute were extensively influenced by concerns regarding classification and job security. He paid heed to this fact in his terms, and by careful wording he directed the attention of the board to such issues, while, at the same time, pointing out that subsection 56(2) (b) of the Public Service Staff Relations Act removed from the scope of bargaining those matters presently covered by certain enumerated Acts, including the Public Service Employment Act. He pointed out further that subsection 86(3) of PSSRA declared that:

> No report of a conciliation board shall contain any recommendation concerning the standards, procedures or processes governing the appointment, appraisal, promotion, demotion, transfer, layoff or release of employees.

In spite of legislative encumbrances Mr. Finklemen felt that problems of job security and the necessity to introduce change would "undoubtedly hang like a pall over the deliberations of the conciliation board in this dispute." So he searched for ways of dealing with them. He observed that subsection 86 of the Act did not state that the report of a conciliation board shall *not* contain recommendations concerning matters set out in subsection 56(2). It follows, according to Finkelman, that if the board "did make recommendations for action by the employer that would infringe subsection 56(2) the law would forbid the employer to carry those recommendations into effect *as part of a collective agreement*."[4]

Mr. Finkelman speculated on the possibility that the government and unions might enter into a collective agreement that included a provision limiting management's rights regarding matters that were preserved as exclusively theirs under Section 7 of the Act. If the employer were to agree to such a provision, said Finkelman, "it would not be bound by that provision.... It would be free in law to repudiate that stipulation the next day." In this case the employer had the unilateral right to determine classifications. If he wished to put a condition into the contract limiting the right and then, subsequently, decided he did not want to live up to it he didn't have to. There was a moral obligation to do so, but no legal obligation.

Terms of reference were delivered to the parties in advance of their official release (October 18). They embraced 56 typewritten pages and covered 62 items. They made it clear that Chairman Finkelman expected the conciliation board to do considerably more than merely listen to the parties and then formulate recommendations on the various outstanding issues. The board was expected to mediate as well. Mr. Finkelman dealt with the matter of technological change at length, pointing out that such issues were of grave concern to employees — reflecting the "fear of employees that their future welfare may be affected, seriously and detrimentally, by technological innovations."[5] Finkelman encouraged open discussion of the matter, pointing out that "if it were not discussed openly, it would insinuate itself in some fashion into the discussion on other items."

"Needless to say," said Finkelman, "no recommendation on this score can be embodied in your report." Nevertheless he suggested that the committee devote "some, but not an undue, amount of time to seeking a formula, apart from the terms of the collective agreement, that would allay the fears of the employees."[6]

Most items in the terms of reference referred to matters of job security and conditions of work. They included job assignments, classification of job duties and the request by the unions for guarantees against layoff, termination, reduction of classification and reduction in pay. Other matters, including the demand for noncontributory pension and a general wage increase, seemed meager by comparison.

THE CODER DECISION

On the same day that Mr. Finkelman officially released his terms of reference for the conciliation board, October 18, the Public Service Staff Relations Board issued its findings regarding the coder operator. The Council of Postal Unions contended that management's introduction of the coder operator in the Ottawa Post Office in May had occurred after notice to bargain had been given and, as such, was a violation of Section 51 of the Public Service Staff Relations Act. Section 51 follows:

> Section 51. *Continuation in force of terms and conditions*
> Where notice to bargain collectively has been given, any term or condition of employment applicable to the employees in the bargaining unit in respect of which the notice was given that may be embodied in a collective agreement and that was in force on the day the notice was given, shall remain in force and shall be observed by the employer, the bargaining agent for the bargaining unit and the employees in the bargaining unit....

The section went on to indicate exceptions in the case where parties come to a voluntary agreement or where the dispute would be submitted to arbitration.

The Board found that the employer "had authority to introduce coding machines into the post office, to assign duties to employees operating the coding machines and to classify the positions occupied by such employees at the P.O. 1 level. "The [employer's] authority in this regard is 'protected' by Section 7 of the Public Service Staff Relations Act...." The Board indicated further that the government had not contravened Section 51 of the Act by introducing the coder after notice to bargain had been given.[7]

The Board went on to find the employer had violated Section 51 of the Act in not endeavoring to establish with the unions an agreed rate of pay for the classification. They pointed out that Section 32 of the expired contract, in force at the time the coder operator was introduced, required that where new classifications are created, the rates of pay shall be fixed by mutual agreement of the parties. Here the employer assigned an hourly rate at Level 1 and failed to confer with the union "in appropriate fashion in an endeavor to establish an agreed rate for the classification."[8]

THE CONCILIATION PROCESS

Since the parties had received draft copies of the terms of references in advance of their actual release everyone was ready to proceed without delay on October 18, the day of their release. On that day, after presentation of formal briefs, parties adjourned to separate suites reserved for them by the Staff Relations Board in Ottawa's Carleton Towers Hotel. The better part of all working days and several weekends for the next six weeks was spent in the hotel by all principal negotiators and the three conciliators.

During the first two days the Board held formal hearings with the two negotiating teams meeting together. After that the parties spent most of their time in separate caucuses, meeting with their respective nominees to the Board — the unions with Mr. Walsh, the management with Mr. Stewart. Chairman Owen Shime divided his time between the parties and meeting with his two colleagues. Shime, Stewart and Walsh were no strangers. Both Stewart and Walsh had appeared many times before Shime in his role as Vice Chairman of the Ontario Labour Relations Board.

Mr. Shime made a series of probes, trying to come to grips with some means by which the Board could help solve the overriding problem. As it turned out, the grievance procedure was his principal device. This had not been a particularly strong issue in earlier submissions, but Section 9.03 of the contract excluded "complaints arising from the classification process" from definition of a grievance. The following section, 9.04, which entitled an aggrieved employee to bring a grievance, contained an identical exclusion. These then became the devices through which a settlement was finally forged but not before a considerable amount of intervening work and anguish.

Owen Shime had recently been involved in an Ontario dispute concerning job classification matters at the Toronto Transport Commission. His work on that case indicated he was sympathetic to a greater role being played by unions in determining classifications. Coupling this with Mr. Finkelman's obvious desire for the parties to find some way to deal with the issues, management negotiators endeavored to work out a solution, anticipating that if they failed to do so Mr. Shime would direct one.

Management was sensitive to union criticisms in the past regarding changes in methods and technology which had been made without any prior consultation. There had been frequent meetings with the unions regarding contemplated changes, but it was apparent in nearly all such meetings that they were information sessions — that management had already made up their minds. The most recent case involving the Ottawa coder had been an example.

Some members of management were themselves cynical regarding consultation with the unions, indicating that the unions had been almost totally negative on such matters — offering little or no help in implementation. Others, recognizing that the philosophy behind consultation could not be legislated through contract language, pointed out that the idea of union-management consultation went to the very heart of industrial relations. By endeavoring to formulate a provision on the subject they might help lead parties toward a basis for better consultation and understanding. For example, if the issue of the Ottawa sorter had been approached in an ideal consultative setting the union might have felt comfortable in suggesting a more appropriate way to construct the job to affect that classification of work. As it was, they listened, became frustrated and walked out.

Through constant probing and some amount of mediating, Mr. Shime secured basic acceptance of several principles regarding technological change and job security:

☐ that there should be full, frank, complete good-faith discussions between the concerned parties,

☐ that protest strikes, walkouts and other forms of pressure tactics in opposition to change should cease,

☐ that existing machinery for discussion of such matters, covered in articles 8 and 31 of the contract, had not been effective,

☐ that consultation, if it occurs, should be something more than mere tokenism and something more than a forum for union representatives to comment on management's unilateral decisions.

In addition Shime obtained agreement from management that two letters of intent would be offered as addenda to the contract. First, there would be a reaffirmation of the letter formulated on September 1, 1970, by then-Postmaster General Eric Kierans guaranteeing that "the planned modernization program for the Post Office would not result in layoffs of present full-time employees during the life of the agreement, provided employees will accept relocation, reassignment and retraining."

The second letter would guarantee that a full-time employee would continue to be paid according to wages specified in the contract for the life of the contract. This guarantee would not apply to those appointed to lower classifications because of incapacity or incompetence, to those voluntarily accepting a lower classification of work, to those who cease to be employed and rehired, and to those who are promoted. In the case of promotions the employee would be guaranteed continuance of his existing pay or assignment of pay for the new job, whichever was higher.

Based on apparent acceptance of the stated principles and knowledge of the two letters of intent, Mr. Shime made proposals which were eventually embodied in the report of the conciliation board as Article 32.

ARTICLE 32[9]

Article 32 provided for establishment of a union-management manpower committee composed of four representatives of the Council, four representatives of the employer and an independent adviser. The committee would have authority to discuss all matters of mutual interest, including:

1. The effect of change on working conditions and the work force,
2. job descriptions and job contents arising from the introduction of change,
3. wages to be paid to new jobs and changed jobs,
4. the relationship between change and hours of work,
5. the coder.

If during the term of the contract the employer proposed to change job content or introduce new jobs, the article required referring such matters to the committee for consultation. The committee then had 75 days after the date of referral to report back to the parties.

The employer would be permitted under the article to implement the proposed changes 90 days after the matters had been referred to the union-management manpower committee provided that the employer shall first have given 15 days' notice to the Council.

If the committee could not agree on wages for the changed or new job the employer could assign a temporary rate, subject to negotiations, and possible retroactive adjustment at the next contract termination.

Nothing in the article would prevent matters referred to the committee from being negotiated at the next contract termination, and nothing could prevent continued discussion on matters resulting from changes even after the employer implemented changes. As part of the article the employer would agree that on introduction or implementation of any changes in job content or new jobs during the life of the agreement, no seniority rights or seniority privileges of persons employed at the date the contract was signed would be adversely affected.

Government negotiators rejected the draft, stating that the article was in part unworkable and that it might prevent successful resolution of the negotiations. They pointed to the earlier discussions regarding the coder, saying that they had sought resolution through consultation, but that dialogue was nonexistent. They saw no indication that the Council was willing to take responsibility for dealing with changes and expressed concern that the recommendations might have contravened sections 56(2) and 86(2) of the Public Service Staff Relations Act.

More specifically, employer representatives pointed out that they had tried in negotiations without success to achieve more flexibility in deployment of the work force. They had tried, for example, to alleviate instances where unassigned letter carriers or supervisory letter carriers sat idly while great mounds of mail remained unsorted. They expressed the belief that the supervisors should help the sorters in such cases. The Council had responded both emotionally and irrationally, refusing even to consider minor changes on an experimental basis. The employer had tried to get changes in seniority rules and jurisdictional taboos – all without success, so they saw little hope that Section 32 would transform overnight what had been a basic problem through the years. As a result of these misgivings Bruce Stewart, management's nominee to the Board, registered a dissent. On the other hand, much to everyone's surprise, the union accepted the article – possibly indicating the start of a metamorphosis.

In early November, after the parties had worked almost exclusively with their Board nominees in separate caucuses for nearly six weeks, Mr. Shime suggested that they should get back together. He proposed doing this through formulation of subcommittees to deal with specific issues. Thus the main teams broke up – three or four to a side – and worked on a number of issues. Agreement was reached in this way on matters of shift premium, overtime work on a day of rest and uniform allowances. No definitive agreement was reached on matters of classification, job security and technological change, but the subjects had received considerable airing, opening the way to a conciliation board report.

THE CONCILIATION REPORT

After requesting and receiving a one-week extension on its deliberations on November 4, the conciliation board heard final positions of the parties on November 27, and delivered its report on December 14. Meanwhile the federal elections were held on October 30. These saw the incumbent Liberal government lose its majority status in Parliament. However the Liberals retained power by virtue of a two-vote majority over the Conservatives. Power for the immediate future would depend on the Liberals' success in forming and maintaining a coalition with various minority factions, most notably the New Democratic Party.

The conciliation board report contained no surprises. It was essentially a unanimous report. The employer's nominee, Mr. Stewart, registered a mild dissent, prompted most particularly by the issue of Article 32. Stewart expressed the belief that there should have been more specific machinery to deal with classification disputes. In addition he considered the failure of the board to make meaningful recommendations on the issue of interjurisdictional problems of the union both "inexplicable and unwarranted." On wages, Stewart expressed the view that a more moderate wage recommendation should have been made. He also had some views on vacations, sick leave and uniforms — but was careful in his conclusion to emphasize that his dissent did "not necessarily mean a call to arms":

> ...it will be up to the employer to determine whether my concerns are serious enough to warrant rejection of the Report and all that such rejection may imply.

The board's report, prepared by Mr. Shime, contained a lengthy preamble dealing with the legislative framework for negotiations, the nature of the parties and the background for the board's recommendations. He dealt with the issue of job security and technological change, expressing the belief that both sides had gone a long way toward understanding on the matters. The employer, according to Shime, had "made a statesmanlike and significant offer to the union," agreeing to provide them with certain guarantees concerning both layoff and wage security for existing employees. Shime pointed out that the offer was "bereft of tactical negotiating advantage and it was a reasonable and humane offer which exceeded the guarantees that are available in private industry."[10]

On the other hand Mr. Shime pointed out that "the negotiating committee of the Council of Postal Unions responded with an equally statesmanlike position because for the first time it agreed as a matter of principle to the introduction of technological change into the post office."

"It only remains," said Shime, "for the union to effectively translate its position to the membership."[11]

Then Mr. Shime dealt with institutional problems facing the parties. He expressed concern that the union bargaining agent was a composite of two separate unions, pointing out that certain matters affect one union and not the other. This inevitably leads to competition for gains, requiring the leaders of one union to assure their membership that they have been able to achieve as much as leaders of the other union. Similarly, issues that may be considered of strike dimensions by one union might not be considered so serious by the other. As a result the unions are forced to negotiate between themselves before they negotiate with the employer. All these are impediments to effective negotiations.

Mr. Shime did not say so in specific words, but he strongly implied that the unions should merge — to remove barriers to effective negotiations, to consolidate on services, thus saving expenses, and to break down structures which prohibit mobility of employees and foster underutilization of manpower by virtue of the inability of members to cross from one union's jurisdiction to another.[12]

Mr. Shime had some words about the employer's institutional problems as well, pointing out that the employer is a composite of the Treasury Board and the Post Office. Some impediments to effective negotiations inevitably occur when the Treasury Board, in considering the particular problems of the Post Office and treatment of the employees in postal operations, relate these considerations to its treatment of other problems and other employees in the public service. Shime said that in these negotiations "one felt that each time the employer was required to reach a decision that it was looking over its shoulder at the remaining government employees."[13] He implied, forcefully, that the government should have a new look at its bargaining setup.

The wage scale put forth by the board was the one eventually adopted. In addition to Article 32 the board put forth two substantive recommendations for contract changes that would deal with job displacement, technological change and classifications. In one, Article 9.03 — the definition of a grievance — was amended to delete a phrase which had previously excluded complaints arising from the classification process from consideration. Now, presumably, classification issues could be raised in a grievance. The second recommendation for contract change was incorporated as Article 43 of the new contract — titled "Unlawful Strikes":

43.01. During the term of this collective agreement the Council of Postal Unions or its constituent unions will take reasonable steps to prevent and stop any strikes (as that term is defined in the Public Service Staff Relations Act) by the employees, and the Employer agrees not to lock out any employees.

This section, in conjunction with the letters of intent regarding maintenance of wages and no layoff (a reconfirmative of the 1970 letter by the Postmaster General) was designed to protect stability in the face of inevitable changes.

Mr. Shime pointed to these matters in commenting on the wage proposal — stating that "the wage security provisions in the event of technological change were tantamount to providing the employees with a guaranteed annual wage."

RANK AND FILE UNREST

Seven days after delivery of the conciliation report a strike would be legal. This would have been December 21, four days before Christmas. As it was, some of the postal workers became nervous long before the report was delivered, giving rise to a series of wildcats.

On Thursday, November 9, about 250 men employed at the main Toronto post office staged a four-hour walkout to protest what they considered slow contract talks and poor working conditions. These men were in the traffic division where mail was shipped and received. While expressing anger at the length of negotiations, some also complained about working conditions and the overloaded bags they had to handle. They pulled fire alarms to trigger the walkout and left a huge backlog of work for the next shift. For this they received letters warning of possible disciplinary action if they repeated the action, giving rise to a a one-hour walkout the following Tuesday, November 14, to "study" the letters.

While there was some feeling among workers that the wildcats would spread, most observers, including members of the union bargaining team, expressed the feeling that a strike was unlikely. There had been a series of rotating strikes during the 1969/70 negotiations with questionable impact, but that experience provided a taste of strike action which helped temper a desire for a fresh taste. More important, perhaps, was the timing. No one wanted to strike at Christmas time; that's when the weather is bad, feelings are good, and bills mount up. Furthermore a strike then would probably have done nothing to enhance the unions' bargaining position. If it had been mid October the politicians would have become involved because of the election; if it were late November the corporations would have been upset, because they depend heavily on the mails then to get bills to their customers. As it was, the timing for a strike was inopportune, so strike action was averted.

THE UNION SPLIT

On receipt of the conciliation board report negotiators for the Council of Postal Unions split on whether to recommend acceptance for their membership. Six favored nonacceptance; four favored acceptance. While reasons for the split were never made official those who opposed acceptance apparently felt that wages were too low and were unhappy in the belief that problems regarding classification had not been solved. On the other hand the four who advocated acceptance expressed the belief that significant gains had been made. They felt that the wage settlement was the best they could hope for, and while the classification issue had not been settled to their complete satisfaction they expressed the feeling that changes in Sections 9.03 and 9.04 had been a step forward. Now, for the first time, they could obtain adjudication of issues involving the classification issue within the framework of the grievance procedure.

The split was aggravated somewhat further when Montreal postal clerks denounced the union negotiators, stating they had lost confidence in the postal council, and they wanted to break away and form a separate union in Quebec.

Following announcement of a split in the negotiating committee, members of the unions were asked to vote on whether or not to accept the majority position of the negotiators. The majority recommendation was sent to members along with a minority report asking for acceptance of the conciliation board's report. Members were scheduled to vote on January 7 and 8, and they did so amid considerable confusion. A "yes" vote meant acceptance of the majority recommendation that the conciliation board's report be rejected. A "no" vote meant acceptance of the report.

Results were announced on January 10, and by a small margin — 10,128 to 9,047 — members had voted to reject the majority recommendation. To some this meant acceptance of the conciliation report; to others it meant a return to the bargaining table. The president of the Montreal local of postal clerks, Marcel Perreault, said the vote indicated no confidence in the negotiators, and said they should resign.

One thing seemed clear to negotiators: they had no mandate to call a strike. As to the resumption of negotiations, they decided to call all union executives to Ottawa for a meeting to ask for "direction." As a result of this meeting, negotiations were resumed, but meanwhile a series of unauthorized walkouts erupted. The most serious of these occurred in Toronto where mail movement dwindled to a trickle. The Toronto strike had started on Wednesday, January 17, when sorters, other inside workers and some carriers set up picket lines at the main downtown postal terminal, and these were honored by other union members. Mail service at the Toronto International Airport was also knocked out.

Since nearly 50 per cent of the national mail passed through Toronto and about 28 per cent of all Canadian mail originated in that city, the walkout had severe crippling effects, causing layoffs in other stations for lack of mail. These, in turn, led to picket lines in protest over the layoffs in Oshawa, Whitby, Belleville and Scarborough. In Winnipeg, about 250 sorters walked off the job at the city's main post office, crippling service there.

All the walkouts were staged in spite of instructions from local union leaders to stay on the job, and they were a source of embarrassment to union bargainers who faced a severe dilemma on how to proceed. It was not a spot for the employer to pour fuel on the fire by imposing discipline, so "he" wisely held back. Finally, a back-to-work movement succeeded when leaders of the Toronto locals pushed for a rule that would in the future prevent negotiations from dragging on for more than 90 days past the expiration of a contract. In all, some mail had been held up by the Toronto stoppages for as long as 10 days to two weeks.

Negotiations resumed on January 11. On January 15 management advised the Council that it would accept the majority report of the conciliation report as a basis for settlement. The same day the Council raised a new issue involving Section 9.04 of the contract. Section 9.04 provided that an employee who felt he had been treated unjustly could present a grievance. However, it contained an exclusion like Section 9.03, as follows: "other than a complaint arising from the classification process." The conciliation board had recommended elimination of the exclusion in Section 9.03, the definition of a grievance, but for reasons unclear to any of the negotiators, they had not dealt with Section 9.04. So the exclusion remained in that section, and negotiators were puzzled.

As a result of the problem regarding Section 9.04, counsel for the unions requested the Chairman of the Public Service Staff Relations Board, Jacob Finkelman, to clarify the matter. The employer contended the section had been considered by the board and was to be left unchanged. Mr. Finkelman, in turn, referred the question to the conciliation board.

On January 22 the board replied, expressing the opinion that Section 9.04 should be amended by the parties, deleting the same words as had been deleted in Section 9.03. This freed the grievance procedure for matters involving classification and seemed to represent the final key to settlement.

In early February preparations were made to conduct a second membership vote. The vote was held February 14, and with more than 24,000 of the 28,000 members voting, 73 per cent of those voting endorsed the new agreement. Thus, more than one year after negotiations had begun, a new postal agreement was assured. While it was a long time in coming it represented a triumph for collective bargaining in the public service. Both sides had come to grips with some knotty, uncomfortable problems, made more so by legislative encumbrances, by internal dissention and from occupying positions in the public spotlight. The problems were not solved to everyone's satisfaction. They rarely are in negotiations. But they had been solved through genuine give-and-take and without resort to a strike.

APPENDIX A

ARTICLE 32

MANPOWER COMMITTEE

32.01

(a) Subject to section 56(2) of the Public Service Staff Relations Act and pursuant to the provisions of Article 8 of the Collective Agreement, the parties recognize that the introduction of change and technolog ical change is a matter of mutual interest. Accordingly the Employer and the Council of Postal Unions agree to establish within thirty (30) days of the signing of this Agreement a manpower committee composed of four (4) representatives of the Council and four (4) representatives of the Employer and each party will notify the other in writing, within the aforementioned period of the names of their representatives. The Council of Postal Unions and the Employer shall retain an independent adviser to assist in the work of the committee and in its deliberations. In the event that the Employer and the Council of Postal Unions cannot agree within a reasonable period of time on the person and conditions of employment of the person to be retained as adviser, such person shall be appointed by the Chairman of the Public Service Staff Relations Board or in the alternative, the Vice-Chairman of the Public Service Staff Relations Board at a rate and for a term to be fixed by him.

(b) In the event that the position of adviser becomes vacant during the term of the Collective Agreement and the parties are unable to agree on a replacement within a reasonable period of time, the Chairman of the Public Service Staff Relations Board and in the alternative the Vice-Chairman shall continue to have the authority to appoint an adviser as a replacement at a rate and for a term to be fixed by him.

(c) The Employer and the Council shall each pay half (1/2) of the wages, expenses and/or fees of such an adviser.

(d) The manpower committee shall have the authority to discuss all matters of mutual interest and, notwithstanding the generality of the foregoing, matters of mutual interest shall include

    (i) the effect of change and technological change on working conditions and on the work force;

    (ii) job descriptions and job contents arising from the introduction of change and technological change;

    (iii) wages to be paid to changed jobs and new jobs in accordance with the wage levels in Appendix "A";

    (iv) the relationship between change and the hours of work;

    (v) the utilization of casual employees and unmanned walks;

    (vi) the deployment of the work force;

    (vii) the coder.

  32.02

(a) If during the term of the Collective Agreement the Employer proposes to change job contents or introduce new jobs, it shall refer such matters to the manpower committee for consultation in accordance with the provisions of this Article. The committee shall report to the parties within seventy-five (75) days after the date that the matter is referred to the manpower committee.

(b) Nothing herein contained shall prevent the Employer from implementing the proposed changes in job contents or new jobs ninety (90) days after the matters are referred to the manpower committee provided that the Employer shall first have given fifteen (15) days' notice to the Council; nor does the implementation of such a change after the ninety (90) day period preclude the committee from consulting further on matters resulting from the changed jobs or new jobs.

(c) In the event that the manpower committee is unable to agree on the wages for the changed job or new job, the Employer shall implement a wage for the changed job or new job which shall be referred to as the holding rate. Such rate shall be considered a temporary rate and if during the life of the Collective Agreement the parties are unable to agree on a permanent rate, the Employer and the Council of Postal Unions shall negotiate the rate of pay at the next open period. The new negotiated rate, if higher, shall be retroactive to the date that the holding rate was applied by the Employer.

(d) The implementation of a changed job or a new job shall not preclude the manpower committee from consulting further on matters resulting from the changes.

(e) Nothing herein contained shall prevent matters that have been referred to the manpower committee from being negotiated during the next open period.

32.03. The Employer agrees that upon the introduction of or the implementation of any changes in job contents or new jobs during the life of the Agreement, that no seniority rights nor seniority privileges of persons employed at the date of the signing of this Agreement shall be adversely affected.

32.04

(a) The manpower committee may at any time appoint a sub-committee to investigate and to report to it with respect to any matter within its jurisdication.

(b) In the event that the adviser deems it necessary he shall retain a technical adviser to assist the sub-committee in its investigations. Such a technical adviser shall be appointed by the adviser at a rate and for a term to be fixed by the adviser after consultation with the parties.

(c) The Employer and the Council shall each pay half (1/2) of the wages, expenses and/or fees of such a technical adviser.

NOTES TO CHAPTER 9

1. Time limits were established under Sections 80 and 86 of the Public Service Staff Relations Act. Under Section 80 (2) the PSSRB Chairman had seven days following his decision to establish a conciliation board to notify the parties to appoint a conciliator.

   Under Section 80 (3) each of the two parties had seven additional days following receipt of notice from the Chairman to nominate a member. Then, under Section 80(5), the two members had an additional five days to agree upon a chairman. In the event that either of these limits were not met, the PSSRB Chairman was required to appoint a chairman. Under Section 86 the Board had 14 days following receipt of its terms of reference from the PSSRB Chairman to deliver its report, or such added time "as may be agreed upon by the parties or determined by the Chairman..." Normally one 14-day extension would be granted. While these limits added up to 47 days some additional time was usually required for the PSSRB Chairman to notify parties of their obligations under Section 80 and to prepare terms of reference for delivery to the board. Consequently 47 days was a minimum estimate. Fifty-nine or 60 days would be more likely.

2. Public Service Staff Relations, Act, sect. 101(2)(b)(i)

3. Ibid., sect. 53.

4. "Terms of Reference," J. Finkelman, October 18, 1972, file 190-2-19 and 20. Underlining is included in original document.

   Sect. 56(2) of the Public Service Staff Relations Act was worded as follows:

No collective agreement shall provide, directly or indirectly, for the alteration or elimination of any existing term or condition of employment or the establishment of any new term or condition of employment, (a) the alteration or elimination of which, as the case may be, would require or have the effect of requiring the enactment or amendment of any legislation by Parliament, except for the purpose of appropriating moneys for its implementation...

5. Ibid., p. 27.

6. Ibid., p. 28.

7. Public Service Staff Relations Act, re: Application for Order Requiring Compliance with sect. 51 of the Act, file no.: 148-2-7, Oct. 8, 1972, p. 3.

8. Ibid., p. 5.

9. Reproduced in full as Appendix A (p. 311).

10. Report of the Conciliation Board, file no. 190-2, 19 and 20, "In the Matter of a Dispute Affecting the Council of Postal Unions and the Treasury Board of Canada," p. 12.

11. Ibid., p. 13.

12. Ibid., p. 19.

13. Ibid., p. 21.

10. BUILDING AN INDUSTRIAL RELATIONS SYSTEM

Industrial relations systems reflect the personalities of those who work within them. Many union-management relationships are the products of careful, step-by-step planning and are extensions of the beliefs and attitudes of the principal administrators. Many others are characterized by uncertainty and lack of direction. There may be a hodgepodge of rules and regulations, a plethora of grievances, a union which seems to be constantly fighting against management — a state of mutual distrust. The latter type of relationship is often the product of top administrators who believe that industrial relations matters are unimportant and not particularly worthy of top management's attention.

Now, with North American businesses experiencing severe competitive pressures from abroad and with increasing discontent among members of the work force regarding the quality of life, many union leaders and company managers are being forced to re-evaluate their industrial relations system. Unions are coming to realize that it takes more than a high wage and an occasional kick in the pants to build job satisfaction and acceptable productivity. Both unions and management are coming to realize that improved productivity is essential for the survival of North American enterprises — that the achievement of improvements is a joint responsibility. Some have come to realize these things too late. The ocean-going maritime industry, for example, virtually priced itself out of the world market by sloppy labor relations practices. The railroads permitted, and even encouraged, make-work practices long after technological changes rendered jobs and skills obsolete. As of early 1974, six of the major railroad systems serving the northeastern United States were bankrupt, and make-work practices shared a substantial part of the responsibility.

With increased concern about the need to work together to build industrial relations systems there is increased attention to systems of participation. While participative management dates back more than a century it characterizes precious few employer-employee relationships. And while more and more managers are coming to realize that employee concern for achievement of corporate goals is desirable, perhaps essential, for the well-being of the enterprise, there have been only a few moves to seek out and incorporate employee input into the decision-making process where important matters are under discussion.

Instances of participative management are well documented.[1] However, instances of companies and unions trying to move toward participation are not well documented. Herein lies a major problem, because the difficulties are severe in establishing a system formed on new beliefs and values. Many managers and union leaders are forced to rethink the basic premises on which they have been operating, and the process is sometimes painful — if not impossible.

The cases in this chapter describe efforts of a large Canadian manufacturer of paper products to institute a participative form of management in one of its small carton-manufacturing plants. Darthom (a disguised name), like many North American paper producers, had experienced nearly a decade of hard times, characterized by increasing costs and severe competition — all brought about by a great expansion in production capacity to meet consumer needs that had not, as of this writing, materialized.

Many of Darthom's manufacturing facilities had piecework incentive systems. Over the years these had become shopworn and outdated. Changes in technology and changes in methods had not always been considered in assigning piecework rates to jobs, so that some jobs provided excellent earning opportunities, while others, calling on essentially the same skills, were assigned more accurate, but tight, rates providing for more controlled earnings opportunities. Inequities were obvious, and many grievances arose over the matter of incentives. Cost accountants and methods engineers alike agreed that the incentive plans were among the principal causes of excess costs and labor discontent. Company officials and their various union leaders were in essential agreement that the systems ought to be overhauled or scrapped. But union leaders insisted that in revamping the method of payment none of their members should suffer loss of earnings. Consequently, management was caught in a dilemma. They urgently needed to cut costs and they saw elimination or revision of the incentive plans as essential toward this end. On the other hand, they were reasonably convinced that cost-cutting efforts in this situation would give rise to severe worker discontent, possibly even strikes, in an effort to maintain earning potential.

Consequently, Darthom decided to move gingerly. Their newest plant, located in Winnipeg, Manitoba, did not have an incentive system. Industrial engineers had been working in the plant to design such a system but had not yet completed the job. Consequently management felt that here was an opportunity to try out a new system of management. They had read and heard about other companies that had cut costs and enhanced profits through participative schemes in which workers and managers worked together to improve performance. In most such instances there were bonus schemes. Workers and managers alike shared part of the savings realized through improved methods. Increased earnings were based on increased productivity of the entire operation, and parties worked together toward common goals. This was a far cry from the usual union-management adversary system which had characterized industrial relations at Darthom for many years, but management believed it was worth a try. If the plan worked at Winnipeg it might have transfer value to other Darthom operations. It could offer a way to escape the existing dilemma.

*   *   *

The Darthom cases (A and B) describe efforts of the company and union to institute participative management at the Winnipeg plant. They are useful in laying out the philosophical ground work for a participative system, for describing the essential elements of such a system and for highlighting the challenges and risks in instituting participative management. The third part of the chapter is titled "Participative Management Mania." It is a sequel to the Darthom cases, explaining in part what happened after the events described in the cases. In addition, it lays down some general principles that should have practical value to all persons who are concerned with the design of industrial relations systems.

DARTHOM INDUSTRIES LTD. (A)

THE MERGER

Nearly seven years ago Dartmouth Paper Co. Ltd. of Canada merged with R.J. Thompson Products Company to form Darthom Industries Ltd., one of Canada's largest companies in the pulp and paper industry. Within four years after the merger Darthom had diversified into other fields and was rapidly becoming one of Canada's most important companies. The company stretched from New Brunswick to British Columbia, with its greatest concentration in the prairie and western provinces of Canada. It also extended into the northwestern United States. In January of last year over 16,000 people were employed by Darthom Industries Ltd. Corporate headquarters were in Vancouver, B.C.

Under terms of the merger two shares of Dartmouth preferred stock were exchanged for one and a half of Thompson Products preferred shares. Common shares were exchanged at the rate of four Dartmouth to one Thompson. Stockholders voted overwhelmingly in favor of the exchange, and six months after the merger all shares were exchanged for new ones carrying the new name: Darthom.

PRESIDENT'S VIEWS ON THE MERGER

Both Dartmouth and Thompson Products Co. had recognized the need for diversification to lessen the impact of economic cycles on their businesses. These cycles were most severe in the paper products and container plants of Dartmouth, and in pulp producing plants operated by Thompson. Commenting on these two phases of the business Mr. Frederick A. Genrich, president of Darthom, said:

> In an industry like the pulp, paper and container industry, size allows for greater utilization of the forests' natural resources and lowers the company's vulnerability to economic cycles.

About 18 months after the merger Darthom called on Scudder, Fenner and Hamilton, well known management consultants, to advise on the appropriate organization, the design of corporate strategy and the setting of implementing policies. Eight months later Scudder, Fenner and Hamilton completed their work and submitted recommendations — most of which were accepted for prompt implementation. Commenting on the consultants' report, Mr. Genrich said:

> We are now in the shakedown period. All the decisions have been made, and we simply have to make them work.

ORGANIZATION

The reorganized company was directed by a management team reporting to the president — each member with responsibility for a segment of the business. The executive team is shown in Exhibit 1 (p.324).

Mr. Genrich believed in centralized control and, while he encouraged discussions among his executives, he reserved the prerogative to make final decisions.

> The team members do not have a vote on every issue. I have never believed in committee management of anything.

COMPANY PERFORMANCE

In the first year following the merger, Darthom's performance was disappointing. Table I-10 compares the performance of the first year after the merger with the combined performances of the prior year.

Four years after the merger, sales had risen to $252 million. The principal component was 821,668 tons of newsprint. Earnings were $20.2 million, and Darthom's total production of paper products was divided as follows:

TABLE I-10

	Net Sales	Net Earnings	Newsprint Production	Newsprint % of Total	Dividends
	(Millions)	(Millions)	(Tons)	Cdn. Market	per share
Year of merger	$234.5	$20.8	861,473	10.2	$2.00
1st year after merger	$242.2	$17.3	800,618	9.9	$1.00

  66.3% newsprint
  22.1% containerboard
   6.3% kraft paper
   5.3% boxboard

Mr. Genrich termed the performance of the past five years in the paper products business "disappointing." He referred to the following factors by way of explanation:

(1) World overcapacity in newsprint, containerboard and market pulp manufacturing facilities,

(2) Higher wages and rising material costs which had not yet been fully offset by productivity improvements or higher selling prices,

(3) High interest charges arising from heavy capital expenditures and other expansion projects which were not yet contributing their potential to earnings.

"Our successes in the non-paper fields has kept us reasonably healthy," said Genrich, "proving once again the value of diversification."

PULP AND PAPER INDUSTRY SITUATION

In the last decade Canadian pulp and paper companies had been caught in an overcapacity squeeze. Massive increases in capacity came on-stream at a time when demand growth temporarily halted. For the next two or three years Canadian mills would most likely be operating at approximately 83 per cent of capacity. A report by George Linton in the Toronto *Globe and Mail* attributed industry problems to three factors:

(1) Rising competition in the United States market,

(2) over-expansion in Canada,

(3) extraordinarily high start-up costs.

No major improvements were foreseen for at least five years, and industry experts were anticipating major shutdowns in most Canadian pulp and paper operations during the next year or two.

Mr. Genrich predicted there would be no significant improvement for Darthom Industries for five years, but he expected dramatic improvement from then on. Genrich expressed the belief tht Darthom's wealth of resources, its sound product planning, and its extensive research programs would ensure excellent long term performance.

WINNIPEG CORRUGATED CONTAINER PLANT

Darthom had ten Canadian plants that manufactured corrugated containers (see Exhibit 2, p.325, for locations). The newest of these plants was located near the Inkster Industrial Park in the northwest portion of metropolitan Winnipeg. It was built at a cost of $3 1/2 million and started production two years ago. The plant was attractive, well designed and had equipment and machinery to match any competitor.

COMPETITION

The southern Manitoba region was serviced by three large and firmly established competitors: Consolidated Bathurst in St. Boniface, Domtar in St. James, and McMillan Company in Brandon. St. Boniface and St. James were considered part of greater Winnipeg — St. Boniface directly across the river to the east, St. James in the western outskirts of the city. Brandon was located 135 miles to the west. About three years ago the officers of Darthom Industries decided that the fast-growing southern Manitoba region could support one more producer of corrugated containers. None of their existing plants were close enough to do an effective job in competing with firms located in the market area.

CUSTOMERS

Some of the principal customers for Darthom's Winnipeg plant were Canada Packers, Labatt's Brewers and Eaton's. Any company manufacturing or selling products that could be shipped in a carton was a potential customer.

MARKET SHARE

By the end of its first full year of operation, Darthom at Winnipeg had reached an annual sales volume of $2.5 million, approximately 11 per cent of the southern Manitoba region. In the past three years there had been an overall market growth of four to five per cent per year. Last year the market share breakdown for sales was:

Consolidated Bathurst	34%
McMillan	33%
Domtar	18%

Darthom	11%
Others	4%
	100%

Last June the Darthom plant's share of the southern Manitoba market amounted to approximately 16 million square feet of production per month.

PLANT ORGANIZATION

The management organization for the Winnipeg plant is shown in Exhibit 3, (p. 326). Exhibit 4, following, shows the position of the Winnipeg manager in the total company's organization.

Mr. Gerald Weatherby, the Winnipeg plant manager, commented about the scope of his position within the total organization:

> The divisional plants run their own operations with very little interference from head office in Vancouver. Only large capital expenditures, for example greater than $5,000, require approval from the head office. Decisions are made at the local level, and we stand or fall on them. Budgets are established by the plant manager and the sales manager. Every nickel has to be accounted for in the budget. Of course, should something be vital, we can deviate from our forecast provided we obtain head office approval. My performance is measured on results versus budgets.

PRODUCTION PROCESS

The production process at Winnipeg is described as follows: Large rolls of liner board and corrugating medium were received at the corrugated container plant from the company's pulp and paper mills. The rolls were fed into a box-plant corrugator which fluted the medium or centre portion of the board and glued it to two sheets of paper called "kraftliner," to form corrugated board. A schematic representation of the box plant corrugator follows:

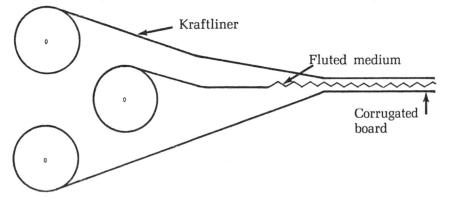

The corrugated board was then transferred to a machine called a "printer slotter." Here it was cut and scored for eventual forming into boxes. In addition it was usually printed with customer and product identifications.

As a final stage in the manufacturing process some of the slotted, printed board was sent to the finishing department for closure. This process was accomplished by taping, gluing or stitching. The final product was then stacked, tied or strapped, and shipped to the customer.

The plant layout is shown in Exhibit 5. The corrugator performed the key operation in the plant. All products went through it, then branched off to other operations depending on the customers' needs.

Plant capacity was rated at 30 million square feet of production per month on a two-shift basis. However, since start-up, the plant had operated almost solely on one shift. Performance figures for the 27 months since start-up are shown in Exhibit 6.

Mr. Weatherby said that the plant had operated well both during and after start-up:

> Almost none of the hourly work force had any industrial experience prior to working here. Thus we had to train them all for the low-to-medium-skilled jobs available. Nevertheless performance has been so good that we are far ahead of our projected production schedule.

Six hourly and 20 salaried (sales, management and clerical) people made up the initial work force. Within two years, the force had grown to 89 hourly and 36 salaried personnel. Approximately one-third of the hourly employees were women. Turnover rates were high (see Exhibit 7). This could be partially explained by the high availability of alternative well-paying jobs in the Winnipeg metropolitan area.

UNIONIZATION

About five months after the Winnipeg plant began operations, the International Woodworkers of America (IWA) organized the plant's production employees, forming Local 3-400. The company did not resist the organization, because most of their work in other locations were represented by some union, and all Darthom production workers in the Prairie Provinces were represented by IWA. Unionization in this industry in this area of the country was viewed as inevitable.

The newly formed local negotiated their first contract in September, about six months after operations began. Its provisions were retroactive to June 20 and would terminate two years later on June 19. The hourly wage scale ranged from $2.33 to $3.50. While incentive plans character- ized all other Darthom corrugated container plants, no incentive scheme was incorporated at the Winnipeg plant. Both management and union agreed that an incentive scheme based on time standards would be impractical in view of the newness of the plant and the inexperience of the employees. Methods of production were likely to change often while men and machines became acclimatized.

UNION-MANAGEMENT RELATIONS

Union-management relations were reasonably cordial in the early days. During those days when adjustments were being made workers were not held to rigid performance standards, and disciplinary regula- tions were not tightly enforced. There were few grievances and no arbitration cases. While a labor-management committee had been formed to air differences and suggest improvements, union leaders expressed the belief that little, if any, constructive changes resulted from these meetings.

Toward the end of the first contract term relations became more strained. Female employees complained that they were not receiving equal pay for equal work. They compared their rates of pay with pay rates of men working in competitor plants on identical jobs. Men on the Titan strippers and semi-automatic stitchers were receiving 20 to 30 cents more in basic hourly pay.

The female employees also complained of having to pay for hospital- ization and insurance benefits when most were already covered on policies held by their husbands. Take-home earnings for women at McMillan and Consolidated Bathurst, including incentive premiums, averaged $.50 per hour more, and this caused still more dissatisfaction at the Winnipeg plant.

Fourteen months after the first contract was signed, Mr. Ian Britney was elected President of Local 3-400 on a platform dedicated to closing the earnings differential between Darthom and competitor plants. Man- agement representatives characterized Britney as considerably more militant than his predecessor. Aside from his "parity" objective he was concerned about lack of interest in union affairs, and sought to stimulate greater participation. Turnout for Local 3-400's monthly meetings was poor, averaging 10 to 15 per cent of the total membership. Ian Britney, when questioned about union support, said:

We don't have quantity but I think that we do have quality in those that actively support the union.

EXHIBIT 1

DARTHOM INDUSTRIES LTD. (A)

Executive Team

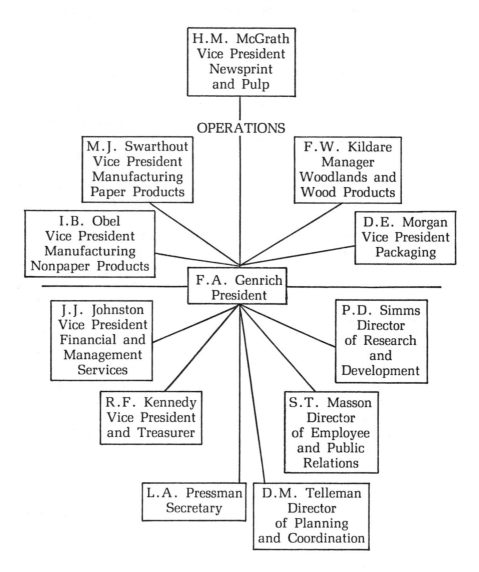

─── EXHIBIT 2 ───

DARTHOM INDUSTRIES LTD. (A)

Locations of Canadian Corrugated Container Plants

Key	Location
1	Halifax
2	Trois-Rivières
3	Elmira, Ontario
4	Winnipeg, Manitoba
5	Moose Jaw, Saskatchewan
6	Medicine Hat, Alberta
7	Calgary, Alberta
8	Kelowna, B.C.
9	Vancouver, B.C.
10	Victoria, B.C.

EXHIBIT 3

DARTHOM INDUSTRIES LTD (A)

Management Organization Chart
Winnipeg Plant, March 1966

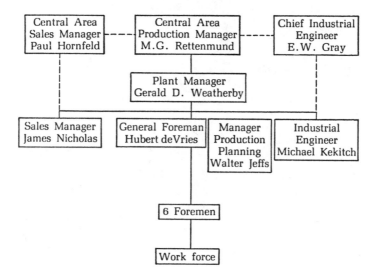

EXHIBIT 4

DARTHOM INDUSTRIES LTD. ORGANIZATION CHART

*Position of Winnipeg Plant Manager
in Total Company
Organization*

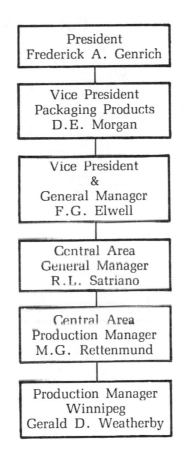

President
Frederick A. Genrich

Vice President
Packaging Products
D.E. Morgan

Vice President
&
General Manager
F.G. Elwell

Central Area
General Manager
R.L. Satriano

Central Area
Production Manager
M.G. Rettenmund

Production Manager
Winnipeg
Gerald D. Weatherby

EXHIBIT 5

Darthom Industries Ltd. (A)

PLANT LAYOUT

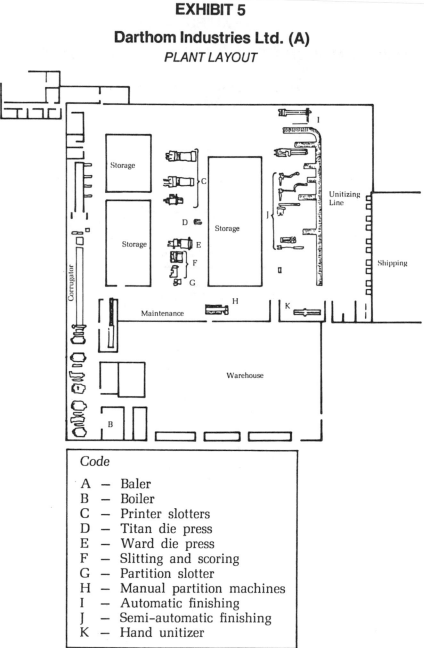

Code

A — Baler
B — Boiler
C — Printer slotters
D — Titan die press
E — Ward die press
F — Slitting and scoring
G — Partition slotter
H — Manual partition machines
I — Automatic finishing
J — Semi-automatic finishing
K — Hand unitizer

EXHIBIT 6
DARTHOM INDUSTRIES LTD. (A)
Monthly Performance Data: start up till present

	Month 1 March	Month 2 April	Month 3 May	Month 4 June	Month 5 July	Month 6 August	Month 8 October	Month 9 November	Month 10 December
a) Production MSF	6,649	7,718	7,589	10,487	12,058	12,646	11,250	11,521	8,723
Shipments MSF	6,042	6,181	4,791	9,353	9,638	13,999	10,507	11,009	7,780
Gross Product Sales	$112,734	115,691	164,496	174,471	177,319	252,259	197,649	222,013	147,026
b) Net Product Sales	111,345	113,256	156,051	169,631	170,886	241,695	189,063	216,350	142,247
c) Net Sales	107,569	108,769	152,683	166,288	165,474	235,497	183,851	207,672	138,596
Direct Costs									
Material	71,950	75,353	95,397	107,110	107,128	154,343	126,006	135,704	93,822
Labor	9,466	9,960	13,289	14,580	14,198	19,831	15,981	18,576	13,641
d) Indirect Production Labor	289	386	1,103	1,519	1,629	1,904	2,526	3,163	2,685
e) Indirect Labor	2,031	3,321	1,935	4,631	4,615	3,785	4,057	5,140	4,597
Supervision and Factory Salaries	3,623	4,192	4,425	4,525	4,495	5,587	6,172	6,517	5,670
Industrial Engineer	755	755	755	755	755	655	655	655	655
Overtime Premium	2,744	1,933	1,116	1,899	1,663	1,740	1,109	1,315	333
Direct Labor Cost/MSF	1.42	1.29	1.54	1.39	1.17	1.56	1.42	1.61	1.56
Total Labor Cost (direct, indirect, supervision)/MSF	2.35	2.36	2.37	2.33	1.99	2.36	2.38	2.68	2.81
Workforce – Hourly	55	55	57	59	61	62	63	71	68
Salaried	17	17	27	26	30	30	30	30	30
Profit before taxes	$(2,050)	(21,128)	(21,415)	(6,032)	6,457	11,010	1,721	3,733	(11,425)
f) Marginal Contribution	$26,073	23,456	45,000	44,598	44,148	61,323	41,864	53,392	31,133
g) Period Costs	$20,566	29,027	32,641	29,251	21,974	34,813	24,643	34,159	27,058

a) MSF: Thousand square feet.
b) Gross Product Sales minus allowances and discounts.
c) Net Product Sales minus freight and delivery costs.
d) Downtime, load transfer costs, rework, rubber die mounting, unreported time, shift premium, lunch breaks, raw material handling, shipping, overtime.
e) Janitors, cleanup, maintenance, training stores.
f) Net sales minus direct costs.
g) Fixed costs minus depreciation (includes factory salaries).
September (month 7) no records available

EXHIBIT 6
DARTHOM INDUSTRIES LTD. (A)
Performance Data: start up to present

	Month 11 January	Month 12 February	Month 13 April	Month 14 April	Month 15 May	Month 16 June	Month 17 July	Month 18 August	Month 19 September
a) Production MSF	11,764	11,136	11,496	12,388	12,540	13,764	14,590	19,445	16,873
Shipments MSF	10,525	10,368	10,713	12,344	12,636	12,601	13,301	18,929	16,451
Gross Product Sales	201,160	201,914	210,805	238,930	238,420	245,011	258,449	353,143	309,989
b) Net Product Sales	195,272	196,334	204,651	230,292	230,000	235,909	252,207	337,785	297,866
c) Net Sales	182,833	189,646	196,411	222,104	221,457	222,979	241,596	327,450	287,247
Direct Costs									
Material	127,231	119,971	128,147	141,602	144,140	151,545	158,771	216,318	186,148
Labor	18,376	18,736	21,016	21,856	20,635	20,983	23,929	27,428	24,775
d) Indirect Production Labor	3,045	3,103	3,529	3,641	2,884	3,144	3,775	4,164	3,726
c) Indirect Labor	3,967	3,736	4,838	5,161	5,083	5,182	4,641	4,940	4,576
Supervision and Factory Salaries	5,836	5,920	6,464	6,614	7,100	7,234	7,497	8,406	8,227
Industrial Engineer	725	725	725	725	725	725	725	725	725
Overtime Premium	1,165	1,749	942	1,402	481	1,363	3,023	3,328	3,757
Direct Labor Cost/MSF	1.56	1.68	1.82	1.76	1.64	1.52	1.64	1.41	1.46
Total Labor Cost (direct, indirect, supervision)/MSF	2.45	2.61	2.87	2.77	2.67	2.47	2.52	2.13	2.27
Workforce – Hourly	68	71	82	77	71	77	76	81	73
Salaried	29	33	33	34	33	33	34	33	34
Profit before taxes	(9,125)	8,804	1,288	10,371	9,423	160	8,743	31,167	24,804
f) Marginal Contribution	37,226	50,939	47,248	58,646	56,682	50,451	58,896	83,704	76,324
g) Period Costs	31,147	26,855	30,680	32,897	31,882	34,872	34,743	37,180	36,079

EXHIBIT 6
DARTHOM INDUSTRIES LTD. (A)
Performance Data: start up to present

	Month 20 October	Month 21 November	Month 22 December	Month 23 January	Month 24 February	Month 25 March	Month 26 April	Month 27 May	Month 28 June
a) Production MSF	14,532	14,793	12,570	14,315	12,848	12,470	15,781	16,751	17,030
Shipments MSF	14,253	14,075	12,252	13,390	11,109	11,171	15,459	15,732	16,985
Gross Product Sales	271,571	260,350	231,877	251,729	220,537	224,778	292,542	297,396	309,625
b) Net Product Sales	261,070	252,069	225,047	244,772	214,987	218,374	282,785	288,640	300,912
c) Net Sales	250,866	242,700	216,704	233,049	205,728	209,176	270,307	275,774	288,992
Direct Costs									
Material	164,018	162,905	144,831	150,304	128,871	131,232	174,391	176,385	186,702
Labor	24,874	25,846	19,800	25,064	23,606	27,022	29,522	29,842	29,165
d) Indirect Production Labor	3,741	4,216	3,219	6,498	6,158	6,654	7,112	7,060	7,589
c) Indirect Labor	4,421	4,311	3,839	3,424	3,251	3,010	3,289	3,214	3,236
Supervision and Factory Salaries	8,583	8,525	8,205	8,607	8,124	8,293	8,458	8,736	8,307
Industrial Engineer	725	725	482	866	866	866	866	866	866
Overtime Premium	2,351	2,305	1,110	472	219	841	1,174	1,436	1,641
Direct Labor Cost/MSF	1.71	1.81	1.57	1.69	1.83	2.16	1.87	1.78	1.71
Total Labor Cost (direct, indirect, supervision)/MSF	2.65	2.73	2.57	2.56	2.79	3.14	2.66	2.54	2.44
Workforce – Hourly	79	82	78	82	82	83	84	92	89
Salaried	34	33	34	35	36	36	36	36	36
Profit before taxes	10,312	1,267	(2,999)	7,802	7,303	5,099	14,700	24,651	20,845
f) Marginal Contribution	61,974	52,545	52,071	57,681	53,251	50,922	66,394	69,547	73,125
g) Period Costs	36,221	36,234	39,560	30,740	28,616	28,444	32,377	29,032	29,718

EXHIBIT 7

DARTHOM INDUSTRIES LTD. (A)

Winnipeg turnover for last 6 months

Labor Force	Month	% Turnover	(voluntary) Quits
80	Jan.	2.5	1
82	Feb.	3.7	1
83	March	2.4	2
86	April	4.7	2
84	May	3.6	3
89	June	6.7	6

Within the union there were at least three discernable factions. The female employees formed the most demanding and vocal group, but their complaints were often viewed as "petty" by the males. The non-production hourly employees — four maintenance men, two rubber die makers, one truck driver and two stationary engineers — formed a second faction. Members of this group had wage rates equivalent to those of McMillan and Consolidated Bathurst's nonproduction employees. Consequently they were more interested in fringe benefits, job security, recognition and prestige. Males in the production force constituted the third major group. They were primarily interested in obtaining earnings comparable to those at competitor plants.

DARTHOM INDUSTRIES LTD. (B)

THE SECOND CONTRACT

The first collective agreement for Darthom's Winnipeg plant was to expire on June 19, 1973. However, negotiations for a second contract began more than nine months before the expiration date as union leaders of the IWA locals at Darthom's four corrugated container plants in the Prairie Provinces expressed their desire to bargain for a master contract covering all locations. These were at Calgary and Medicine Hat in Alberta, Moose Jaw in Saskatchewan, and Winnipeg. The two agreements in Alberta were to expire seven months earlier (in November 1972), the one in Moose Jaw four months earlier (March 1973). The final master agreement would not be signed until agreements had been reached for all locals, but newly agreed upon provisions would be applied to the various locations as their contracts expired. Ostensibly all locations were involved in all talks, but there were occasions when talks progressed without any representatives from the Winnipeg plant.

One of the coordinated demands put forth by the union was that all incentive programs then in existence be abolished. The union wanted the company to buy out the plans. The company, in spite of problems with the incentive programs, balked, because other companies in the industry had suffered serious productivity losses when they had eliminated their incentive programs.

After lengthy bargaining the various incentive plans were retained and Darthom's Winnipeg plant, which till then had no incentive program, became committed to one. However, there was some feeling that a better, more realistic incentive scheme could be devised instead of the traditional MTM piecework systems used in the other plants. Consequently the form of the Winnipeg plan was not decided. Section 13D of the new contract simply called for some form of incentive scheme for Darthom's Winnipeg plant by January 1, 1974, giving the parties several months to explore various alternatives:

Section 13 D

It is agreed that incentives will be applied by January 1, 1974 or alternatively a committee will be established to study and recommend some other type of plan. If the existing plan of the Corrugated Division is implemented it will apply to the existing machine centers

2 Existing printing presses
Scoring machine
Manual stitcher
S & S auto taper
2 semi-auto tapers
Ward die press
Titan die press
Scrap slitter
Partition slotter
Corrugator
Semi-auto stitcher

In the event of the existing program being decided upon and not implemented in the above noted machine centers, a penalty clause as outlined in the master agreement Incentive Clause will apply to employees in these machine centers.

The reopener on the incentive clause in respect to the Winnipeg plant will be at the midpoint of the contract between the date of signing and termination.

The master agreement penalty clause called for a payment to all employees of 10 per cent of their hourly base rate during the first 60 days in which no incentive plan was in use. The initial 10 per cent was to be increased by a 5 per cent payment for each additional 30 days in which no incentive plan was installed to a maximum of 25 per cent.

Mr. David Wilson

Mr. David Wilson, Darthom's Industrial Relations Manager for pulp and paper products, was instrumental in the formulation of Section 13 D. Mr. Wilson had joined Darthom in April of 1973 and was only superficially involved in the negotiations. However, he took a special interest in the Winnipeg plant. Here was a relatively new factory with excellent prospects for growth. The workforce was young, and the plant was small enough that everyone could see how his contribution affected the final product. In addition, there were many opportunities for improvement. Given the proper atmosphere Mr. Wilson believed that men and women in the shop would contribute to these improvements. They might be receptive to a relationship that Mr. Wilson termed "participative management." Mr. Wilson drew his ideas from the writings of Professor Frederick Herzberg of Case Western Reserve University and the late Douglas McGregor of the Massachusetts Institute of Technology. These men had found that traditional authoritative management was often inadequate to motivate today's workers, because the lower level human needs on which the traditional approach rely were no longer important determinants of behavior. (Two books frequently cited by Mr. Wilson were: Herzberg, Frederick et. al., *The Motivation to Work,* Wiley and Company, 1967 and McGregor, Douglas, *The Human Side of Enterprise,* McGraw Hill, 1960.) According to Herzberg and McGregor today's worker is most likely to derive satisfaction from activities appealing to his higher-level needs — the needs for social interaction, for recognition and for self fulfillment. Management can appeal to higher-level needs by giving workers an opportunity to direct their activities toward the goals of the organization — to make suggestions for improvement, to help implement those suggestions and to share in the benefits. Many companies had successfully implemented participative management programs, and Mr. Wilson had read extensively about their experiences. He was particularly interested in companies using Scanlon plans, expressing the belief that a Scanlon-type plan might be appropriate for the Winnipeg plant. Contract Section 13 D could open the way to such a plan.

Mr. Wilson hoped that if successful at Winnipeg the participative management plan could be transferred to other plants. If Darthom's output per manhour could be improved by such a plan, it would give the company an advantage over its aggressive competition and, at the same time, result in a highly motivated workforce.

With these thoughts in mind Mr. Wilson tested some of his ideas on members of management. He circulated articles on participative management throughout the executive levels of the Darthom organization.

Meanwhile he sought the advice of a labor relations consultant experienced in the installation of participative management schemes. After several phone calls Mr. Wilson was referred to Dr. James Forsyth, Professor of Labor Law at Winnipeg's St. Francis University. He told Dr. Forsyth about the current negotiations, described Section 13D and its purpose, and asked if Dr. Forsyth would be willing to meet with Darthom's management, to look at the Winnipeg plant and offer his opinion on the possibility of installing a workable scheme.

Dr. Forsyth accepted the invitation. During the telephone conversation he explained to Mr. Wilson that participative plans require considerable maturity on the part of both labor and management. He stated that such maturity often depends on the parties having enjoyed a relatively long relationship. However the elements of youth and newness, plus the strong desire of both union and management to avoid problems associated with piece work systems, might make the Winnipeg plant an exception. Certainly it was worth exploring.

Approximately three weeks after Mr. Wilson's initial contract, Dr. Forsyth received a call from Mr. Edward Gray, Chief Industrial Engineer of Darthom. Gray invited Professor Forsyth to the Winnipeg plant to meet himself and other management members. The first meeting was scheduled for Wednesday, June 27.

On June 27 Dr. Forsyth visited the Winnipeg plant. He was met by Edward Gray and Michael Ketitch, Chief Industrial Engineer for the Winnipeg plant. Messrs. Gray and Kekitch had done a considerable amount of reading about the theories of participative management and about specific participative management schemes.[2] They intended to discuss these plans with Dr. Forsyth and to show him the Winnipeg operations. They wanted Dr. Forsyth's opinion on whether ideas from such schemes were applicable to their plant. Both Mr. Gray and Mr. Kekitch were experts in piece-work plans, but they had been instructed to postpone installing piecework standards at Winnipeg during the exploration of alternative systems. Experience with piecework plans at other Darthom locations had been bad. People were taking home pay checks in some locations that bore little relationship to their work effort. There were out-of-line rates and excessively high numbers of grievances. Furthermore, productivity levels at these plants were disappointing.

THE WALKOUT

June 27 was the scheduled date for formal signing of the new contract. Union and management representatives from each of Darthom's four corrugated container plants in the Prairie Provinces had gathered at Winnipeg's Fort Garry Hotel, along with the Industrial Relations Manager for pulp and paper products, David Wilson, to affix their signatures. Gerald Weatherby, the Winnipeg plant manager, was ill that day, so he designated General Foreman Hubert deVries to attend on his behalf. Local 3-400 was represented by Ian Britney, president, William Linton, vice president and Samuel Harwood, secretary.

Although the formal signing was scheduled for 11 a.m. some members of the Winnipeg plant's workforce had other ideas. At 9:30 a.m., coffee break time, the entire production operation at the Winnipeg plant shut down. The workers had staged a protest walkout.

Soon after the walkout Walter Jeffs, Head of Production Planning, phoned Mr. Kekitch in the conference room where Kekitch was meeting with Messrs. Gray and Forsyth. He said that all the workers were outside in front of the plant and that newspaper reporters had arrived on the scene. The meeting ended while steps were taken to find out what was wrong.

Walter Jeffs and Michael Kekitch were the highest-ranking members of management at the plant. They decided that Ketitch and George deHaviland, Senior Foreman, should go outside, talk to the workers and try to find out what had caused the walkout. They suspected it was a protest against union leaders; consequently they were reluctant to issue any ultimatums or warnings. Ketitch soon confirmed the suspicions, and a decision was made to telephone the union leaders and Mr. deVries at the Fort Garry Hotel.

When word of the walkout reached the Fort Garry Hotel the contract-signing was postponed. Hubert de Vries, Ian Britney and the other local 3-400 officers made plans to drive back to the plant immediately. Meanwhile the work force stayed outside in the sunshine, talking to reporters. Gray, Kekitch and Dr. Forsyth resumed their conversations, then took a tour through the quiet, abandoned plant. Dr. Forsyth expressed doubt at that time whether any form of participative management program could work. There appeared to be a lack of communication within the union as exemplified by the walkout and a communications gap between management and members of the workforce, as exemplified by management's surprise when the walkout occurred. Nevertheless the men agreed to explore the situation further — paying particular attention to the outcome of deliberations when Messrs. de Vries and Britney returned.

* * *

Ian Britney and the other Local 3-400 officers arrived back at the Winnipeg plant before 11 o'clock. They talked briefly to workers standing in front of the plant and arranged to meet later in the afternoon. The turnouts at this and a subsequent meeting that evening were reported to be the "best ever." Members aired their complaints about the contract, and officers explained their positions. The most significant complaint reported by the Winnipeg *Free Press* was that the membership had not been kept informed about the progress of negotiations. The *Free Press* article, dated Thursday, June 28, is reproduced below:

UNION REVOLT

STRIKERS PROTEST LACK OF CONTRACT INFORMATION

Jerome Hilton, *Free Press* Labor Reporter

WINNIPEG — Hourly-rated employees at the Darthom Industries corrugated container plant here walked off their jobs Wednesday, shortly before a contract was to be signed at the Fort Garry Hotel by union and company representatives.

The workers, members of Local 3-400, International Woodworkers of America, were protesting a lack of information on the new contract.

The workers — about 40 on the day shift loft their jobs — said they were not informed about the full contents of the contract.

"There's been a breakdown in communications between the union, the company and the membership," a worker said.

"There are only three guys who know what's going on," another worker added, after pointing out Local 3-400 president Ian Britney, vice-president William Linton and secretary Samuel A. Harwood were to sign the contract without informing the membership of its details.

The workers said some contract agreements were reached at a Wednesday meeting between union and company representatives and the membership was not informed about them.

"We want to know exactly what the contract consists of, we have the right to know," a female worker said.

"We went out because we want equalization and incentive standards," another female added.

Contract at the Winnipeg container plant, which has about 70 Local 3-400 workers, expired June 19.

On Thursday, the 28th, all workers reported back to their jobs. No disciplinary action was taken against any employees for staging the walkout, and no changes were made in the contract. The local membership was far from satisfied, however, as reflected by their subsequent 26 to 7 vote against ratification. Nevertheless the contract become effective, because the majority of workers in the four plants affected by its terms voted in favor.

Ian Britney had commented to reporters on the day of the walkout that the contract was a good one — blaming the misunderstanding on "people who don't go to union meetings [blowing] it all out of proportion." Sometime later Britney said that he was not particularly happy with the agreement and expected that there would be a return to local bargaining the next time. According to Britney: "The coordinated approach did not work very well from our point of view."

*   *   *

The new contract became effective on Thursday, the 28th retroactive for the Winnipeg plant to June 20, 1973. It would run for two years — expiring on June 19, 1975. Section 13 D had been incorporated in full — causing Messrs. Gray and Kekitch to express a desire to meet further with Dr. Forsyth. A diary of the subsequent meetings follows:

July 5

Dr. Forsyth returned to the Winnipeg container plant and talked with Michael Kekitch and Hubert deVries. He wanted to see the plant in operation and to learn about the intraunion problems that had caused the June 27 walkout.

After some investigation Forsyth discovered that the precipitating cause of the walkout had been a remark made by Ian Britney when he was preparing to leave for the Fort Garry Hotel on June 27. A union member had asked, "Where are you going?" Britney replied, "Downtown to sign the contract, but don't tell anyone!" It wasn't long before everyone in the shop knew of the comment. When Britney returned on the 27th and explained the contract terms the women objected vehemently. The new contract called for them to receive $2.96 and $3.01 on laboring jobs — $.25 and $.19 below rates for men on jobs which they said were comparable. In addition, when they compared themselves to workers in other plants on similar jobs they found they were receiving less money. For example, in Moose Jaw the two men operating semi-automatic finishing machines were classified as operators and received identical pay. Both men worked on all phases of the job. The new contract called for one man and one woman to operate similar machines in Winnipeg. The woman, classified a feeder, was specifically assigned to feed product into the machine. The man, called an operator, took the product from the machine and bundled it. He also adjusted the machine for new runs and filled the glue pots. During the setup time for a new run, the feeder was usually idle. In Winnipeg, feeders received $3.01 per hour while operators received $3.26.

* * *

Dr. Forsyth's skepticism about a participative management scheme for Winnipeg was aggravated further when he saw the organization chart for Darthom Industries. Mr. Weatherby, the plant manager, was located five levels below the company's president (see Exhibit 4 of Case A) and, apparently his decision-making authority was severely restricted. Nevertheless, Dr. Forsyth agreed to continue discussions. He said that the apparent *savoir faire* of Messrs. Kekitch and deVries, coupled with their desire to begin laying the groundwork for change, gave him some amount of encouragement. Both men, according to Dr. Forsyth, seemed to recognize that the proper atmosphere for such a plan might not exist for several years — well past the January 1 deadline for implementation of Section 13 D.

Dr. Forsyth briefly described the kind of atmosphere that would have to exist in order for participative management to work. It would require a new concept of the roles that representatives of management and union would play. Managers would solicit the complete involvement of workers in decision making. When new machines were contemplated, the workers to be affected would be consulted. When new products were considered workers would be informed. If orders were cancelled or cut back, workers would receive an explanation. Eventually under such a system employees and management would develop confidence that both their best interests were served when they cooperated for the well-being of the firm. Evidence that the system was beginning to work would be observed in reduced absence and turnover rates, in fewer grievances, in reduced lateness, in plant-wide concern for company production problems, in heated but constructive arguments between workers and members of management over problems that in the past were considered strictly the prerogatives of management.

The role of union leaders would also change under such a system. Without sacrificing their own need to police the contract and represent employees in grievances, union leaders would find themselves becoming concerned with long range planning and would participate in decisions involving new acquisitions, employment policies, and marketing practices.

Dr. Forsyth explained that participative management schemes usually center around some sort of bonus-sharing scheme. Bonuses are based on improvements in performance and are paid on a group basis. Such schemes must be simple, easily understood by all and derived by union and management working together. At all times, however, it should be clear that the bonus-sharing scheme is only a tool — a device around which new attitudes are built and genuine participation obtained.

Dr. Forsyth then expressed a desire to meet with leaders of Local 3-400, to see whether they would be receptive to such a scheme. Arrangements were made for a meeting to take place on July 10. Meanwhile, Michael Kekitch agreed to accumulate company performance figures for the past two and one half years so that he and Dr. Forsyth could make some preliminary calculations toward development of a bonus-sharing plan.

July 10 — Meeting with Union Representatives

Dr. Forsyth met with officers of the Union: Ian Britney, President, William Linton, Vice President, Samuel Harwood, Secretary, and Linda McArthur, Steward. Dr. Forsyth explained that he had been invited by company representatives to offer advice on implementing Section 13 D of the contract. He asked the union representatives what they expected to realize as a result of this section. Mr. Britney said: "We want a plan that will guarantee us a 25 per cent increase!" Dr. Forsyth asked why they had not negotiated this. Britney replied: "We tried!" After further discussion Mr. Britney conceded that his real desire was to obtain a plan that the union could police and that was fair to the workers.

Then Britney talked briefly about piecework plans, expressing his desire to avoid problems that seemed to accompany such plans. When asked about his reaction to a group savings-sharing plan Britney and the others showed interest. Dr. Forsyth cautioned that such plans had not, to his knowledge, been tried in the paper products industry, but then he described several company-union situations in other industries where such plans had been successfully introduced. All involved close union-management co-operation and called for union involvement in management decision making. Mr. Britney expressed doubt whether Darthom management would go along with such a plan. He cited some earlier experiences with a labor-management committee — a group formed to consider suggestions for improvement. Britney said that several suggestions had been considered by the committee, but not one had been implemented. Furthermore, no explanations had been given for the failure to implement the suggestions. The union representatives agreed that for all practical purposes the union-management committee was ineffective.

Design of a Formula

Michael Kekitch and Dr. Forsyth met twice, July 7 and again on July 14, to study the company performance figures gathered by Mr. Kekitch and to design a tentative bonus-sharing formula for consideration by the parties. The figures from which they worked were reproduced in Case A, Exhibit 6.

Messrs. Kekitch and Forsyth used the following criteria to guide their work:

1. The bonus plan should be simple — one that all workers could understand.

2. The plan should reflect, as closely as possible, conditions that could be influenced by the participants. (This criterion ruled out profit-sharing plans, because profits are sometimes dependent on matters over which men in the shop have little control, such as changes in depreciation rates. It also ruled out any plan based on shipments, because management sometimes decided to produce for inventory.)

3. The plan should be based on a realistic standard, and improvements on that standard should be shared on a group basis.

4. The plan should be flexible enough to reflect changes in product mix.

5. It should be possible to change standards with relative ease if it becomes obvious that they are out of line — at least in the early stages.

After agreeing on the criteria Messrs. Kekitch and Forsyth made a sample bonus calculation which related labor costs to production output. For illustrative purposes they compared the months of May and June as follows:

	May	June
Shipments per 1000 sq. ft.	15,732	16,985
Direct labor cost	$ 29,842	$ 29,165
Indirect labor cost	3,214	3,230
Factory supervision	9,602	9,173
Total labor cost	$ 42,658	$ 41,574

The total labor cost per square foot produced in May was $.0027 (42658 ÷ 15,732,000). If May were used as the base month the $.0027 figure would become a standard to be applied in all future months. In June the actual production was 16,985,000 square feet. Applying the $.0027 standard we would expect a labor cost of $45,859(16,985,000 x .0027). The actual labor cost for June was $41,574, a saving of $4,285 over the base. This saving would be divided among participants.

Messrs, Kekitch and Forsyth believed that a fair, attainable standard could be derived through this sort of comparison and that improvements on that standard should be shared by those who made the improvements possible.

They recognized that the formula they had been considering did not reflect changes in product mix. These changes were not controllable by the labor force and did influence the degree of difficulty with which production could be accomplished. To include a factor reflecting product mix changes would result in a more accurate standard but would cause two problems: one, it would make it impossible to calculate a standard in advance, so participants could know the goal at which they were shooting; and two, such inclusion would complicate the formula. Kekitch and Forsyth were convinced that a fair standard could be derived which would take into account various product mixes over time. Such a standard would be known in advance and attainable, but parties would retain the flexibility to change it if it was obviously out-of-line. However, they hesitated to suggest such a standard because of their desire for simplicity.

July 17

Dr. Forsyth met with Gerald Weatherby, the plant manager. He described the proposed formula for bonus sharing and asked for Weatherby's comments. Mr. Weatherby supported the concepts and agreed to attend a meeting with union representatives later that day in order to show his support.

Dr. Forsyth had translated the actual performance figures into hypothetical figures for illustrative purposes. However, he sought permission from Mr. Weatherby to disclose actual figures to union representatives if such disclosure seemed appropriate. Professor Forsyth said he doubted whether they would be requested but pointed out the importance of demonstrating a policy of complete disclosure with the union, starting immediately. Mr. Weatherby, while supporting the concept of full disclosure, said he could not give permission — that such permission would have to come from someone else in the organization.

It was with some trepidation, then, that Messrs. Kekitch and Forsyth entered the meeting with the union. The meeting could not wait, because union leaders might interpret a delay as another example of management's insincerity — thus ruining the chances of any participative management scheme before it got started.

Professor Forsyth, using hypothetical figures, described the bonus-sharing plan tentatively devised by Mr. Kekitch and himself. The bonus calculation related direct labor costs to production — thereby avoiding reference to indirect and supervisory costs.

Sample Bonus Calculation
given to union representatives
on July 17

Assume, based on past experience, that it had cost the company $1.40, on average, to make 1,000 square feet of finished product.

Assume in month X the
following:

Actual production:	10,000,000 sq. ft.
" direct labor cost:	$12,000
Employees	50
Bonus Calculation:	
Expected labor cost	
(1.40 x 10,000) =	$14,000
Less: Actual labor cost	$12,000
Difference	$ 2,000
Share per person (2000 ÷ 50)	$ 40

Dr. Forsyth showed how the bonus calculation could be made and posted on an accumulative daily basis. He then cited two matters that required caution:

1. There would be some months when actual costs would exceed standard. Past experience showed that January, February and March had been typically poor. It would be important for everyone to know that no bonus could be paid in such months, and it would be advisable, in Professor Forsyth's opinion, to set some money aside during bonus months to offset loss months. The company should not be expected to absorb the complete loss in poor months if participants expected to receive the total gain in good months.

2. The union leaders should be careful not to oversell the bonus plan. Employees' expectations should not be inflated beyond what could be realistically expected. In fact, figures used for illustrative purposes should be intentionally deflated. Thus actual performance would hopefully yield a bonus in excess of the examples, and the plan would be looked upon favorably by the employees.

Mr. Weatherby attended part of the session and expressed his support of the concepts. Union leaders expressed a considerable amount of enthusiasm and said they were anxious to translate the proposal into something workable.

Dr. Forsyth cautioned against proceeding too rapidly. He suggested that Mr. Kekitch and other management representatives derive a realistic standard. They might consider an experimental dry run of two months before making any final determination. Dr. Forsyth gave the union several matters to think about and suggested they be prepared to put forth their views at a future meeting. These matters included the following:

1. Who should share in the plan: supervisors? service employees? probationary employees?
2. How should bonus shares be calculated? Should everyone share equally? Should shares be based on a worker's present wage? Should those who work only part of a month receive the same as those who work the whole month?
3. Under what conditions should the base be changed?
4. How much should be set aside in good performance months to compensate for months when performance fails to meet standard?

Dr. Forsyth stressed again that the bonus formula was only a small part of total participative management plan. The more important part would be union participation in the management decision-making process. A suggestion committee consisting of union representatives and management would replace the so-far ineffective union-management committee. The new committee would consider ideas for improving performance and would have power to implement suggestions, within certain as-yet-undefined limits. Union members were urged to consider how the committee members would be appointed and within what limits the committee would operate.

Union representatives indicated some preliminary sentiments about the plan. They seemed unanimous in their desire that *everyone* participate — stating that through full participation members of management and union leaders alike would demonstrate their interest in making the plan work.

The representatives agreed that a two-month trial period would be advisable, and there was general agreement that September and October would be the best months for such a trial. This way various "bugs" which showed up could be ironed out well in advance of the January 1 deadline.

As a final matter the union was asked to designate two persons who would work along with Michael Kekitch and Hubert deVries of the company to formulate a detailed experimental plan based on the ideas already discussed.

*   *   *

Following the July 17 meeting members of management and Dr. Forsyth expressed optimism. Both management and union appeared sincere in their desire to work together.

Hubert deVries suggested that the foreman be informed of what had happened and arranged a meeting for Dr. Forsyth to speak with them that same day. Dr. Forsyth outlined for the foremen the various events that had transpired since his involvement. Then he illustrated the bonus-sharing plan as he had done earlier with union representatives. Dr. Forsyth cautioned that the bonus-sharing plan was only a tool — a symbol of a new relationship. Among the most important keys to the success of the new relationship were first line supervisors. Foremen under such a system would be expected to manage. Clerical duties would be done by clerks. Foremen would be responsible for education of the workers, for placing them in jobs, seeing that conditions were ideal for top performance, and soliciting new ideas. Foremen would be judged not only on their performance related to budget targets, but also on how well they stimulated and successfully implemented new ideas that would improve performance.

The foremen responded enthusiastically to the meeting, expressing a strong desire to be active participants in the bonus-sharing plan. Some of them expressed personal thanks for having been informed about the progress of discussions and said they hoped they would be informed of future developments.

*   *   *

Following the meetings on July 17, Messrs. Kekitch and deVries met with Edward Gray, the company's Chief Industrial Engineer, in an effort to derive a realistic standard from which a monthly bonus could be calculated. They encountered difficult problems in deriving such a standard, because the plant had only operated for 27 months. No consistent pattern was apparent from past performance records. Furthermore, the frequent changes in product mix, caused by factors over which the work force had no control, apparently had a direct effect on output. From month to month they could cause variations in the bonus. Nevertheless, the men were optimistic and expressed that optimism to management in Vancouver — men who eventually would be called upon to approve or disapprove any participative management plan. With this in mind Edward Gray contacted David Wilson, the company's Industrial Relations Manager for Pulp and Paper Products, and the two men arranged a meeting for July 23 to review the status of the plan. Dr. Forsyth was asked to attend.

July 23

The following were in attendance:

David Wilson, Industrial Relations Manager, Pulp and Paper Products.
Edward Gray, Chief Industrial Engineer
Stanley Lehroux, Director of Manufacturing Services
Marvin Rettenmund, Area Production Manager
Dustin Nickerson, Manager of Production Control
Jack Owens, Assistant Industrial Relations Manager
Gerald Weatherby, Manager, Winnipeg Plant
Michael Kekitch, Chief Industrial Engineer, Winnipeg
James Forsyth, Consultant

After being introduced by David Wilson, Dr. Forsyth gave a chronological summary of the meetings that had taken place since June 27. He expressed optimism that a participative management plan could work but cautioned that short run dramatic results probably could not be expected. "My greatest concern," said Dr. Forsyth, "is whether management can be open-minded and flexible enough to adjust to the form of management needed to make the program work." Dr. Forsyth stated he was echoing doubts expressed by the union leaders. An important symbol of management's sincerity could be the prompt and effective implementation of an experimental bonus-sharing plan. The figures would be posted, but no payments would be made. He noted that Messrs. Kekitch and deVries, along with two designees from the union, were planning meetings to derive an acceptable formula.

Dr. Forsyth pointed out that Darthom was embarking on a plan that was different. They would be pioneers. There would be frustrations, but the returns in job satisfaction and improved performance could be huge.

During the discussion which followed, the bonus-sharing formula illustrated on July 17 to the union members was reviewed. Mr. Lehroux expressed some doubt whether the union would accept any plan which called for setting aside an amount as a contingency against losses. Dr. Forsyth said he believed this was an important feature of the plan— that all participants should be continually reminded that the company, in instituting a plan of this nature, was assuming greater-than-normal risk. There was the risk that labor costs, by virtue of no ceiling, would skyrocket, or that performance, by virtue of no controls, would drop. And there was the further risk of management frustration as the traditional rights to manage without interference would be encroached upon.

Dr. Forsyth expressed confidence that union leaders had already accepted these concepts— provided they could be assured of management's sincerity in making the plan work. He thought an important symbol of this sincerity would be wholehearted participation in the plan by all members of the Winnipeg plant's work force, including management personnel.

When everyone appeared to be reasonably well acquainted with the ideas behind the proposed plan, Dr. Forsyth outlined a four-step action plan which he said should be implemented as soon as possible in order for matters to proceed:

1. Gain complete understanding of the proposed plan— its strengths and its weaknesses.
2. Give approval, in principal, to the scheme so that local management and union people could proceed with implementation on an experimental basis starting in September.
3. Take whatever steps were necessary to allow local management autonomy to implement suggestions promptly and conduct their industrial relations program without having to check each item with the head office.
4. Give approval in advance to the concept of complete participation in the plan— by everyone from plant manager to laborer.

Commenting on the final point, Mr. Lehroux said that an incentive plan for all management personnel was currently under consideration at corporate headquarters. He expressed reservations about recommending that Winnipeg plant managers participate in two plans "After all they are managers," said Mr. Lehroux, "and deserve separate treatment from members of the factory force. Furthermore we don't want to get ourselves into the position of giving Winnipeg managers preferred treatment."

Mr. Lehroux expressed additional concern about the degree of autonomy that should be given to the local manager. He noted that Mr. Weatherby at present had authority to approve and implement all capital expenditures of less than $1,000. Anything over that needed head office approval.

Dr. Forsyth suggested that the members in attendance resolve these issues as soon as possible, and made it clear that he believed complete participation and considerable autonomy for local managers were important ingredients of success. The members agreed that, while head office pondered these questions, Messrs. Kekitch, Gray and deVries would proceed with designated union members to design an experimental plan. They were given a tentative deadline of September 1.

Following the management meeting, Michael Kekitch, Hubert deVries and Dr. Forsyth met with Ian Britney, Samuel Harwood, Linda McArthur and Susan Randall of the union to report on the results of the management meeting. When she arrived in the conference room Mrs. McArthur asked Dr. Forsyth, "Well, did the shit hit the fan?" Dr. Forsyth replied "No, not really. We think we made some progress." Then he described what had happened— pointing out the two areas of apparent concern. He reported that agreement had been secured to continue with the experimental plan. The union had decided that Mr. Britney and Mrs. McArthur would work with Messrs. Kekitch and deVries to design a plan for a trial run in September.

ITEMS FOR DISCUSSION

1. Based on the information available to the company and union representatives what type of bonus-sharing plan would you advise?
   a) State the objectives of your plan.
   b) State how you would implement those objectives via a detailed plan.
2. How would you appraise the probabilities of success of a participative management plan for the Winnipeg plant? What factors are in its favor? What factors are against it?
3. Comment on management's handling of the June 27 walkout.
4. What is your assessment of the Section 13D contract provision?

PARTICIPATIVE MANAGEMENT MANIA [2]

This is a sequel to the Darthom Industries case series. Darthom,[3] one of Canada's largest producers of paper products, had employed a well-known consulting firm to help institute a participative style of management in one of their operations. The final result was failure. However, there is much to be learned from Darthom's experience so that others might avoid a similar fate.

It seems clear that more and more companies will have to seek greater participation in management from all levels of the work force as a matter of survival in this increasingly competitive world. Some have already done so, with spectacular success.

Others, like Darthom, have tried and failed. In looking at some of the failures it is reasonably clear that success might have been secured through application of a few simple, but important, principles. Here we attempt to set forth some of the important elements of successful participative management and to raise storm warnings for those who might leap into ill-considered changes in management style.

On February 20, 1974, Ian Britney was suspended! Britney was president of Local 3-400 of the International Woodworkers Association of Darthom Industries Ltd. Winnipeg, Manitoba, corrugated container plant.[4] The reasons for Britney's suspension: "Gross insubordination and disrespect for his supervisor."

The facts leading to Britney's suspension were simple. At about noon on February 20 the production superintendent received a call from the sales manager asking whether it would be possible to shut down the corrugator, change it over, and run through sufficient corrugated board of a different size to accommodate a customer's emergency need for 240 boxes. This customer had been courted by the sales manager for more than a year and represented a significant sales dollar potential if Darthom could gain his business. The particular run of 240 boxes would be a money loser, but goodwill generated by it could have long-term positive impact.

Production superintendent Hubert deVries recognized what was at stake and gave immediate orders to carry out the sales manager's request. This resulted in a 30-minute shutdown of the corrugator, and idled six production workers. More important to Ian Britney and the union members, however, the shutdown represented a loss of take-home pay, because the workers received a group bonus based on the amount of corrugated board produced. Union members recognized that any delays or shutdowns on the corrugator had a direct effect on their wallets. As a result Britney went looking for deVries.

After inquiring in the production superintendent's office, in the plant manager's office and around the shop Britney finally located deVries in the cafeteria having a cup of coffee. Several other employees, including three women, were there too. Britney went up to deVries and, in a loud voice that all could hear, shouted a series of obscenities that made doubting references to the superintendent's origins and his morals. Amid his cursing Britney demanded to know why the corrugator had been shut down. DeVries, both surprised and angered by the confrontation, said, "It's none of your business!" This lead to further obscenities and, after several minutes of heated argument, deVries told the union president to leave. He was suspended for two weeks!

Hubert deVries promptly reported the incident to the plant manager, Gerald Weatherby. Weatherby said he believed deVries had done the proper thing under the circumstances and pledged his support in the event that the suspension was appealed. Britney did appeal, and the case went before an impartial arbitrator.

The decision of the arbitrator in Ian Britney's case is not important. What is important is that Manager Weatherby and Superintendent deVries could have used this incident to further the cause of participative management — a concept of management which both of them had helped initiate in the Winnipeg plant only seven weeks before.

The participative management plan at Darthom Industries' Winnipeg plant had been designed by a well-known consulting firm. (Darthom had engaged the consulting firm to develop a more sophisticated standard for the bonus plan. Professor Forsyth had not been directly involved with the plan after the new consultants were called in.) It featured a finely engineered group bonus-sharing scheme whereby all hourly employees would participate in the fruits of productivity improvements. Improvements were measured in square feet of corrugated board produced, and the principal influencer of production was the corrugator. In selling the plan to the management and union the consultant's representatives made it clear that the real benefits from this new plan were not in the bonus scheme but in the atmosphere of participation that would surround its implementation. A production improvement committee was formed where delegates from the company and union would meet regularly to consider suggestions regarding production facilities. They had power to recommend implementation of any useful suggestion. The consultants said that eventually union members would become interested in matters that were hitherto the strict concern of management. Decisions on marketing, finance and production would be subject to scrutiny, and arguments about them would sometimes be heated. Union members would be encouraged to challenge management's actions, and a mark of a good manager would be his receptivity to suggestions for improvement. Increased enthusiasm through participation, decreased absence, decreased employee turnover and less tardiness would be indices of the program's success. Workers would begin to arrive early and would sometimes offer to stay after prescribed quitting times to work on an important job. Workers would voluntarily help each other when production bottlenecks appeared. They would develop their own techniques for improving productivity and willingly pass on their ideas to others. They would share a genuine concern for the company's well-being, knowing that their own well-being and the company's were interdependent. Eventually all distinctions by classification and department would break down, and employees would consider themselves part of a unified team with a single objective.

Gerald Weatherby served as chairman of the production improvement committee. Herbert deVries was a member. So was Ian Britney, up until the time of his suspension. The consultant had long since collected his fee and departed.

In the meeting of the production improvement committee following Britney's suspension some of the union members sought to discuss the matter. Gerald Weatherby refused to talk about it, observing that the consultant had insisted that productivity meetings should not be contaminated with grievances. The latter, according to the consultant, should be handled through normal contract procedures. One of the members said Britney had been suspended because he was expressing his concern about problems of productivity, and this was something the new plan had been designed to encourage. Weatherby replied that this was a matter to be decided in the grievance procedure.

Not long after the Britney suspension it became clear that participative management for Darthom Industries Ltd. in Winnipeg was not working. Issues discussed by the production improvement committee became less and less meaningful; attendance at the meetings dwindled; and bonus amounts fell to virtually nothing. Union members began agitation for elimination of the bonuses and replacement by a substantial pay increase.

*   *   *

The failure of participative management at Darthom's Winnipeg plant was one more in an increasing list of such failures. Many of these can be traced to a management mania brought on in recent years by behavioral scientists. Behaviorists have put forth convincing evidence that companies which recognize the influx of a new consciousness among members of the work force and open the doors to worker participation can make significant strides toward greater profits. Their views have been enhanced by the spectacular successes of companies which have adopted participative management schemes, such as Texas Instruments, Motorola, Donnelly Mirrors and Hewlett Packard. Some managers came to believe that a sure-fire formula had been devised for instant success. Some management consultants nurtured this belief by devising and selling participative schemes which were eagerly accepted by managers. In many cases there was only meager awareness of the wholesale changes in management style which such programs require and, in addition, only token willingness to make the necessary changes.

The following section puts forth the basic ingredients which are considered essential for successful participative management programs. It demonstrates how the Britney case, in a successful participative management setting, could have been made to work toward furtherance of the scheme itself. And it urges managers to determine whether their own style of management can be comfortably adapted to the requirements of participative management.

Elements of a Successful Participative Management Scheme

1. *Everyone should participate.*

Gerald Weatherby, Hubert deVries and other supervisory people at the Winnipeg plant did not share monthly bonuses with production and maintenance employees. Instead they were part of a corporate-wide profit-sharing plan. As a result the production improvement committee meetings were characterized by an aura of insincerity. When union members argued for short-term improvements that would have an immediate impact on their take-home pay, managers often came to assume that these arguments were prompted by money, nothing else. There was no meaningful opportunity for managers to share elation for good performance or to share concerns about poor performance.

A manager whose bonus is derived the same way as everyone else's can talk with passion about his own expectations. The feeling of comaraderie when manager and employee both receive a bonus check is one of the binding forces that makes participative management work.

Aside from the feeling of comaraderie, participation by everyone forces attention to matters that sometimes are considered exclusive management prerogatives. It forces management to justify expenses for supervision, engineering, research and maintenance, and opens up meaningful channels of communication toward reduction of these expenses. In some cases these expenses have been substantially reduced as a result of production workers enthusiastically taking over the functions of inspection, maintenance and first-level supervision, thus providing themselves with added responsibility and contributing to greater job satisfaction. It also sweetened the bonus pot.

A word of caution is appropriate here. Some production improvement committees have become over-eager when given authority to recommend reductions in nonproductive labor expenses. They have cut maintenance, engineering and research to the bone and succeeded in making immense, immediate improvements in bonus yields. But the company's long range competitive edge was lost as machines started to deteriorate through lack of adequate preventive maintenance and as other companies gained competitive advantages through more vigorous research and development activities.

2. The bonus scheme should be simple.

The scheme at Darthom Industries' Winnipeg plant was complicated. It contained provisions for changes in product mix, for carrying over losses from one month to another, for dealing with parochial interests and status needs of various worker groups, and for coping with the possibility of technological changes. Most workers did not understand the plan. But most were unwilling to reveal their ignorance. As a result they sat back skeptically, waiting to see results.

While bonus schemes are important ingredients for most participative management plans they often attract a disproportionate amount of attention. The bonus plan should serve two purposes: One, it should motivate those who are primarily concerned with money, and two, it should be a focal point around which participative management can develop.

The plan should reflect matters that can be controlled by those who share. Furthermore, it should be flexible enough to fairly reflect changing conditions. When there is a choice between accuracy and simplicity, between unchallengeable legal language and layman's understanding, it is best to err on the side of simplicity and understanding.

3. There should be full participation in formulation of the plan.

Darthom's plan was formulated by a consultant, purchased by management, and presented to the workers' representatives as the best conceivable plan for the distinctive needs of the Winnipeg operation. Not one operating manager or worker representative contributed to its formulation. Consequently no one was committed to making it work.

Participative management plans are most likely to succeed if participants participate from the beginning. This requires joint consideration of the nature of the operation: its strengths, its weakness and its problems. It involves joint awareness of costs, income, potential markets, plans for expansion and knowledge of technological changes which are under consideration. Finally it involves joint determination of a bonus-sharing plan. The plan itself may be less sophisticated than one which is designed by an experienced consultant, but this is not important. The process of formulation is far more important: a process which in itself, can establish commitment to mutually shared goals.

Before proceeding with such a plan managers must ask themselves if they can live with a program where traditional management rights to make decisions are regularly subjected to scrutiny and criticism by members of the work force. If they cannot they should not go ahead!

4. Don't oversell.

There is a tendency with persons enamored of the virtues of participative management to inflate the expectations of potential participants. There are firms where profit improvements, cost savings and bonus yields have been spectacular, and it is difficult to ignore them. Thus we find consulting firms submitting illustrations to their potential customers with figures designed to seduce.

It is important to exercise restraint when speculating about the potential success of such a plan. There is some merit in intentional deflation of illustrative figures, so that initial enthusiasm for adoption of the plan can be most vividly focused on its participative aspects, not on its potential monetary returns. Then if actual performance exceeds expectations there will be additional enthusiasm. However, even then, it is important to downgrade the performance results and to exhibit cautious optimism. In this way principal attention is focused on the need for constant attention to improved performance. Persons who are intimately involved with a participative management plan should never express satisfaction, no matter how well things are going. To do so invites complacency and degeneration.

5. Losses should be shared.

In the three years prior to institution of its participative management plan Darthom Industries' Winnipeg plant experienced profitable months during the summer and fall and losses during January, February and March. Knowing this, Darthom's management urged initiation of the plan at the start of the profitable period so as to start things off with a bang. Furthermore, some members of management expressed belief that the company should absorb any losses. They reasoned that no responsible union leader could stay in office long if monthly take-home pay fluctuated downward. These views betrayed ignorance of the philosophy by which participative management works.

Members of the work force should understand the nature of business fluctuations. They should be concerned about downtrends and willing to share in ups and downs. Thus, when things go bad everyone should feel the impact. An amount should be set aside in each good month as an insurance fund. Some predetermined percentage of the fund would be paid back to the company in the event of a loss month. This percentage should be related to the extent of the loss, but it should not be so great that hopes of near-term replenishment are smashed. The sole purpose of the insurance fund is to remind participants that bad times affect everyone. If employees and their leaders are not willing to accept this reminder they are probably not ready for participative management.

There are examples of firms which experienced difficult times following institution of participative management programs. In one instance a company, engaged in production of electronic components for the U.S. space program, experienced a severe setback through sudden cancellation of over $300,000 in orders. This meant that profits in the next several months would be nil until new orders could be generated. In addition, expenditures for necessary capital improvements would have to be cut, thus jeopardizing the company's competitive edge. When the workers learned about this they insisted that management cut everyone's wages in order to help pay the bills. "We've shared generously in the good times," said one worker, "now we'll assume some of the burden for the bad times."

6. Engage the services of a strong catalytic agent.

The best catalyst is someone in the leadership ranks of management or labor who has had prior experience with participative management. Such a person is especially important during early stages in order to nurture the plan through the inevitable growing pains.

The catalyst should possess an aura of trust. He should act as a sounding board for frustrations. He is both an educator and counselor. He provides an outlet at the early stages so that parties can talk freely if they want to, without fear of betrayal.

If such a person had been on the scene in the Darthom situation he might have been able to help turn the Britney suspension into an incident for improving the new relationship. Here was a demonstration by Britney, the union president, of extreme interest in a management decision. His methods were crude and his motives, perhaps, questionable. However, a dispassionate catalyst might have seen this as an opportunity to build understanding. Britney, as union president, was under pressure from his members to explain why the corrugator had been shut down. Furthermore, as a party to the new bonus-sharing scheme, he bore some responsibility for improved earnings. If he had been apprised in advance about deVries' telephone conversation with the sales manager he might have participated in the decision to shut down operations. Even if he did not agree with the decision he would have known why it was made, thus avoiding the need to seek out deVries.

The presence of a catalyst would not likely have avoided the Britney-deVries confrontation. But following the confrontation he could have helped management look at the case more openly, to raise the question of how this situation might be used to the best advantage of the plan. In considering the question Weatherby and deVries might have determined that Britney's suspension was best for the plan. On the other hand, they might have decided that an apology was in order and that Britney should be brought back with a pat on the back for expressing such passionate interest in a management decision, and a plea that he restrain himself in his choice of language in the future.

7. Cast aside preconceptions about employer-employee relations.

Participative management requires revolutionary changes in ways of running a firm. As an example, managers are called upon to stimulate new ideas among their subordinates, to encourage challenges to traditional methods. For some managers such changes represent a threat to their security. For others they represent an opportunity to plan more fully, to coordinate and to motivate.

During the transition period employees, employee leaders and managers often experience frustration. Sometimes, as in the Britney case, they revert to autocratic assumptions about traditional superior-subordinate relationships. Some find it impossible to adjust and they are quickly identified. If there is a commitment to participative management and it is clear that some members of the organization cannot adjust, these persons must be eliminated!

Contrary to popular belief, participative management is tough management. In Darthom it became clear, after a short time, that Gerald Weatherby was unable to cope with constant questioning of his decisions by those who had hitherto accepted and executed his orders without question. Weatherby did not recognize the opportunity for furthering concepts of participative management when he was confronted with the Britney case. By letting the case fester through grievance and arbitration proceedings he opened an irreparable wound. By stifling suggestions he helped ruin any hopes that the program would succeed. Weatherby's superiors recognized these symptoms at an early stage but were reluctant to do anything about them. Eventually, after months of dismal performance, Weatherby was replaced. It should have happened much earlier.

8. *Employee leaders must be tough-minded, yet flexible.*

Unions are not required for successful participative management programs. However, they can be useful, provided they are blessed with tough-minded leaders of their own. Sometimes union interests and management interests appear to be at odds. When this is the case, employee leaders need to tread a fine line between the two. Sometimes union and management interests must be neatly separated in order to appease those who assume that the two are inco patible. For example, the union leader must fight vigorously as a negotiator for improvement in wages, hours and working conditions. He must fight equally hard for his members in grievance meetings and, if necessary, in arbitration. If members detect any soft spots he will likely lose strength and become a liability toward the furtherance of those interests which seem to be compatible. At the same time he must retain his identity as a representative of membership interests and as a leader of his members toward the furtherance of management's goals.

If union leaders or members come to believe that participative management is a device by which company managers seek to emasculate the power and identity of the union they will likely fight a battle for survival. Such battles are usually irrational, often bitter, and can spell the demise of participative management. Thus company managers must constantly respect the role of the employee leader and offer him opportunities to demonstrate his strength — both as an advocate of parochial interests and as a supporter of joint interests. At the same time managers must maintain control, lest they force employee leaders into a takeover position. The line between genuine participation in decision making and anarchy is clear, but it takes a strong, skillful manager to guard against crossing the line.

9. Leadership must be patient.

Most firms experience difficult times during the first several months of participative management. Costs rise, profits dip and tempers wear thin. Sometimes there are no positive results for a year or two. Any manager who wants to show immediate, short-term improvements would be well advised to adopt a more tightly controlled management style, even to consider piecework incentives. Gerald Weatherby's successor at Darthom Industries' Winnipeg plant did just that, with spectacular early results.

A leader who believes in the philosophies behind participative management is content with gradual improvement over time, and is constantly bolstered by the faith that good performance will be a natural result of utual trust and respect. He constantly nurtures and reaffirms that trust. He shares responsibility for bad performance and gives credit to others for success. He takes action, when necessary, to educate. He eliminates persons who do not measure up. And he reasserts his faith in the face of impatience by his own superiors.

CONCLUSION

More and more executives are considering the need for changing their styles of management as a result of new expectations among members of the work force. There is increased recognition that the members of the work force are becoming more thoughtful, more sensitive, and that they respond best to a form of management that gives recognition to each person and provides maximum opportunity for self-expression and participation toward attainment of mutually derived goals. Along with this greater awareness we have seen a number of consulting firms which advocate participative management, and they sell it in a neatly tied bonus-sharing scheme with insufficient regard for the wholesale changes in management style that must accompany such a change.

Bonus-sharing schemes are useful, but not essential, devices around which successful participative management plans can be built. They derive strength from participation in their formulation. Once formulated they become a focal point for building a new atmosphere. Such building takes time and patience and recognition of new roles that must be played by employees, employee leaders and managers.

The creation and nurturing of these new roles involve changes of major importance, all directed in unswerving fashion to the merits of participative management.

Successful participative management plans have a number of important characteristics in common. They include lower-than-normal absence, lateness and turnover rates. They involve few, if any, formal grievances. They are characterized by workers helping each other, by an open atmosphere of self-analysis and criticism, and by conversations which center on matters of importance to the firm itself. The greatest assurance of success comes from full participation in the plan's formation and implementation, from simplicity and understanding, from abandonment of traditional employer-employee assumptions, from leadership strength, and from patience.

NOTES TO CHAPTER 10

1. See for example, the following:
   Fred Lesieur and Elbridge Puckett, "The Scanlon Plan Has Proved Itself,"*Harvard Business Review,*September-October, 1969.
   Fred K. Foulkes,*Creating More Meaningful Work,* American Management Association, 1969.
   Alfred J. Marrow et al,*Management by Participation,*Harper & Row, 1967.
2. Reprinted by permission from *The Business Quarterly,*Canada's Management Journal.
3. Disguised name.
4. Personal names, the company name, and the location are disguised.